1 MONTH OF
FREE
READING

at

www.ForgottenBooks.com

By purchasing this book you are eligible for one month membership to ForgottenBooks.com, giving you unlimited access to our entire collection of over 1,000,000 titles via our web site and mobile apps.

To claim your free month visit:
www.forgottenbooks.com/free779187

ISBN 978-0-266-51699-6
PIBN 10779187

NCIDENTS AND REFLECTIONS

· CONTAINING

ILLUSTRATIONS

OF

CHRISTIAN TRUTHS.

COLLECTED BY JOSEPH WALTON.

PHILADELPHIA:
AT FRIENDS' BOOK STORE, 304 ARCH STREET.

1888.

Wm. H. Pile's Sons, Printers,
treet

PREFACE.

In preparing the present volume, the writer has endeavored to show that the tender mercies of the Lord extend to all the creatures whom He has made; that his dealings with men are designed to make them "partakers of the Divine nature, having escaped the corruption that is in the world through lust;" and that this happy result is effected through his own Divine power and spirit, acting immediately on the mind, or through such means as He may see fit to use.

The desire of the author will be answered, if, through the Lord's blessing, some of his readers may be instructed in the way that leads to peace, and may be encouraged so to follow the leadings of the Spirit of Christ as to receive the full fruition of those blessings which his outward coming among men was designed to procure for mankind.

In the anecdotes which have been introduced, care has been taken not to make use of any incidents of whose authenticity there was a reasonable doubt. Many of them are taken from the autobiographies of writers whose statements are thoroughly to be relied upon. Of the remainder, several occurred within the knowledge of the author himself, or of persons whom he knew and confided in.

Some foot-notes have been introduced, giving short sketches of some of the persons mentioned, and occasional references to sources whence further information may be derived.

CONTENTS.

PART I.—OPERATIONS OF DIVINE GRACE.

PAGE

CHAPTER I.—Teaching of Divine Grace. Among Barbarous People. The Young Man of Feeble Intellect. Martha Routh when a Child. The Friend of Bush River. Theodore Parker and the Water Turtle. John Churchman when Young. Job Scott's Early Impressions. Are we Christians? The Boy that Died a Martyr. The Norwegian Boy. Tenderness of Conscience in Children. Tempted to Buy a Cigar. William Williams and the Little Girl. The Child and the Tavern-keeper. The Boy in a Street Car. William Hone and his Daughter. Dr. Vinton and his Patient. Mary Capper's Experience. John Fothergill's Childish Oath, ... 9

CHAPTER II.—Converting Power of Divine Grace. The College Student. Mary M——. The Young German Baptist. John Flavel's Message. E. Worth's Neighbor. Daniel Stanton's Experience. The Scotch Virago Reformed. Edward Wright's Awakening. Special Seasons of Visitation, ... 27

CHAPTER III.—Conversion by Instrumental Means. Gospel Ministry. John Ashton. John Estaugh's Preaching. Baptizing Power of True Ministry. Effect on Joseph Pike. Samuel Neale's Awakening. "What Can this Old Fool Say?" William Williams' Reproof. Dreams. David Ferris. Of the Unworthy Captain. Of the Pasture Field. Of Giving Way to Provocation. Of Washing Linen. Of the Dangerous Ferry Boat. Of Helping a Neighbor. Of Going to Hell. Warnings and Accidents. S. Grellet at St. Gilles. Racing Horses. The Privateer "Tartar." The Singer and the Poor Laborer. The Widow of Lyons. Example. Effect of on an Infidel. "Aunt Mary's Practising." "Master's Life." Madagascar Convert. Mountebank Preacher. Acknowledging

the .Wrong. German Rationalist Convinced. "His Life a
Sermon." French Hospital Matron. Swearing Pilot. The
Blood of the Martyrs is the Seed of the Church. The Clerks
and their Bibles. Mechanic and Lady. Responsibility for
Influence. Presbyterian and his Store Boy. Thomas H.
Benton's Mother. The Coachman's Mother. Consistency.
The Unfaithful Cooper. The Irritated Professor. John
Churchman and Armed Vessels. Blessing on Cards, . . 40

CHAPTER IV.—Obedience Essential. Secret Society. Use of
Wine. First-day Train. Samuel Neale's Gunning. Wine
Merchant. · Beer Saloon. The Clerk who could not Swear.
James Kennedy. The Man who would not Travel on First-
day. Fruits of Disobedience. Resisting Conviction. Jane
Pierce's Friend. John Churchman. Job Scott. Joseph Hoag.
Work of Regeneration. John Richardson. Job Scott. Samuel
Neale. A Stratagem of Satan. Thomas Ellwood. John
Griffith. John Thorp's Advice. James Naylor's Testimony.
Source of Spiritual Knowledge. John Cowper. David Ferris.
Thomas Story. "What will become of us?" Taulerus.
Danger of Delays. Hannah Gibbons. Joseph Hoag. The
Travelling Salesman. The Man Without Hope. A Neglected
Duty. Elizabeth Collins, ... 80

PART II.—FRUITS OF THE SPIRIT.

CHAPTER V.—Repentance. Confession. Restitution. Boy in
a Store. Young Woman who had Stolen. Young Man who
had Burnt a School-house. The Stray Sheep. Let him that
Stole Steal no more. The Honest Coal Merchant. Dr. Johnson's
Repentance. Dr. John Todd. The Tramp. Abraham Lin-
coln's Honesty. The Boy who couldn't be Dishonest. The
Robber and the Gold Watch. Self-Restraint. The Little
Shoes did it. Warning in a Saloon. Samuel Bettle's Sermon.
Edward Wright and the Drowning Boy. Plainness. Daniel
Wheeler. John Richardson. Job Scott. God Does not Need
These. Jacob Green and the Skeleton. Joseph Booth. The
Early Methodists. She took up the Cross in all things.
Michael Robson's Convincement. David Ferris. Samuel

PAGE

Neale. Unprofitable Amusement. Half an Hour to Live.
Cardinal Mazarin. Playing Cards. Could not Give Up the
World. Dr. Johnson and David Garrick, ... 121

CHAPTER VI.—Love. Benevolence. The Kind Scotchman.
Widow Green's Wood. The Strong to Help the Weak.
Genius for Helping. Abraham Lincoln and the Pig. A. Lin-
coln and Cogdal. Joseph Rachel's Bond. Lending to the
Lord. The Chicago Children. Road Mending. Measuring
Wood. Robert Moffat and the African Woman. Dying for a
Friend. Peace Making. Thomas H. Benton and John Wilson.
Duke of Wellington on War. Humility. Keep Inward.
Foreign Travel. Giving Up Religious Conviction. Watch-
fulness. John Richardson. Abigail Bowles. Resist Temp-
tation. The Banker's Clerk. The Backsliding Methodist.
Submissiveness. The Child and the Cemetery. The Sick Son.
Bounty Money. Abraham and Richard Shackleton. Learning
to Chew Crusts, ... 159

PART III.—THE LORD'S CARE OVER HIS PEOPLE.

CHAPTER VII.—Divine Help, Healing and Protection. Thomas
Story and Drinking Healths. John Richardson Healed.
Joseph Hoag and the Woman in Despair. Joseph Hoag's
Injury. Endre Dahl Shipwrecked. The Highland Weaver.
The Railroad Engineer. John Wesley's Prayer. Providential
Preservation. Daniel Stanton in a Storm. Vessel on the Coast
of Norway. The Poor Schoolmaster. Unexpected Relief.
The Honest Costermonger. The Conscientious Mechanic.
Bishop Gobat and the Hyena. Catharine Phillips and the
Hostile Fleet. The Convicted Colonel. The Uneasy Captain.
Trusting in God. Support under Suffering. William Leddra.
James Renwick. Dying Grace for Dying Hours. The Re-
signed Cripple. "Couple Heaven with it." John Churchman
in the Dead Timber. Old David's Weapons. Nicholas Waln.
Thomas Story. Friends During Indian Wars,   .   .   . 196

CHAPTER VIII.—Faith. William Bray. The Crippled Man.
The Timid Slave. Abraham Lincoln's Trust in God. Emancipation Proclamation. The Doctor taken at his Word. Divine

PAGE

Guidance. David Sands and Remington Hobby. George Withy's Impression to go Home. John Knox Saved from being Shot. Matthew Warren's Wife. Elizabeth L. Redman and the Escaped Prisoner. Prepare for Death. A Lantern for the Footstep. Joseph Lybrand and his Stolen Child. Healing a Breach. Thomas Waring. R. Bourdman Saved from Drowning. Dr. Guthrie and the Paralytic. Daily Bread. Widow Safford. Changing Residence. John Richardson. Joseph Hoag. The Decayed Meeting-house. Joseph Hoag and the Slaveholders. Thomas Story and the Practice of Law. John Richardson and his Step-Father. Frederick Smith and his Wife, ... 231

PART IV.—SERVICES TO BE PERFORMED BY THE FOLLOWERS OF CHRIST.

CHAPTER IX.—Concern for Others. Restore thy Brother. John Churchman and his Drowsy Friend. William Baily. Elizabeth Bathurst. Job Scott. Christian Woman and her Drunken Brother. Joseph Hoag and the Elder. Reproof for Swearing. The Moorish King and the Sack of Earth. Frederick of Prussia and the Mill. James Naylor. Andrew Fuller. The Swiss Colporteur. Mary Swett. John Wesley and the Swearers. Satan's Book. A Box on the Ear. The Motion was in Himself. Bishop Simpson and Brother Swank. Illustrations. The Two Mines. The Queen has sent for Him. Geraldine Hooper and the Dress. The Soldier who did not Intend to Fight. The Drowsy Committee Woman. The Remedy that Cures. John Churchman and the Watch. Food in Winter. The Potter's Care. The Polished Clam Shell. Rowland Hill and the Pigs. The Snuffers. The Pilot, . . 267

CHAPTER X.—Prayer. Thomas Chalkley and the Privateer. The Religious Wife. Prayer for Bread. Ministry. Thomas Story and America. John Churchman and Great Britain. Job Scott's Prospect. Job Scott Shut Up. Willing to be Silent. Resolved to do Better. The Emptied Pitcher. Burning the Bad Bushel. . Waiting on the Lord. Robert Barclay's Testimony. Tennent's Extremity. The Norfolk Preacher. Women Preachers. Mary Collet. Mary Brantingham and the Poacher.

PAGE

George Withy and the Unitarian Minister. James Naylor's Preaching. The Trumpeter. Conscientiousness in Small Things. Thomas Willis. Elizabeth L. Redman and the Slave Dealer. "Ephraim is a Cake not Turned." "Quench Not the Spirit." How to Listen to Preaching. John Finch Marsh. Richard Jordan at Richmond. Barbara Everard. Job Scott's Care. Thomas Wilson. Isaac Penington, ... 295

CHAPTER XI.—Ministry Continued. Prophetic Visions. John Richardson. Joseph Hoag. Peter Gardiner. Miles Halhead. John Roberts. Dr. Leifchild's Sermon. James Simpson's Sermons. James Simpson and the Deist. Maintenance of Ministers. Remarks of John Richardson. Of Thomas Story. Joseph Hoag's Experience. Industry. Daniel Stanton. John Parker. John Banks. John Simpson. When to be Silent. Thomas Story. Joseph Hoag. William Bray. John Churchman. Without Outward Information. Joseph Hoag. John Churchman. Communion of Spirits. Thomas Story. Robert Scotton and the Indian Woman. Richard Shackleton's Advice, 323

CHAPTER XII.—Religious Meetings. Individual Labor. Drowsiness. George Withy. William Hunt. Grace at Table. John Richardson. David Ferris. Meat *versus* Bones. Dr. Manton's Sermon. Balaam's Ministry. Religious Opportunities. John Richardson at Bermuda. Thomas Story at Bristol. Cuthbert Featherstone. Sarah Grubb and Ann Baker. Joseph Oxley. Religious Controversy. Thomas Story and Dr. Gilpin. Thomas Story and a Priest. Job Scott and a Baptist Preacher. Isaac Penington. A Crooked Spirit. Religious Conversation. William Lewis. Richard Shackleton. The Two Merchants. The Teacher's Influence, . . . 354

PART V. REWARDS OF FAITHFULNESS.

CHAPTER XIII.—Joy. Hope. Peace. Job Scott. Thomas Wilson. Thomas Thompson. William Hornold. Thomas Camm. Samuel Bownas. A. F. Priscilla Richardson. Epidemic in Philadelphia in 1699. John Fletcher. Peter Gardiner. John Churchman. Death of a Skeptic. Mary Griffin. Comfort Collins, ... 381

PART I.

OPERATIONS OF DIVINE GRACE.

CHAPTER I.

Teaching of Divine Grace among Barbarous People. The Young Man of Feeble Intellect. Martha Routh when a Child. The Friend of Bush River. Theodore Parker and the Water Turtle. John Churchman when Young. Job Scott's Early Impressions. Are we Christians? The Boy that Died a Martyr. The Norwegian Boy. Tenderness of Conscience in Children. Tempted to Buy a Cigar. William Williams and the Little Girl. The Child and the Tavern-keeper. The Boy in a Street Car. William Hone and his Daughter. Dr. Vinton and his Patient. Mary Capper's Experience. John Fothergill's Childish Oath.

THE great and blessed doctrine that our Saviour, who came into the world to redeem man from sin, visits the hearts of all by his Spirit, and shows unto them how they should walk to secure the Divine favor, so lies at the foundation of all practical religion, that it is illustrated by almost every incident of a religious nature; and is thus being perpetually brought into notice.

A few years ago, I was listening to the remarks of a friend, who told us of a conversation he had had many years before with a man in England, who was probably a sea-captain. He was speaking of barbarous people among whom he had travelled, among whom he said there was no trace of religion at all. After some time, my friend asked him whether

these degraded people seemed to know the difference between actions, as to their being right or wrong—for example, between telling the truth and lying; being honest and
stealing, &c. "Oh, yes," said the Captain, "they know all
about that." In their further conversation the question was
put, as to how these people came to know the difference in
the moral character of their acts? After a little thought, as
if it were a subject new to his mind, the Captain replied,
"It must be from the Divine Spirit, you know."

It was interesting to observe the testimony thus borne to
the truth of the Apostle's declaration, that "The Grace of
God, which bringeth salvation, hath appeared unto all
men;" and teaches them to "live soberly, righteously and
Godly." This teaching is often present and effective in the
minds of those who might be supposed almost incapable of
appreciating it, from want of mental development; and
who are quite unable to form any clear intellectual concep-
tion of many points of theological dogma. As an instance
of this, may be mentioned the case of a young man of feeble
intellect, who desired to become a member of a religious
body in New England. He presented himself to the church
committee. The first question put to him was:

"Do you understand the doctrine of the Trinity?"

"No; I can't say I do."

"Can you give the committee a definition of regeneration?"

"I don't think I can."

"Well, what do you understand by foreordination?"

"Take plenty of time to answer," said a kind-hearted
old deacon, thinking the candidate was confused.

"I don't know much about it," said the young man.

"Can't you give us some opinion respecting God's decrees?"

"I'm afraid not," he replied.

"Well, then," said the minister, a little impatiently, "what
do you know?"

Promptly came the answer, "I know that I am a sinner,

and I know that Christ died to save me, and I want to join the church to get more help from Christ and his people."

Every member of that committee felt rebuked, and one of them said afterwards, "I learned from that moment to respect the spiritual knowledge of the humblest man or woman, and not to think so much of that knowledge which comes from the head alone."

Those quite young in years are often made sensible of the visitations of the Grace of God, showing them those things in their conduct which are displeasing to their Heavenly Father, and awakening a sincere desire to become his obedient children.

It is related of Martha Routh,* a ministering Friend of England, who visited America near the beginning of the present century, that being placed at a day-school where she had not much of the company of other Friends' children, she deviated from the simplicity of language inculcated by her parents at home. Sometime afterwards, two Friends, ministers, came to visit the families of the meeting to which she belonged: "At which" she says, "I greatly rejoiced, though I did not expect to be so found out and melted down under that ministry as proved to be the case. After reminding us who were children, of the example of our parents, how carefully we had been brought up, and the steady attention manifested in the discharge of their duty, that we might act consistently with the principles of Truth; they said, 'What a loss and pity it would be, if any of us should deviate therefrom when out of the sight of our parents, in not using the plain language'—which I well knew was my own case. I seemed like one broken to pieces, and could scarcely forbear weeping aloud.

"As soon as I could get to my cousin Mary Beadley— who had learned to write before me—I got her to write me a letter, which I directed to a scholar to whom I was much

---

*Martha Routh was born in Worcestershire, England, in 1743, and died at London in 1817. She was a fervent laborer in the ministry of the Gospel; and visited America in that service in 1794, and again in 1801. See *Memoir in Friends' Library*, vol. 12, p. 413, etc.

attached, expressing a hope that she would not be offended that I could not any longer give her the title of 'Miss,' but must call her by her proper name, as well as the other girls, though I should love them no less but rather better, because I knew it was acting contrary to the mind of my parents, and the way in which Friends spoke to one another.

"When I went to school again on Second-day morning following, it was under as much weightiness of spirit as mind or body could well bear; but going early, few were in the school, and I took my seat close to that of my governess, whom I loved much. When she came in, she spoke to me in her usual kind way, as did the other girls, and took no notice of my change of language or more serious deportment."

A writer in "The Journal" of Philadelphia, who was born a member of the Society of Friends, in the limits of Bush River Meeting in South Carolina, in giving some reminiscences of his early life, relates the following incident :—

"I remember about this time being left in the nursery by my parents under the care of the housekeeper on a First-day afternoon, whilst they made a social call, when my choleric temper was soon quite aroused by having my childish privileges curtailed, as I thought, by my brother and sister. I immediately retired in disgust to the kitchen to vent my angry feelings in a boyish pout, but in this state, I heard a still small voice saying, 'Now this is all wrong; go right back to thy brother and sister, overcome this angry feeling, and enjoy thyself in their company and their innocent sports and plays.' Then I immediately, like Paul, conferred not with flesh and blood, but obeyed the injunction. O, the sweet peace that accompanied it. Nothing since has ever surpassed its serenity and heavenly enjoyment, easing every burthen, and making all things light, not only for that afternoon, but through all my boyish labor of the following day. This peace of mind was afterwards lost by boyish unfaithfulness."

The remark that the peace of mind which followed submission to the Divine command was afterwards lost by unfaithfulness, is alas, a too common experience of poor, frail man. There can be no advance in our heavenly journey, nor any of that sweet comfort which attends a sense of the Lord's approval, without filial obedience to what He requires of us—without seeking in all things to know the Divine will, and to be conformed thereto.

Theodore Parker* relates an instructive incident that occurred to him in his childhood.

"I saw a little spotted turtle," he writes, "sunning itself in the shallow water. I lifted the stick in my hand to kill it; for though I had never killed any creature, yet I had seen other boys, out of sport, destroy birds, squirrels and the like, and I had a disposition to follow their example. But all at once something checked my little arm, and a voice within me said, clear and loud, 'It is wrong.' I held my uplifted stick in wonder at the new emotion, till the turtle vanished from sight.

"I hastened home and told the tale to my mother, and asked what it was that told me it was wrong. She wiped a tear from her eye, and taking me in her arms, said, 'Some men call it conscience, but I prefer to call it the voice of God in the soul of man. If you listen and obey it, it will speak clearer and clearer, and always guide you right; but if you turn a deaf ear or disobey, then it will fade out little by little, and leave you in the dark without a guide. Your life my son depends on heeding that little voice.'"

There are many witnesses to the truth, that the Grace of God which bringeth salvation, which is the Spirit of Christ our Redeemer shining in the heart, visits the minds of young children, causing them to fear their Creator, and pointing out what they must do and leave undone. And

*A Unitarian minister, and a voluminous writer on theological and literary subjects. Born at Lexington, Massachusetts in 1812; died at Florence, Italy, in 1860.

2

there are few things that bring more true pleasure to the heart of the sincere Christian, than to see those young in years bending their necks to the yoke of Christ; and becoming followers of the Saviour. He can rejoice over such, because he knows they have entered on the only path in life which leads to pure and unmixed felicity. It is sweet indeed to trace the dealings of the Lord with those who yield their hearts to Him in early life. Such are often made a blessing to others in a far higher degree than they themselves can know.

John Churchman* thus relates his experience: " I early felt reproof for bad words and actions, yet knew not whence it came, until about the age of eight years, as I sat in a small meeting, the Lord by his heavenly love and goodness, overcame and tendered my heart, and by his glorious light discovered to me the knowledge of Himself. I saw myself and what I had been doing, and what it was which had reproved me for evil ; and was made in the secret of my heart to confess that childhood and youth, and the foolish actions and words to which they are propense, are truly vanity. Yet blessed forever be the name of the Lord! in his infinite mercy and goodness, He clearly informed me, that if I would mind the discoveries of his pure light for the future, what I had done in the time of my ignorance, He would wink at and forgive: and the stream of love which filled my heart with solid joy at that time, and lasted for many days, is beyond all expression.

Job Scott† says: "I can well remember the serious impressions and contemplations which, at that early period of

*Born in Nottingham, Pennsylvania, in 1705; died 1775. He travelled extensively as a minister in America; and in 1750 crossed the ocean and labored in the service of the Gospel for more than four years in Great Britain, Ireland and Holland. See *Journal in Friends' Library*, vol. 6, p. 176, etc.

†Born at Providence, Rhode Island, in 1751; deceased at Ballitore, Ireland, while on a religious visit to that country in 1793. A deeply spiritual minister of the Gospel. For an account of his travels in America and Great Britain, see published *Journal*.

life, [ten years of age] and for some years before my mother's decease, attended my mind, as I sat in meeting with her, and on my way home. I even had longing desires to become truly religious and to serve and fear God, as Abraham, Isaac and Jacob did, and others that I read or heard of.

" I am fully persuaded of the great advantage, and spiritual usefulness to children and others, resulting from frequent silent waiting on the Lord. I have seen lively and convincing evidence of it, even in children very young in years; and fully believe the impressions of Divine goodness have been such to their minds at some such seasons, even when there has not been a word uttered vocally, as have lastingly remained and powerfully tended to beget the true fear and love of God in their young and tender hearts. And oh! that parents were more generally concerned to do all they could towards leading their tender offspring into an early acquaintance with, and relish of Divine things; best learned, and most livingly and experimentally sealed upon the soul, in a state of silent introversion, and feeling after God.

" Almost as early as I can remember anything, I can well remember the Lord's secret workings in my heart, by his grace or Holy Spirit; very sensibly bringing me under condemnation for my evil thoughts and actions, rudeness and bad words, (though not frequent in the use of them); disobedience to parents; inwardly wishing, in moments of anger, some evil to such as offended me; and such like childish and corrupt dispositions and practices; which over and beyond all outward instruction I was made sensible were evil, and sprang from a real root of evil in me."

Anna Shipton* relates that when travelling in Italy, she stopped at a large hotel. She says: " Great was my astonishment in the evening when I descended to the table d'hôte, to find a small table spread for me alone in a large and magnificent saloon lighted by one solitary lamp and warmed by the faint flame of a wood-fire recently ignited.

" The rain poured in torrents; the wind howled through

* An English writer, the author of several small books of a religious nature.

the long corridors, and echoed through the solitary saloon with its fresco paintings and gorgeous decorations.

" At the close of my dinner, a lady in deep mourning, enveloped in a mantle and shawl entered the room. Supposing from her appearance that she had just arrived in that tempestuous weather, I hastened to offer her the seat I had occupied, and stirred the pine wood into a cheerful blaze.

" As the pale face of the stranger became lighted up by the kindling flame, I was struck by the deep dejection of her countenance, that told of some recent sorrow.

" She was lately a widow, and now mourning an only child, a fair, promising daughter of seventeen, in the dawn of life's morning given to God. She had returned for the last time from the seminary where her education was completed, and the still youthful mother welcomed her companionship, to be no more interrupted ; both had awaited this day with impatience.

" On the first evening of her return, with her arm clasped around the waist of her mother, and her blooming face pillowed on her breast, the young daughter told forth her happiness. And then there was a long pause, as if some perplexing thought had entered her mind and shadowed the face that seemed to have known no cloud of care ; and then she said slowly,

" ' Mother ! Are we Christians ?'

" ' Yes,' replied the widow, a little startled at the earnest tone of the question, ' Christians ! Yes, I hope so !'

" ' Then,' continued the daughter, ' we do not live like Christians. We are just like other people. We take the same amusements, do the same things. If we are Christians, should we not live for Christ ?'

" These words from the lips of her child, who had never known the trials and sorrows of her own life, awakened in the mother new views of a future, which she had imagined was to be one of social enjoyment and cultivated talents. Mother and daughter took counsel together how Christians could serve Christ, and both personally desired to know how this new life could be lived.

" They had not long to wait to know the way of God more

perfectly. Fever broke out in the neighborhood, and the widow's only child was one of the first to sicken and fade.

"It was the messenger of the Lord to prepare the way before Him. Six long, anxious weeks of hope and fear passed by for the mother, marked by an amount of heaven-taught wisdom in the child that I never before traced in one of her years,—so much of the trial and temptation more common to riper age was comprised in her experience. The Lord was moulding and maturing the young spirit for its eternal home.

"'I only wish to live to serve Christ!' was the expression on her lips, whenever a dawn of hope brightened the heart of those who watched beside her. And the Lord heard it.

"A lady left her own family of five children to help the mother to nurse her only child; and when remonstrated with on the danger and cruelty of incurring the risk of infection to her children, she meekly replied that she had obeyed the Lord in coming, and she trusted her children to his care, who bade her leave all to Him. Her family and herself were preserved from the fever. The words and example of this young disciple, 'whom Jesus loved,' were made instrumental in the religious awakening of the eldest son of her nurse and of several other persons.

"A physician of great eminence, who was also a friend of her family, was called in to see her. She inquired of him if he thought she would recover. He replied that most assuredly she would. On which she reproved him with a sternness which startled him, telling him that he knew the falsehood that he had spoken; and with a power and clearness that came from the Holy Spirit's teaching alone, she set before him the Saviour whom he rejected, and the wisdom and power of God which he despised.

"During these six weeks this girl of seventeen, with so little [outward] instruction in the things of God but with a heart that longed to serve Him, lay down upon a bed of fever and suffering to accomplish the desire of her heart in ways she knew not; and died to live with and serve Christ forever, where neither tears nor death can come."

It is interesting to note the manner in which young

2*

persons are sometimes visited by the Day-spring from on High, and the effect produced on their susceptible minds by the company and appearance of those who are endeavoring to walk in the footsteps of Christ's flock.

When Richard Mott* was on one occasion travelling in western Pennsylvania he stopped at a public house. A boy there seemed particularly impressed with his appearance, and asked him why he dressed plain. Continuing near him, he asked many questions about the Quakers, and finally told him that he wanted to go and live with him, and be a Quaker. As Richard was then going from home, he could not comply with the boy's request. Sometime afterwards being at the same place, he asked the landlord if he could tell him about that boy. The landlord replied, " he died a Quaker and a martyr."

From the day after his conversation with Richard, he had never been known to use the plural language to one person. He had also had a plain suit of clothes made which he wore. These things exposed him to great ridicule and persecution by his school-fellows. One day some of them seemed determined to make him fight, which he positively refused to do. One of them, in order to provoke him into a fight, flourished his fist in his face, and without intending to injure him, struck him on the head. The lad fell down dead! Thus the testimony was left behind him, that he died a Quaker and a martyr.†

When travelling in Iowa some years ago, I met with a Norwegian who had joined in membership with Friends after coming to this country. He attributed the first turning of his mind in that direction to the impression made upon him when a boy of perhaps six years old, by the visit

* A minister among Friends who resided at Mamaroneck, New York. Died in 1856, aged eighty-nine years. He paid a religious visit to the Southern and Western States in 1805 and 1806, at which time it is probable the incident related in the text occurred

† Although true religion leads to plainness and simplicity in dress and behavior, yet these do not constitute religion, which is the work of Divine grace in the heart of man.

of some Friends to his father's house. He was eager to see them, but was not permitted to go into the parlor, probably because he was too ragged or dirty. But he contrived to gratify his curiosity. Their solid behavior and appearance so affected him that the impression never wore away.

As illustrations of the tenderness of conscience produced by the work of the Spirit, and of the early age at which it is manifested, the two following cases may be cited:

A beloved child who was ill of a mortal disease, spoke to his mother desiring her forgiveness. She could not recollect that her boy had ever offended her. But he replied, that although he might have performed what she commanded him, yet he had not obeyed with that willingness which he ought to have felt. His shortcoming in this respect caused him uneasiness. Another child, not yet three years old, ill with small-pox, made use of some angry and improper expression to a person who attended it; but soon felt the reproofs of conscience for the offence. It acknowledged the fault to its mother, and when the attendant again entered the room stretched out its little arms in token of desire to be reconciled.

I knew well a man, who, when a boy of six or seven years of age, was tempted to imitate other boys whom he saw smoking. So he asked his father for a penny, not without many smitings of conscience at the use to which he intended to put it, and some fears lest his father should inquire about the purpose for which it was intended. The penny was given without any questions being asked, and the child went at once to the nearest cigar store, for he felt as impatient as he was unhappy about getting the cigar. The woman who tended the shop gave him what he asked for, and turned about to go to her work. Under conviction that he was doing wrong, the child said to her, "Does thee think I had better take this?" She replied,

"Did'nt you ask for it?" "Yes, but does thee think I had better take it?" She replied that she thought it was worth the money; but as he took hold of the door-knob to go out, he again queried, "Does thee think it is *right* for me to take it?" She asked if he had ever smoked any, and finding he had not, told him it would make him sick, and she could not advise him to begin. So there was a second exchange of money and cigar; and the child, who had been struggling •with the convictions of grace and dallying with temptation, felt a measure of that peace and joy which is graciously given to those who yield themselves to the Divine will; and he went out of the cigar store far happier than he entered.

The journal of William Williams,* a minister in the Society of Friends, who resided in Tennessee, contains the following interesting incident:

I think proper to relate here, also, a singular circumstance concerning a little girl,† whose father rode sometime with me, when I was first in the State of New Jersey, and at whose house I lodged the night before I left that State to go to New York. The child was then under eight years of age. I had a sitting in the family, which was a watering time, for the presence of the Master was to be felt, and the dear little daughter (as well as I remember, the youngest of a large family) was tendered, and felt her mind much attached to me in tender love, which I was sensible of at that time. This was in the Fifth Month, 1811, and as I returned from the eastward in the Sixth Month, I sent for some linens which I had left there, and when I opened

---

* William Williams was born in North Carolina about the year 1763, removed from thence to Tennessee, and finally to Indiana, where he died in 1824. He labored extensively as a minister of the Gospel.

† The name of this child was Mary Black. At the time of her death, she was not quite seven years old. Her father, who travelled considerably in New Jersey in company with William Williams, resided near Columbus, New Jersey.

them, I found a small present from this child to my little daughter at home, whom I had told her of. On the 8th day of the Second Month, 1813, I left home again, and in the course of this visit also, I got to her father's house; and when I got there, I soon looked for the little daughter, but saw her not. I then asked for her, and saw the tears start in the eyes of her mother at the hearing of her name. We sat awhile in solemn silence, and I spoke and said, "is the child gone to rest?" she said "she has;" and then told me about her latter end, which I thought I would then write; but I put it off at that time, yet it made so deep impressions on my mind, that it could not be erased. The child was taken sick, and in a little time afterwards she told her mother that she should not live to get well again, but should die; and her mother asked her if she was willing to die. She said there was but one thing that she wanted; that was to see that friend who was from Tennessee; "if I could only see him once more, and hear him, I should be willing then to go to my Heavenly Father, and leave all my dear friends behind;" and thus she continued for many days, often saying, 'O Heavenly Father! I am willing to die, and come to thee, yet I wish to see that endeared friend, and hear him preach to my father and mother, and to my brothers and sisters, if it is thy holy will, O Lord! but not my will be done." And one day, as her mother was sitting by her bed with another friend, Mary lay still, as though she was asleep or in a doze, for an hour or more; then she stirred, and her mother asked her if she wanted any thing, (meaning drink or any refreshment) she said no, she wanted nothing, but to die; and added, "I have wanted to see dear William Williams, but I shall not see him, but shall die: you will see him." "O, no, Mary," her mother said, "he lives a great way from here." "No matter for that, he is on his way now, and in time he will be here, in this land, and thou wilt see him and hear him; and then give my love to him, and tell him, I go to my Father, and his Father, there to wait for his coming." So, on the next day, she quietly departed this life, when I was in Virginia, on my way to those parts.

It sometimes pleases the Lord to make use of young and feeble instruments to awaken those who are older to a sense of their situation, or to perform other services. In such cases, the effect produced depends on the power of Divine Grace which accompanies the message or service, and which brings conviction to the one to whom it is addressed; and this Grace may be extended through weak agents, who, without its assistance would 'have no power to effect any good.

In my school-boy days, I knew a little boy, the son of one of my teachers,* who died at an early age perhaps eight or nine years. He was a thoughtful child, and one day asked permission of his mother to visit a neighbor who kept a house of entertainment for travellers, and sold spirituous liquors to such as wanted them. He was a man of wealth and respectability, and the owner of a large landed property, and his house was one that was regarded as reputably kept; I never heard of anything like carousing or disorderly conduct being permitted about the premises. The mother discouraged her child from making the visit, thinking one so young would not be able to accomplish any good. But the impression of duty was so imprinted or renewed on his young mind, that the request for permission to go was repeated at intervals, until the mother was unwilling longer to prevent the visit. Accordingly the child went alone. It would be interesting to know what took place at the interview which followed, but there was probably no one present but themselves, and it is not known. But I believe it was not long after that the proprietor discontinued the sale of liquor.

I recently met with a narrative which brought the above

*The late Daniel B. Smith, of Germantown, Philadelphia, then a teacher at Haverford School, now College, incident to my recollection. The writer of it, was riding in a street car in one of our cities, when there entered a man about seventy years of age.

He says: "I noticed that he walked unsteadily, but thought it due to the motion of the car. His actions after he was seated, however, convinced me that he was intoxicated. By my side sat a little boy, aged about eight years; he, with his father, and the old gentleman, before mentioned, and myself, constituted the sole occupants of the car. I remarked, that after a few moments close scrutiny of the old gentleman by the boy, he addressed his father. I could hear but imperfectly what he said, but I distinguished a 'Please, papa, let me speak to him.' The father answered, 'No, my boy, he will not understand what you say.' Still the boy pleaded, and finally I saw him go to the side of the old gentleman. Laying his little hand on the old man's knee, the boy said, 'Please, sir, I am sorry for you.' The half stupid man raised his head and said, 'Eh! what did you say?' The boy repeated his first remark and added: 'I know what is the matter with you, for I have seen a great many who had been drinking; but I know how you can stop, and I am sure you want to know too.' 'How,' answered his hearer.' 'Pray,' answered the boy. 'Mamma has told me whenever I felt tempted to do wrong to pray, and God would help me by taking the temptation away: and I know He does help me, for many a time when I have wanted some fruit I have prayed, and God *always* made it easy for me *not* to take any. You see,' said the boy in explanation, 'I was very sick a year ago and the doctor thought I would die; but I got well, and the only way I can keep well is not to eat fruit. Now, if you would pray I don't believe you would want *rum*. I know you have friends who hate to have you sick as much as my friends do me; so won't you try and keep well? I am going to pray for you, anyway.' "

"I did not hear this, but the gentleman told me afterwards what the youthful preacher had said. What I saw, however, was this: *tears* streaming down the face of the old man opposite, and I heard him say, 'Pray! yes, I will, and you must *pray* for me.' The little boy, under the guidance of the Spirit, had wrought a good work."

The writer adds, that since that time he had seen the man exposed to great temptation, but that he had never fallen into the ensnaring habit. His safety resulted from looking to the Lord for help to overcome the sin that so easily beset him. His feelings towards the lad who spoke the "word in due season" are thus indicated: "He is *beloved*, and I have heard a white-haired gentleman, with a voice tremulous with emotion, say: 'And a little child shall lead them.'"

William Hone,* the author of the "Every-day Book," was at one time a noted infidel and an active opposer of Christianity. A little girl of his, coming under the saving influence of truth, became much concerned for her father, and obtained a Bible, but knew not how to put it into his hands, for she feared his displeasure. She retired to seek Divine guidance. Her father, passing the door of the apartment, heard the voice of his child; it was the voice of prayer; she prayed for him; he became affected, agitated and distressed. After a little while the family assembled at the tea-table, the beverage was handed round, but he could not partake. "Is there a Bible in the house?" he said. "My dear," replied his wife, apprehensive of the proposed repetition of the act, "did you not burn every Bible that we had, not leaving so much as one?" "Is there any good book then?" he inquired. His little daughter, thinking that God might be answering her prayer, arose, took him by the hand, and asked him to go with her, and when they had left the room, looking into his face, said, "Father, surely you won't be angry with me; I know you won't be angry with me; come with me and I will get you one," and she brought him and gave him the Bible which for this very purpose she had procured.

* Died in 1842, aged sixty-three years. He was a native of Bath, England, and for many years a publisher and bookseller in London. He was the author of many political pieces and other works, of which *The Every Day Book* is the most valued.

He felt deeply, and, trembling while he handed it back to her, said, "My child, I cannot read this book; will you read it for me?" She did so, and then taking her in his arms he kissed her and said, "Tell me, my child, where did you get this book, and how did you obtain this knowledge of it?" She told him all. That very evening he accompanied her to the chapel. As they entered the minister was engaged in prayer; his manner and address made a powerful impression on the father's mind, for he seemed to talk with God. The sermon aided in deepening the impression. It was an interesting sight when, two or three weeks afterward, that father appeared in that chapel with his wife and nine children, and openly renounced his infidelity.

It is related of Dr. Vinton, that when a young skeptical physician, a friend persuaded him to read "Butler's Analogy." This book satisfied his reason. Intellectually he was no longer a sceptic. Things stood thus with him when he was called to attend a little girl dying of consumption. Lying on her sick bed, she whispered she had something to say to him; and when encouraged to speak, said she had not the courage, but confessed that it would relate to his being at peace with God. "To-morrow morning," she added, "when I am stronger, I will tell you." And *to-morrow morning* she was dead. The incident made a permanent impression on Dr. Vinton. He could not cease to ask himself what that little girl would have said to him on that matter. He framed one thing after another, and thus called up before his conscience the persuasions he himself invented for the little girl. He became a pious man.

Mary Capper* relates the following incident, which shows that the Spirit of Christ operates on the minds of children in very early life.

"One occasion, I think I cannot forget, because it is sealed by mercy and by experience to this day; though the thing was, in itself, comparatively little, and I was then

---

*A minister in the Society of Friends. She died at Birmingham, England, in 1845, in the ninety-first year of her age. See *Memoir in Friends Library*, vol. 12, p. 1, etc.

young. Being tempted to take some fruit in a garden where I was unobserved, and being on the point of gathering it, a sudden check arrested me. I cannot distinctly describe it, but I walked from the spot with a sweetness of inward peace, indescribable, such as I think I had never before known; and it arose in my heart and has remained in my understanding, this is the teaching of the Grace of God; or, in other words, of the Holy Spirit! This, we had been taught to believe, would enable us to overcome evil; but it is not sufficiently understood; and when gently developed in the still, small voice, it is frequently not obeyed; and the quick sense of its secret monitions becomes less discernible."

In John Fothergill's Life,* occurs the following passage: "When I was between six and seven years old, as near as I can recollect, being at some little play with another boy, through the force of a sudden temptation, I swore an oath, which notwithstanding it was to a truth, yet such secret conviction of the evil of so doing in the sight of the Almighty God, so affected my mind with sorrow and remorse, as made a lasting impression on my judgment; and also imprinted that warning and fear in my heart in this respect that I never did the like since on any occasion.

"Wherefore as I cannot but believe that the pure law of God, which is light, makes its appearance against evil in all, and often in tender years; so if a careful regard were yielded in youth to this inshining of the day of God in secret, many evil practices and defiling liberties would be prevented, and would never get that room in the mind, and in use, which with sorrow we too often observe they do."

The preceding incidents and testimonies show that the Holy Light of Jesus impresses a sense of right and of wrong on the mind; and brings those who disregard it under a sense of condemnation. This accords with the testimony

* A faithful minister in the Society of Friends, residing in Yorkshire, England, where he died in 1744, aged sixty-nine years. He thrice visited America in the service of the Gospel. See *Life in Friends' Library*, vol. 13, p. 352, etc.

of the Apostle John, that He who was in the beginning, and who "was made flesh and dwelt among us," "was the true Light which lighteth every man that cometh into the world." And with the declaration of our Saviour himself, that "This is the condemnation, that light is come into the world, and men loved darkness rather than light, because their deeds were evil." In the following pages, illustrations will be produced of the blessed truth, that to as many as receive Christ in the way of his coming to their souls, and believe in and obey his commands, He still gives power to become the sons of God.

CHAPTER II.

Converting Power of Divine Grace. The College Student. Mary M——. The young German Baptist. John Flavel's Message. E. Worth's Neighbor. Daniel Stanton's Experience. The Scotch Virago Reformed. Edward Wright's Awakening. Special Seasons of Visitation.

THE poet Cowper forcibly expressed a most important truth when he wrote:

"Transformation of Apostate man
From fool to wise, from earthly to divine,
Is work for Him that made him."

This transformation is the same thing as the experience of that regeneration, without which, as our Saviour told Nicodemus, a man "cannot see the kingdom of God." This is effected through the renewed visitations of the Holy Spirit, or Grace of God, mercifully given to lead man from sin and misery to purity and happiness.

Our Saviour said there is more joy in heaven over one sinner that repenteth than over ninety and nine just persons who need no repentance. No wonder, then, that the accounts of the conversion of sinners, and of the various means used by Divine Grace to arrest their attention, and turn them from darkness to light, should be of ever-fresh interest to the lovers of the Lord Jesus. A few of these narratives are here grouped together.

The *Episcopal Recorder* relates the case of a young man at a college, where a deep interest in religion had been awakened among the students. He had left the breakfast-hall, and stood upon the steps of the building, gazing thoughtfully on the scene before him. It was early in summer; the college grounds were covered with their richest verdure, and the leafy tresses of the overshadowing elms hung motionless in the balmy atmosphere. One by one the students were passing to their rooms, exchanging with each other here and there a morning greeting, but mostly silent, as if feeling the awe of an invisible Presence resting upon all hearts.

The person spoken of was struck with this peculiar aspect of stillness and solemnity. For several weeks the Spirit of God had been working there. Many were deeply impressed; some seeking to resist their convictions by affected levity, others borne down by them as by an insupportable burden.

Young S—— had been trained by pious parents, and was irreproachable in principles and habits. But he was not a Christian. The visible solemnity which rested upon the college excited his attention, and pressed that fact with unwonted force upon his heart. The thought of the venerated father and saintly mother, who, he knew, prayed for him daily with unutterable desire, rushed as never before upon his mind. Suddenly the inquiry sprung up within him, "Why should I not be a Christian, too? Often have I promised myself that I would attend to this subject. Is not this the time? Why not now?"

He descended the steps of the breakfast-hall, and slowly sauntered to his room. The inquiry rung in his ear, Why not? He entered his room and seated himself for study. But he hesitated. A silent voice within disquieted him: the thought of God, of eternity, of his own guilt and need of salvation, pressed upon him with unwonted force, and urged him to defer the momentous decision no longer.

"What," thought he at length, "is it to be a Christian? *How shall I begin?*"

"To be a Christian," he said, "is to love God, and to live to please Him. This I know I have not done. I have been a diligent student, but it was because I was interested in my studies, and was ambitious to excel. I have come to college in hope of fitting myself for distinction in life. Alas! I have not thought of God in all this; I have not cared to please Him; I have not asked his will. This was all wrong. Of course, therefore, if I would be a Christian, I must entirely change my life in this respect. I must begin to act as God would have me; *I must begin by doing the first thing I have to do, to please Him.* This lesson," laying his hand on his book, "is to be learned from regard to Him; this day, in all its duties and occupations, is to be given to his service; my college training is to be made preparatory to a life devoted to his glory. And so I am to give *myself* to Him—my soul, my body, my talents, my acquisitions, my all."

"Yes," said he, after some moments of profound thought, "*I will.* First, I will kneel down and say so to Him, and ask his aid and his blessing." He did so. Had his resolve stopped at that first act, it would have been of little worth. As related by himself to the writer of the narrative, it was the *turning-point* in his course, from which he dated the commencement of his religious life. He then entered the school of Christ, and receiving humbly the first of its lessons, was prepared by it for others in due time until he attained a well-balanced and most devoted piety.

It was the Light of Christ—the Spirit of his Saviour—which enabled this young man to see that he was not living in the fear of God; and, as he turned to its reproofs, gave him power to form the holy resolution to devote himself wholly to the Lord's cause. This enabling power will never be wanting to him who in sincerity seeks it. For, as Wm. Penn says: "Never did God convince people, but, upon

3*

submission, He impowered them." "They that want power are such as don't receive Christ in his convictions upon the soul; and such will always want it; but such as do [reçeive Christ] they receive power (like those of old) to become the children of God."

A writer in the *American Messenger* describes the religious awakening of a young woman, Mary M——, in one of our New England towns. She had been piously brought up, but had married into an irreligious family and had drifted away from her early associations, until she seemed to have no concern left about her spiritual welfare. A younger brother of her husband, named Edwin, lived with them, and out of curiosity he attended a religious meeting, where a deeper feeling was awakened in his mind. On the next occasion he asked Mary to accompany him. She laughingly objected; but consented at the suggestion of a young friend who was visiting them, that they might at least derive some amusement from going.

On their return the young women noticed that Edwin seemed sad, and they determined, if possible, to erase all serious impressions from his mind. So they jested about the meeting and the preacher, and religious meetings in general, and at length Mary laughingly said, "Now let us have a prayer meeting; brother Edwin will please pray with us."

Edwin before this had sat silent and thoughtful, but now he aroused himself, and gravely replied, "Yes, let us pray, for we all need help from above;" and to the surprise of the others he kneeled and poured out his soul to God.

When he began, Mary was more angry than ever before in her life, but when he prayed for her, that "God would forgive her for sporting with religious things, and bring her to himself," she began to feel alarmed, and when the prayer was concluded she was shedding tears which she vainly strove to hide.

She hastened to her room with feelings far different from those when she left it. Her sins rose up to condemn her, and she spent the night in great agony of mind. The conviction of her sinfulness, thus remarkably fastened upon her mind, worked its proper effect in leading her to repentance and amendment of life; and her fervent petitions to the Lord for mercy, were, in due time, answered by a sense of forgiveness of the sins that were past.

This narrative reminds the writer of the relation of her own experience given to him some years ago by an elderly woman, a member among the German Baptists, who was a religiously-minded person.

When a young woman, like many others at that time of life, she was thoughtless and giddy. A young man belonging to a neighboring family, with whom there was considerable intimacy, seemed seriously inclined, and would frequently, after being at meeting, make some remark which indicated that the religious services had made an impression on his mind. But she, in her thoughtless frivolity, would ridicule his seriousness, and tell him, " You are getting religious."

One day his sister came in haste across the field to her home, telling her she must immediately come to their help, for her brother was taken very ill, and said he was not fit to die. This brought her into a very close trial—for she felt that her influence over him had been unfavorable, and it would be awful indeed if he should be taken in an unprepared state, and the responsibility rest upon her.

He lived about two weeks from that time, and before his death was favored with an evidence of acceptance with his Heavenly Father. But what she then passed through had a sobering effect upon my informant, and that period of time proved to be a turning point in her spiritual career.

Two hundred years ago, John Flavel,* of Dartmouth,

---

* An eminent Nonconformist minister, a native of Worcestershire, England. He was the author of many religious pieces. He died in 1691, and his works have been several times republished. "An excellent man, full of zeal in the cause of religion."

England, driven out of his pulpit by the persecuting Act of Uniformity, was preaching in the open field. With his wonted earnestness and affectionate fervor of address, he spoke of the dreadful curse resting on all who loved not the Lord Jesus. Among the listeners on that day was a youth of fifteen, who heard the solemn words of the preacher, and went away as though he heard them not. Some of noble birth and high intellectual culture were so deeply affected that they fell senseless upon the ground. But that thoughtless young man only listened and looked on as if he were a disinterested spectator. Soon afterwards he began a roving life upon the seas, and finally settled down for a permanent home, a fatherless and a prayerless man, in America. Eighty-five years passed by from that day of field preaching at Dartmouth, and the boy of fifteen was now a man of a hundred years, and a wanderer from God. The quick susceptibilities of youth had died in his old and guilty heart long ago. No ordinary faith could have believed that the seed-corn of divine truth, planted by John Flavel's preaching eighty-five years before, on the other side of the ocean, still survived, and was destined to spring up and bear fruit unto life eternal. It chanced on a certain day that he found himself alone in an open field belonging to his farm, with no weeping multitude around him to awaken his sympathies, and no preacher's solemn voice to tell him of his sin. Moved, he knew not how, that old man, in his hundredth year, passing over all the intervening space, felt himself back again in the fields at Dartmouth, hearing the fearful words, "If any man love not the Lord Jesus, let him be accursed." And the message of heaven, which the thoughtless youth so easily rejected, was mightier when speaking from the remembered past than when heard from the living voice. Then first the aged sinner found strength to roll the burden of the threatened curse from his heart, through the exercise of penitent and trusting love. He lived to the extraordinary age of one hundred and sixteen years, believing and rejoicing in the Saviour whom for a century he had rejected.

In the Ninth Month of 1868, when in company with that good man, Ebenezer Worth, of Chester County, Penna., he related to the writer the case of one of his neighbors, which illustrates the long-suffering loving-kindness of the Lord, who wills not that any should perish.

This neighbor had been a rough man, giving little evidence of regard for religion, and became ill with what proved to be his last sickness. Ebenezer went on a First-day afternoon to see him, and found him in a suffering state, and his nerves rendered irritable by the disease, so that he looked "fierce." After kindly inquiring into his wants, and whether he was supplied with suitable food and fuel, and finding that the neighbors had attended to these wants, the way opened to make some remarks on the comfort and support which religion furnishes in times of sickness and suffering. The sick man replied that he did not believe in hell as preached by the Methodists, &c.; but seemed a little softened before Ebenezer left him.

The next First-day E. again visited him, and found him in a milder mood, though still disposed to cavil at some of the truths of religion. In the course of the conversation which followed, the sick man related an incident that had occurred to him many years before. He said at one time he was walking and carrying a bag of meal, when an impression came over his mind to pray. This was so unusual, and seemed so strange to him, that he knew not what to make of it. He thought that if he should make the effort, he would not know what to say in his prayer. But the impression was so strong, that finally he laid down his bag of meal and knelt beside it. The feelings and thoughts that then came into his mind, and the words that were put into his mouth, were surprising to himself; and he arose from the ground with a quiet, comfortable feeling, that continued about him for several days. As he related to Ebenezer this remarkable visitation of Divine Grace, a portion of the same feeling which had accompanied it seemed to revive on his mind, and E. parted with him in a more satisfactory condition than he had been in. Before the close of his life came, Divine mercy accomplished its work in his case, and he died the death of a Christian.

When Daniel Stanton* was quite young, he lived in a part of New Jersey, where he had no opportunity of attending a place of religious worship. "But the Lord," he says, "was pleased, by his grace and good visitations, to operate on my mind, that I was made to dread and fear the great Almighty Being, and it was given me to know that 'God is a spirit, and they who worship Him must worship Him in spirit and truth;' and through the blessed knowledge of God by his Holy Spirit, I had great reproof in my own breast for sin and transgression, and dreaded to speak bad words, or do what was evil, and was brought by inward conviction to mourn and seek for mercy to my soul. And at a time when I heard of the suffering of my dear Saviour on the cross, and how He suffered unto death, my heart was broken before the Lord, and I went alone and wept, being much affected with a sense of his suffering by that hard-hearted people, the Jews, and of his being crucified. Great was the goodness of the Almighty to me, in giving me a sense of many things appertaining to godliness, in the time of this tender visitation; and I found by the divine witness in myself, that if I would be a disciple of Christ, I must take up my cross daily to that which displeaseth God, He being greatly to be feared and obeyed, and was worthy of the deepest reverence that my soul, body and strength could ascribe to his all-powerful name."

Daniel Stanton was one of many witnesses to the fulfilment of the gracious promise, "they shall be all taught of God." For the Apostle declares, "The grace of God which bringeth salvation hath appeared unto all men, *teaching* them, &c.," so that it may truly be said, "there is no speech or language" where the voice of this Divine Instructor is not heard.

One of the most marvellous instances of the transforming

---

* A resident in Philadelphia, where he was born in 1708, and died in 1770. He labored in the ministry of the Gospel in various parts of America and the West India Islands, and also in England, Wales and Scotland. See *Life in Friends' Library*, vol. 12, p. 146, etc.

power of Divine Grace is that related by John B. Gough,* of a woman whom he encountered in Edinburgh, Scotland, where he had gone to labor in the interests of temperance.

He attended a meeting in the wickedest part of that city. He had never before witnessed such degradation, misery and filth, as were visible among the outcasts there assembled. Among the audience was one of the most desperate characters known to the city authorities. She had served fifty-four terms in prison. Not one of the police force would attempt to arrest her without help, and when she was excited by rum or passion, the thieves and outlaws among whom she lived would flee from her.

Some one on the platform pointed her out to J. B. Gough, and was telling him her character, when she noticed that they were looking at her. She immediately arose, went on to the platform, and in a defiant manner asked Gough whether he would give the temperance pledge to such an one as she. His companion greatly feared a scene of fighting and confusion and whispered to Gough not to notice her— that she would never keep a pledge to abstain from liquor. She demanded in a threatening way, Is he ready to give me the pledge? He replied, yes; but there is a man here that says you will not keep it. Terribly excited at this, she screamed at the top of her voice, and demanded to know who and where he was that had so said. Her excitement was calmed by Gough who again said he would give her the pledge, and that he would take her word to keep it as quick as he would the word of any woman in Edinburgh. Touched by his confidence, she stood quiet and thoughtful for a minute, and yielding to the visitation of Divine love to her soul, afresh extended at that critical moment, she promised to give up her drinking habits.

Four years after, J. B. Gough held another meeting at Edinburgh. Two women sat in front of the platform, listening attentively. The tears and emotion of one of them touched his heart deeply. When the meeting closed one of

* A celebrated temperance lecturer. Born in Kent, England, in 1817, and removed to the United States when twelve years old. Died 1886. The author of several auto-biographical works.

the women came up to the platform and asked him if he knew the woman that sat sobbing in front of him. He said no. "Well," she said, "that is my mother. And oh how proud I am of her. But the fire and rum is all taken out of her now, wherein the neighbors were all afraid of her when she drank. Now, when they have trouble or sickness, the worst of them will say, bring me the good angel, for she has got the comfort that serves all." There she sat clothed, and in her right mind. She that was as ferocious as a tiger sits with streams of joyful tears, wetting her cheeks, so subdued and humble that she shrinks from making herself known even to the man that dare trust her word when no living creature would believe her. Gough asked her how she got along. "Oh sir, the struggle was hard, hard, hard, very hard. Often I have dreamed that I had gone back to drink, and that I was fighting with the neighbors with a worse nature than ever before. The dreams have been so real to me that I have often awakened out of sleep and rolled out of bed onto my knees, crying at the top of my voice for God to save me, and I would never drink or fight again.

"The voice of my daughter has often called me to consciousness, in times of such despair. She would cry, 'Mother, mother—you are safe; it is only a dream you had.' As I passed from that anguish, at the thought of falling, I had some idea of the misery of a lost soul, And when I threw myself on the floor of my little quiet, clean room, with my saved daughter by my side, Oh how the joy of a heaven on earth flooded through my soul. Praise God I am not only saved from drink, but saved from sinning against such a merciful and loving God as I have found in Jesus."

J. B. Gough made inquiry from others how she got along and spent her time. He found that she hired a little shop and sold eatables, such as the poor around her used, at a lower price than they could buy at other places. Her daughter and she made common sacks. They lived on thirty cents a day, and were able to help scores of poor families. As soon as the drink got out of her own system, she began to labor with others like herself. Her first effort was with a woman that was counted the next hardest case in Edinburgh. She never left her until she was reclaimed. When she went after such ones, she was never known to fail. She believed when she felt for them, God felt for them, and had laid the burden on her for them. There was no sacrifice too great for her to make, in view of rescuing another immortal soul. She generally brought them to her house, and kept them there, until she broke up their hardened hearts with her love. She would watch every move that they would make. She would wait on them, wash their feet, comb their hair, pat their cheeks, and kiss them as but few mothers can. She knew her work, and had the assurance that she was successfully wooing them for Christ. She was never idle in her new Master's work. Many were lifted up from the lowest depths of sin through her instrumentality.

She lived to the honor of her Redeemer, Jesus Christ, over twenty-seven years. She died in great joy, praising God for his power to save to the uttermost all that come to Him through Jesus Christ, the only mediator between God and man.

The mayor of Edinburgh, with the city officers, and ministers of the gospel, and Christians of every denomination, together with thousands of the citizens, mourned with a heartfelt grief as her remains were lowered into the grave.

A remarkable instance of the convicting and converting power of Divine Grace is that furnished by the case of Edward Wright,* of London.

He was a dissolute man, given to fighting, fond of drinking, and one who often resorted to thieving and other dishonest ways of obtaining the means of supporting himself and family. At the time that he was thoroughly awakened to a sense of his spiritual condition, he was under training for a projected prize-fight, in which he was to participate. After tea he asked his wife to accompany him in a walk, so that if any of his companions should call that night, with a view of persuading him to drink, he might escape a temptation

---

* *Incidents in the Life of Edward Wright.* London, 1870.

that would materially interfere with his prospects of success.
They had not gone far before they were met by a boy who
was distributing invitations to a meeting.   On the circular
were the words, "All seats free, no collections;" and they
concluded to spend the evening at the meeting.

The preaching did not greatly affect him; but at the close
of the services, the preacher cried with a loud voice, "Young
man, where will you spend eternity?"   This he repeated
six times causing an interval of solemn quiet to pervade
the meeting between each cry of "Eternity."

During those awful moments the Holy Spirit brought to
his remembrance his past history; the thought came, "Am
I prepared to die?" and he remembered the words of the
preacher "The wicked shall be turned into hell, with all
the nations that forget God."   So great was the agitation of
his feelings, that at last he swooned.

Whilst in this partly unconscious state, the intellectual
faculties were still awake, and to his strongly excited feelings the realities of the Day of Judgment seemed actually
present.   His conscience being greatly stirred, he felt himself standing as a wretched sinner before the great Judge
without any thing to say in his own defence.   In this awful
condition, feeling his guilt, and with broken heart seeking
for pardon and forgiveness, he was impressed with the conviction that there was hope for him through the mercy of
God in Christ Jesus.

When he was restored to consciousness, the perspiration
was streaming from his brow, and tears channelling his
cheeks.

His wife also was deeply impressed on the same occasion,
and they returned home fully determined to walk hand in
hand on the heavenly journey.

The next morning brought with it a test of the sincerity
of his newly formed resolutions.   He felt that he could not
fulfil his engagement to take part in the prize-fight.   So, the
first thing after breakfast he went to the friend by whom
the matter had been arranged, and announced his intention.
Of course, he was met with many bitter reproaches; called
a cur, and a fool; and one remarked, "Poor Ned, he's gone

off his chump (*i. e.* mind) at last." Ned overheard the free criticism, and observed, " No, I was never in my right mind before ; but I am now, thanks be to God.

Like the Apostle Paul, who also was met with in a sudden and very wonderful manner, Edward Wright was not disobedient to the heavenly vision. His narrative furnishes an interesting instance of what Robert Barclay says, in speaking of the Spirit of Christ, that it " Comes upon all at certain times and seasons, wherein it works powerfully upon the soul, mightily tenders it, and breaks it; at which time, if man resist it not, but closes with it, he comes to know salvation by it. God moves in love to mankind, at some singular times, setting his sins in order before him, and seriously inviting him to repentance, offering to him remission of sins and salvation : which, if man accept of, he may be saved." " This then," he adds, " O man or woman, is the day of God's gracious visitation to thy soul, which if thou resist not, thou shalt be happy forever."*

The memorable evening when E. Wright was providentially led to a place of religious worship, appears to have been to him, such a " *singular time*," and it was indeed an unspeakable favor to him, that he was enabled to submit to the Divine visitation. He often afterwards spoke of it as the time of his " conversion"—and so it truly was in the proper sense of the word, which signifies a turning or changing ; for his thoughts were turned from the pursuit

---

* *Barclay's Apology*, Prop. V., VI., Sec. 16. Robert Barclay, who belonged to a noble family in Scotland, joined the Society of Friends while still young, and was the author of several works in which he defended its principles with great learning and ability. His *Apology*, first published in 1675, has been translated into several languages, and often reprinted, both in England and America. He died in 1690, aged forty-two years. For a fuller account of him, see *Sewel's History of the Quakers,* Evans' *Friends of the Seventeenth Century, Biographia Britannica, Allibone's Dictionary of Authors*, etc.

of merely sensual gratifications towards the possession of heavenly treasures. But he experienced, as all true Christians do, that though his feet had been happily *turned* into the path that leads to Heaven, yet many struggles and conflicts were to be encountered in his journey thither.

CHAPTER III.

Conversion by Instrumental Means. Gospel Ministry. John Ashton. John Estaugh's Preaching. Baptizing Power of True Ministry. Effect on Joseph Pike. Samuel Neale's Awakening. "What can this old fool say?" William Williams' Reproof. Dreams. David Ferris. Of the Unworthy Captain. Of the Pasture Field. Of Giving way to Provocation. Of Washing Linen. Of the Dangerous Ferry-boat. Of Helping a Neighbor. Of Going to Hell. Warnings and Accidents. S. Grellet at St. Gilles. Racing-horses. The Privateer "Tartar." The Singer and the Poor Laborer. The Widow of Lyons. Example. Effect of on an Infidel. "Aunt Mary's Practising." "Master's Life." Madagascar Convert. Mountebank Preacher. Acknowledging the Wrong. German Rationalist Convinced. "His Life a Sermon." French Hospital Matron. Swearing Pilot. The Blood of the Martyrs is the Seed of the Church. The Clerks and their Bibles. Mechanic and Lady. Responsibility for Influence. Presbyterian and his Store Boy. Thomas H. Benton's Mother. The Coachman's Mother. Consistency. The Unfaithful Cooper. The Irritated Professor. John Churchman and Armed Vessels. Blessing on Cards.

Although the glory of man's conversion and salvation is due to the Lord alone, yet He operates not only immediately by his Spirit, but also through various instrumental means; in all which cases, the good effected must be ascribed to the Divine blessing that rests upon them. Among these means, is the exercise of Gospel ministry, which has often proved effectual in awakening the careless and unconcerned, as well as in edifying and comforting those who are endeavoring to walk in the footsteps of Christ's companions.

The general subject of the Ministry will be referred to further on, but some illustrations of the effects which have been produced by it will be introduced in this place.

It is related of John Ashton, of Killconinmore, Ireland, in the early days of the Society of Friends, that being desirous of further discoveries of the knowledge of God and way of salvation, he, with his wife, went to a meeting at Birr, when both of them were convinced by the powerful ministry of Thomas Wilson: and were obedient to the manifestation of truth in their hearts. On coming out of the meeting they said to each other, " The way of everlasting happiness has been clearly laid down before us, and *we are resolved to walk in it*, come life or come death."

Not long after, he was thrown into prison for his Christian testimony against tithes, where he was kept six months, and bore his confinement with exemplary patience and resignation; and being accustomed to industry and averse to idleness, he learned to make gartering and laces for his support during his imprisonment.

When at liberty he and his wife constantly attended the meeting at Birr, twice a week, generally going on foot about seven miles of a very bad road, and having a river to wade through both going and returning. When crossing this river in winter, they sometimes had to break the ice, and John frequently wept to see the blood on his wife's limbs in coming through it.

When Friends travelling in the service of the gospel, came to his house, his zeal for the propagation of the truth and love to the souls of his neighbors was manifested in the great pains he took to invite them to come and partake of the benefit of their labors; for which purpose it was his frequent practice to ride several miles round, and this in the night, as well as day, and even in the depth and severity of the winter season; and though some returned scoffs and abusive speeches, yet many came and were well satisfied; several were convinced, and among the rest some of his own servants.

4*

We doubt not that many in this day are convinced by the Spirit of Truth of what the Lord requires of them. Happy would it be for all such, if like this Friend and his wife, they would resolve, when the way of life and salvation is set before them, *" to walk in it, come life or come death. "*

When Daniel Stanton* was a boy, he was brought into a serious state of mind, and persuaded a relation to accompany him to a Friends' meeting at Newtown. "In this blessed opportunity," he says, "through the power of truth and the good testimony of that dear servant of Christ, John Estaugh, being attended with the authority of the word of life, my heart was greatly contrited, and my spirit baptized in the presence of God; it was a joyful day of good tidings to my poor seeking soul; and the eminent and powerful advice that did attend that worthy instrument in the Lord's hand for my salvation, has been 'like bread cast upon the waters, that has been found after many days.' He adds, "I went from that meeting much satisfied with the way of worship of Friends."

In his Journal, D. Stanton gives an illustration of the effect produced by a true exercise of spirit, when, in speaking of a religious visit which he paid to England, he says:

"In some of the counties in which I had been, some dear young people, who were libertine in the shew of pride and finery of the world, became sober, solid and exemplary; and one young woman in particular was so reached, as I sat in a Friend's house, though I had nothing by way of testimony in words. to her condition, yet the weight and exercise attending my mind at that time, so reached her understanding, she became a plain solid Friend; and before I left England I heard her in the ministry at a meeting, and, as I thought, to the general satisfaction of Friends present."

Joseph Pike† relates that in the year 1669, when he

*See note, p. 34.
. †A member of the Society of Friends, who resided at Cork, Ireland. Born 1657, died 1729. See *Life in Friends' Library*, vol. 2, p. 340, etc.

was about twelve years of age, "William Edmundson* of Rosenallis, that worthy and honorable Friend and father in Israel," was concerned to visit Friends at Cork, where he resided. He says, "To this meeting I went, with great heaviness and sorrow upon my soul, under a mournful sense of my repeated transgressions against the Lord; and also with earnest cries, that He would be pleased to forgive me, and for the time to come grant me power and strength over the temptations of the enemy; for I clearly saw that I was not capable, by any ability of my own, to preserve myself from the least evil, agreeably to the saying of my blessed Lord, 'Without me ye can do nothing.' I sat down in the meeting full of sorrow; and William Edmundson's testimony so reached my inward state and condition, and pierced my very soul, that I could not refrain crying out in the meeting, under a sense of my sins and the Lord's terrors and judgments, which I then felt beyond what I had ever before experienced. And I was at that time as *truly baptized* by the powerful preaching of the word of life by him, as those were to whom the apostle Peter preached." Acts ii. 37.

At one period of Job Scott's† life, he had imbibed the belief that baptism with water was a Christian ordinance. The argument which produced this conclusion, he thus states:

" ' Christ commanded his disciples to baptize: no man can baptize with the Holy Ghost; therefore the baptism He commanded was not that of the Holy Ghost, but that of water.' This then appeared to me conclusive and unanswerable. But it was my ignorance of that baptizing power which attends all true Gospel ministry, that made me assent to this false position, 'No man can baptize with the Holy Ghost.' Man himself, in his own mere ability, I know cannot; but I also know, that of himself, he cannot preach the

---

*An eminent minister in the early days of the Society of Friends. Born in Westmoreland, England, in 1627. Removed to Ireland about 1652. Twice visited America in the service of the Gospel. Died in 1712. See *Journal in Friends' Library*, vol. 2, p. 84, etc.

†See note, p. 14.

gospel. This assertion, 'no man can preach the gospel,' is just as true as that, 'no man can baptize with the Holy Ghost.' As man merely, he can do nothing at all of either; but it still stands true, man can, man does, through Divine assistance, do both. The real gospel was never yet preached, but 'with the Holy Ghost sent down from Heaven.' Thus the apostles preached it, and thus alone it is still preached; and so preaching it, it was a baptizing ministry. As they spake, the Holy Ghost fell on them that heard them; that is, where faith wrought in the hearts of the hearers, and the living eternal word preached, through the power of the Holy Ghost, was mixed with faith in them that heard it; the Holy Ghost fell on them, baptizing them into a living, soul-saving sense of the power of God unto salvation, which is the true life of the Gospel. Thus the apostles fulfilled the commission; they taught *baptizingly*."

When Samuel Neale,* of Cork, Ireland, was a young man, he indulged in many sinful pleasures and liberties, and was far from submitting to the restraints of the cross of Christ. In an account of his life which was left among his papers, he describes the manner in which he was aroused to an earnest pursuit after heavenly riches. He says:—

"I remember being at a play one evening, up late that night; and lying pretty long next morning, which was First-day, an acquaintance asked me to go to meeting, and at the same time informed me there were strangers to be there, telling me who they were. I said, I would, for at my worst state I generally attended meetings. So to meeting I went, and it was a memorable one to me; for in it my state was so opened to that highly favored instrument in the Lord's hand, Catharine Payton† (who with my beloved

---

* A resident of Ireland. Paid a visit to America as a minister of the Gospel. Died in 1792, aged sixty-two years. See *Life in Friends' Library*, vol. 11, p. 1, etc.

† Afterwards Catharine Phillips. Visited as a minister, America and Holland. Died in 1794, aged about sixty-eight years. See *Memoirs in Friends' Library*, vol. 11, p. 188, etc.

friend, Mary Peisley,* was visiting the churches) that all I had done seemed to have been unfolded to her in a wonderful manner. I was as one smitten to the ground, dissolved in tears, and without spirit. This was a visitation from the Most High, beyond all others that I had as yet witnessed. I was so wrought upon by the power and Spirit of the holy Jesus, that, like Saul, I was ready to cry out: "Lord, what would'st thou have me to do?" I was almost ashamed to be seen, being so bedewed with tears, and slunk away from the meeting to get into a private place. * * I abode still and quiet, and kept near these messengers of glad tidings to me. I went with them to Bandon and Kinsale; and the same powerful dispensation of Divine virtue followed me, breaking in upon me, and tendering my spirit in a wonderful manner, in public meetings as well as private opportunities; which drew the attention and observation of many. When I returned to Cork, I kept as private as I well could, and resolved to quit all my worldly pursuits, and follow the gentle leadings of that heavenly Light, which showed me the vanity of worldly glory, and that the pleasures of sin are but as for a moment."

As Samuel Neale continued to walk in the way which the Lord cast up before him, he was soon constrained to open his mouth in testimony. Returning to Dublin, which was then his home, he says:

"I had much reasoning with flesh and blood, such as, what would the people think or say of such an one as I, who had been a gay young man, a libertine, and a persecutor of the holy Jesus in his spiritual appearance, to appear now as a preacher of righteousness. When the meeting-day came, my fears increased; and in this state I went to meeting. It was on a First-day; there was a very large gathering, amongst whom were divers of my associates and old companions. I was concerned to bear my testimony, which I did in great fear and trembling. The subject was

*Afterwards Mary Neale. She lived in Ireland. Visited America in company with Catharine Payton. Married Samuel Neale and died three days afterwards, in 1757, aged about forty years.

Paul's conversion: 'Saul, Saul, why persecutest thou me?' It was spoken in great brokenness,—I did not say much, but it had an extraordinary reach over the meeting; many wept aloud, and for a considerable space of time. After meeting I endeavored to get away unperceived, though one man (not of our Society), caught me in his arms and embraced me. Thus I was sustained and strengthened in my setting out in the work of the ministry; and had an evidence that the people were much reached and powerfully affected that day."

On one occasion, Thomas Wilson,* whom Thomas Story describes as one of the most powerful ministers of his time, was at a meeting in London where there was a great concourse of people, and among them two persons of high rank in the world, who sat very attentively whilst a Friend was speaking, and seemed to like what was delivered. But when Thomas stood up, being old, bald, and of a mean appearance, they despised him; and one said to the other: "Come, my lord, let us go, for what can this old fool say?" "No," said the other, let us stay, for this is Jeremiah, the prophet; let us hear him." So, as Thomas went on, the life arose and the power got into dominion, which tendered one of them in a very remarkable manner; the tears flowed in great plenty from his eyes, which he strove in vain to hide. After Thomas had sat down, this person stood up, and desired he might be forgiven of the Almighty for despising the greatest of his instruments under Heaven.

The following incident, related by William Williams* in his journal, is an interesting illustration of the manner in which the Spirit of Christ in the bearer often bears witness to the truth of the messages which are delivered by Divine authority; and thus makes them effectual for reproof, for correction, for instruction in righteousness.

* An eminent minister in the Society of Friends. Born in Cumberland, England. Removed to Ireland in 1694, and died in 1725, aged seventy-one years. He travelled in Great Britain, Ireland, and America. See *Life in Friends Library*, vol. 2, p. 310, etc.

*See note, p. 20.

He says:—"Now I think proper to relate a circumstance which took place as I was travelling, which is as follows:

" I was alone, and put up at a professor's house, to lodge. After I had been in the hall a little while, the landlord asked to be excused, and walked out to order his evening business, so that I was left alone, which gave me a better opportunity to hear what passed in an adjoining room, where one of the company raised her voice in singing praises to her Maker (as she called it), and after a very short line it broke off into very loud laughter. The singing then commenced again, and then the laughter, and so on for four times; so that I thought that I should be under the necessity of telling them my thoughts, if I should get an opportunity. Supper was soon set in the hall, and they were invited to sup, whereupon the landlady and five young women came in, and we sat down and supped. After we were done, before we left the table I brought on the discourse I wished, by observing to the landlady that I hardly thought these were all her daughters. She answered that two of them were her daughters, and the other three were neighbors, who had come on a visit. I thought I could mark out the singer; so I spoke and said, 'It is likely I may give you reason to think that I am a meddling traveller, for I have some remarks to make to you, from what I have heard since I came here.' I then told them what I had heard as above related. I told them not to misunderstand me, for I was not speaking against praising their Maker, if it was done with the Spirit; but against its being interrupted by loud unbecoming laughter; a thing that ought to be beneath the dignity of so noble beings as they were, at any time, much more when engaged in that exercise.

" I told them, it brought to my remembrance the words of the apostle, where he was speaking of the unruliness of the tongue, with which, saith he, ' we bless God and curse men ; these things ought not to be so;' said I, ' these things ought not to be mixed together.' When I was done, the noble young woman, whom I had marked out in my mind, spoke and said, ' I thank you kindly, sir, for your rebuke. I am the very one, and I knew I was doing wrong when I did it; yes,' said she, 'there was something here,' (clapping her hand on her breast) 'which told me that it was wrong.'

"The landlord then took up the subject and said something on the imperfection of man, but I do not recollect what he said, nor what I answered; but my answer was such that he said no more. The young woman then observed that the leprosy was out of the power of man to cure. I said it was;—but did she not think that Christ was as able to heal the leprosy now, as He was when here on the earth? She said He was. 'But,' continued she, 'we read that it gets into the wall; then the wall has to be taken down and rebuilt before it can be cleansed,' and this she said, was a great work. To which I agreed, and asked if it was not a necessary work to salvation. She said it was. I asked if she did not think it was a possible work through the assistance of the spirit of Christ. After a solemn pause, she said it was. So I told her, if we have a great work to do, and a necessary work, it is no matter how soon we begin, in faith, to do it. To which she acknowledged and was silent.

"Then I took the opportunity, in a few words, to open to her, and the rest, that to do this work, was to attend to that in the breast, which tells us when we do wrong. For instance, if thou (directing my discourse to the young woman) had'st attended to that within at the first, perhaps thou would'st not have been overtaken in the first breach of good order, much less to have repeated it. For that which spoke in thy breast and told thee that thou wast doing wrong, was Christ within, the saint's hope of glory, who has descended into the hearts of the children of men, in order to heal them and cleanse them from all sin and leprosy, and make them a pure people, and enable them to praise God in humility of spirit, and purity of mind; then this degrading thing of loud laughter would be far from our minds, and we should be preserved from being overtaken by that fault, as well as by all others.

"We then rose from the table, and it was taken into the other room. After a time the women withdrew, and the landlord pretty soon spoke of going to rest. I said I was ready to lie down; so he stepped to the door and called for a candle to light me to bed. When these young women heard this, they all came in again, and the young woman whom I have mentioned before spoke as for all, and said, 'You are a traveller, and will, likely, be up and gone in the morning, before we shall come down from our chamber; and we thought we could do no less than to come in and take our solemn leave of you, and once more thank you for your advice and counsel, hoping we may never forget it, nor you.' So said they all as they bid me farewell, with tears flowing from their eyes, which they did not try to hide, for the truth had tendered their hearts. So we parted in great tenderness and love. Oh! that people would attend to that which teaches within, so that they might become the children of light, and dwell no longer in darkness; for as many as are led by the Spirit of God are sons of God; and God is light, from whom cometh that which teaches within, being the true light that lighteth every one that cometh into the world, which is the Spirit of God, which leads up to Him, and enables us to become his children."

Among the instrumental means which are used to awaken man to serious reflection are dreams. Some persons pay a superstitious respect to dreams, which are often but the unbalanced and unrestrained operation of the mind when the controlling power of reason is wholly or partially at rest. Yet there is abundant evidence that it does please the Almighty Dispenser of wisdom, sometimes to speak to man in the visions of the night, when the head is reclining in slumber. *Such* dreams are accompanied in the waking hours which follow, with an impression that a lesson is to be learned from them; and have often been a means of conveying instruction, warning, or comfort.

David Ferris[*] relates in his journal that when he was

[*] Born in Connecticut in 1707. Settled in Wilmington, Delaware, in 1737. Died in 1779. See *Memoirs*, several times reprinted.

5

under preparation for the work of the ministry, and sensible of the Divine call, yet unwilling to yield obedience, he was at a meeting on Long Island in company with two women Friends, travelling in the ministry. On this occasion a concern came upon his mind to say something, but he refused to comply. The following night, one of the women dreamed, he says, "that she saw me sitting by a pleasant stream of water; before me a table was spread with all manner of dainties; but I was chained, so that I could not reach any of them; at which she was troubled, and asked the master of the feast why I was deprived of the liberty to partake of the good things on the table. He answered that the time had been, when, on certain conditions, I might have enjoyed them to the full, but that I had refused the terms, and therefore was now justly deprived of them. She inquired of him, whether this must always be my case. He answered perhaps not; that if I would yet submit and comply with the terms, it was not too late to partake of all the good things she saw. The interpretation of this dream was easy and plain. It rested on my mind for several years, as cause of humbling instruction, and incitement to future care, diligence and obedience."

How many of us are like David Ferris, prevented from partaking of the rich bounties of the Lord's spiritual table, by a want of faithful obedience to his requirings! We would fain be reckoned as on his side, yet hold back part of the price. We are afraid to trust ourselves unreservedly in his hands, not having that living faith in his goodness and mercy, which would enable us to believe that all his dealings with us would be for our good. Therefore we want to retain the government of our lives, in part at least, in our own hands, and so our course is a sad mixture of inconsistencies, in which little spiritual progress is discernible; and but little is known of the enjoyment dispensed to the true-hearted follower of the Saviour. "Trust in the Lord with all thine heart, and lean not to thy own understanding." "They that trust in the Lord shall be as Mount Zion which cannot be removed, but abideth forever."

On another occasion David Ferris says : " Being from home at a meeting, I was concerned to say something to the people; but I postponed it till a more convenient season. On this account I left the meeting in great heaviness and sorrow, for my disobedience. On the following night I dreamed that I saw two generals drawing up their armies in order for battle. Each captain had his men in order ready to obey the command of their general, and stood at their head waiting for orders to march and stand in the engagement where he should command them. One of the generals came to a captain who stood near me, and said to him, ' You are a valiant man and skilful in the art of war; therefore march into the right wing of the army, and in front of the battle.' But the captain objected to the post assigned him, and pleaded his unfitness for it, saying, ' It is a place of danger, and requires a man better qualified for such a post.' The general answered that he was well qualified for the place allotted him, and that if he took it, he might by his skill and valor, do eminent service for his king and country, and gain great honor, which would be a means of promoting him to places of higher trust. He, however, desired to be excused and could not be persuaded to take the post assigned him. I stood by and heard all the general's arguments to persuade him to comply, until I was filled with indignation at the captain's obstinacy, especially as the general had *absolute* authority to *command,* and yet was so kind as to use entreaty and persuasion. I then said to the general, ' It is my judgment this captain is not worthy of the place assigned him, since he refuses to serve his king and country according to his capacity, and rejects the honor and promotion he might obtain. Were I in the general's place, I would set him in the rear of the army, where he will have less opportunity of promotion, and may lose his life as well as in the front.' To this the general replied, ' The decision is just, and in the rear he shall stand,' where he was accordingly stationed.

" I awoke from my sleep in great distress; under a sense

of the just judgment which (like David) I had passed on myself."

The two following dreams, related by that eminent minister of the gospel, Samuel Fothergill,* are probably familiar to some of my readers,—but there are others to whom they may be new, and I believe they may be useful to all.

Samuel Fothergill, in a meeting at Lurgan, in order, as is believed, to arouse the negligent to diligence ere it might prove too late, told those present of a Friend, a relative of his own, who, when he was young, was earnestly concerned for the salvation of his soul, and was also well-affected toward the truth. About this time, and whilst he was still undecided, he dreamed that he found himself in a beautiful pasture field surrounded by a wall, in which were a number of well-conditioned lambs who fed upon it; there was also a well of pure spring water for them to drink. Whilst he looked upon the lambs an axe was given him, and he was instructed to guard the well from pollution, and to repair any breaches which might be made in the wall. This dream, as well as the following, he related to Samuel Fothergill in America, when near the close of life, and when it was not with him as in days that were past, he not having taken heed to the intimation received, but permitted the cares of life and the love of the world to choke the good seed, so that he neglected to exercise the gift bestowed upon him, and was in consequence thereof, plunged in darkness, distress, and sorrow of heart.

Second dream.—That he found himself again in the same pasture field, but it had lost its verdure; the lambs were distempered, and the wall was much broken down; the water in the well was muddy, and there were serpents in it which hissed at him when he went near. Having lost the weapon he had been entrusted with for its defence, he was unable to dislodge or overcome them, and as he looked

---

* An eloquent and favored minister in the Society of Friends. Born in Yorkshire, England, 1715. Travelled in America, Ireland and Scotland. Died in 1772. See *Memoirs in Friends' Library*, vol. 9, p. 83, etc.

upon the lambs and beheld their condition, he thought he heard a voice say, 'All these will I require at thy hands.'

It is frequently the case that we can trace a connection between previous trains of thought, and the visions that float over the mind in our sleeping hours, so that we can find a rational cause for these vagaries of the imagination. But even in such cases it may please the Good Shepherd, who watches over his flock, to make the impressions thus left on the mind a means of instruction or help to those who are looking to him for counsel and direction.

This is illustrated by a dream which I heard related by the person to whom it happened.

My friend was a fellow-member of a meeting with a man of contentious and unreasonable disposition. On one occasion this person came to his house and acted so unhandsomely, that my friend lost the command of his temper, and requested the other to leave, as he was unwilling to be so treated in his own house. Almost immediately after his visitor had left, he felt condemned for his unwatchfulness, and passed through a season of severe mental suffering before his peace of mind returned and he felt that his fault had been forgiven. About a year afterwards, long after the breach had been healed, in his dreams he passed through the same experience. He thought that he again lost the control of his feelings, and again strongly and distressingly felt the sense of condemnation; and was greatly relieved on awaking to find it was but a dream. Soon after this, after being at their religious meeting, he called in at the house of this acquaintance—when something occurred to call forth his contentious spirit. The combative feelings of my friend began to rise under this fresh provocation, when his dream came freshly before his mental vision, as if a curtain had been lowered before him. The warning was sufficient, and

5*

checking his anger, he quietly turned and walked away, truly thankful for the caution extended in the time of need.

When Stephen Grellet* was a boy at school at Lyons, France, he had a dream, or "religious opening," which made a deep impression on his mind, and the remembrance of which helped to sustain him in many subsequent exercises and trials.

"I thought I saw," he says, "a large company of persons, or rather purified spirits, on one of those floating vessels, which they have at Lyons, on the Rhone, occupied by washerwomen. They were washing linen. I wondered to see what beating and pounding there was upon it, but how beautifully white it came out of their hands. I was told I could not enter God's kingdom until I underwent such an operation,—that unless I was thus washed and made white, I could have no part in the dear Son of God. For weeks I was absorbed in the consideration of the subject—the washing of regeneration. I had never heard of such things before, and I greatly wondered that, having been baptized with water, and having also received what they call the sacrament of confirmation, I should have to pass through such a purification; for I had never read or heard any one speak of such a baptism."

The experienced Christian learns that it is through much tribulation that the righteous enter the kingdom, that it requires "much beating and pounding," to remove the defilement of sin. The Divine Grace which effects this change is spoken of under the similitude of a fire and a hammer—and the process is compared to the removal from the precious metal of the dross, the tin and the reprobate silver. Yet, while passing through those baptisms, there is often granted a sustaining hope that the effect thereof

---

* Born in France in 1773. Came to America in 1793. Joined the Society of Friends in 1796. Made four religious visits to Europe, and travelled extensively on that continent and in America. Died in 1855. See L*ife*, edited by B. Secbohm.

will be peace, and quietness and assurance forever; and there are times when the truly devoted servant of the Lord is filled with peace and holy joy—a foretaste of that glorious inheritance promised to all those who faithfully follow their Lord and Saviour.

Years ago, J. A., of Leeds, England, was travelling in Scotland. In descending a hill, at the foot of which a river meandered, he found himself forcibly struck with the scene, not only on account of its beauty, but because he was certain he had seen it before. As he never before had been even to the borders of Scotland, he could not at first account for this strange though clear remembrance of the country around him. After a few minutes, he recollected a dream in which he thought he was descending the same hill in order to cross the river by a ferry at the foot of it; and that a little ragged boy opened him a gate, and held his horse while he got into the boat, and then followed him with it; that when they reached the middle of the river the boat sunk and all were drowned.

As this was passing in his mind, the same little ragged boy whom he had seen in his dream, opened a gate for him. However, startled at the strange coincidence, he reasoned that it would be an unworthy thing in a man of sense and intelligence to be guided by a dream, which might be a mere vagary of the imagination when unrestrained by the reason; and he determined to go on. But the impulse to avoid the ferry was too strong to be set aside by such reflections, and he concluded to cross the river by the nearest bridge which was about twenty miles off.

Some weeks after, as he was returning from his journey, he stopped to dine at an inn on the opposite side of the same ferry. The landlord observed him with a melancholy earnestness which distressed him. "Are you not sir," he said with great emotion, "the gentleman who, a few weeks ago, refused to cross the ferry, and went around Stirling bridge instead?" "Yes," he answered, "I am, why do you ask?" "Then, sir, you may thank God for it; for either by the boat's being too much laden, or from some unknown cause, it sank in the middle of the river, and every one, among whom was my son, perished!"

The caution felt by J. A. not to place too much dependence on the warnings of a dream was a prudent one ; and the same remark is true respecting those impressions which sometimes form on the minds in our waking hours. Without such caution a person may become the victim of imaginary and delusive suggestions. But the testimony of holy men of former days, and the experience of those in modern times who endeavor to walk in obedience to the will of the Saviour, abundantly evince that man is often favored with a degree of light and wisdom superior to his own, coming immediately from the Source of all our blessings, and that the discoveries of this Light are attended with a degree of authority and power which satisfies the obedient soul that it is safe to follow their guidance.

S. Carlett states in his Life, that he owed a sum of money which was due on a certain day, and he was very anxious not to disappoint his creditor. He says, "When the day arrived, notwithstanding all my care, I lacked twenty dollars to make the amount I owed. This was rather strange to me, as I thought I had done my best. On the morning of the day I rose early and meditated on the matter. Some persons might think twenty dollars a small matter to meditate upon ; but I wished to see where, if at all, I had erred. True, I had given away some money to the poor. I had not kept account how much. Had I displeased God in this? or why was Providence seemingly suffering me to feel the regret of a broken promise made to my neighbor? I took no breakfast, but went to a secluded place, and bowed to God in prayer. Before I arose from my knees I was impressed with a strong assurance that the twenty dollars would be in my possession by the hour I needed it. I had not gone far before I was accosted by a man—a good Methodist—with these words, ' My brother, just stop, I have something for you. I had a dream last night. In it I was told to let you have twenty dollars, the extra profit of my business last week.' Saying which, he took from his pocket-book four five dollar notes, and laid them down before me. I took the money and paid my debt, with an increasing confidence in the providence of God."

Many years ago, a man lived near Freehold, N. J., who was an habitual drunkard, and spent much time, particularly in the evenings and on First-days, with people of like habits. This man dreamed one night that he had a fit of sickness and died ; and, as he had always expected, after death went to hell. Hell did not appear in his dream what he had expected to find it, but seemed to him like a very large tavern filled with people. He was so shocked by what he saw there that he begged the landlord to let him return to earth again ; who, after many entreaties, consented that he should, if he would make a solemn promise to return there at the end of a year. This the man promised, and awoke.

The dream filled his mind with great horror ; and in the morning he went and related it to one of the Tennents.* Tennent desired him to reform and lead a new life ; for this seemed to be a special warning.

The man did reform, and for six months avoided his old companions. At the expiration of that time he was returning from work one evening, and was met by several of them near a tavern. They began to ridicule him for becoming religious, and dared him to go in and take one drink with them. The man felt confident in his own power over himself, and said he would go in and take one drink to show it would not hurt him. He took one drink and then another, till he was much intoxicated. From that time he returned to his old habits, and grew worse and worse.

His family lived in the second story of a house, to which there was a stair-case on the outside. One night when he had drank more than usual, he made shift to get up stairs and to bed : but in the morning, when he went out of the door to go to work, he was still under the effects of liquor, and pitched off the stairs to the ground and broke his neck.

* Several of the family were Presbyterian ministers in Pennsylvania and New Jersey, during last century.

The news was carried to Tennent, who recollected the man's dream, and on looking at a memorandum found it was a year that day since the man told it to him.

Allusion has been made to the Divine warnings extended to the careless and disobedient by means of dreams. But the Almighty has other ways also of teaching his people. His anointed ministers of the Gospel have often been commissioned to "sound an alarm" and call upon the wicked to forsake their ways, and to turn unto the Lord and seek for pardon for their sins.

When Stephen Grellet* was travelling in the South of France, in the year 1832, he held a religious meeting on the day called Christmas, at a place called St. Gilles. The meeting was very large, and respecting it, S. G. thus writes:

"I thought there were pious persons present to whom the word of comfort and encouragement was preached; but there were others with whom I did earnestly plead of righteousness, temperance and judgment to come. Whilst I was proceeding, my own heart being much affected with the awfulness of it, I stated how solemn it was thus to join in company with those who are met together to worship God, and publicly acknowledge and bow down in spirit before Christ Jesus, the Saviour of sinners, who came into the world for the very purpose that He might save us from our sins. But that, possibly, whilst some keep this day as a memorial of the coming in the flesh of the eternal Son of God, thus to be unto us a Saviour and Redeemer, they have concluded on and made preparations to spend this very evening and night perhaps in a riotous and sinful manner. As I was uttering this, a man fell down from his seat on the floor. There was some bustle for a short time, they carried him out, and I continued to speak, a considerable increase of solemnity appearing over the meeting. After the conclusion, I heard the people say to one another, 'He is dead, he is dead!' I was then told that this very

* See note, p. 54.

man had made extensive preparations for a sumptuous banquet that night, when a variety of diversions were to be introduced; that on coming, he had boasted how he would honor the Lord and sanctify this day by going to a place of worship first, and then close it in feasting and revelling. Some persons, hearing him speak so had reproved him for it, which he answered by impious expressions. The people appeared struck with astonishment at the awfulness of the event. I received a deputation from the inhabitants in the evening, requesting that I would have another meeting with them; but I did not feel it my place to do so. To the Lord and his Spirit, I leave and commit them."

It is one of the evidences of the Lord's goodness that He does not permit those who are rejecting his government to go on undisturbed in the way they have chosen, but visits them from time to time with the reproofs of his Holy Spirit; and oftentimes by outward warnings and chastisements, calls upon them to return to Him in whom alone there is safety and peace. An instance of this is related by Elizabeth Collins* in her memoirs respecting a person whom she knew. Her narrative is as follows:—

" A singular instance of the love and mercy of Almighty God, as also of his just judgment, in the case of a young man, happened in my early life. He lived at a public house, and was one who took great delight in company, vanity, and horse-racing. One day, as he and one of his companions were running horses, at the end of the race-ground he was dashed with great violence against a tree, the horse taking the opposite side from that he expected to go, which brought his head directly against the tree. He was taken up and carried into a house for dead. A doctor was sent for, who gave no encouragement of his recovery; but after a time he revived, and in a few days recovered his understanding.

* A minister of Upper Evesham, New Jersey. Born in 1755, died in 1831. See *Memoirs in Friends' Library*, vol. 11, p. 450.

"Oh! the distress and anguish he was then in, having no other prospect but shortly to be summoned before an offended God, to receive the sentence, 'Depart from me, thou worker of iniquity.' Bitter were his moans, and sore his lamentations, and fervent his cries for mercy. I went to see him in his distress, when it was not in the power of man to relieve him. His petitions were for mercy and for time: he asked only for one year, that he might live a new life, be an example and warning to his companions, and honor and glorify his God and Creator. The Lord in mercy heard his petition, and in great condescension granted his request, even to a miracle, as it was thought impossible for him to be raised, and gave him not only one year but several.

"For a time he lived a sober, watchful and orderly life, but for want of breaking off from his old companions, and living a more retired life, he at length, by little and little, fell away, and got into the same paths of folly and dissipation. He was not, however, suffered to go on long in this way, for one evening, as he was riding with several of his companions, one of whom he expected to be joined in marriage with in a few days, his horse, without any fright that they could discover, ran off, threw him in the road and killed him. I was told he never drew breath after they reached him, that they could discover. This event happened in the evening, after spending the First-day afternoon in lightness and vanity.

"As this solemn instance of Divine mercy and justice has from time to time been revived in my remembrance, I have thought it best to commit it to writing, as a caution and warning to my dear children, to beware of loose and unprofitable company, and of breaking their covenants."

Daniel Stanton* mentions in his Journal that some great men in Philadelphia were concerned in fitting out vessels for the wicked business of privateering. This brought a deep engagement on his mind, and it came upon him as a weighty duty, to go to one of these men, faithfully to warn

* See note, p. 34

him against this unrighteous way of getting riches.   He
says :—

"I got a friend to accompany me, and cleared my spirit
of a heavy burden : he pleaded for the practice, but used
me civilly.   A new vessel was fitted out sometime after,
called the Tartar, which was much talked of to do great
matters in privateering ; but, as I have been informed, she
sunk before she got out to sea, and many or most of the
people on board were drowned.   I had peace of mind for
having discharged my duty, although I much lamented the
unhappy circumstances of these poor fellow-mortals, losing
their lives in such an evil undertaking."

Anna Shipton* in one of her works, describes the case
of a poor laboring man whom she knew, who was one of
those who are rich in faith.   He went to live in a village
where few, if any, cared for much beyond this present life.
His home here was a poor thatched cottage on the outskirts
of the village ; and when his day's work was done, seated
by the low casement of his room, in summer time, he held
communion with his Heavenly Friend.

As he communed with God aloud, and poured forth his
soul in prayer, a woman of ill character passed by the cottage door ; the sound of his voice arrested her steps, and she
lingered by the casement, and listened.   It was a new language to her ears, and she went on her way, astonished and
perplexed.   Her occupation was a degrading one.   She possessed a voice of remarkable power and sweetness ; her husband frequented the taverns in the neighborhood, and she
accompanied him, and by her songs procured from the
landlord or his guests, the liquor that he thirsted for.

Day by day, the singer marked this humble disciple of
Christ, to see if his life corresponded with the desires after
holiness expressed in his prayers.   She watched for his
halting, week after week, but watched in vain.   He probably
passed through many a conflict ; and in humble brokenness
of spirit may have felt himself but a cumberer of the
ground, as far as bringing any honor to God was concerned ;

* See note, p. 15.

6

and he little dreamed that the Lord was making use of his unconscious ministry, and his example, to disturb the orgies of sinners to whom he had never spoken and who had never heard of his existence. The woman's heart became heavy, and she could not sing. Under Divine conviction for sin, she turned away in bitterness of spirit from the scenes in which she had before been content to dwell. The anger of her husband was kindled against her; his gains were gone, and the means of procuring his evening's unholy revelry were over. His persecution added to her distress. The burthen of her sins pressed heavily upon her, and there seemed no way of escape. Satan whispered that "in death there was no remembrance;" but he added not, "and after death the judgment."

Despairing of relief, she determined to rid herself of a life which had become intolerable to her. One morning, when she thought herself secure from interruption, she went to a neighboring stable, prepared to end an existence too miserable to be borne. But at that awful moment there came into her mind the expressions of praise which she had overheard from the poor laborer, and his heartfelt thanksgiving for redemption through the precious blood of Jesus. She, too, knelt in prayer, the floodgates of her tears were opened, and a sweet sense of the pardoning mercy of God in Christ Jesus came over her mind. The prey was taken from the mighty and the captive delivered. When evening came, and the good man who had been an instrument in the Lord's hand in awakening conviction in her heart, returned to his cottage, he found her there—rejoicing in the mercy of which she had partaken—the fruit of those days that seemed of no account, save that he walked in fellowship with Jesus. He had lived near the fountain; the stream that flowed in refreshment through his own soul, had been used to awaken the life in another.

An aged widow woman lived in the city of Lyons. Her parents were very poor, and her husband had nothing but his industry to depend on. As long, however, as he was able to work, they honestly gained their daily bread, though they were never able to put anything by for a rainy day;

but, when the old man died, leaving his poor widow childless and infirm, want entered her desolate dwelling as an armed man. She sold everything but what was indispensable, and removed to a miserable garret to spend the remainder of her days.

One day, as she was sitting alone in her comfortless, half-empty room, it struck her that there was a singular outline on the beams of the wall. The walls had been whitewashed, but she thought it looked as if there had been a square opening in one of them, which had been carefully closed with a kind of door. She examined it closely, and the thought occurred to her, " Perhaps there is some treasure hidden there;" for she remembered as a child the fearful days of the Revolution, when no property was safe from the men of liberty and equality. Perhaps some rich man had concealed his treasure there from rapacity, who had himself fallen a victim to the Revolution before he had time to remove it. She tapped with her finger and the boards returned a hollow sound. With beating heart she tried to remove the square door, and soon succeeded, without much difficulty; but, alas! instead of the gold and silver she hoped to see, she beheld a damp, dirty, mouldy old book! In her disappointment she was ready to fix in the boards again, and leave the book to moulder and crumble away; but a secret impulse induced her to take it out, and see if there were any bank-notes or valuable papers in it; but no, it was nothing but a book, a mouldy book!

When she had a little recovered from her vexation, she began to wonder what book it could be that some one had hidden away so carefully. It must surely be something extraordinary. So she wiped it clean and set herself to read. Her eyes fell upon the words: " Therefore I say unto you, Take no thought for your life, what ye shall eat, or what ye shall drink; nor yet for your body, what ye shall put on. Is not the life more than meat, and the body than raiment? Behold the fowls of the air; for they sow not, neither do they reap, nor gather into barns; yet your heavenly Father feedeth them. Are ye not much better than they?" And the words that she read appeared to her so sweet and precious that she read on and on. The next morning she sat down again to the damp old book, the words of which made a deep impression on her soul. Her little chamber no longer looked so desolate. Her food, which had so often seemed to her as the bread of tears, now appeared to be more like bread from heaven; and her solitude was relieved by the presence of the great King.

She had the book cleaned and bound, and it was to her as meat and drink, until she was permitted to close her eyes and enter into the joys of her Lord. She related this history in the latter days of her pilgrimage, to a beloved pastor in Lyons. It is Amelotte's edition of the New Testament, of the time of the Huguenot persecution.

Our blessed Saviour commanded his hearers, " Let your light so shine before men, that others seeing your good works may glorify your Father who is in Heaven." The example of an upright Christian, is often a more powerful means of convincing others of the reality of religion and of inducing them to yield to the convictions of the Spirit of Christ, than any preaching.

The *Young Mens' Christian Magazine* describes the case of a young man who had become an infidel, and rejected the Bible and its teachings. In his father's house a young woman resided who was a relative of the family. Her fretful temper made all around her uncomfortable. She was sent to a boarding school, and was absent some time. While there she became a true and earnest Christian. On her return she was so changed that all who knew her wondered and rejoiced. She was patient and cheerful, kind, unselfish and charitable. The lips that used to be always uttering cross and bitter words, now spoke nothing but sweet, gentle loving words. Her infidel cousin George was greatly surprised at this. He watched her closely for some time, till he was thoroughly satisfied that it was a real change that had taken place in his young cousin. Then he asked her what had caused this great change. She told him it was the grace of God which had made her a Christian and had changed her heart.

He said to himself, "I don't believe that God has anything to do with it, though she thinks He has. But it is a wonderful change that has taken place in her, and I should like to be as good as she is. I *will* be so." Then he formed a set of good resolutions. He tried to control his tongue and his temper, and keep a strict watch over himself. He was all the time doing and saying what he did not wish to do and say. And as he failed time after time, he would turn and study his good cousin's example. He said to himself, "How does it happen that she, who has not as much knowledge or as much strength of character as I have, can do what I *can't* do? She must have some help that I don't know of. It must be as she says the help of God. I will seek that help."

His seeking was not in vain; for He who is long-suffering, and abundant in mercy, was pleased to hear and answer his petitions.

A somewhat similar incident is related of one who had gone to live with her aunt when she was a self-willed, thoughtless, headstrong young girl, leaving the house of her parents because they opposed her marriage to a young man who proved, as she soon found, entirely unworthy of her love. The aunt who was a Christian in life as well as in profession, received her lovingly, and with patient and gentle kindness and good sense, gradually led her to see the error of her course, and to receive in love the lessons she endeavored to impress, till in the end they brought forth fruit an hundredfold, and the niece became a warm-hearted and faithful Christian. And, when some one asked, "under whose preaching was she converted," with a smile she replied, "Under nobody's *preaching*, it was under Aunt Mary's *practising*."

A writer in referring to this incident, remarks, "There is a world of meaning in the answer, for example is ever more powerful than precept, and a holy life is the mightiest of all arguments for religion. 'It wasn't master's sermons, but it was master's life that did it,' said a servant—who had been awakened to think of her sin—of her master who was a clergyman. Christian reader can it be said of us that our home life is a daily sermon which every one in the house can read?"

An anecdote is told of a native of Madagascar, who had embraced Christianity; and who was asked by a sea-captain what it was that first led him to become a Christian. "Was it any particular sermon you heard, or book which you read?"

"No, my friend," replied the chief, "it was no book or sermon. One man, he a wicked thief; another man he drunk all day long; big chief, he beat his wife and children. Now thief, he no steal; drunken Tom, he sober; big chief, he very kind to his family. Every heathen man get something inside him, which makes him different, so I became a Christian too, to know how it feel to have something strong inside of me to keep me from being bad."

While good example does exert an influence over others for good, there are many mournful illustrations of the truth, that a conduct inconsistent with his profession in a professor of religion, is often very hurtful to others. Ford describes the case of a man, whom he visited on his dying bed, and who passed away from this life in a state of despair. He ascribed the ruin of his soul to a popular preacher, who, on some public occasion, he heard deliver a sermon which deeply affected him; and whom at the close of the service, he was delighted to meet at the house of a mutual friend. But great was his disappointment; the individual, who, in the pulpit was a Boanerges, in the parlor played the mountebank, and in either character seemed perfectly "at home." His adventures, jokes and anecdotes kept the company till past midnight in a roar of laughter. The consequence may be easily imagined. The unhappy man who was doomed to witness that incongruous scene, pursuaded himself that Christianity was disbelieved by its professional advocates, and henceforth he treated it as unworthy of notice.

Dr. Dwight relates that a man of his acquaintance who had a vehement and rigid temper, had a dispute with a friend of his, a professor of religion, and had been injured by him. With feelings of resentment he made him a visit for the avowed purpose of quarrelling with him. He accordingly stated to him the nature and extent of the injury done him, and was preparing, as he afterwards confessed, to load him with a train of severe reproaches, when his friend cut him short by acknowledging, with the utmost readiness and frankness, the injustice of which he had been guilty, expressing his own regret for the wrong which he had done, requesting his forgiveness, and offering him ample compensation. He was compelled to say he was satisfied, and withdrew full of mortification that he had been precluded from venting his indignation, and wounding his friend with keen and violent reproaches for his conduct. As he was walking home he said to himself: "There must be more in religion than I have hitherto suspected. Were any to address me in the tone of haughtiness and provocation, with which I accosted my friend this evening, it would be impossible for me to preserve the equanimity of which I have been a witness, and especially with so much frankness, humility and meekness to *acknowledge the wrong* which I had done; so readily ask forgiveness of the man whom I had injured, and so cheerfully promise a satisfactory recompense. I should have met his anger by anger, &c. There is something in religion that I have hitherto been a stranger to." He soon after became a Christian.

An illustration of the power of an upright Christian life in convincing others, was related as follows in the *Christian Advocate* :—

" A plain, earnest Christian was recently rehearsing in our presence the circumstances by which he was providentially led to an experimental knowledge of Christ. Years ago he had been employed as a common laborer on a farm owned by a well-known local preacher of Central New Jersey. He was at that time a confirmed rationalist, having a few months before emigrated from Germany. He saw how his employer consecrated his means in aiding churches in that vicinity and in adjacent communities; how he earnestly sought to save souls; how he was the friend of the disconsolate and the needy; how he encouraged education and promoted the circulation of a healthful literature; how he stood foremost in temperance reforms, declining civil preferments when offered by a political party under the domination of rum; and how he stood firm for the protection of the poor slave when a fugitive fleeing from human bondage. Under circumstances which carried an almost irresistible influence he became powerfully impressed with the reality of religion. He bowed before the cross. He experienced the saving power of that Gospel which he had once despised. The memory of that employer can never fade away. He delights in nothing more than to speak of his tender associations during those months of toil. " He has gone," said he, " gone to dwell with Christ and with the redeemed in heaven, and I will meet him there by and by."

Some years ago a young man, who gave clear evidence that he was truly a subject of the regenerating grace of God, was asked what had led to the change in him, as he had been wild and thoughtless. Was it any sermon or book that had impressed him? He answered, " No!" " What was it, then? Did any one speak to you specially on the subject of religion?" The same response was given.

" Will you, then, state what first led you to think of your soul's eternal welfare?" The reply was:

" I live in the same boarding-house and eat at the same table with J. Y."

" Well, did he ever talk to you about your soul?"

" No, never till I sought an interview with him," was the reply. " But," he continued, " there was a sweetness in his disposition, a heavenly-mindedness, a holy aroma about his whole life and demeanor, that made one feel that he had a source of comfort and peace and happiness to which I was a stranger. There was a daily beauty in his life that made me ugly. I became more and more dissatisfied with myself every time I saw him; and though, as I said, he never spoke to me on the subject of personal religion till I myself sought the interview, yet his whole life was a constant sermon to me."

It has' often been said that there is no preaching more effective than that of a truly godly life. As an illustration of its power, the following incident is narrated.

One of the largest hospitals in a city in the south of France, had a matron who was a faithful follower of the Lord. She had learned by grace, that a meek and quiet spirit was of great price in the sight of Him who was meek and lowly of heart.

On one occasion a patient, angry at a rule of the hospital being enforced, spat in the matron's face, in the presence of the assembled ward; she quietly wiped her face, saying, "I have been greatly honored to share the indignity offered to my blessed Saviour." The outrage was never repeated.

Afterwards, when a new patient was admitted, and placed in bed, the matron sent her daughter to remove the apparel from the ward to another apartment, as no clothing was allowed to be retained in the sleeping room. As the young girl stooped to gather the clothing together, the woman, enraged that it should be removed, bent over her and raising one of her heavy wooden shoes, struck her violently and repeatedly on the back.

All looked on in wonder and dismay at this undeserved cruelty to one who had never offended, feeling that this must touch the mother's heart far more severely than any indignity offered to herself. The matron calmly continued her duties. In the evening the culprit beheld her approach her bed. She waited for some word of reproach—none came; for some expression of displeasure on her face—none was seen. Carefully she arranged the pillows, tenderly she spoke to the woman while performing offices of kindness. The heart of the harsh and violent woman melted. She watched and listened to the matron as from day to day she ministered of the "good things" promised by her Heavenly Father. Before leaving the hospital she declared that the meek forgiveness of injury thus manifested by one who walked with God, had broken her heart, and prepared her to follow in the foot steps of the flock of Christ's companions.

It is related that the captain of a vessel sailing down the Mississippi, had his vessel so injured that there was great danger of losing both vessel and cargo. He was a pious man, and though placed in this perilous position, manifested a composure which evidenced that his mind was stayed upon God, while at the same time he omitted nothing that could be done to save the property entrusted to his care. While things were in this situation, there came to his aid one of the pilots on that station, who, by his own account, neither feared God nor regarded man. After offering his services, he began to storm and swear. After a little time, however, he began to contrast his own conduct with that of the captain, and said to himself, "How is it, that while I have nothing at risk I am swearing as though it were mine? And the captain, who has property and reputation at stake, seems perfectly calm? It must be his religion, and as I have a Bible on board my boat, I will commence reading it, and see if I can find what his religion is."

The conviction of his own sinfulness, forced upon him by the contrast with the consistent course of the captain, was the commencement of a change for the better, and through the power of Divine Grace, he was enabled to forsake the evil of his ways and to live a more Godly life. He afterwards called upon the captain and informed him of what the Lord had done for his soul.

It is a common remark that the blood of the martyrs is the seed of the church; for nothing so convinces beholders of the value of the religious principles professed as to see men patiently enduring suffering and death rather than desert them. It is indeed a strong proof of the value of that crown of righteousness laid up in store for those who endure to the end. One Adrianus, in ancient times, seeing the martyrs suffer such grievous things in the cause of Christ, asked, "What is that which enables them to bear such suffering?" One of them replied, "Eye hath not seen, nor ear heard, neither hath entered into the heart of man, the things which God hath prepared for them that love Him." So powerful was the effect of these words, and such the conviction sealed by the Holy Spirit on the mind of Adrianus, that he became a convert to Christianity, and himself suffered martyrdom.

In a conversation at a tea-table on religious subjects, one of the company stated that when he was a young man of about eighteen, he was a clerk in Boston, and his room-mates at the boarding-house were clerks of the same age. When First-day morning came, during the hours between breakfast and meeting-time, he said : "I felt a secret desire to get a Bible, which my mother had given me, out of my trunk, and read in it, but I was afraid to do so before my messmates, who were reading miscellaneous books. At last my conscience got the mastery, and I rose up and went to my trunk. I had half raised it when the thought occurred to me that it might look like over-sanctity or pharisaical, so I shut my trunk and returned to the window.—For twenty minutes I was miserably at ease. I felt I was doing wrong. I started a second time for my trunk, and had my hand on my Bible, when the fear of being laughed at conquered the better emotion, and I again dropped the top of my trunk. As I turned away from it, one of my room-mates, who observed my irresolute movements, said laughingly :

"'I say, what's the matter? You seem as restless as a weathercock !'

"I replied by laughing in my turn ; and then conceiving the truth to be the best, frankly told him what was the matter. To my surprise and delight, they both spoke up and averred that they had Bibles in their trunks, and had been secretly wishing to read in them, but were afraid to take them out lest I should laugh at them." The result was that all three took out their Bibles.

The next First-day morning, two of their fellow boarders came into the room, and finding how they were engaged, requested that a chapter be read aloud. That evening the three room-mates agreed to have a chapter read every night in their room. A few evenings after, four or five of the other boarders happened to be in the room talking when the nine o'clock bell rang. One of the room-mates opened the Bible, and another explained to their visitors their custom. " We'll all stay and listen," they said.

The practice spread, till finally every one of the sixteen clerks boarding in the house spent his First-day mornings in reading the Bible, and the moral effect on the family was of the highest character.

F. N. Zabriskie, in an article on the *unconscious* influence which we exert over each other, mentions the case of a woman who had occasion to stop for a moment in the street to speak to a mechanic, and walked on, the interview quickly passing from her mind. A year after he came and told her that he had not touched a drop of liquor since that day. She wondered why he should tell her of it, until informed that on that occasion she had stepped a little aside while talking with him,—as he supposed, because his breath was offensive to her from the fumes of liquor. He had instantly said to himself, with a sudden consciousness of degradation : " Have I reached the point where this lady shrinks from me as from one unclean? It is time for me to stop short!" She surprised him by saying that her move- ment had no such motive. But the effect had been the same, and her unconscious influence had done more to sober him than a good many temperance lectures would probably have done.

When we reflect on the wide-reaching extent of the in- fluence we exert over one another, and the unexpected way in which it often operates, we can appreciate the force of the following caution :—" One can no more escape from the obligation of guarding his personal influence at all times and in all places than he can escape from the necessity of breathing.   There is no moment in conscious life where a man should not be on guard for the right use of his personality, any more than there is any moment when the heart should cease, for a time, to beat, and for nerve and brain to become paralyzed."

A valued friend many years ago related to me an occurrence in his own early experience, which shows how great is the responsibility which rests upon all for the influence they exert over others.

When a boy he was placed in the employment of a mercantile firm, one of whose partners was a Presbyterian. My friend had been brought up to the regular attendance of meetings on week-days as well as First-days, and conscientiously believed it his duty to be faithful in this matter. But he soon found that his new master was unwilling to spare him from his store duties for that purpose, telling him he might go to meetings on First-days, and in the evenings, but that business hours belonged to his employer, and must not be diverted from attention to his interests.   The boy was thus brought under deep trial and conflict to know his real duty in the position in which he was placed, and earnestly prayed to his Heavenly Father for light and strength.

On the morning of week-day meeting, he was told to unpack an invoice of goods recently received from China, evidently with the intention on the part of his employer, that there should be no opportunity for going to the place of worship; and soon after received a sample-card of a case of Chinese buttons which was in the invoice, and a list of persons in the city who dealt in such goods; and was sent out to endeavor to effect a sale.

Pleased with the commission with which he was entrusted, our young friend went from one store to another, but met with no success—none were in want of the article, and he was told that a new style of buttons had been latterly introduced which had largely superseded the Chinese article. Somewhat discouraged by these continued rebuffs, he found himself at the end of his list of names, at the store of a merchant, as I think, in Second Street, near Vine, and close to the meeting of Friends, then held in New Street (or Keys' Alley) below Second Street. This last merchant was, like the others, unwilling to purchase, but gave permission to the boy to leave his card on the store counter, while he went to the meeting to wait upon the Lord, and receive from Him comfort and help in his troubles.

While he was thus communing with his Creator, a person entered the store of the merchant, picked up the sample-card of buttons, was pleased with some of the patterns, and asked the storekeeper if he had those buttons in stock. The storekeeper replied that he could furnish him with any of those represented on the card; and accepted an order for some of them which was given him by his customer.

On the return of the boy from meeting, to claim his card, the merchant told him that he had changed his mind, and would take part of the case offered him. He was told that the case was not to be divided; so, as he had already sold a part, he agreed to purchase the whole, and our friend returned to his own establishment, much gratified with the events of the morning.

On entering the store, he said to his employer, that he had sold the case of buttons. He was pleased to hear it, and remarked, "That was much better than going to meeting," "I did go to meeting," was the reply, "and if I had not gone, I would not have sold the buttons." From that time forward, the subject of meeting was never mentioned, nor was any allusion made to what had occurred, but it was well understood that no opposition should be made to the performance of his religious duty in this respect.

Years rolled on, and the time came in which his former master felt that he was drawing near to the dark valley of the shadow of death. He lingered for some months in declining health; and during this time, his former boy, now his faithful friend, was often with him, nursing and caring for him. At this period, for the first time, he referred to their former conflict, saying, in substance, to my friend—"I cannot tell you how thankful I feel that you were faithful to your convictions, and did what you believed to be right. If you had given up your meetings, in deference to my wishes, and violated your conscience, it might have been the beginning of a downward course for you; and now, with the prospect of death before me, I might feel that your blood was required at my hands."

Among the means used by our Father in Heaven for directing the steps of the young in the right way, are the counsels and prayers of Godly parents.

The following tribute to his mother, by the late Thomas H. Benton,* who was long in public life and exposed to many temptations, shows the value of the influence which she exerted over him.

"My mother asked me never to use any tobacco, and I have never touched it from that time to the present day; she asked me not to game, and I have not, and I cannot tell who is winning or who is losing in games that can be played. She admonished me, too, against hard drinking, and whatever capacity for endurance I may have at present, and whatever usefulness I may attain in life, I attribute it to having complied with her pious and correct wishes. When I was seven years of age she asked me not to drink, and then I made a resolution of total abstinence, at a time when I was sole constituent member of my own body, and that I have adhered to it through all the time, I owe to my mother."

The labors, prayers and tears of pious parents for their offspring are often blessed, even though they may be for a time rejected, and apparently of no use.

Some years ago, a coachman was living in a gentleman's family near London. He had good wages, a kind master and a comfortable place, but there was one thing which troubled and annoyed him. It was that his old mother lived in a village close by, and from her he had constant

* A native of North Carolina. For thirty years he represented the State of Missouri in the Senate of the United States. He was the author of several historical works. Born in 1782, died in 1858.

visits. You may wonder that this was such a trouble to him, but the reason was that whenever she came she spoke to him about Christ and the salvation of his soul. "Mother," he at last said, "I cannot stand this any longer. Unless you drop that subject altogether I shall give up my place and go out of your reach, when I shall hear no more of such cant." "My son," said his mother, "as long as I have a tongue I shall never cease to speak to you about the Lord, and to the Lord about you." The young coachman was as good as his word. He wrote to a friend in the highlands of Scotland and asked him to find him a place in that part of the world. He knew that his mother could not write and could not follow him, and though he was sorry to lose a good place he said to himself, "Anything for a quiet life." His friend soon got him a place in a gentleman's stable, and he did not hide from his mother that he was glad and thankful to get out of her way.

The coachman was ordered to drive out the carriage and pair the first day after his arrival in Scotland. His master did not get into the carriage with the rest of the party, but said he meant to go on the box instead of the footman. "He wishes to see how I drive," thought the coachman, who was quite prepared to give satisfaction. Scarcely had they driven from the door when the master spoke to the coachman for the first time. He said, "Tell me if you are saved." Had the Lord come to the coachman direct from heaven it could scarely have struck him with greater consternation. He simply felt terrified. "God has followed me to Scotland," he said to himself. "I could get away from my mother, but I cannot get away from God." And at that moment he knew what Adam must have felt when he went to hide himself from the presence of God behind the trees of the garden. He could make no answer to his master, and scarcely could he drive the horses, for he trembled from head to foot.

His master went on to speak of Christ, and again he heard the old, old story, so often told him by his mother. But this time it sounded new. It had become a real thing to him. It did not seem then to be glad tidings of great joy, but a message of terror and condemnation. He felt that it was Christ, the Son of God, whom he had rejected and despised. He felt that he was a sinner. By the time the drive was over he was so ill from the terrible fear that had come upon him that he could do nothing else. For some days he could not leave his bed, but they were blessed days to him. He came as the poor prodigal, with the cry, " Be merciful to me, a sinner ; " and as he submitted to the work of grace in. his heart, he was favored to feel that there was hope for him in the mercy of God, through Christ Jesus.

The first letter he wrote to his mother from Scotland, contained the joyful news of the change in his purposes and feelings.

The effect upon others of an upright, consistent life is very great. But when a professor of religion, however zealous in some things, shows a self-indulgence or want of faithfulness in other matters, it sadly mars the good that he might have done. If his " candle" is really lighted, it is so " hid under a bushel" that others do not glorify our Father in Heaven on his account.

An incident related by John Richardson* as having happened in Virginia, some time before his visit to that country, illustrates how certainly those who are unfaithful to their own profession forfeit the esteem and respect of sensible men. He says :

" The governor wanted a cooper to mend his wine, cider and ale casks, and some · told him there was a workman near, but he was a Quaker ; he said if he was a workman, he made no matter what he professed : so the Quaker, such as he was, was sent for, and came with his hat under his arm. · The governor was somewhat at a stand to see the man come in after that manner, and asked if he was the

---

* A native of Yorkshire, England. Died in 1753, in the eighty-seventh year of his age. He twice visited America in the service of the Gospel. See *Life in Friends Library*, vol. 4, p. 60, etc.

7*

cooper he had sent for? He said, Yes. Well, said the governor are you not a Quaker? Yes, replied the man, I am so called, but I have not been faithful. He then asked, How long have you been called a Quaker? The poor man said, About twenty years. Alas for you poor man! said the governor, I am sorry for you.

"By this we may clearly see, that such who walk most up to what they profess, are in most esteem among the more thinking and religious people; and the unfaithful and loose libertine professors of Truth are slighted, and I believe will be more and more cast out as the unsavory salt, which is good for naught in religion, and is indeed trodden under the feet of men."

John Churchman* mentions an incident which occurred probably in his early childhood, and which illustrates the need of watchfulness over their conduct even in little matters, by those who make a profession of religion. He says:

"I remember a person was once at my father's, who spoke about religious matters with an affected tone, as if he was a good man; and when he mounted his horse to go away, taking a dislike to some of his motions, he called him an ugly dumb beast, with an accent which bespoke great displeasure, and grieved me much. I believed that a man whose mind was sweetened with Divine love, would not speak wrathfully or diminutively, even of the beasts of the field, which were given to man for his use: and I relate this instance as a warning to be careful of giving offence to the little ones."

Another passage in the Journal of John Churchman shows his care to practise that consistency in his own case, which he recommended to others. In 1761, he had a concern to pay a religious visit to Barbadoes, and some of the adjacent islands, and says: "I went to Philadelphia, to inquire for a passage, when my friends informed me of five vessels, three of which were nearly ready to sail; but understanding that all of them were prepared with guns for defence

* See note, p. 14.

I felt a secret exercise on my mind, so that I could not go to see any of them. I kept quiet from Sixth-day evening until Second-day morning, when I went to the meeting of ministers and elders, where I had a freedom to let Friends know, 'That I came to town in order to take my passage for Barbadoes, but found myself not at liberty to go in any of those vessels, because they carried arms for defence; for as my motive in going was to publish "the glad tidings of the Gospel, which teacheth love to all men," I could not go with those who were prepared to destroy men, whom Christ Jesus, our Lord and Master, laid down his life to save, and to deliver from that spirit in which wars and fightings stand.' I further added, "If I had a concern to visit in Gospel love, those now living at Pittsburg or Fort Duquesne, do you think it would become me to go in company with a band of soldiers, as if I wanted the arm of flesh to guard me; would it not be more becoming to go with a few simple unarmed men? I now tenderly desire your sympathy and advice.' One honest Friend said, 'Keep to the tender scruple in thy own mind, for it rejoices me to hear it;' and several said they believed it would be best for me to mind my own freedom.

I then begged that Friends would consider weightily whether it was right for any professing with us, to be owners, or part owners, charterers, freighters or insurers of vessels that a Friend could not be free to go passenger in on a gospel message. As I returned to my lodgings, I felt so much peace of mind in thus bearing my testimony, that I thought if my concern ended therein, it was worth all my trouble, though at that time I did not think it would, yet was quite easy to return home and wait until my way appeared more open. As my concern went off in this manner, I have been since led to consider that I could not have borne that testimony so fully and feelingly, if I had not been thus restrained."

It is said that William Romaine* was one evening invited

* An English clergyman; the author of many treatises on religion and theology. Born in 1714, died in 1795. There have been many editions of his works; especially of his treatises on Faith.

to a friend's house to tea, and after the tea things were removed, the woman of the house asked him to play at cards, to which he made no objections.   The cards were produced, and when all were ready to commence the play, the venerable minister said: " Let us ask the blessing of God."

"Ask the blessing of God?" said the woman in great surprise; " I never heard of such a thing at a game of cards."

Romaine then inquired, "Ought we to engage in anything on which we cannot ask his blessing?"   This gentle reproof put an end to the card playing.

CHAPTER IV.

Obedience Essential. Secret Society. Use of Wine. First-day Train. Samuel Neale's Gunning. Wine Merchant. Beer Saloon. The Clerk who could not Swear. James Kennedy. The Man who would not Travel on First-days. Fruits of Disobedience. Resisting Conviction. Jane Pierce's Friend. John Churchman. Job Scott. Joseph Hoag. Work of Regeneration. John Richardson. Job Scott. Samuel Neale. A Stratagem of Satan. Thomas Ellwood. John Griffith. John Thorp's Advice. James Naylor's Testimony. Source of Spiritual Knowledge. John Cowper. David Ferris. Thomas Story. "What will become of Us?" Taulerus. Danger of Delays. Hannah Gibbons. Joseph Hoag. The Travelling Salesman. The Man without Hope. A Neglected Duty. Elizabeth Collins.

THE operations of the Spirit of Christ in the heart of man, are designed to bring him into a state of purity and acceptance with his Heavenly Father, in which he may know a holy communion with Him, and feel that precious peace which is bestowed upon the true-hearted followers of Christ. A very little thing—a small withholding of full submission —is sufficient to prevent the reception of the Divine blessings.   How light and impalpable is fog or mist, and yet how completely it will hide the sun and interpose a barrier to the shining of his rays upon us!

A writer in *The Earnest Christian* says, that coming under religious conviction, he believed it right to resign his connection with a secret society of which he was a member. But he fought against the Light of Christ which pointed out to him this evil in his ways. "I was willing," he adds, "to give up anything or everything but that lodge—it seemed impossible to abandon it; I had so built on it. Was I not providing for my wife and family? I saw members of nearly all the churches identified with one order or another. Why should God require such a sacrifice at my hands? But He did. Oh, how I struggled and fought with my conscience." For want of yielding to the manifestations of the Light, he went backward in religious things, falling into one after another of the old habits which he had once forsaken, until he became wretched, without joy, or hope, or peace. "Inwardly," he says, "I knew what was the matter. I knew no person could help me. I had the Light, but was too great a coward to walk in it. None but God knows the wretched months that I passed."

At length under a fresh visitation of Divine Grace, he was induced to seriously consider his situation. He says: "It was plainly set before me: Either hold on to the lodge, carry about this load of misery and wretchedness, perhaps enjoy the good opinion of the world in a measure, and finally lose my soul; or by God's assisting grace, give up my lodge, come out and be separate, and touch not the unclean thing, and do what I knew was my whole duty." Yielding to the conviction with which he was favored, and giving up that which had been shown to him to be evil, peace and joy followed, and the gracious promises were brought to remembrance—"I will never leave thee nor forsake thee," "They that put their trust in me shall never be confounded," and many others.

> Whatever passes as a cloud between
> The mental eye of faith and things unseen;
> Causing that brighter world to disappear,
> Or seem less lovely, or its hopes less dear;
> This is our world, our idol, though it bear
> Religion's impress, or devotion's air.

An anecdote is recorded of a wealthy woman in a heathen

country, who was induced by the example of a friend, to seek for consolation in the religion of Christ. Her friend had lost a sweet child, and been supported under the sore affliction by the hope of meeting her in the heavenly country. And she felt the want of love and comfort, which she had sought in vain by offerings in the temples and visiting the shrines of her ancestors.

The assurances of the love of God, manifested in the sending of his beloved Son into the world, and the instructions she received in the doctrines of Christianity failed to bring peace to her soul; for there was one evil habit which she was loth to resign—the excessive use of wine. She was asked if she was willing to give up everything for Christ. She hesitated a moment and replied, "Yes, everything but —but—," "But your wine?" "Yes, all but that," she cried with tears. "And I will drink at night and sleep off my disgrace, and never disgrace Him. Then He will not be ashamed of his new disciple." For some time she clung to the delusive hope that God would accept of such a partial offering, but she could not obtain his peace until she was made willing to bear his cross, and sacrifice everything that He required of her.

How many nominal Christians are like this poor woman, —longing to have the assurance that they are the Lord's, and desiring to partake of the blessings which He bestows on his faithful ones, yet keeping back part of the price, unwilling to resign themselves unreservedly to his government, afraid to trust themselves in his hand lest He should require more than they are willing to part with or to do, having only a half-confidence in his goodness. Such double-minded persons are unstable in all their ways. They would fain be heirs of two kingdoms—which is an impossible thing.

But the Lord often does give a blessing even in temporal things, to those who faithfully give up to his requirings, and makes a way for them where there seems to be no way.

The *Congregationalist* records the experience of a railroad conductor, who was a professing Christian, and who, in the summer of 1873, received an order to run an extra train on a First-day morning to accommodate a travelling circus. He felt that the act was one which he could not do with a clear conscience, yet to decline might cost him his position. He had worked hard nearly nine years as a brakeman, and had recently been promoted to conductor. Could he afford to lose all by refusal to do as ordered? As he thought of the family dependent upon him, he said, I cannot throw away all these years of hard toil to satisfy conscience. Then he remembered his religious associations, and felt that his influence for good would be destroyed by yielding. The notice had been received on a Third-day morning, and the remainder of the week was a time of much conflict between the opposing feelings in his own mind. Sleepless nights and weary days were passed, and prayers for Divine help and wisdom were put up to Him who heareth the petitions of his children. His mind became settled under a clear conviction that duty required him to decline obeying the order.

His father was a deacon in a congregation, and he says, "I went to him and told him the story, reserving my decision to myself, and asking his advice what to do. I knew well what he would say. What a look went over his face as he spoke! 'But,' I said, 'Father will you help me to get something to do? I shall lose my position, I have devoted nearly my whole life to this business, and now I must turn to something else.' 'Trust God, my boy,' he answered promptly, 'and I will help you too.'" He returned to the office, walked up to the manager, and respectfully told him, that he had been detailed to run the circus train, but that he could not do it. The manager looked him in the face, and, to his joyful astonishment, replied, "You been detailed to run Sunday trains! I am surprised! You go home, and don't worry about Sunday trains." He adds, that since that time he had never been called on to perform such work.

After Samuel Neale* of Ireland, had been awakened to a sense of his sinful condition, and had entered on a course of

* See note, p. 44.

life more in accordance with the will of his Heavenly Father, he accompanied an innocent, goodly Friend, named Garratt Van Hassen on a short religious visit. On their return, they staid a few nights at Christians-town, where the following incident occurred; " I had been used," he says, "in · former times to walk out with my gun and dog; it was a retired way of amusing myself, in which I thought there was no harm; and reasoning after this manner, though I was very thoughtful about leading a new life, yet now I went out as formerly. I remember I shot a brace of woodcocks, and on my return home it rained, and I went to shelter myself by a stack of corn; when it struck my mind as an impropriety thus to waste my time in this way of amusement, so I returned home rather heavy-hearted. Dear Garratt and I lodged together; and next morning he asked me if I was awake, I told him I was. 'I have something to say to thee,' said he. I bid him say on. 'It has been,' said he, 'as if an angel had spoken to me, to bid thee put away thy gun; I believe it is proper thou should'st put away that amusement. To this purport he spoke, and that same night I dreamed that it was said to me, intelligibly in my sleep, that if I would be a son of righteousness, I must put away my gun, and such amusements. It made a deep impression on my mind, and I concluded to give up everything of the kind, and take up my daily cross, and follow the leadings of the Lamb, who takes away the sin of the world."

The *British Friend* of Fifth Month, 1885, contains the experience of one of the members of a Women's Temperance Association at Dublin, Ireland, as related by herself, the truthfulness of which is vouched for, and which shows how a faithful surrender to the Divine leadings is often attended with both inward and outward blessings. It is in substance as follows:

" We lived in a flourishing town in the South Riding of Tipperary, and carried on an extensive business as wholesale and retail grocers and wine and spirit merchants. Most of the gentry in the neighborhood were our customers; and our business, which was the principal one in the place, was looked upon as a great public convenience.

"For some years I had been anxious to serve the Lord. I had abundant means at my disposal, and, so far as earthly things are concerned, all that might be desired to make me happy; yet I was not satisfied. My life was on the whole miserable, an alternation of sinning and repenting. I longed to realize something better. By the help of the Holy Spirit, I was enabled, though not without a struggle, to make a full surrender of all that I had, and all that I was to God. Certain costly articles of dress had long proved a snare to me. I now saw the vanity of such profuse expense, and forthwith proceeded to abolish the idols. This self-denial brought gladness to my heart.

"But another and more trying surrender was soon to be made. The most profitable branch of our business, and that which seemed essential to success in the grocery department, was inseparably mixed up with much that was evil. No drink was consumed on the premises, but the demon was there. I knew what a snare it was in the houses where it went. I knew the desolation it was working in certain families, and when I thought that I was, to some extent, abetting this work of ruin, my soul got clouded. Happily, my husband shared my scruples, and became equally anxious to escape from Satan's toils. But what were we to do? If we gave up the wine and spirit business, we saw clearly that most of our customers would leave us altogether; our grocery business would be destroyed, and financial disaster would overtake us. Still, we heard God's voice calling and saying distinctly, 'Come out from among them, and be ye separate, and *touch not the unclean thing;*' and at length we felt compelled to make our choice between disobedience to God and worldly ease, and obedience to Him and the probable forfeiture of earthly goods. Unhappily, in our extremity we thought of a compromise. We decided to give up the liquor business for a year or two, but with the mental reservation that if the experiment failed we should commence it again.

"The experiment did fail, just as we expected; and I am

8

sorry to confess, that we embarked again in a trade that we were feeling keenly was opposed to the law of Christ. Nevertheless our Heavenly Father did not leave us to ourselves; but from undreamed-of sources rained upon us trials thick and fast. Our hearts were overwhelmed with divers sorrows. We saw the loving hand of our God in it, and at last determined to obey. Through the help of the Holy Spirit, we decided to give up our business altogether, and separate ourselves forever from the accursed thing. We sold out our entire stock at a sacrifice of several thousand pounds. Then with aching hearts, and a sadly diminished exchequer, we went forth, literally not knowing whither we went.

"By a wondrous chain of providence, God led us to a most suitable business house in a leading thoroughfare in the city, which for years had remained empty because the estate-agent refused to allow it to be used for the drink traffic. And now three years have gone by and God has never ceased to bless us. We can say from the depths of our hearts, we would not go back to the liquor traffic for the bestowal of a kingdom. Since we finally gave up our license my husband and children have been savingly brought to a knowledge of the truth. Rescued from Satan's snares, we rejoice together in the sunshine of our Father's love."

In the dealings of our Heavenly Father with his children, it is instructive to notice how one step in the right direction seems to open the way for another, until, through obedience to the pointings of the Divine finger, he who had been walking in the broad way that leads to destruction is found among those whose faces are turned Zionward. Such a case is mentioned by J. B. Gough* in his "Sunlight and Shadow," of an Englishman with whom he had met."

He was a sporting man, and being very popular, he resolved to open a beer-house, which should serve as a place of resort for his associates. One day he noticed a poor woman, with two or three children, whose husband was drinking in his shop, looking anxiously in at the door. The thought of the meanness of selling beer and making

* See note; p. 35.

money out of the poverty of this family struck him quite forcibly; and the impulse to get out of the miserable business came on him with such power that he said to his wife, "See here, lass, I'll work my fingers to the stumps before I'll keep a box like this; and I'll get out of it." When it was known that he proposed giving up the business, he was advised to advertise and sell it. " No, no," was his reply, " I give it up because it's bad; and I'll put no man in a bad business for money." To a brewer who offered to put him in a larger and more profitable house, he said, " No, I would not do it for all the world. I'd die first."

At that time he saw no evil in the drink itself, only in its abuse. He therefore secured a house, and took to it several barrels of ale and porter for moderate use: but becoming further enlightened, he went to his cellar and turned the tap of every barrel, telling his wife, who asked how she was to care for the children without ale, that she must use porridge instead.

His next good impulse was to go to a place of worship, having never been into one before. The only religious exercise he remembered was part of a prayer by a street preacher. The first sermon he heard was from a passage in Timothy: "Godliness is profitable unto all things, having the promise of the life that now is, and that which is to come." The preacher was neither learned nor eloquent, but his homely phrases were understood, and the effect produced through the Divine blessing, was shown by the remark, after the discourse: "If it's true what that chap says, it will just suit me. Only think! good for this life and good for t'other. All right now, and all right then. Safe here and safe there. That's just what I want, and I'll have it."

This was the commencement of a consistent Christian life. His fifteen years recklessness had left him in debt; so he did what every Christian should do,—began to pay his debts. He had seven little children, and was owing one hundred and fifty pounds, without a penny to meet his obligations. He went to his principal creditor, to whom he was indebted seventy-five pounds, and engaged to pay five shillings per week, which he did, never missing a week for more than five years. To another creditor, who had never even mentioned the debt to him, he went, three years after the change in his life, and said:

"I believe I owe thee seven pounds. Now, I've a pig that I've fed instead of feeding the publican, and thou canst have the pig."

"Well, lad," was the reply, "I'll take the pig; and if there's aught over, I'll pay thee the balance."

The pig was killed, weighed, and the balance of three pounds ten shillings was paid over.

On one occasion, an old companion, who did not understand the great change wrought in him, called at his shop to obtain some sporting information, and wished to know who was likely to win in a certain race. He replied that he knew nothing about it, that he had but one more race to run.

"Another race art thee going to run? Another race? Who is it with? Hast thee made another match?"

"Ay; I have made a match with the Devil for eternal life and my own soul, and it will take me all the days of my life to beat him."

When Gough parted with him, he had been a consistent Christian for twenty-nine years, with a family of six sons and two daughters walking with him in the right road. He occupied a respectable position, had been blessed in basket and store, and had been a means of blessing to others.

When any one has been brought to that condition of mind, that to love, honor and obey God is the ruling principle of his life, the fruits of this principle will soon become apparent in his conduct.

One of the old numbers of the *Moral Almanac* contains the following interesting account of the experience of a man, who under great trials, was enabled to maintain his faithfulness to his convictions, and was finally brought out of all his distresses. The person who gives the relation says:—

"About the year 1815 I became associated in the Committee of the London Female Penitentiary with an excellent man, who very shortly afterwards became a visitor at my house, and who related to me his very interesting history, which was as follows :

"He told me that in early life he had been placed in the general post-office, whence he had risen to the situation of first clerk in the receiver-general's or accountant-general's office—I think the first ; with a salary of £500 per annum ; that he was at that time very gay, frequenting with his wife, the theatre, and places of public amusement, and spending year by year, very nearly the income he received. But he was not happy, for he had an impression on his mind that things were not right between him and God. In the gayety of his heart he read novels, but he had never been in the habit of reading the Bible or attending the place of worship. In consequence of the disquiet of his mind he began to read the Bible, but being unacquainted with its contents, he knew not where to look for those parts which might be most profitable to him. He went to a neighboring place of worship, and some of the prayers seemed interesting, but there was nothing in the sermon which came home to him. He went to other places, but with no better result. One morning, in passing through White Hart Court, Gracechurch Street, he saw the Friends going into their meeting-house, and he determined to go in too. In the course of the service an aged Christian man spoke with much feeling of the difficulties which some men felt in coming to God, stating that it had been his own case. He then referred to those parts of Scripture which he had found to be of an encouraging nature. The gentleman told me he was quite thunderstruck at finding the good man expressing the very feelings and referring to the very difficulties of which he had been the subject for some months previous. The address of this aged Friend had excited an interest he had never felt before, and he went home and searched those parts of the Scriptures to which he had referred.

"He then determined to tell his wife where he had been, not having done so on the previous occasion. He met, as he expected, with sneers and contempt, and, ' Oh,' said the

8*

good man, 'could I expect anything else? If she had taken
that course a few months previous, when my mind was given
to vanity, I have no doubt I should have said pretty much
what she did.' He persevered in attending, notwithstanding
her remonstrances, and very soon afterwards purchased the
works of the Quaker writers. He little thought at the
time, as he said, to what this would expose him; but in his
reading he found what he considered very strong arguments
against the taking of an oath, which he was required by the
course of the office to take once a quarter to the accuracy
of his accounts. After a very serious examination of the
subject, he came to the decision that he ought not to take
it; and the clerk who stood next to him in the office,
having no such scruple, he requested leave of his principal
to change places with that clerk: by doing this he would
lose £100 a year; but that he was willing to sacrifice for
conscience sake. On mentioning this to his wife, he told
me that he brought the most bitter reproaches upon himself
for neglecting the interests of his family, in giving up that
of which they ought to have the benefit; and he was charged
with cruelty towards her and his children. But this was
not his greatest trial, for his principal positively refused to
allow of the exchange, wishing, as it afterwards appeared,
for an opportunity of placing another person in his office.
The quarter-day approaching he again applied, stating that
the second clerk had gone over the account with the
vouchers, and was prepared to swear to its accuracy; but
this was again refused, and, on the day on which they were
to be presented, he was called before the principal, asked
whether he was prepared to swear to the accounts, and
declining to do so, he was at once superseded, and another
person put into his place; who swore to them the same day,
after an hour's examination.

"The storm and the tempest which he had to encounter
when he went home and told his wife that he was dismissed,
was, as he said, tremendous. The children were presented
to him, one by one, and he was told that he would be their
murderer; and each day only brought fresh reproaches.
He immediately made inquiries for means of obtaining a

subsistence, but could hear of none. After a time, the little money he had saved was nearly expended, and poverty seemed to stare him in the face: still, as he told me, he was enabled to trust in God.

"One day, as he came out of the Friends' meeting-house, two of the elder brethren took him aside, desiring to speak to him, and they asked him whether it was true that he had given up his office sooner than violate his conscience? He told them it was. They desired him to meet them the next day, and then inquired particularly into his circumstances. He told them frankly everything, and they called at his house and satisfied themselves, by inquiring of the persons to whom he referred them, that his statement was correct; and having done so, they told him they were willing to give him a trial, but that it must be in a subordinate situation; and learning that he had been intended for a chemist, and had begun to learn the business when his father had obtained for him the situation in the post-office, they made an arrangement for his serving in a chemist's shop, and afterwards assisting in the warehouse of a wholesale chemist, each for six or eight months, they allowing his family during the time two guineas-a-week, 'for which,' as he said, 'I was thankful.' At the end of that time, his employers certifying that he was qualified to go into business, they set him up in a shop, lending him £300 to begin with, and giving him a running credit with a wholesale druggist for £300 more God prospered him in his business, and when I first made his acquaintance, he was a man of good property; and his wife, who had long before become a Friend, was quite satisfied with the course he had taken."

The Earnest Christian of Sixth Month, 1886, gives some instructive reminiscences of James Kennedy, of San José, California, with whom the editor of that paper had made his home some years before. He was a native of Scotland, who had removed to this country in early life. In 1852, in company with many others, he went with teams across the plains to California. He was chosen leader of the caravan, and every Seventh-day went into camp, and did not allow a wagon to be moved till Second-day morning. After a few weeks some of the company became impatient, and drove ahead on the First-day, without waiting for the rest. Others followed their example, so that he was left alone with his own family and teams.   But he persevered in his course, and got through in safety, with his cattle in good order, having lost none, and without being once molested by the Indians.   After about ten days, the first of those who had left him arrived, and others came straggling in for two weeks more.   They had lost a number of cattle and those that lived were poor.

After he reached California, J. Kennedy engaged in the " packing business."   In those days there were no railroads and no wagon roads to the mining camps in the mountains. Their roads were narrow trails, often up the steep sides of mountains, and through and across deep ravines; and only men, or small, sure-footed mules could pass over these mountain trails in safety.   Supplies were carried to the miners by trains of mules having on them pack-saddles, on which were loaded, meat, flour, vegetables, canned goods, clothes, and everything wanted in a mining camp.   From a dozen to twenty mules constituted a train.   When J. Kennedy loaded up his first train at Sacramento, the merchant of whom he bought, a brother Scotchman, said, " You must load one mule with whiskey."

" Not a mule of mine will ever pack any whiskey," was the prompt and decided answer.

" You will fail then in business; for it is of no use for you to attempt to trade with miners unless you keep whiskey."

" Then fail it is ; for they will never get any whiskey by means of me."

The mule that the merchant intended should carry whiskey was loaded with onions.   This proved a most profitable venture, for the scurvy had broken out in camp, and onions were in great demand.   At the close of the season it was found that he had done better than any of the traders who carried whiskey.

The feeling on the subject of slavery ran high in those days.   Everywhere men met on the American continent the subject was agitated.   Kennedy often had to defend in the mining camps the cause of human freedom. On one occasion, the landlord, though he had formerly been a college professor at the north, defended slavery with marked ability. Kennedy answered his arguments so well that the listeners insisted upon a public discussion. Arrangements were speedily made, and the question of slavery was debated with warmth and skill until two o'clock in the morning. The vote of the audience was very largely in favor of freedom; and they were all unconsciously being prepared to take the right side in the great struggle which was to determine the fate of slavery in this republic.

When the war broke out, J. Kennedy was toll-keeper on a turnpike owned mostly by Southerners. He sometimes had in his hands from two to three thousand dollars. Yet during all this time he never kept a revolver, or arms of any kind; and no attempt was ever made to rob him though the mill and the store near by were robbed.

News that the conflict had actually begun reached them when one of the directors, a hot-headed Southerner, was with him.

"I would like," said this director, "to cut the heart out of the first black republican I meet."

"You had better," said Kennedy, "begin on me. You will not find a better one."

The Southerner, ashamed of himself, changed the subject at once.

Some of his friends urged Kennedy to be more careful of what he said, as he might lose his position, the directors being generally Southerners. He replied that if he did, it would make no difference; he should stand by the right, come what would.

But he was confident they would not discharge him, for they wanted an honest man in his position and they knew it was difficult to get one. He kept his place till the war closed, and he voluntarily resigned.

He died in the eighty-second year of his age, in the hope of a blessed immortality.

Although a faithful attention to the directions of conscience, and to the monitions of the Spirit of Christ, may

sometimes be attended with pecuniary loss or outward suffering, yet there are many instances where a blessing has
evidently attended such faithfulness.   One such was related
by Neal Dow in the *New York Observer*:

A friend of his, yet young, who had been in business in
a small way, thought he would go to New Orleans, live
there, and try his fortune.   He put all his property into a
certain kind of merchandise which he knew the market in
New Orleans would readily take, embarked on board a brig
and sent her off, while he resolved to go by land.

In those days there were no railways.   From Philadelphia he took stage over the mountains to Pittsburg.   On
Seventh-day night there was talk among some of the passengers on the question of travelling on First-day; N. Dow's
friend said he would not travel on that day—he would stop
over at the hotel where the passengers had supper.   He had
never travelled before, and some old stagers represented to
him the possible, if not probable consequences of his resolution.

On Second-day the stage might have no place vacant
and he must necessarily wait another day, and perhaps
another and another, before he could continue his journey.
In that case, on arrival at Pittsburg, he might find the
steamer gone, and another delay would result from it.   He
considered the matter carefully.   His orders to the ship-
master were to await him at New Orleans so many days, if
he should fail to arrive he was to warehouse the cargo, a
costly affair in New Orleans.   He had hoped to sell it from
the vessel.

He said: " I will stop over."   The stage with his pleasant
companions went on without him.   He remained in the poor
country inn, with no books, no company, no church.   On
Second-day the stage was full and he could not proceed, on
Third-day the same, on Fourth-day he found a seat, and on
his arrival at Pittsburg there was no steamer and would be
none for two weeks.   He took passage on a flat-boat for
Cincinnati, where he arrived after a tedious passage, and
was obliged to wait there three days for a steamer for
New Orleans.   All looked very dark to him.

If he had kept on without stopping over he would have found a steamer at Pittsburg all ready to start, by which he could go without change to New Orleans. On arriving at his destination he found his cargo in a warehouse as he had feared, and besides, he missed an admirable opportunity to sell the whole of it from the vessel, to a merchant in undoubted credit, who importuned the captain to sell and thus save storage. All looked very dark, but in two days after his arrival, the merchant failed who had endeavored to buy his cargo. The sale would have been "on time," and the entire cargo would have been lost. In the meantime his merchandise greatly advanced in the market, was very quickly sold at a large profit and for cash, the transaction being the foundation of a handsome fortune, which he employed always wisely and well, not for himself and family only, but most liberally in every good work.

Our Saviour has declared, "Him that cometh unto me, I will in no wise cast out;" and so it will be with all those who listen to his voice, and through the assisting power of his Spirit, take up their cross and follow Him in the way of self-denial. But there is such a thing as resisting his call and the pleadings of his Spirit, till its visitations are withdrawn, and it no longer strives with us. In that awful situation, there is neither power nor will to change. In illustration of this condition, the following incident is introduced:

A minister at Plymouth, Massachusetts, was requested by a woman to visit her daughter, who was at the point of death. On entering the room, and inquiring of the sick woman why she wished to see him, she replied, that she had only consented for the sake of gratifying her friends; that it would do her no good to be visited by him or any other minister. On further conference, she told him that there had been a time when her mind was powerfully wrought upon by God's Spirit, and was occupied with serious thoughts about her eternal welfare. She felt convicted for sin, and that she needed pardoning mercy. Under these convictions she struggled for months.

At length she was invited to be present at a ball or party of pleasure, and urgently solicited by some of her young and thoughtless acquaintance to attend. But conscience strongly remonstrated. She felt convinced that if she went to that scene of vain amusement, it would jeopardize the interests of her soul. While she was preparing to go, and while on her way to the place where the gay circle were to meet, she felt that she was doing wickedly, and that if she joined them, perhaps God would leave her to herself, and her soul be lost forever.

As she came near the house she hesitated, doubting whether to go in or not; but at last she yielded to the temptation, and tremblingly crossed the threshold. But no sooner had she entered and begun to participate in the evening's amusements, than her convictions all left her. Since that time, she said she had no compunctions of conscience whatever; preaching, personal appeals, judgment and mercies, and even the firm belief that she must soon die, had not affected her hard heart, or awakened the least anxiety of mind. Her case she said was hopeless. She knew that Christ had saved the thief on the cross, and was able to save all that came unto Him for mercy, but she had no desire to come—the Spirit had taken its flight and left her to hardness of heart.

This poor girl died without giving any outward sign of repentance—anything on which her friends could find ground for consolation and hope—yet there may have been a secret work of grace, which no mortal eye saw, and mercy may have been extended as at the eleventh hour. However this may be, what a striking commentary does this incident furnish to the prayer of David—a prayer which has thousands of times since been offered by contrite hearts—" Take not thy Holy Spirit from me?"

Sad indeed are the results of an obstinate refusal to bow in submission to the Great Ruler of all things; and of rejecting his government, which is designed to promote our own happiness. A striking example of this is furnished by the case of a young woman in Philadelphia, many years ago, a member of a wealthy family there. She believed it required of her to appear as a minister, but was unwilling to yield to the requisition ; and having long resisted it, was brought into great distress of mind, because of her disobedience. After a time, the call to this service was withdrawn ; and then, hoping to obtain relief from her mental anguish, she presumed to offer unbidden sacrifices. But these appearances in the line of the ministry brought no comfort to herself or to her friends.

Her mind probably became unsettled by her anxiety and distress; and her temper being unrestrained, grew to be so unreasonable and violent, and her demeanor so disagreeable, as to unfit her for much social intercourse with others. For a long period, she remained most of the time in her own room, waited upon by an Irish nurse, who felt such a contempt for her patient, that she usually spoke of her by some disparaging apellation.

The late Jane Pierce, out of her feelings of compassion and Christian interest, was accustomed to visit her frequently. On one occasion a female Friend, a minister of the Gospel, being at her house, Jane took her to visit the poor creature. After a time of silence, the Friend addressed the invalid with a Gospel message, in which she expressed her belief that a renewed visitation of the love of God would be extended to her soul, and that a door of mercy would be opened before her. Jane Pierce could scarcely believe that this would be the case, so great had been the fall of her neighbor. But the event proved that the prophecy was a true one. One morning the nurse came for Jane, desiring her to come and see the sick woman, of whom she then spoke in terms of respect, no longer calling her by any opprobious term. She said she thought she was going to die, for she had been praying all night ! Jane went and found her greatly changed; she had become gentle as a lamb, and so continued till her close came.

This is a striking instance of the long forbearance and abundant mercy of our Father in Heaven, who willeth not that any should perish, but that all should return, repent

9

and live.   But how sad it is to think of the years of misery, and of the loss of happiness and of usefulness, which her disobedience caused this poor woman!

The experience of John Churchman* illustrates the manner in which some through disobedience or unfaithfulness, have been led to imitate the foolish man who said in his heart, "There is no God."

John Churchman had been tenderly visited by the Spirit of the Lord when a young child, and had been brought into a state of filial obedience to his Heavenly Father.   But through unwatchfulness, he lost his good condition, and for some years endured much conflict and distress.   He says: "During this time I was diligent in attending meetings, hoping at seasons that the Lord would condescend once more to visit me ; for a saying of an eminently pious man was revived in my remembrance, 'That if there remained a desire in the heart after redemption, as it was kept to, the Lord would again assuredly visit such in his own time.'   I was therefore fearful of neglecting meetings, lest I might miss of the good intended for me ; yet the subtle working of the power of darkness was very great, suggesting to me that all things came by nature, and that there was no God, no heaven, no devil, no punishment for evil, religion a jest, and painful care about futurity a silly whim, propagated to deprive people of pleasure.   But, blessed be the Lord! He preserved me from this snare ; for while I felt his judgments for sin, I believed in his being and holiness; and I am indeed fully of the mind, that no man can be an atheist before he acts contrary to knowledge, when, to allay the horror and anguish of mind he feels for the commission of sin, he closes in with this temptation."

When Job Scott* was growing toward manhood, he passed through much conflict of mind, through unwillingness fully to yield up his own will to that of the Lord, and to refrain from those gratifications which the Holy Spirit

* See note, p. 14.

clearly showed him were wrong, and condemned him for. Of this period of his life, he says:

"One time under deep exercise, after reasoning and hesitating great part of a day, whether I had best give up with full purpose of heart, to lead a religious life or not; at length I gave up, and entered once more into solemn covenant to serve God, and deny myself, according to the best of my understanding. Almost as soon as I had thus given up and come to this good conclusion, in stepped the grand adversary and blundered and distressed my mind; powerfully insinuating that a certain number were infallibly ordained to eternal salvation, the rest to inevitable destruction; and that not all the religious exercises of my mind could possibly make any alteration in my final destination and allotment. I might set my heart at rest, and live just such a life as would most gratify my natural inclination.

"I did not, indeed, so drink down this stupefying potion of false doctrine, as to relinquish my purpose of amendment all at once; I held out a few weeks, when, mournful to relate, the influence of young company, and my vehement desires for creaturely indulgence, through the tolerating influence of the aforesaid insinuations, broke through all my most solemn engagements, threw down the walls and fortifications, and exposed me an easy prey to the grand enemy of my soul's salvation. Again I took my swing in vanity, amusements and dissipation. The prince of darkness followed me with temptation upon temptation to evil, and with various subtle insinuations and dark notions, to rid me of all fear, restraint or tenderness of conscience. At length, notwithstanding all I had felt of the power of God upon me, in reproof for sin, and invitation to holiness, yea, though I had had some true relish of Divine good, the holy witness became so stifled, that I began to conclude there was *no God;* that all things came by chance, by nature, by the fortuitous jumble and concourse of atoms, without any designing cause or intelligent arrangement; that it was idle, chimerical, and delusive to think of serving, or fearing a being who had no existence but in imagination."

It has been the experience of many, that as they have yielded to temptation, and departed from the law of God written in their hearts, the light that is in them has become darkened, and those spiritual truths which they once knew have been hidden from their sight, until they have become sadly blinded and bewildered. In this deplorable state, nothing but a fresh visitation of love from the Saviour of men,—even from Him who is the Light of the world, and who alone can open the eyes of the spiritually blind,—can restore the lost faith, and enable the poor wanderer to return to the fold of peace and safety.

This is instructively shown in the account which Joseph Hoag* gives of what he passed through in his young years. He says:

"Soon after arriving at the age of fifteen, I thought it my duty to speak to a difficult subject, then before the Monthly Meeting, but I forbore from a fear of opposition. This want of faithfulness brought great distress upon me for a while. In about three months after, it was laid upon me to bear public testimony in our meetings of worship, which requisition I suppressed and reasoned away from time to time for about six months. At the expiration of this time, those manifestations of duty left me, and with them all comfort and peace. My light became darkness, and truly great was that darkness. In this I groped about seeking rest, but finding none; some times reclining under the fences, and at other times seeking solitary places, and bitterly bemoaning my situation. At length I concluded that all hope was lost; that there was no place of repentance left for me, and that I might as well be merry and take all the comfort I could. In this state of mind I rejoined my young companions, and ran into mirth at a rapid rate,

---

* Born in Dutchess County, New York, in 1762. Removed to Vermont, where he died, in 1846. He travelled extensively as a minister in various parts of the United States and Canada. See *Journal* published in 1860.

carrying the anguish of my soul with me wherever I went, and was often met with renewed conviction, which caused me to tremble, yet I concluded there was no return for me, and that I might as well go on; and in this situation I dragged along for several months, sometimes down in the extreme, at other times as much in the air.

"About this time hearing a discourse on the principles of infidelity, where it was held up that the Scriptures were uncertain records, and that the idea of the divinity of Christ was a foolish one, that God had no need of a Son, and that there was no future punishment; this pleased me, and I wished to have it so. I laid hold of this sentiment willingly, and endeavored to soothe all my feelings, in the hope that this doctrine was correct; yet it was a long time before I could bring my mind to believe these statements, neither could I accept them, before I concluded that all the openings of truth which I had witnessed were the effects of dubious stories which had been told me. When fixed in this idea, the anguish of my soul was inexpressible—it seemed as though all light had left me, and I had little or no power to govern my temper or tongue; of all states that I ever witnessed for hardness of heart, this seemed the most remarkable. Although for a while my distress was indescribable, I persisted in vindicating these principles till I became a believer in them. In this state, gross darkness was my portion, where neither sun, moon, nor stars were seen—oftentimes my days were wearisome and my nights tedious, yet through all this bewildered state I was preserved from gross evils.

"In this way I struggled along till I was nearly eighteen years of age, when it pleased the Lord to send his faithful servant, Abel Thomas,* into our part of the country; who, in a large meeting, addressed a certain state, and was enabled to speak to my condition so clearly that I could not deny a single word. He described my progress from

---

* An industrious laborer in the ministry of the Gospel. Born at Merion, near Philadelphia, and finally settled at Monallen, in Adams' County, Pennsylvania, where he died in 1816, in the seventy-ninth year of his age. He met with severe trials in his journeys during the war of the Revolution. See *Memoir in Friends' Library*, vol. 13, p. 470.

9*

the first religious impressions which I was favored to experience, to my then condition, more correctly than I could
have done it myself; clearly showing me from what I had
departed, and that this departure was the occasion of the
distress which I had undergone. When he took up my
principles of infidelity, he placed his eye upon me, and in a
wonderful manner unfolded my reasoning, laying waste all
my arguments, and then warned me, in a solemn manner,
to return to the Truth from which I had departed, closing
in these words: 'That Jesus, whom thou hast denied, has
revealed to me thy state and condition.' Learning after
meeting that he had travelled a number of miles to reach
it, and that he had lodged far from the meeting place—no
Friend knowing that he was in that part of the country, I
was persuaded he had no opportunity of obtaining information of any particular state among us. This circumstance
served to enforce the weight of the testimony on my mind,
and so fully convinced me, that it overthrew my castle: I
durst trust it no longer, and I went into the wood and wept
till I could weep no more.

"Now the potent enemy of all happiness poured in upon
my mind a mighty flood of reasoning, after this manner:—
That the Friend was not sent for my salvation, but only to
stop my mouth from speaking blaspheming principles, so
that I might not deceive others. That I had blasphemed
the Father, Son and Holy Ghost; that I had sinned against
it, and therefore no mercy was extended towards me, for
the justice and holiness of God would never be reconciled
to such a monster as I was:

"These reflections sunk me below all hope. I became so
disordered that I was watched day and night: my sleep
went from me, and my stomach refused food. I pined away
like one in a decline, for my distress and horror were beyond
the scope of language to describe. I fancied I saw the re-
gions of endless torment ready to receive me. In this situation I remained for a number of weeks.

"Here I would exhort the reader to stop, and reflect for
a few moments. Behold what I passed through for departing from the Truth, and letting in unbelief! Let it be a

warning to all, for my cravings are that another may never have the distress to go through from disobedience which I had; so narrowly escaped the Jaws of eternal destruction.

"The above-mentioned Friend, Abel Thomas, with his companion James Thomas, passing on to the southward, went through our Yearly Meeting, expecting to go home from Long Island. I then lived at Nine Partners. Our Quarterly Meeting, then held at Oblong, came on about the time that these Friends had finished their visit; but instead of finding liberty to return home, they felt their minds forcibly arrested to return back more than a hundred miles to attend our Quarterly Meeting, to which my father had taken me, fearing to leave me at home. On seeing them come in, I was exceedingly shocked, and concluded they had now come to denounce my final doom.

"After sitting awhile, Abel Thomas arose and brought into view the state for which he had been led to feel, when in our land before; and in a tender manner declared 'that he perceived the enemy had taken advantage of the poor penitent, and had made him believe that his damnation was sealed, and the Lord had no mercy for him! He then feelingly testified that the enemy was a liar, and was so from the beginning; and that whom God cast off, he no longer strove with, neither did he strive with the damned; therefore, while the striving of his spirit was felt to caution against evil, it was an evidence that the day of mercy was yet continued; and if there was faithful obedience to the manifestations of the Spirit of Christ within, and an entire giving up to the Lord for his disposal, even unto life or death—a patient endurance of the needful baptism, and a submission to the chastening of the rod that was lifted up, thus reconciling the hand that shook it; the days would come when the individual would have to go forth to tell others what great things the Lord·had done for his soul.'

"When these words dropped, I said to myself, 'It is enough, I now believe.' He stopped, as though he heard me speak, and turned to another subject."

When passing through trials and afflictions of various kinds, it is a source of comfort to the Christian to remember, that " whom the Lord loveth, He chasteneth; and scourgeth every son whom He receiveth." Exposed as we are in this state of existence, to many sources of suffering; we may yet experience even these bitter portions of our cup to promote our ultimate good, if we truly love and fear God. Indeed it is nearly always through the dispensation of suffering, that we are made willing to submit to the government of Christ. Jolm Richardson* thus describes his own experience in the work of regeneration:

"I now came to witness that scripture to be fulfilled, which saith, that when the Lord's judgments are in the earth, or earthly hearts of men, the inhabitants learn righteousness. And notwithstanding there was an aversion in my wild nature to the people in scorn called Quakers, as also to the name itself, yet when the afflicting hand of the Lord was upon me for my disobedience, and when, like Ephraim and Judah, I saw in the Light my hurt and my wound, I bemoaned myself and mourned over that just principle of light and grace in me, which I had pierced with my sins and disobedience; and although that ministration of condemnation was glorious in its time, yet great were my troubles, which humbled my mind, and made me willing to deny myself of everything which the Light made known in me to be evil; I being in great distress, and wanting peace and assurance of the love of God to my soul; the weight of which so humbled my mind, that I knew not of any calling, people, practice or principle, that was lawful and right, which I could not embrace or fall in with. This was surely like the day of Jacob's troubles, and David's fears; I saw that the filth of Zion was to be purged away by the spirit of judgment and of burning; this is the way of deliverance and recovery of poor men out of the fall, and the time of the restoration of the kingdom to God's true Israel."

The testimony of Job Scott* is very similar. He had

* See note, p. 77.   † See note, p. 14.

wandered far from the fold of Christ, and long done despite to the Spirit of Grace, but when he yielded up his heart to its government, and gave up in faithfulness to some requisitions which were hard to obey, he was rewarded with a sense of heavenly joy, "which," he says, "sprang in my bosom as a well-spring of living waters. And yet this flow of divine consolation lasted not long at this time; for though I gave up to whatever the Lord required of me, yet as I had so long and so stubbornly rebelled against Him, He saw meet in his infinite wisdom, soon to hide his face from me again, and close me up in almost utter darkness, which rendered my days truly tedious, and my nights wearisome to my soul. I was fully convinced that God was to be known inwardly, in power and great glory, by those who obey Him and wait upon Him. My heart was inflamed with love towards Him. I had seen a little of his comeliness; He had become the beloved of my soul, the chiefest among ten thousands; therefore I often retired alone, and in profound reverential silence, sought after Him, and pressingly solicited a nearer acquaintance with Him. But He, knowing what was best for me, graciously hid his presence from me. And though this was a painful suspension, yet I could not be easy to give over seeking Him; I still continued my ardent silent approaches or waiting. * * Oh the mourning and lamentation, the distress and bitter weeping, that almost continually overwhelmed me for several months together, for the want of the soul-enlivening presence of my God! * *

O my God; thou leddest me through the desert, thou weanedst me from the world, and alluredst me into the wilderness; there thou did'st hide thy face from me for a season; until the longings of my soul after thee were intensely kindled: then liftedst thou up my head and spake comfortably to me; blessed be thy holy name forever!"

Samuel Neale* in speaking of his own case, says: "The Lord was pleased to be with me, contriting my spirit, and humbling me under his mighty hand. The mount of Esau was still on fire, which at times was very affecting and hard

* See note, p. 83.

to be borne; and were it not for the Divine hand that sustained, I could not have abode the fierceness of the furnace; but it is a gradual work and must be accomplished; the kingdom of sin and Satan must be destroyed, before the kingdom of the holy Jesus becomes established in the hearts of men. The house of Saul grew weaker and weaker, and the house of David stronger and stronger, until it became established: so, in a religious sense, conversion is a gradual work; the sinful nature declines through the efficacy of the Holy Ghost and fire, which purges the floor of the heart, and makes it a fit temple for the Spirit of the Son of God to dwell in."

The essence of religion consists in being brought under the dominion of the Divine Life and Power of Christ; and knowing it to regulate our whole course of life. Where the enemy of all good sees that any are thoroughly awakened to the necessity of this, so that they are no longer his willing servants, one of his stratagems is to clothe himself so as to appear as an angel of light, and to suggest various duties and even acts of self-denial. However helpful these might prove, if Divinely required, yet if they are performed at the suggestion of the Evil one, they tend to bewilder the mind, and to keep it in bondage to him. This is a more common temptation than some may suppose. Many of those who have attained a good degree of religious experience, in looking back over their lives can remember travelling over this rough and rocky ground.

Thomas Ellwood,* in his interesting and instructive autobiography, relates how he was for a time entangled in this snare, " I, not then knowing the wiles of Satan, and being eager to be doing some acceptable service to God, too readily

* A native of Oxfordshire, England. A friend of John Milton, to whom he suggested writing *Paradise Regained*. Born 1639, died in 1713. Author of *Sacred History*, and other works. See *Life in Friends' Library* vol. 7, p. 342, etc.

yielded myself to the conduct of my enemy instead of my friend."

"He thereupon, humoring the warmth and zeal of my spirit, put me upon religious performances in my own will, in my own time, and in my own strength; which in themselves were good, and would have been profitable to me and acceptable to the Lord, if they had been performed in his will, his time, and the ability which He gives. But being wrought in the will of man, and at the prompting of the Evil one, no wonder that it did me hurt instead of good.

"I read abundantly in the Bible, and would set myself tasks in reading; enjoining myself to read so many chapters, sometimes a whole book or a long epistle at a time. And I thought that time well spent, though I was not much the wiser for what I had read, reading it too cursorily and without the true guide, the Holy Spirit, which alone could open the understanding, and give the true sense of what was read.

"I prayed often and drew out my prayers to a great length; and appointed certain set times to pray at, and a certain number of prayers to say in a day; yet knew not, meanwhile, what true prayer was. This stands not in words, though the words that are uttered in the movings of the Holy Spirit, are very available: but in the breathing of the soul to the Heavenly Father, through the operation of the Holy Spirit, who maketh intercession sometimes in words and sometimes with sighs and groans only, which the Lord vouchsafes to hear and answer.

"This will-worship, which all is that is performed in the will of man, and not in the movings of the Holy Spirit, was a great hurt to me, and hindrance of my spiritual growth in the way of Truth."

John Griffith[*] records that after he had been divinely visited, and been made willing to deny himself in all things which appeared inconsistent with the Divine will, Satan, "taking advantage of the ardency of my mind, suggested

[*] Born in Wales in 1713. Removed to Pennsylvania in 1726. Returned to England in 1750. Died there in 1776. He four times crossed the ocean on religious visits. See *Life in Friends' Library*, vol. 5, p. 329.

that my work would be much easier in obtaining a complete victory over evil, were I to refrain for awhile from
some of the necessaries of life, particularly from eating and
taking my natural rest in sleep, except Just as much as
would preserve my life; and that I must constantly keep
my hands employed in business, as idleness is the nursery
of vice; neither was he wanting to bring Scripture, and
passages out of other religious books, to confirm these requirings."

In his effort to conform to these requirings of a hard task-
master, his strength failed, and he almost sunk into despair.
But the Lord, whom he still loved, awakened a concern in
the mind of one of the members of his meeting, who visited
him, closely inquired into his condition, and showed him
that he was under a delusion of Satan.   John Griffith says:
"Being thus, through the Lord's mercy, delivered from the
wicked designs of my enemy, which undoubtedly was to
destroy both soul and body, I had in reverent thankfulness to rejoice in his salvation.   I then clearly saw that
Satan, in his religious appearances, is also carefully to be
guarded against; as nothing in religion can be acceptable
to God, but the genuine product of his unerring spirit."

It was probably a similar concern to that which John
Griffith's friend felt for him, that led John Thorp,* in one
of his excellent letters, to extend the following caution to
his friend Francis Dodshon, whose spirits were long in a
depressed condition ·—" I would have thee in anywise comply
with whatever thou thinkest may conduce to thy bodily
health in meat, drink, sleep and exercise; to do anything
to injure our health, or shorten our lives is certainly a fault.
The blessing of natural life and health, deserves our gratitude and attention ; and I believe it equally offensive to
defile or to destroy."

* A minister among Friends, who resided at Manchester, England.
Died in 1817. His collected letters have been several times published.
The last edition, by Friends' Book Store, Philadelphia.

The testimony born by James Naylor* in his treatise, "Love to the Lost," as to the danger of being deceived by the Enemy of all good, is substantially the same as those of Thomas Ellwood and John Griffith. He says:

"When the creature hath been out in the world and unrighteous ways thereof, doing that which is evil, then the Spirit of Christ in the heart condemns for the evil and neglect of good; then the same mind runs to act a worship to get peace, when both the evil and the worship is in one nature, and so the prayer becomes abomination. For the Evil-worker hath not only his hand in the deceitful works of the unrighteous mammon but in the deceitful works of worship too. For, did he not deceive in worship to hide his wickedness with pretence of godliness and long prayers, he could not keep his people in any peace in his wicked ways."

From these remarks it appears, that those who are endeavoring to do their Heavenly Father's will are often brought into some conflict in deciding whether certain things which are presented to them to be done, are of his requiring or not. These seasons of doubt and perplexity are humbling to those who are exercised thereby, and are, we believe, designed to preserve them in a dependence on the Lord, and to promote their spiritual advancement.

A somewhat similar exercise of spirit has been felt by many in their attempts to learn what are the true principles of the Gospel of Christ. They have found by experience that it is the "Lion of the tribe of Judah,"—the Spirit of the Lord Jesus—which alone is able to open the book and make known to them the mysteries of the kingdom of God. Near the end of his life, John Cowper, a brother of the

---

* A noted minister among the early Friends. He fell away, but was afterwards restored. He died in 1660, in the forty-fourth year of his age. See *Sewel's History of the Quakers* and Evans' *Friends in the Seventeenth Century.*

10

poet, who had long been a respectable and studious clergyman, came to see his dependence on God for light and
salvation as he had never seen it before, and bore this
testimony :

" I see the rock upon which I once split, and see the rock
of my salvation.   I have learned that in a moment, which
I could not have learned by reading many books for many
years.   I have often studied these points, and studied them
with great attention, but was blinded by prejudice ; and
unless He who alone is worthy to unloose the seals, had
opened the book, I had been blinded still.   Now they appear so plain, that though I am convinced no comment
could ever have made me understand them, I wonder I did
not see them before.   Yet, great as my doubts and difficulties were, they ·have only served to pave the way ; and
being solved, they make it plainer.   The subjects crowd
upon me faster than I can give them utterance.   How plain
do many texts appear, to which, after consulting all the
commentaries, I could hardly affix a meaning ; and now I
have their true meaning without any comment at all."

In the lively narrative which he has left of his religious
experience, David Ferris* describes the manner in which
he became convinced of the truth of the doctrines of which
he afterwards became a consistent professor and a faithful
supporter.   He says :

" I clearly perceived that all right understanding in
spiritual concerns must proceed from the immediate revelation of the Holy Spirit ; and that we could not come to the
knowledge of God, nor of anything relating to his kingdom
without it."

" Being very desirous to know the truth in all things, I
made application to Him who I believe to be the only
teacher of his people ; and as I waited upon Him for instruction, my understanding was gradually enlightened, so
as to perceive many errors in my former creed."   The doc-

* See note, p. 49

trine which stood most in his way was that of unconditional election and reprobation, in regard to which he says:

" It pleased the Lord to open my understanding clearly to perceive the error of this doctrine; and I was enabled to believe that Christ, who ' gave Himself a ranson for all,' would ' have all men to be saved, and come to the knowledge of the truth." After some further remarks, he adds:

" I ascribe all my knowledge in divine things to the inward manifestations of grace and truth, the teaching of the Holy Spirit. It was Christ, the light of the world, the life of men, who opened to me the Scriptures, and gave me a discerning of their meaning; and as I was faithful and obedient to the pointings of truth, I was favored with further and clearer discoveries thereof."

Thomas Story,* in writing to a correspondent in the year 1676, expresses his belief that the things of God, spoken of in the Holy Scriptures, "are rightly to be understood and truly known only by the openings and inshinings of the light of the same Divine Word, by which at first they were dictated. After saying that he had ever depended on this Word, since he was favored with the knowledge of God, and not upon his own reason as a man only. He adds:—

" And now, dear friend, know that I am not a contemner of the Holy Scriptures, but do love them, and have searched them from my youth, and have often been much comforted, and my heart has often glowed within me, whilst the blessed and holy spirit of Christ, which was in the prophets and apostles, brought the Scriptures to my remembrance, and opened the mysteries thereof in me: and therefore, to the Word of God, which the noble Bereans received with all readiness of mind before they searched the Scriptures, do I refer thee; even to the ingrafted Word, which is able to

* Born in Cumberland, England, in 1667. Visited America as a minister of the Gospel in 1698. Was appointed Recorder of the city of Philadelphia by his intimate friend, William Penn. Returned to England in 1714. Died in 1742. See *Life in Friends' Library*, vol. 10, p. 1, etc.

save thy soul, if thou believest therein; that, by the light
and power of it, thou mayst read and understand, and have
the Scriptures (as well the divine law of God written in
thy heart, as the letter of the book) opened unto thee."

The following incident illustrates the great difference
there is between a theoretical assent of the mind to the
truths of religion, and that living conviction of their reality
which flows from the revelations of the Light of Christ, and
the experience of his work in the heart.

A minister of great ability, who, years ago, preached in
the vicinity of New York, was remarkable for the earnestness with which he set forth the doctrine of self-denial, and
the cross. This was distasteful to some of his hearers, one
of whom, in consequence, for a long time absented himself
from the congregation. One morning, he concluded again
to go and hear the preacher, that he might ascertain
whether his preaching was any more to his taste than formerly. The discourse was on the "narrow way, and of a
new creature in Christ, or eternal condemnation." During
the sermon, the question was forced on the conscience of the
hearer—"How is it with myself? Does this man declare
the real truth? If he does, what must inevitably follow
from it?"

These thoughts took such hold on him, that he could not
get rid of them in the midst of his business or amusements.
He at last resolved to go to the preacher and ask him upon
his conscience if he was convinced of the truth of that
which he preached. He went and said to him with great
earnestness, "I was one of your hearers when you spoke a
short time since of the way of salvation. I confess to you,
you have disturbed my peace of mind, and I cannot refrain
from asking you solemnly before God and upon your conscience, if you can prove what you asserted, or whether it
was unfounded alarm."

The preacher, not a little surprised, informed him that it
was the doctrine of Holy Scripture, and therefore infallible
truth. "What, then, is to become of *us?*" replied the
visitor. The word "*us*" startled the preacher, but he rallied

his thoughts, and began to explain the plan of salvation. But the inquirer, as though he had heard nothing of what the preacher said, interrupted him in the midst of it, and repeated with increasing emotion the anxious exclamation, "If it be truth, sir, I beseech you, what are we to do?" Terrified, the preacher thought, "*We!* what means this *we?*" But he endeavored to stifle his inward uneasiness, and resumed his exhortations. Tears came into the eyes of the visitor; he smote his hands together and exclaimed, "Sir, if it be truth, *we* are lost and undone?" The preacher stood, trembling and overwhelmed with astonishment. He soon, however, kneeled in supplication with his visitor, after which the latter departed.

The preacher then shut himself up in his closet, and for two weeks was not seen by his congregation. He then appeared before his hearers, pale and worn by inward conflict, and acknowledged to them that before his recent experience, he had never really entered in at the strait gate. The Light of Christ had shown him in measure the difference between the wisdom of man, and the grace and power of God.

This striking narrative brings to mind the somewhat similar case of Taulerus,* a celebrated preacher who resided at Strasburgh, Germany. About the year 1340, when in the height of his popularity, he became acquainted with a layman of deep religious experience, who saw that Taulerus preached from a knowledge of the Scriptures, and by the aid of his own reason; and that he knew not experimentally those truths which he so eloquently and learnedly proclaimed to the people. The labors of this layman were blessed to the opening of the eyes of his friend, who ceased for a considerable time to minister to others, and passed through a season of retirement and humiliation, in which he was divinely instructed in the things of God, and prepared to speak, now in the demonstration of the Spirit, and with power. He saw that while he had proclaimed to others the necessity of self-denial and perfect submission to the Divine will, his own life had not corresponded therewith;

* A clergyman of the order of St. Dominic. Born 1290, died 1379. Resided at Strasburgh, Germany.

10*

and that to love, honor and obey God, had not been his ruling principle.

A stratagem of Satan, which has been often successful, is to suggest to those who are under Divine visitation, and who would not dare to directly refuse obedience, to put off till a more convenient season, their yielding to Divine requirings. The experience of many shows how important it is for those who are favored with Divine impressions, to be on their guard against improper delay in attending to the duties pointed out to them.

On one occasion, as our late valued friend, Hannah Gibbons,* was going from Birmingham to her home in West Chester, her mind was brought under religious exercise, with an impression that it would be right to call at a house by the roadside, with whose inmates she had no acquaintance. She mentioned her concern to the Friend who drove the carriage. He expressed his willingness to do whatever she desired, but suggested that as the day was waning, and the roads deep and heavy, it might be better then to go on home, and promised to take her to call on the family, when a suitable opportunity presented. To this suggestion Hannah yielded, and they pursued their journey without calling.

The opportunity for the discharge of a religious duty, which was thus allowed to pass unimproved, never returned. For, on a subsequent visit to the house it was ascertained, that the family had removed in the interim to a distant part of the country ; and the burden of an unfulfilled duty doubtless rested uncomfortably on the mind of this conscientious and tender-spirited Friend.

When Joseph Hoag* was a young man, he had occasion to go about twelve miles from home on business, into a part of the country where he had no knowledge of the people.

---

* A minister in the Society of Friends, who died at West Chester, Pennsylvania, in 1868, aged ninety-seven years.
* See note, p. 100.

He says: "As I came in sight of a house, I felt it my duty to stop and go into it. As I continued to approach the house, this sense of duty increased with so much weight, that I was afraid to pass by without attending to it. I accordingly alighted and went in. As I entered the door, this portion of Scripture powerfully ran through my mind: 'Set thine house in order, for thou shalt die and not live.' I was exceedingly struck with the language, and instead of expressing it as I ought to have done, I sat down and reasoned, until a cloud came over my mind, when I thought that I was too young, and had not arrived at that degree of experience, which would justify me in delivering such a solemn and awful message; querying with myself, how did I know but that it was all the work of the wicked one to destroy me. I arose and went away, carrying with me a heavy heart and a distressed mind for this omission of duty, which continued with me for a long time. After accomplishing my errand, on passing the house as I was returning the next day, the same impression came over me, but I rode by and went home, losing my peace and my testimony, which did not return to me for months. All this I kept to myself.

"About a year after, as I was passing the same house, my former exercise came fresh in my remembrance, and I thought I would call at another house near, and inquire after the family, where I was told that a great change had taken place in it; that the parents with twelve children all living at home had neither witnessed death nor sickness of any serious consequence till within the past year, but that lately the mother and seven of the children had died of a fever . within a few weeks of each other. I then inquired if they were religious people, but was informed that they were not at all so. Previous to hearing this, I had passed through deep sufferings and sore chastisings for my want of obedience, thinking at times if I could have my peace restored, I would accomplish any duty required of me hereafter, if I could only be sure it was a right requisition, for I greatly feared being deceived, or running without right authority, and desired to know for a certainty whether I had done wrong or not in withholding as I did. 'At length this language opened to my mind : ' As thou didst it not through wilful disobedience, but through fear of being deceived, there is forgiveness for thee ;' and my peace in good measure returned to me, and I appeared in public again a number of times to my own comfort.   But on hearing of the deaths in this family, I was beset by the enemy, who insinuated to my mind, 'that now I knew for a certainty that I had disobeyed the word of the Lord ; that I had not warned the wicked, and they had died in their sins; that now their blood was required at my hands, and cried against me as Abel's cried against Cain ;' and thus I was sorely buffeted by Satan, who tried to persuade me that the idea of my finding forgiveness was only imagination, till I was almost driven to despair ; so that had not the Lord in mercy rebuked the serpent, I should have sunk under the affliction, for which favor I desire to praise his ever-adorable name.

"Here I can but remark, that had I, instead of entering into reasoning, turned my mind to the Lord with a humble prayer that He would preserve me from all delusion, and give me strength to do his will, no doubt I should have been enabled to do my duty, have enjoyed peace and a tranquil mind, and escaped the buffetings of Satan.   Oh ! I should have been spared the loss of much time, missed an abundance of sorrow and woe, and have been better able to fill up my duty, both in a temporal and in a religious line.   I have suffered almost every way on account of my remissness herein, for when my mind was so much perplexed, I was not able to manage my temporal affairs to good account.   May these portions of sorrowful experience be lessons of lasting instruction to my posterity."

The *National Farmer* relates a case in which the prompt use of a passing opportunity enabled a watchful Christian to be helpful to a brother and to fill his own eyes with tears of gladness.   He was a travelling salesman, and on his way to the depot, in a town in Illinois, was accosted by a stranger, a young man of about twenty-five years of age, and invited to stop and have a glass of beer.   "I do not drink," was the reply.   "Come, have a cigar, and let us enjoy a game of cards," persisted the stranger, pointing to a saloon near by. "I don't smoke nor play cards. Won't you walk with me to the depot?" said the traveller. It was the one opportunity to do good, and it was not lost. As they walked on together the evil course of the stranger and its inevitable results were clearly and kindly pointed out. His mother was brought to remembrance, and there was an earnest and affectionate appeal to be reconciled to God.

The stranger broke down in tears and was again urged to give his heart to Christ. As the train came up, with tears streaming down his cheeks, he promised not only to join a temperance society, but also that he would try to be a Christian.

For some days frequent and earnest prayer was offered for him, but soon business matters forced the thoughts of the man from the mind of the traveller.

Two years or more passed, and one morning, in a town in Northern Ohio, the one who had been faithful to an opportunity was called to his door to receive from a stranger the greeting: "Don't you know me?" Grasping his hand with an expression of gladness, the stranger gave a name which recalled the incident in Illinois. He was the young man. He had kept his promise and had come to Christ, and the eyes of him who had been instrumental in turning a sinner from the error of his ways, and of him who had been turned, were both filled with tears of gladness.

There is no case in which the importance of being "instant in season" is more vitally pressing, than where the visitations of heavenly love are extended to the soul, inviting man to submit himself to the government of God, to take up his cross and follow in the way in which his Saviour would lead him. Thousands have had cause bitterly to lament that they turned aside from these invitations, and deferred to a future day that work which man cannot do of himself, and which depends upon that assisting Grace— of whose renewed visits he has no control.

What a warning is contained in a narrative given in the *American Messenger* of a young man of good moral character, and respected in the community in which he lived, but who seemed insensible to religious impressions at a time when much interest was awakened on such subjects among his associates! To one who conversed with him on his indifference, he made the following statement:—

"I do not doubt that this is the work of God. I rejoice in your success. But as for myself I feel no interest. I know full well that I am not reconciled to God, and that I am hastening on to a sinner's doom; but clearly as I perceive this, I feel no alarm. These precious calls, these offers of mercy, this pardon of sin, this salvation, this peace and joy, is for others, but not for me. A life of darkness, an end of utter darkness, lies before me. For others there is hope. For me there is no hope. Once I too might have turned and found eternal life. Now it is too late.

"When I was in college, I passed through scenes similar to these we are now witnessing. Then the Spirit of God came, and many obeyed his call. I too was so distressed that I could not study. I felt that my soul demanded my immediate attention. But to attend to my soul I thought I must give up the studies in which I was deeply interested, and sacrifice the literary mark I had set before me. After struggling awhile with my convictions, I deliberately resolved to put off all consideration of the interests of my soul till I was through college, and then give my undivided attention.

"No sooner was this determination formed, than I felt that the Spirit had left me. I was troubled with no anxiety, no seriousness. Others were burdened and distressed, but I was free to plunge into my books. Others found peace and sang a new song, but even this did not disturb me.

"I passed through that revival, callous to every gospel appeal. My college life is now over. The time that I had fixed to seek the salvation of my soul has come. The Spirit of God is again poured out, but the anxiety I once had does not return. I have not the least disposition to act.

I believe the truth of the message you bring. I have the fullest conviction of the reality of the judgment of eternal life for those who come to Christ, and of eternal death for those who do not come, and yet my heart is not moved. I know that my companions are pressing into the kingdom while I am left behind, yet this does not disturb me. I have so grieved the Spirit of God, that I have no hope the Spirit will ever return to bid my soul live."

Whether this individual was ever favored with a renewal of the offers of grace, we know not; but his experience may well remind us of the petition of the Royal Psalmist, when he had greatly offended: "Take not thy Holy Spirit from me."

A writer in the *Christian Soldier* gives the following incident, which was related to him by a Christian brother.

Some few years ago, I was clerk in a store. One day a hired man of my employers, whom I knew to be destitute of religion, came into the store. I felt it my duty to speak to him on the subject of his soul's salvation; but my wicked heart invented a thousand excuses—He may not receive it kindly, thought I, since I am younger than he; I had better keep silence until a more favorable opportunity. Conscience told me these excuses were vain, and a voice seemed to say, "Speak to the man:" but I refused to listen. But mark the result. The next day he was taken sick, became dangerous, and on the third day he died. Oh that I had listened to the voice of God's Spirit, and done my duty! Perhaps I might have been instrumental in the saving of his soul from perdition; at least I might have cleared my own skirts, and washed my own hands in innocency.

In the Memoirs of Elizabeth Collins* of Upper Evesham, N. J., she mentions that as she was sitting in a meeting at her home, under exercise, a few words presented to express, but for want of attending singly to the opening, she gave way

* See note, p. 59.

to reasoning, and put off expressing them, until the meeting was nearly over; when the language was intelligibly spoken in her inward ear, "If thou art not more faithful, thy gift shall be taken from thee." She says, "The language was awful; I was brought to see the deplorable situation I should be left in, if after receiving so precious a gift, I should neglect to improve it, and it should be taken away, and I left poor and distressed   I was led to cry for mercy and for strength to be more faithful; and in fear and trembling I arose and expressed what was before me."

PART II.

FRUITS OF THE SPIRIT.

CHAPTER V.

Repentance. Confession. Restitution. Boy in a Store. Young Woman who had Stolen. Young Man who had Burnt a School-house. The Stray Sheep. "Let Him that Stole, Steal no more." The Honest Coal Merchant. Dr. Johnson's Repentance. Dr. John Todd. The Tramp. Abraham Lincoln's Honesty. The Boy who Couldn't be Dishonest. The Robber and the Gold Watch. Self-restraint. The little Shoes did it. Warning in a Saloon. Samuel Bettle's Sermon. Edward Wright and the Drowning Boy. Plainness. Daniel Wheeler. John Richardson. Job Scott. God Does Not Need These. Jacob Green and the Skeleton. Joseph Booth. The Early Methodists. She took up the Cross in all Things. Michael Robson's Convincement. David Ferris. Samuel Neale. Unprofitable Amusements. Half an Hour to Live. Cardinal Mazarin. Playing Cards. Could not give up the World. Dr. Johnson and David Garrick.

ONE of the early effects of Divine Grace on those who yield themselves up to its government and guidance, is repentance for their past sins, and confession and restitution, so far as is practicable, to those who have been wronged.

A lad who was employed about the store of a mercantile firm, was once tempted to take a few cents belonging to his employers, to obtain the means of procuring some gratification which his appetite craved. He knew that the act was wrong, but endeavored to quiet his conscience by determining to replace the money at a future time. The same thing

11

was frequently repeated, until his indebtedness had increased from a few cents to a few dollars; and if it had not been for the preserving care of his Heavenly Father, whose tender mercy is over all his works, and who seeks to reclaim his wandering children from the paths of sin, the erring boy might have gone to still greater lengths in the way to ruin. He still kept in his mind the sum which he had clandestinely taken, and never lost sight of the purpose of restoring it. Coming more under the influence of serious impressions, his convictions for the wrong step he had taken were strengthened; and the feeling gradually settled on his mind, that before he could hope to experience Divine forgiveness and the return of true peace, he must humble himself so far as to make confession of his fault to the person wronged. He clearly saw that it would not be sufficient secretly to restore the money. The natural will struggled strongly against bearing this cross; but he found there was no other way to obtain relief than to submit to the judgments of the Lord, and to lie as with his mouth in the dust, so that he might obtain hope. He was strengthened to yield up his will in this matter, and to resolve that as soon as he was able, he would return the money, with an open acknowledgement of the cause which required it. Some years elapsed before he was in a position to earn anything by his own labors—and the discharge of this obligation was one of the earliest uses to which his earnings were applied. He received a kind letter in response from one of his former employers, acknowledging its receipt. During the years in which this load rested upon him, before it was thus happily thrown off, he kept among his papers a written statement of the transaction; so that it might be made known to those interested, if any accident should prevent the fulfilling of his resolution.

This anecdote is by no means a singular one; but simple as it is, it has seemed to the writer to be instructive, and to furnish an illustration of the Scripture declaration, "He that covereth his sins shall not prosper: but whoso *confesseth* and forsaketh them shall have mercy."

In the Acts of the Apostles it is said that Paul continued

on one occasion for two years in Ephesus, " disputing and persuading the things concerning the kingdom of God."— Special miracles were wrought by his hands, and the word of God mightily grew and prevailed. One effect especially noticed of this work of Divine Grace was, that " many that believed came, and *confessed and showed their deeds.*"

An interesting case of this kind is mentioned in the Memoirs of the late Charles G. Finney,* the President of Oberlin College. On one occasion he resided for a time in the city of New York ; and while there was visited by a young woman, whose conscience had been awakened. She had been in the habit of pilfering from her childhood ; taking from her schoolmates and others, handkerchiefs, breast-pins, pencils, and whatever she had an opportunity to steal. She made confession respecting some of these things, and asked what she should do. He told her she must return them, and make confession to those from whom she had taken them. Her convictions were so deep that she dare not withhold, and so she began the work of making confession and restitution. As she went forward with it, she continued to recall more and more instances of the kind ; for her thefts had extended to almost every kind of article that a young woman could use. From time to time she would call on her friend, and report what she had done. He relates what took place in one particular instance, as follows:

One day she informed me that she had a shawl, which she had stolen from a daughter of Bishop Hobart, then bishop of New York, whose residence was on St. John's Square, and near St. John's Church. As usual, I told her she must restore it. A few days after she called and related to me the result. She said she folded up the shawl in a

---

* Born in Connecticut in 1792. Was President of Oberlin College, and noted as a revival preacher   Died in 1875.. See *Memoir*, published by A. S. Barnes & Co., New York.

paper, and went with it, and rung the bell at the bishop's door; and when the servant came, she handed him the bundle directed to the bishop. She made no explanation, but turned immediately away, and ran around the corner into another street, lest some one should look out and see which way she went, and find out who she was. But after she got around the corner, her conscience smote her, and she said to herself, " I have not done this thing right. Somebody else may be suspected of having stolen the shawl, unless I make known to the bishop who did it."

She turned around, went immediately back, and inquired if she could see the bishop. Being informed that she could, she was conducted to his study. She then confessed to him, told him about the shawl, and all that had passed. " Well," said I, " and how did the bishop receive you?" " Oh," said she, " when I told him, he wept, laid his hand on my head, and said he forgave me, and prayed God to forgive me." " And have you been at peace in your mind," said I, " about that transaction since?" " O yes!" said she. This process continued for weeks, and I think for months. This girl was going from place to place in all parts of the city, restoring things that she had stolen, and making confession."

The result of this thorough work was what might have been expected—humility, brokenness of heart, contrition of spirit, and finally, love, joy and peace. When the time drew near for C. G. Finney to leave New York, he mentioned the case to his friend A. G. Phelps, who promised to watch over her for good. She subsequently married, and appears to have maintained a consistent Christian character.

The same author gives the experience of a young man, who resided in Oneida County, New York, which strikingly portrays the pernicious effects produced on the minds of young and excitable people by reading works of a sensational character. This young man having been visited by Divine Grace, and brought under deep conviction for sin, made the following statement:

Several years ago, a book was put into my hands called,

"The pirate's own book." I read it and it produced a most, extraordinary effect upon my mind. It inspired me with a kind of terrible and infernal ambition to be the greatest pirate that ever lived. I made up my mind to be at the head of all the highway robbers and bandits and pirates, whose history was ever written. But my religious education was in my way. The teaching and prayers of my parents seemed to rise up before me, so that I could not go forward. But I had heard that it was possible to grieve the Spirit of God away, and to quench his influence so that one would feel it no more. I had read also that it was possible to sear my conscience, so that that would not trouble me. After my resolution was taken, my first business was to get rid of my religious convictions, so as to be able to go on and perpetrate all manner of robberies and murders, without any compunction of conscience.

After a little while I made up my mind that I would commit some crime, and see how it would affect me. There was a school-house across the way from our house; and one evening I went and set it on fire. I then went to my room and to bed. Soon, however, the fire was discovered. I arose, and mingled with the crowd that gathered to put it out; but all our efforts were in vain, and it burnt to the ground.

The first step which the awakened sinner felt impelled to take, was to call on one of the trustees of the property that had been so wantonly destroyed, and make to him a full confession. He was a religious man, and was deeply affected by the recital. He undertook to inform the other trustees of the circumstance; and told the penitent youth, that he believed they would all unite in forgiving him for what had been done.

But the mind of this returning prodigal was not yet at case. A public meeting for religious worship was to be held in the evening. To this he went, and meeting Finney at the door of the house, told him that he must make a public confession: that several young men had been suspected of this thing, and he wished the people to know who had done it, and that he had no accomplice. He added, "Mr. Finney, won't you tell the people? I will be present, and say anything that may be necessary to say, if any body should ask any questions; but I do not feel as if I could open my mouth. You can tell them all about it." His family were well known and much beloved in the community; and the statement of the facts made a great impression. The people sobbed and wept all over the congregation.

The experience of the awakened sinner in all ages, is typified by the parable of the Prodigal Son. The work of the Holy Spirit on his heart ever leads him to adopt the language, "I will arise and go to my Father, and say unto him, Father, I have sinned against Heaven, and in thy sight, and am no more worthy to be called thy son." And those who have submitted to the government of the Prince of Peace, and have enrolled themselves under his banner, when they see such returning wanderers, will still partake of that joy which is felt in heaven over every sinner that repenteth.

The duty of confessing our sins and making restitution when we have wronged others, is so strongly impressed upon the heart of him who truly repents, that where we find persons unwilling to submit to it, there is room to doubt whether they have yet fully yielded their hearts to the convicting power of Divine Grace. There may be and probably are, many cases in which the awakened sinner is not led to make open confession of his former evil deeds; because there may be reasons which would render it improper; yet he ought in every instance to be so humbled under the power of God, as to be made willing to take shame to himself, and to do whatever he is convinced is called for at his hands. This humility and surrender of self are essential to enable any one to go through the narrow, "*strait*," gate which is the only entrance to the highway that leads to the Kingdom of Heaven.

Among the hills of northern New England were two infidel neighbors. One of these heard the gospel message, was impressed therewith, and enabled to bow in heart to the visitations of that Grace which hath appeared unto all men, and which bringeth salvation to those who are guided by it. This Grace, the apostle says, teaches us, among other duties, to live *righteously;* and the convicted sinner felt that he had wronged his neighbor. No doubt his pride rebelled against making the acknowledgment of his fault; but the terrors of the Lord for disobedience are a fearful burthen to an aroused conscience—as the Scriptures query, "A wounded spirit who can bear?" So he visited his infidel neighbor and informed him of the change that had taken place in his feelings as to religion. The other replied that he had heard of it, and was surprised, because he had thought him about as sensible a man as there was in town.

"Well," said the Christian, "I have got a duty to do to you, and I want you to stop talking and hear me. I haven't slept much for two nights for thinking of it. I have four sheep in my flock that belong to you. They came into my field six years ago; and I knew they had your mark on them, but I took them and marked them with my mark; and you inquired all around and could not hear anything of them. But they are in my field, with the increase of them; and now I want to settle this matter. I have lain awake nights and groaned over it, and I have come to get rid of it. And now I am at your option. I will do just what you say. If it is a few years in State's prison I will suffer that. If it is money or property you want, say the word. I have a good farm and money at interest, and you can have all you ask. I want to settle this matter up and get rid of it."

The infidel was amazed. He began to tremble.

"If you have got them sheep you are welcome to them. I don't want nothing of you, if you will only go away; a man that will come to me as you have—something must have got hold of you that I don't understand. You may have the sheep, if you will only go away."

"No," said the Christian, "I must settle this matter up

and pay for the sheep; I shall not be satisfied without. And you must tell me how much."

"Well," said the skeptic, "if you must pay me, you may give me what the sheep were worth when they got into your field, and pay me six per cent. on the amount, and go off and let me alone."

The man counted out the value of the sheep and the interest on the amount, and laid it down, and then doubled it, and laid as much more down beside it, and went his way; leaving a load on his neighbor's heart almost as heavy as that which he himself had borne.

One result which followed from this honest confession and restitution, was the conviction forced on the mind of the man who had lost the sheep, that there was something real in the power of religion; and he himself was afterwards frequently seen in the assemblies of those met to worship the Lord.

It is related of — Nott * a missionary to one of the islands in the Pacific Ocean, that he preached a sermon one day on the words, "Let him that stole steal no more." In the sermon he said that it was a duty to return things that had formerly been stolen.

The next morning when he opened his door, he saw a number of natives sitting on the ground around the house. He was surprised to see them there so early, and asked why they had come. "We have not been able to sleep all night," they said. "We were at the chapel yesterday, and heard you say that Jehovah commanded us not to steal; whereas we used to worship a god who we thought would protect thieves. We have stolen, and all these things we have brought with us are stolen goods." Then one of the men held up a saw, saying, "I stole this from the carpenters of such and such a ship." Others held up knives and various tools.

"Why have you brought them to *me?*" asked the missionary. "Take them home, and wait till the ships from

* Probably Samuel Nott, Jr., born at Norwich, Connecticut, and for many years a missionary in the East Indies. In 1856 he published a treatise on Slavery.

which you stole them come again, and then return them, with a present besides." Still the people begged him to keep the things until they could find the owners. One man, who had stolen from a missionary, then being on another island, took a voyage of seventy miles, to restore the goods.

That is the only way to improve by preaching—doing what it says. How many people form good resolutions when they hear a sermon which touches the heart and conscience; but how few such resolutions are *set to action.*

"Be ye doers of the word, and not hearers only, deceiving your ownselves."

A recent writer speaks of a friend, naturally of a gloomy turn of mind, who had much peace and joy during a long illness that ended in death. Speaking to his widow as to the cause of this, which seemed in one of his temperament somewhat remarkable, she said that her husband gratefully noticed the fact, and next to the hope of salvation which he had through Jesus Christ, he thought that it was because he had *never once knowingly cheated any one of a lump of coal,* his business being that of a coal-merchant.

It is often the case that wrongs have been committed, for which there is no way of atoning, however sincere the repentance.

There is a touching story of the famous Dr. Samuel Johnson, * which has had an influence on many a boy who has heard it. Samuel's father, Michael Johnson, was a poor bookseller in Lichfield, England. On market day he used to carry a package of books to the village of Uttoxeter, and sell them from a stall in the market-place. One day the bookseller was sick, and asked his son to go and sell the books in his place. Samuel, from a silly pride, refused to obey.

Fifty years afterwards, Johnson became the celebrated

* Born in 1709, died in 1784. One of the most distinguished of English writers. Author of an English Dictionary and of numerous other works.

author, the compiler of the "English Dictionary," and one of the most distinguished scholars in England, but he never forgot his act of unkindness to his poor, hard-toiling father; so, when he visited Uttoxeter, he determined to show his sorrow and repentance.

He went into the market-place at the time of business, un-covered his head, and stood there for an hour in a pouring rain, on the very spot where the book-stall used to stand. "This," he says, "was an act of contrition for my disobedi-ence to my kind father."

Many a man in after-life has felt something harder and heavier than a storm of rain beating upon his head, when he remembered his acts of unkindness to a good father or mother now in their graves.

Dr. John Todd,* of Pittsfield, the eminent writer, never could forget how, when his old father was sick and sent him away for medicine, he (a little lad) had been unwilling to go, and made up a lie "that the druggist had not got any such medicine."

The old man was just dying when little Johnny came in, and said to him, "My boy, your father suffers great pain for want of that medicine."

Johnny started in great distress for the medicine, but it was too late. The father on his return was almost gone. He could only say to the weeping boy, "Love God, and always speak the truth, for the eye of God is always upon you. Now kiss me once more, and farewell."

Through all his after life Dr. Todd often had a heartache over that act of falsehood and disobedience to his dying father. It takes more than a shower of rain to wash away the memory of such sins. Dr. Todd repented of that sin a thousand times.

The *Episcopal Recorder* describes another case, in which the person would most gladly have relieved his conscience,

---

* A Congregational minister. Author of numerous popular works. Of *The Student's Manual*, 170,000 copies have been sold.

by recompensing one to whom he had been unkind, but who had passed beyond his reach. The account says:

"I shall never forget that poor body. Long years have passed away since I saw her. I have had children born, and they have grown up and gone forth into the world, and have married, and their children are growing up; but that poor woman with her half-starved babe—again and again has it passed before my mental vision, and up to the present hour, it always brings with it a feeling of sorrow. Yes, God has forgiven that hasty word; but he who uttered it can never forgive himself. 'As far as the east is from the west, so far have I removed thy transgressions from thee.' So the Lord speaks; and the transgressions may be removed and the sins may be covered; but there the mother was, and I seem to see her still. She had broken some sticks out of the hedge, had made a fire by the roadside, and was sitting down thereat, warming herself and her little babe."

We speak in our friend's own words. "Yes, I have made every excuse for myself, but all will not do. I lived near the high road, and my fields adjoined it; and again and again were my hedges torn and burned by tramps as they passed along the road—one party first, and then another and another, kindling a fire on a small piece of waste ground adjoining. I was young then, and was often vexed, and sometimes angry—very angry—but vexation and anger only made the matter more unbearable. The remembrance of anger cleaves to one, as it has to me for many long years; and, now that the cares of business are laid aside, memory goes back, and the paths of former days are traversed over again. There were hasty words then as well as angry feelings; and that morning from a distance, I saw the going up of the smoke, and I rode quickly to the spot, and I saw the hedge torn and the wood burning, and I spoke to the poor woman who was sitting by the fire. I mentioned the policeman and the prison, and I threatened the one and the other. In a moment she sprang to her feet. She was a miserable object to look upon. She stood before me trembling from head to foot. She had not time, nor did she care, to adjust her dress. The babe was hanging on her bosom, which

was browned by exposure and want. There stood the
trembling mother, and there I sat on my horse, and the
thought rushed over me of my own home and my babe,
and its fond and loving and ailing mother. Yes, she had
been sick, and the poor woman before me had evidently
been sick ; but one had every comfort that love could provide, and the other, from sheer want, had broken my hedge
to gain a little warmth for herself and babe. The contrast
was very great. There were two mothers and their two
babes, and who made the difference ? That thought crossed
my mind, and perhaps the verse from Dr. Watts, did, but I
cannot remember :—

> '"How many, helpless in the street,
> Half-naked I behold!
> While I am clothed from head to feet,
> And sheltered from the cold.'"

" Who made one to differ from the other ? In a moment
these feelings had passed through my mind. There stood
the woman trembling before me. My anger was gone, but
I could not easily pacify the poor creature. I gave her
some kind words : I gave her something more substantial
than words ; but she went on her way trembling as an aspen
leaf, and methinks I see her now. God taught me a lesson
on that day which I shall never forget. A spark of pity
for sorrowing ones fell upon my heart, and burnt its way
into my soul.

" I have sometimes thought, ' Perhaps that poor woman
was in the covenant of grace, and I was a professor. Were
we a son and a daughter of the Lord God Almighty ? Was
she a sister of Jesus ? Was she my sister in Him of whom
the whole family in heaven and earth is named ?'"

So spoke my friend ; and may God bless these remarks
to whom He will. May He use them to stir up others to
avoid hasty words, and never let us forget that we have all
one Father, and that one God hath created us.

Another " fruit of the spirit" which will be manifested by
all those who have been " changed from darkness to light,"
is strict honesty and conscientiousness.

A pleasant anecdote is related of Abraham Lincoln, who at one time acted as Post Master of a small office. Several years elapsed after he had resigned the position before his accounts were adjusted, and the agent of the department called on him for a settlement. He produced the amount which, during all that time, he had kept carefully laid away, remarking that he *never used any man's money but his own.*

Because they have not acted on this principle of *never using any man's money but their own,* many have suffered in reputation, and have found themselves entangled in almost inextricable difficulties without any dishonest intention. They have allowed money belonging to others in their hands to become mingled with their own; the feeling that funds were at their control has encouraged expenses which might have been avoided; the want of strict business habits, which would lead them closely to scrutinize their income, outgoings, and liabilities, has in some cases added to their embarrassment; and a time of reckoning has caught them when unprepared to meet it. We doubt not there are thousands who have had cause bitterly to repent that they had not been as scrupulous in this respect as Abraham Lincoln.

The anecdote above narrated illustrates what was a usual habit with him. He had always a partner in his professional life, and, when he went out upon the circuit, this partner was usually at home. While out, he frequently took up and disposed of cases that were never entered at the office. In these cases, after receiving his fees, he divided the money in his pocket-book, labelling each sum (wrapped in a piece of paper) that belonged to his partner, stating his name, and the case on which it was received. He divided the money so that if by any casualty he should fail of an opportunity to pay it over, there could be no dispute as to the exact amount that was his partner's due.

12

The same honesty was exhibited in Abraham Lincoln's conduct after he had been admitted to the bar, and came to practice as a lawyer. His biographer says of him: "If a man went to him with the proposal to institute a suit, he examined carefully the man's grounds for the action. If these were good, he entered upon the case, and prosecuted it faithfully to the end. If the grounds were not good, he would have nothing to do with the case. He invariably advised the applicant to dismiss the matter, telling him frankly he had no case and ought not to prosecute. Sometimes he discovered, in the middle of a trial, by the revelation of a witness, that his client had lied to him. After the moment that he was convinced that justice was opposed to him and his client, he lost all his enthusiasm and all his courage. He would not strive to make the worse appear the better reason for any man. As a citizen, as a lover of good order, as a man who believed in truth and justice, he was, by every instinct of his nature, opposed to the success of villainy and the triumph of wrong, and he would not sell himself to purposes of injustice and immorality. He repeatedly refused to take fees on the wrong side of a case. When his clients had practised gross deception upon him, he forsook their cases in mid passage; and he always refused to accept fees of those whom he advised not to prosecute. On one occasion, while engaged upon an important case, he discovered that he was on the wrong side. His associate in the case was immediately informed that he [Lincoln] would not make the plea. The associate made it, and the case, much to the surprise of Lincoln, was decided for his client. Perfectly convinced that his client was wrong, he would not receive one cent of the fee of nine hundred dollars which he paid. It is not wonderful that one who knew him well spoke of him as "perversely honest."

A sheep grower sold a number of sheep at a stipulated average price. When he delivered the animals, he delivered many lambs or sheep too young to come fairly within the terms of the contract. He was sued for damages by the injured party, and Lincoln was his attorney. At the trial, the facts as to the character of the sheep delivered were proved ; and several witnesses testified as to the usage by which all under a certain age were regarded as lambs and of inferior value. On comprehending the facts, Lincoln at once changed his line of effort, and confined himself to ascertaining the real number of inferior sheep delivered. On addressing the jury, he said that from the facts proved they must give a verdict against his client, and he only asked their scrutiny as to the actual damage suffered.

An interesting illustration of that honesty which flows from the fear of God, is related in one of the volumes of *The British Friend*. It occurred at a time when great distress prevailed in some parts of England, particularly in Lancashire, owing to the suspension of work in the cotton factories.

An old woman in humble life, who resided in that district, although not herself a " mill hand," found from the general depression of trade, that her little means were getting less and less, until the pressure grew too great to bear. In her sore poverty, she resolved to pack up the few articles she had left, and go to Preston, where she had a daughter who was married, and with whom she might live. She went to take leave of a minister of a congregation of which she was a member ; and on hearing her plan he endeavored to dissuade her from it ; urging her if possible to remain where she was in hope of better times, and adding that perhaps her daughter might be even worse off than herself. " That cannot be," said the old woman, " for I am very poor and have nothing left to live on ; I will go to my daughter, for that will be shelter for me at any rate." The minister finding that she had so miserable a prospect if she remained in her old dwelling, kindly gave her the amount of her railway fare to Preston and half a crown besides.

When she reached Preston station, a crowd of boys surrounded her, begging to carry her box ; which she refused, as all the money now left in her purse was a half-crown and three pennies. One poor lad with a piteous look, besought her very earnestly to let him take it for her, adding, " I will take it to any part of the town for two pence : do let me, for it is the only way I have to get a bit of bread, and we're clemming (starving) at home." Small as was the sum the old woman had to begin anew her struggle with the world, she had a pitying heart, and the appeal thus made was enough. The lad shouldered the box, and followed her through the lamp-lit streets to a humble part of the town, where she knocked at the door of one of the houses; and, after waiting awhile and receiving no answer, she found it was locked.

Supposing the daughter might be out on some errand, she desired the boy to put down the box; and paying him for his services, she seated herself on it by the door to await the daughter's return. After awhile the latter came up, and, on finding her mother come to settle with her, burst into a lamentation : " Oh! why have you come? for we are starving. I have been out trying to get a morsel for the children and I can't. What can we do?

Her mother calmed her a little, and begged her to open the door. " Let's go in anyhow, I have a half-crown in my pocket, and you can take that and buy something; and that will carry us over to-morrow at any rate." They entered, and the old woman drew forth her purse to take the half-crown, when, to her dismay, she found she had paid it to the boy in the dim light of the evening in mistake for a penny. This was too much to bear and both the women sank down and cried long and bitterly over the prospect before them. The mother, however, was a truly Christian person; and when the first burst of sorrow was past, her faith rose triumphant over all. " Well," said she, " never mind, we have the two pence left, and let us be thankful to God for that, and for a roof over our heads: You take it; it will buy bread for you and the children to-night, and I will go to bed, for I shan't want anything, and let us hope God will provide for to-morrow when it comes." The daughter did accordingly and that night passed away with its griefs and sorrows.

With the early morning came a tap at the door, which the daughter opened. A boy stood there before her, who introduced himself rather briefly with, " Didn't I bring a box for an old woman here last night." " Yes, you did." " Where is she?" " Up stairs." " Then tell her to come down, for I want to see her." Very soon the mother made her appearance and was greeted with " Missus, do you know you gave me a half-crown last-night instead of a penny? because you did; and I have brought it back, and here it is." " Yes, my lad, and I am very much obliged to you for bringing it back again. But I want to know how you came to do so, for I thought you told me you were clemming at home." " Yes, we are very bad off," said the boy, brightening up as he spoke, " but I go to Sunday-School and I love Jesus, and I couldn't be dishonest."

Precious indeed is that holy fear and confidence in God, which enabled this poor boy to resist the temptation to keep that which had been given to him in mistake, and led him to seek out its rightful owner. " This is the victory that overcometh the world, even our faith."

Another illustration of conscientiousness was furnished by the head of a family named P—— who lived in the south of Ireland many years ago, and were much respected, not only for their wealth and station, but for moral worth and benevolence.

They were connected with the Society of Friends, and lived consistently with their principles of peace and non-resistance, in the trying days of the commotions in Ireland in 1798. One night in those troublous times their house was broken into and spoiled by a band of robbers, who seemed fully aware of what valuables they might expect to obtain—a knowledge probably derived through some of the servants. As they were about to depart with their booty, one of them said to the wife, " You have a gold watch?" She had put it in her bosom at the attack, and now quietly replied, " No, I have not." Her husband was standing by, and when he heard her denial, he turned on her such a look and such a reproof, as she never met before from him. " Mary," he said, " I am ashamed of thee! Would'st thou then barter thy sweet peace by an untruth, for the sake of thy gold watch?" The rebuked wife stood abashed before

12*

her husband, and taking the watch from her bosom handed it over to the robber.

Sometime after, the husband was sent for to the county town on an unexpected errand. The party of robbers had been arrested for another robbery, and he was sent for to identify his property, which was returned to him safely. In jail suspicion first rested on the leader of the gang, from the watch having been seen with him bearing her initials.

That Divine Grace which brings salvation, not only teaches man "to live righteously" towards others, but to "live soberly"—that is with proper self-restraint over his appetites and inclinations.

The Apostle Paul in one of his epistles, uses this suggestive language, "I keep my body under and bring it into subjection, lest by any means, when I have preached to others, I myself should become a cast-away." Of the need of such watchful care, and the sad consequences which flow from its neglect, we have thousands of mournful proofs, in the multitudes around us who are ruined by indulgence in the use of ardent spirits. We believe there are few, if any, of these victims of a depraved appetite, but have heard the warning voice in their souls, which would have saved them, if it had been heeded. We believe also, that there are few, if any, true Christians, but have known the cross to be laid on their appetites, and have felt that it was necessary for them to follow the example of the apostle, and bring the body "into subjection:" and this not only with reference to the use of spirituous liquors, but in all things.

Among the many incidents connected with this subject, that float along the tide of public prints, there is a simple one that is interesting and touching; showing how Divine Grace sometimes uses the power of natural affection to restrain the drunkard and awaken him to a sense of his responsibilities.

A young man who had been reclaimed from the vice of intemperance, was called upon to tell how he was led to give up drinking. He arose, but looked for a moment very confused. All he could say was, "The little shoes, they did it!" With a thick voice, as if his heart was in his throat, he kept repeating this. There was a stare of perplexity on every face, and at length some thoughtless young people began to titter. The man in all his embarrassment heard this sound, and rallied at once. The light came into his eyes with a flash—he drew himself up and addressed the audience: the choking went from his throat. " Yes, friends," he said in a clear voice, " whatever you may think of it, I've told you the truth—the little shoes did it ! I was a brute and a fool : strong drink had made me both, and starved me into the bargain. I suffered; I deserved to suffer; but I didn't suffer alone—no man does who has a wife and child, for the woman gets the worst abuse. But I am no speaker to enlarge on that; I'll stick to the little shoes. It was one night, when I was all but done for, the saloon keeper's child holding out her feet for her father to look at her fine new shoes. It was a simple thing ; but, friends, no fist ever struck me such a blow as those little shoes. They kicked reason into me. What business have I to clothe others with fineries, and provide not even coarse clothing for my own, but let them go bare? said I; and there outside was my shivering wife and blue-chilled child, on a bitter cold night. I took hold of the little one with a grip and saw her chilled feet. Men, fathers! if the little shoes smote me what must the little feet do? I put them, cold as ice, to my breast; they pierced me through. · Yes, the little feet walked right into my heart, and away walked my selfishness. I had a trifle of my money left; I bought a loaf of bread and then a pair of little shoes ; and from that day I have spent no more money at the public house. That's all I've got to say—It was the little shoes that did it."

The South Bend *Sun* tells of a prominent professional gentleman, who one morning stepped into a saloon to get his customary drink. After passing the ordinary salutation with three or four loafers who were hanging about the place, he went up to the bar and called for whiskey, which was handed to him As he filled the glass and was raising it to his lips, a miserable, wretched, drunken tramp stepped up beside him and said :

"Say, Squire, can't you give *me* a drink out of that bottle?"

Not wishing to be annoyed by associates of that class, the gentleman roughly told him to go away and mind his own business. The tramp angrily replied that he need not be so cranky about the matter, for before he got to drinking he was just as respectable as he was, and wore as fine clothes as he did, "And what is more," he said, "I always knew how to act the gentleman."

The gentleman stood for a few moments eyeing the man from head to foot, noting with deep disgust his blood-shot eyes, his bloated face, his long unkempt hair, his filthy, ragged garments, and his mismated boots, after which he said,

"Then it was drinking that made you an outcast from society and the miserable man you are?"

"Yes," said the tramp.

" *Then it is time for me to quit;*" said the gentleman, and pouring the glass of whiskey on the floor, he turned and left the saloon, never to enter it again.

The following account was related by Samuel Bettle, Sr.,* in a very remarkable communication, on First-day, the 16th of Eleventh month, 1823, in a meeting in Merion:

He was acquainted with a man of strong and fine natural abilities, of excellent character, and good fortune or property ; but this man had one darling sin, one failing which, given way to, sullied all his virtues, and this was, inebriety. Though he strove in his own will against it, yet it still gained and kept dominion over him, until it destroyed his constitution, and ruined him in character and substance. Thus, a poor, wretched, miserable being, he found himself

---

* For many years a minister and a prominent member of the Society of Friends in Philadelphia. Remarkable for his wisdom and foresight. Died in 1861, in the eighty-seventh year of his age.

progressing rapidly to destruction; and all his strong re-solves and re-resolves availed him nothing. One day he was coming down stairs to take his usual potation, yet sensible of the consequence of so doing; but, of a sudden, he prayed for help to resist the temptation. He uttered no words; he sighed from the bottom of his soul that God would help a poor lost creature; and his prayer was heard. On reaching his room, instead of taking his bottle, he took his seat and remained in silence about half an hour. The Divine and healing Power broke in upon his mind; he wept and prayed, and was preserved. The next day the temptation was renewed, but having been favored once to get the victory, he was enabled to persevere to the end. I saw," said S. B., "the death-bed of the man, just before he was called to his account. Oh, how humble, how changed, and how happy! With triumphant hope he joined the assembly of the saints of God."

It is recorded of Edward Wright,* of whose conversion some account was given in a former page, that, before he came under the government of the Spirit of Christ, he was greatly addicted to the use of strong drink.

He was standing on the steamboat pier at the river Thames, when he heard the cry, "A boy overboard!" Hastening to the spot, and looking carefully into the water, he observed bubbles, "and in a moment the thought occurred to him that these bubbles were probably caused by the last breathings of the drowning lad. Instantly, with the quickness of an apparition, he plunged into the river, dived beneath the surface, and while the crowd on the shore and pier were awaiting in breathless suspense his re-appearance, he dived to the bottom, and there lay the body, as if dead. Passing one arm under the lad, and with the other raising himself and his burden to the surface, Ned was seen with his prize above the water, and was greeted with a simultaneous shout from the spectators. A boat was meanwhile sent to his assistance, the boy put in it and conveyed to a public-house, and Ned, amid such plaudits as nearly bewildered him, swam safely to the pier.

*See note, p. 37.

"As he was going away, the captain of one of the steamboats cried out, 'Hold on! we are going to make a collection for you.' 'All right, was Ned's response; 'while you are doing so, I'll just run up and see how the lad is getting on.' The boy had been so long under water that he appeared as one dead : and although stimulants were freely given, and every appliance obtained for restoring animation, it was feared for some time that the case was hopeless. The means were at last successful, and the frantic mother, whose wild shrieks of sorrow had been heard from outside, pushed her way into the room, clasped her child fondly to her bosom, and having relieved herself by a flood of tears, inquired, 'Where is the man who saved my child?' The brave rescuer was pointed out, and falling at his feet she thanked him repeatedly, asking what she could do to reward him for his bravery. Ned laid his hand on her head and said, 'All right, mother; I've a little one of my own.'

" Returning to the pier, he found that the collection had been made by the captains of the two steamers, and the man in charge of the pier, and his jacket pockets were filled with coppers, and his trousers pockets with small silver. Of course, he could not resist the temptation to drink too much rum, and the consequence was that he spent all he had that night in the public-house, going home drunk and penniless! He could expose his life to danger, to rescue a drowning child; but he could not be brave enough to resist the temptations of drink. He could sympathize with a mother's sorrow and a child's suffering; but in the midst of these allurements to drink he could forget his young and hungry wife, and neglect the wants of his infant child."

This incident occurred during the time of his spiritual darkness, when he was a willing servant of the Evil one; but when he came under the government of the Spirit of Christ, he was enabled to turn from the temptation to indulge in strong drink, and to "live soberly," as well as "righteously."

Those who have submitted to the visitation of Divine Grace, and through its transforming power have come to be of the Lord's children, are early made to feel the force of the

Scripture language, "Ye are not your own," and the consequent necessity of glorifying God with their bodies and their spirits. They soon learn that it is their duty to obey the injunction, "Be not conformed to this world, but be ye transformed by the renewing of your mind;" and that the Cross must be taken up in many things which the world considers allowable. Among the things in which the Christian is often led in a different path from that which he had before trodden, is the observance of plainness and simplicity in dress and behavior. A testimony on these subjects is not peculiar to any one religious Society, but belongs to the Church at large—being founded on the commands of our Saviour and his Apostles, and of the Holy Prophets; and also on the openings of the Spirit of Christ in the hearts of his obedient followers. Many indeed are the instances of those who have been brought under a living concern for their own salvation and been made willing to bend their necks to the yoke of Christ, who have felt the force of the command, "put away thine ornaments from thee;" and who have seen that they could no longer comply with many customs which others thought harmless.

This has been the case in all true revivals of religion. The early members of the Society of Friends were led into great simplicity in their manner of life, and watchfulness over their words and actions. Their liberty stood in the liberty which the Spirit of Christ gave them.

When Daniel Wheeler* had submitted to those Divine visitations which were the means of redeeming him from

---

* A noted minister in the Society of Friends in England. He spent more than four years in a religious visit among the islands of the Pacific Ocean, returning in 1838. He twice visited America in the service of the Gospel; and, during the second of these visits, died at New York city, in 1840, aged sixty-eight years. See *Life in Friends' Library,* vol. 7, p. 1, etc.

sin and transgression, he found, as his children state in his Memoirs, that the only path in which he could walk with safety, was that of self-denial. "Much mental conflict was at this time his portion; but peace was only to be obtained by an entire surrender of the will; and in conformity with what he believed required of him, he adopted the plain dress. He once recounted to a friend in lively terms, the trial it was to him to put on a different hat to that which he had been accustomed to wear; especially as in going to the meeting at Woodhouse, he generally met a number of his former gay acquaintances, whom he crossed on the way to their place of worship, which he had himself previously been in the practice of attending. In this instance it was hard to appear openly as a fool before men; he thought if his natural life might have been accepted as a substitute he would gladly have laid it down; but this was not the thing required. He diligently examined his heart, and believed he saw clearly his Master's will in the requisition; and that it was a discipline designed to bring him into a state of childlike obedience and dependence. In great distress he cried unto the Lord for help; and a passage of Scripture was powerfully applied to his mind, "Whosoever shall confess me before men, him will I confess also before my Father which is in heaven.' His resolution was immediately taken; he put on the hat, and with his mind staid on the Lord, set out to join his friends at meeting."

John Richardson* who was also an instrument in the Lord's hand to proclaim the way of life and salvation, and who travelled for that purpose both in England and America, relates that there was in his "wild nature," an aversion to the strict living and demeanor, plainness of habit and language of the "people called in scorn Quakers;" and that he learned none of these things from them, for he says, "When the Lord changed my heart, he also changed my thoughts, word and ways, and there became an aversion in me to vice, sin and vanity." "Now I came to be clearly convinced about hat-honor, bowing the knee, and the corrupt language, as well as finery in habit; all which for con-

* See note, p. 77.

science-sake, and the peace thereof, I came to deny, and take up the cross to, and had great peace in so doing."

The experience of Job Scott* is very instructive. When he submitted his heart to the holy work of Divine Grace, he was early convinced that "religion was an internal life in the soul," and "that men generally rely too much on external performances and appearances." Thus his understanding was opened to see "that a plain, decent, and not costly dress and way of living, in all things, was most agreeable to true Christian gravity and self denial."

"Thus instructed," he adds, "I bowed in reverence; and as it became from time to time necessary to procure new clothing, I endeavored to conform my outward appearance in this respect to the dictates of Truth, in which I found true peace and satisfaction. Also, He instructed me to use the plain Scripture language, THOU to one, and YOU to more than one. The cross greatly offended me in regard to these things. This form of language in particular, looked so trifling and foolish to the wordly-wise part in me, and the fear of the 'world's dread laugh' so powerfully opposed it, that I gave way to carnal reasoning. 'What good can this exactness of language do. May I not as well serve God in a less singular and less contemptible way?' Such reasonings as these, and many more, presented in opposition to the holy injunction. But the Lord showed me, that if I would be wise, I must first become a fool; if I would be his disciple, I must first deny myself, take up my cross daily, in whatever He required of me, and follow Him in the way of his leading.

"It was very hard and trying to my natural will to give up to this duty. This exercise beset me day and night for some time, during which I had many sorrowful and bitter tears, pleaded many excuses, and greatly wished some substitute might be accepted instead of the thing called for. But he who called me into the performance of these foolish things (to the world's wisdom), was graciously pleased to show me with indubitable clearness, that He would choose his sacrifice himself; and that neither a right hand nor a

*See note, p. 14.

13

right eye, neither thousands of rams, nor ten thousands of rivers of oil, would by any means answer instead of his requirings. If he called for so weak or foolish a thing as the words *thou* and *thee* to a single person, instead of *you*, nothing else of my substituting would do instead of it." "Perhaps," says Job Scott, "few will believe the fulness of heavenly joy which sprang in my bosom, as a well-spring of living waters, after my giving up in faithfulness to this requisition."

That self-denial in matters of dress is a testimony that should be borne by the whole Church, and ought not to be confined to any one branch is shown by the following case, described in the *Journal* of Eighth Month 27th, 1884, by Mary G. Smith, of Hoopestown, Illinois.

An intimate friend of mine, a member of the Methodist society, who has been one from her earliest years, related to me the power of grace upon her, as regards dress. She had ample means before and after marriage to indulge in the gay and ornamental robing of the body. She said that when growing up and for years, her rich jewelry did not interfere with her religion. But at last, an impression was felt that she must live closer to God, and seek to know more clearly his will for her; and in the quiet of her own home, she received a baptism that opened the seal of the inner sanctuary and disclosed many inconsistencies, hindering the pure worship of God. When she next went to prepare herself to go to meeting, not thinking about what she should put on, she took up her jewelry, which she had been in the habit of wearing, when a voice told her, "God does not need these." She was startled by the thought, and again she put forth her hand to place the ornaments on her person, when lo! the same clear voice said: "Thou dost not need these to worship me." Then there arose a contest in her mind as to what her friends would think of her strange appearance, when once more she heard: "Art thou not mine?. be obedient and thy soul shall live." She left her ornaments in the box, and went forth a monument to the effect of a dedicated heart and to the voice of God in the soul.

But the next time she went out, the contest arose between the desire of her natural will to conform to her usual attire, and the spiritual light which convinced her that ornaments were injurious to the salvation of her soul. She said:

"I never afterward wanted to put them on," and she felt compelled to remove the ruffles and trimmings from her clothes.

A person who had been brought under religious conviction found, as many others have done, that her fondness for dress was one of the things which had to be brought under the crucifying power of the Spirit of Christ. At the time of her awakening she had just finished a dress—but it was never worn. She joined in religious fellowship, I believe, with the Methodists. She says:—

"When I went home [from the meeting at which she had become a member] the Lord let me see that I had more trimmings on my hat than was for his glory, and I took the flowers off; but at meeting that night the light kept shining, and I pulled the feather off in meeting, and I have never had any on since. The Lord let me see I could not wear these things and be a true Christian. And I cannot see how any one that has a Bible experience, and is willing to walk in the Light and obey God, can conform so much to the world in their dress."

A few years since, a Friend, who was paying a religious visit in some parts of the Southern States, had an appointed meeting among the colored people at Raleigh, N. C. In the audience he observed a nice-looking, plainly dressed young woman, in whose appearance he was much interested. In a subsequent conversation he found that she was a member with the Methodists, who had felt it to be her duty to preach among her people. In relating her experience, she said that at one time she was fond of wearing ornaments like other young women; but as she came under the power of Divine Grace, one after another of these had been dropped from a sense of duty. She further stated that there were several other women in her religious society, who had been led into the ministry, and all of them had been led into the same self-denial and plainness as to dress, that she had seen to be the allotted path for her to walk in.

Though the strong testimony on the subject of plainness in attire borne by prophets and apostles of old seems to be much lost sight of by many who profess to be Christians— yet persons who are brought under deep religious conviction are very often led into a Christian simplicity—and a following of the fashions of the day is felt to be inconsistent with the self-denying life of a follower of Christ.

Mary Bosanquet,* who afterwards married John Fletcher, says, in her life: "I saw clearly that plainness of dress and behavior best became a Christian. I will therefore, make it my rule to be clean and neat, but in the plainest things, according to my station; and whenever I thought on the subject, these words would pass through my mind with power: 'For so the holy women of old adorned themselves.'"

Jacob Green, an Irish Friend, who, about 1840, paid a very acceptable visit to America, as a minister, related on one occasion, that when he was a young man, before he had joined the religious Society of Friends, he entered a grave-yard, where he beheld the skeleton of a human being. This made so deep an impression on his mind that he never after felt the least inclination to adorn his person.

When Thomas Story† was in America, he had a meeting in the year 1699, at Mispillion, in Delaware. Here he met with a man named Joseph Booth, who asked him many questions on religious subjects, all of which were answered to his satisfaction; and, after the meeting, he expressed his full convincement in what he had heard.

"But," says T. Story, "I found he stuck at the cross; he

* A friend of John Wesley, and a very pious and exemplary woman. See *Life*, by Henry Moore.
† See note, p. 111.

could not submit to the plain language of thou and thee to a single person, nor become unmodish in keeping on the hat, and declining the customary ways of address, nor break off that heathenish custom of calling the days and months by the names of their imaginary gods; which he thought too low for matters of religion; concerning all which we discovered next morning, as he set us on our way; and in some of these points he was better satisfied before we parted. Yet the cross was hard for him to bear in these small things; and why? Because submitting to the practice of them immediately subjects a man to all the scoffing and contempt with which we are treated by the world at this day; no-way agreeable to the natural and carnal mind. And that which rendered things harder to him was, the station and character he supported in the world; for he was a justice of the peace, and the most sober and knowing person in these parts."

At those favored seasons in the history of the Church, when the Lord has been pleased, in a remarkable manner, to pour forth his Spirit on the hearts of the people, and to cause them to turn with sincerity and earnestness to Him, the revival of true religion has been accompanied with a corresponding simplicity in life and dress, in accordance with the precepts of Holy Scripture. It was so with the early members of the Society of Friends. Without any formal regulations on the subject, they soon came to feel that it was beneath the dignity of one whose affections were set on Heavenly things, to follow the varying fashions of the day; and the plainness and simplicity they manifested in their apparel as well as conduct, were the legitimate fruits of their devotion to the cause of Christ.

The early Methodists were also a plain, self-denying people, and this was manifested in their personal appearance, as well as in other things. As their congregations have increased in wealth they have come more under the influence of pride and fashion; and their places of worship

13*

are now very often expensive and ornate structures, especially in the large cities. This is greatly to be regretted, as it must lessen the influence for good of that people. The change that has taken place has affected their dress, as well as their meeting-houses. A few years since, as a Friend who was from home on a religious visit, was standing at a ferry in company with his companion, he was accosted by a stranger who remarked that he supposed they were ministers of the Gospel, and that he also was one, though they would not suppose it from his appearance. He was a Methodist preacher, and he further said, that in former times a person would be known to be a member of their Society by his appearance, but now they had become ashamed to bear this open testimony to religion in the face of the world.

Alas, of how many of the members of the Society of Friends must it be acknowledged, that they too have "become ashamed" of the unmodish dress of a consistent Quaker!

The writer was greatly interested some months ago in meeting with an aged woman of another religious profession, who was evidently green in old age. She informed us that she had become deaf, and could hear nothing save the still small voice in the inmost recesses of her soul. She dressed much in the manner of a plain Friend of the last generation ; and some allusion being made to it in our intercourse (by means of a slate and pencil), she said she had been asked whether she was a Quaker, and when she replied in the negative, the question was put, Why did she dress so plainly? To this she answered, that when she yielded to the power of Divine Grace and became a Christian, she took up the cross in *all* things, dress as well as others.

The influence which may be exerted on others by plainness of dress, when it is connected with uprightness and consistency in other respects, is illustrated by an account furnished by Samuel Chadbourne of Orleans County, N. Y. respecting Michael Robson, who resided at Hartland, Niagara County of that State, S. C. says :—

"I being a stranger, an immigrant, seeking a place of settlement in this country, had been recommended to call on this Friend; and after an evening of social converse, which seemed to cement our hearts in the union and fellowship of Christ, I had retired. He came very early to my room, saying he could not sleep, believing it required of him to inform me how he was convinced and became a Friend. He then said: He was a wicked sailor boy, and had persuaded himself that religion had been established to keep people in subjection to the powers that be; and was very strongly inclined to infidelity. The vessel had put in the port of Scarboro, England, and as he was sauntering about the streets, some plain-dressed Friends appeared, going to meeting. Their plainness and demeanor struck him so forcibly, that it occurred to him, what if religion should be true,—I would like to know more about this people. He followed them; then ventured to look in the meeting; some one beckoned him to a seat. The appearance, solemnity and silence, deeply affected him. When the meeting ended, he felt a desire to be good, and concluded he would try to know more; but the enemy suggested, it may be only form—he would like to know whether they were really what they appeared to be. In order to try them, he soon found some of their shops (or stores), bought some trifles, laid down more money than the real cost, to see if they would take it; but no—the money was returned,—now he was more convinced he would like to be good, and be a Friend; but how could he amongst the sailors? What to do he did not know. The vessel was ready for sea, but the wind was contrary; he again attended meeting, and so it happened the wind still contrary, which continued for three weeks; at the end of which time he concluded to go to sea no more, but remained on shore, learned gardening, and became acquainted with nursery business. After a suitable time he was admitted to membership, finally emigrated to this country and settled as above, and was a steadfast pillar in the Society, and deceased in the year 1853, at the advanced age of ninety-three.

David Ferris* was brought up in Connecticut, and in early manhood was led by the Spirit of Christ into a self-denying course of life, and ultimately joined in membership with the Society of Friends. At the time to which the following extract from his memoranda refers, he had had but little intercourse with that people. He says:—

"After I had been some time at home, new objections arose in my mind against a compliance with the customs of those among whom I resided; such as bowing and scraping; putting off the hat; saying, 'your servant, sir, madam,' &c., and against using the ungrammatical, corrupt language of 'you' to a single person. Although, in past years, I had known various exercises, and though I had learned many hard lessons, yet I found much in me that required mortification, and that I had yet many things to learn. To refuse the use of the plural language to a single person, although it seemed a small matter, yet I found it hard to submit to. I was convinced that the common mode of speaking in the plural number to a single person, was a violation of the rules of grammar and unscriptural. I also believed the pride of man had introduced the custom; yet I thought it was not necessary to make myself ridiculous to all about me for a matter of so small importance. So long, therefore, as no necessity was laid upon me to take up the cross in that respect, I continued to use the language of my education. Yet I used compliments sparingly, because the disuse of them was not so observable. However, it was not long before I found it my duty to say 'thee' and 'thou' to every individual. Nevertheless, I found an inclination or temptation so to turn the conversation as to shun this mode of speech; yet this did not afford peace. Small as the matter appeared, I could not be easy without being entirely faithful in every

* See note, p. 49.

respect; and my duty in this particular being clearly manifested, I reasoned no longer with flesh and blood, but submitted to the requiring. And thus I obtained peace.

"About this time, several scholars coming from the college, invited me to accompany them on a visit to the minister in our settlement; and accordingly I went with them. We walked with our hats under our arms, and so entered the house. Just as we were about to depart I was required to bear a testimony against the hat-honor. So I rose, put on my hat, went to the priest, and bade him farewell, without putting my hand to it, or bowing my body. This being the first time I had refused these compliments, it was a close trial; and it appeared remarkable that it should be required of me at such a time, and in such company; but neither the priest nor my companions took notice of it, so as to make any remark. My obedience afforded me great peace; and, by yielding to these inward motions of the Sure Guide, in small things, I gained strength; and was more and more confirmed that I was right in making such a change.

Samuel Neale * relates the following instance of the outward respect, as well as the inward peace, which accompanied his acting consistently with his profession:

" When I was with my old master, T. S., as an apprentice, he had occasion to pay rent to the Bishop of Clogher for one of his correspondents. I was sent with the money, and addressed the Bishop, not as though I was one called a Quaker. He took but little notice of me; I thought he treated me rather with contempt. It stung me to think I had played the coward, and was ashamed to address him as a Quaker; I therefore entered into an engagement that if ever I went again, I would address him in the plain language. The season came that I was to go, and I was warned in my mind to remember my engagement. I went in some degree of fear; he was just stepping into his coach to go into the country: when I addressed him as a Quaker, he very politely received me, and treated me as if I had

*See note, p. 44.

been his equal. When I had done my business, I returned with a pleasure far transcending anything I had felt before, for such an act of obedience. I thought I could leap as an hart, I felt such inward joy, satisfaction and comfort. So that I would have the beloved youth mind their Guide, and not dishonor that of God in them; for as we are faithful in a little, we shall be made rulers over more; and we shall have more of the praise even of men, by keeping to our religious principles, and be in higher esteem by those in authority, as our forefathers were."

There are many ways in which a worldly-minded spirit manifests itself. There is one form of this which often attracts the unwary; and that is the indulgence in those kinds of amusements which are calculated to wean the affections from our great Creator, and which expose the individual to many temptations to evil.

The Testimony of the Monthly Meeting of Philadelphia respecting Daniel Stanton,* a valuable minister, who deceased in 1770, states :—" He was of late deeply exercised in consideration of the evils of the horse-races, stage-plays, drunkenness, and other gross enormities, encouraged and increasing in this city; closely exhorting our youth against those pernicious and destructive devices of the enemy of mankind ; and, under the awful sense that God will judge and punish the wicked and evil doers, he was often fervent in public supplications, that the Lord would lengthen out the day of his merciful visitation."

I met some time ago in one of the public papers with a sad illustration of the folly of wasting life in a round of such amusements. I have no means of testing the accuracy of the narrative, but there is nothing improbable in its statements.

A wealthy young woman in the South, who had been a thoughtful girl, anxious to help all suffering and want, and

*See note, p. 34.

to serve her God faithfully, married a resident of New York, and entered into the whirl of fashionable life. She and her husband soon seemed to have no object before them but enjoyment; and an almost constant round of excitements occupied their time. Some years ago she was returning alone from California, when an accident occurred to the railroad train in which she was a passenger, and she received a fatal internal injury. She was carried into a wayside inn and there, attended only by a physician from a neighboring village, she died.

The doctor said it was one of the most painful experiences of his life. "I had to tell her that she had but an hour to live. She was not suffering any pain. Her only consciousness of hurt was that she was unable to move, so that it was no wonder she could not believe me.

" 'I must go home,' she said, imperatively, 'to New York.'

"Madame, it is impossible. If you are moved, it will shorten the time you have to live."

"She was lying on the floor. The brakemen had rolled their coats to make her a pillow. She looked about her at the little dingy station, with the stove stained with tobacco in the midst.

" 'I have but an hour, you tell me?'

"Not more."

" 'And this is all that is left me of the world. It is not much, doctor,' with a half smile.

"The men left the room, and I locked the door, that she might not be disturbed. She threw her arms over her face and lay quite a long time, then she turned on me in a frenzy. 'To think of all that I might have done with my money and my time? God wanted me to help the poor and the sick! It's too late now! I've only an hour!' She had not even that, for the exertion proved fatal." The doctor added, "No sermon that I ever heard was like that woman's despairing cry, 'It's too late!' "

But life may be wasted, not merely in trifling or sensual amusement, but in any course of conduct which conflicts with our Saviour's command, "Seek *first* the kingdom of Heaven and the righteousness thereof." Who can but pity Cardinal Mazarin,* the great minister of Louis XIV. It is recorded of him, that when he was near the end of life, a courtier, loitering without leave in the apartments of the sick statesman, heard a slippered foot dragging itself with difficulty along the carpet of an adjoining room, and hastily hid himself behind some tapestry. He saw Mazarin creep feebly in, and gaze around, little suspecting that he was himself being watched. From all sides shone on him the art treasures he had collected—the only objects except wealth and power, he cared for. He looked on them long and regretfully ; his eye wandered from picture to picture, from statue to statue, till at last his anguish vented itself in words. " I must leave all that. What pains it cost me to acquire these things! I shall never see them where I am going!" The courtier, Count Louis de Brienne, whose ears caught that dying groan, remembered the speech, and when Mazarin was dead, put it in print, unconsciously as a warning to all those who lay up treasures for themselves, but are not rich toward God.

That the Light of Christ leads those who obey it out of worldly amusements, is shown by the experience of Thomas Chalkley.† In his Journal he says :

" I remember that, unknown to my parents, I had bought a pack of cards, with intent to make use of them when I went to see my relations in the country. At the time called Christmas I went to see them, and on my way went to a meeting at which a minister of Christ declared against the evil of gaming, and particularly at cards ; and that the

* An Italian by birth, but a noted French statesman during the minority of Louis XIV. Died in 1661.

† Born in London in 1675. Travelled extensively as a minister of the Society of Friends. Removed to Pennsylvania. Died in West Indies at Tortola while on a religious visit. See *Journal in Friends' Library*, vol. 6, p. 1, etc.

time which people pretend to keep holy for Christ's sake, many of them spend mostly in wickedness, sports and games. From this meeting at Wanstead I went to the house of my relations, where the parson of the next parish lodged that night, who used to play cards with them sometimes, and the time drawing near that we were to go to our games, my uncle called to the doctor, as he called him, to me, and to my cousin, to come and take a game at cards; at which motion I had strong convictions upon me not to do it, as being evil. And I secretly cried to the Lord to keep me faithful to Him; and lifting up my eyes, I saw a Bible lying in the window, at the sight of which I was glad. I took it, and sat down and read to myself, greatly rejoicing that I was preserved out of the snare. Then my uncle called again, and said, 'Come, doctor, you and I, and my wife and daughter, will have a game at cards, for I see my cousin is better disposed.' Then he looked upon me, and said, 'he was better disposed also.' So their sport for that time was spoiled, and mine in that practice forever; for I never, as I remember, played with them more, but as soon as I came home offered my new and untouched pack of cards to the fire. And of this I am certain, the use of them is of evil consequence, and draws away the mind from heaven and heavenly things; for which reason all Christians ought to shun them as engines of Satan; and music and dancing having generally the same tendency, ought, therefore, to be refrained from."

In reply to a question whether "Card-playing is dangerous to good morals?" the editor of the *Sunday-School Times* points out the evil effect of the prominence which card-playing gives to chance or "luck" as an element of success or failure. He thinks there is hardly any "dividing line of equal moment in its practical bearings upon the affairs of one's personal life, with that which separates the two questions: Am I to succeed in life by the blessing of God on my endeavors? or am I to succeed in life by my luck?"

As to the practical effect of card-playing, the writer says:

14

"That he was accustomed to play cards in his early life: but that from his observation of its injurious effects on the players—among 'the best people'—he abandoned it, while he was not a professed Christian, or even a nominal church-member ; and that all his observations in varied spheres of life, since that time, have confirmed his conviction that the influence and tendency of card-playing is injurious in any and in every home, under the most favorable conditions whatsoever. He could point to instances of persons ruined in life from among 'the best people,' by a course that clearly grew out of the influence of early card-playing on the mind and character. He has never seen a home where card-playing was sanctioned, which he did not believe either to be itself harmed, or to be a means of harm to other homes, by this sanction. His counsel is, unqualifiedly and emphatically, to all parents, to keep card-playing out of their homes, to keep their children from card-playing: and to all pastors to do their best to keep card-playing out of the households in which they are interested, or which they can influence for good."

An anecdote is told of a young woman, who on her way home from a religious meeting remarked to a companion, that she could not give up the world. A person who heard the remark, told her that if that was the case, she need not attend meetings any more. She might as well attend places of amusement, and be as happy as she could in this world, for it would be the only heaven she would ever have. God had marked out the path of self-denial which all must walk in, who would reach the abodes of blessedness and peace ; and if she would not walk in that path, but decided to keep the world, she had better enjoy it while she could ; for it was a pity to lose both worlds by being undecided. This view of the matter so impressed her mind, that under the convicting power of Divine grace, she was enabled to forsake her worldly amusements, and give up her heart to the Lord without reserve.

When Dr. Samuel Johnson* visited his friend David

*See note, p. 129.

Garrick, at Hampton Court, the latter showed him his fine house, gardens, statues, pictures, &c. "Ah! David, David," said the Doctor, "these are the things which make a death-bed terrible." Not that the possession of the comforts and conveniences of life is wrong in itself, but whenever the affections and thoughts become absorbed by these things, then the commands of our Saviour are violated, and our treasure is laid up on earth instead of in Heaven.

The feelings of Dr. Johnson on this occasion were proba-bly similar to those of a visitor at the house of a ministering Friend in Philadelphia many years ago, where there was much evidence of luxury and display. In the course of conversation she intimated that she had but little to say in the way of public ministry. "No marvel," thought her visitor, "whilst thou hast so much of the world's glitter about thee. Where is self-denial, simplicity and the daily cross?"

CHAPTER VI.

Love. Benevolence. The kind Scotchman. Widow Green's Wood. The Strong to Help the Weak. Genius for Helping. Abraham Lincoln and the Pig. A. Lincoln and Cogdal. Joseph Rachel's Bond. Lending to the Lord. The Chicago Children. Road Mending. Measuring Wood. Robert Moffat and the African Woman. Dying for a Friend. Peace-making. Thomas H. Benton and John Wilson. Duke of Wellington on War. Humility. Keep Inward. Foreign Travel. Giving up Religious Conviction. Watchfulness. John Richardson. Abigail Bowles. Resist Temptation. The Banker's Clerk. The Back-sliding Methodist. Submissiveness. The Child and the Cemetery. The Sick Son. Bounty Money. Abraham and Richard Shackleton. Learning to Chew Crusts.

ANOTHER of the "fruits of the Spirit" which is one of the marks of true conversion, is a love for mankind and a willingness to sacrifice our own ease and means for the good of others. The poet Whittier has written:

> "Kindness to the wronged is never
> Without its excellent reward,
> Holy to humankind and ever
> Acceptable to God."

And higher authority than he has given as a test of disciple-ship, " By this shall all men know that ye are my disciples, if ye love one another." In the sacred writings, " to love mercy" is associated with " to do justly" and " to fear God," as a summary statement of human duty. Even the natural and instinctive desire to relieve those in distress, which is so helpful in promoting the happiness of mankind, is a very amiable trait of character. But where this is purified and ennobled by Divine Grace, it becomes one of the virtues held up to view in the Holy Scriptures as incumbent on a Christian to practise. A reward is promised for even a cup of cold water given in the name of a disciple, or out of love and allegiance to our Father in Heaven.

A writer in *The Christian Statesman* relates the following incident, which was observed by one of his friends, when travelling a few years since from San Francisco to New York.

" The train had reached the junction where the two Pacific Roads meet. Every one was dusty and weary and glad to leave the car for a breath of air and a draught of fresh water, as well as for a relief from the cramped up quarters they had occupied so long. All sorts of people came out to exchange friendly greetings and sentiments and conjectures on the weather, the probable length of the journey and similar topics which occupy the thoughts of travellers on the same roads.

" One old Scotchman, who was particularly brusque, crabbed and querulous, just looked out and then returned to his own corner. Two merry, dainty young Englishmen, with their charts and maps and rugs, and gay young hearts, had been out on the plains for a fishing and hunting excursion. They seemed quite critical, and had a merry word or question for their American cousins.

Seated a little way from the depot, on a string-piece, was a forlorn-looking woman, seemingly careless of her surroundings. Her two children, a boy and a girl, were looking towards the town, as if in wonder or waiting for their mother to rise. By her side was a rough pine box, which looked familiar to the travellers who had left the train. One more curious than the others, perhaps more sympathetic, went to the group and addressed the woman. This was her story:

"She and her husband had left the East years before and settled in Kansas, and were doing pretty well; blessed with three children, the oldest a fine, brave girl, who was the stay, the joy and the comfort of the family! The father, hoping to improve his chance, heard of an opportunity further to the southwest, whither he removed with his belongings, but soon began to experience all the trials of an emigrant's life. He' was unsuccessful. His daughter, only fourteen, did all in her power to encourage her parents and to supplement with her own labor, the work that her father, now fallen ill, could not do. The father died. The widow, with the three children, toiled on in hopes of better days to come. The daughter fell sick and died.

Alone, dejected, friendless and far from home, the mother in her widowhood thought of her former home in Kansas, and of the friends she had left there, and resolved to return.

The Southern Pacific Road gave her a pass for herself and her children, and the rough box that contained the remains of her daughter. She had now come as far as the junction, and had learned that the pass was valueless on the other side. She had pleaded in vain with the officers. No one had authority to pass the party on free, and there she sat with a few pennies in her purse, alone among strangers, with her dead child at her side, and two others, almost helpless, stranded, as it were, on a desolate island. She was too heartbroken even for tears. The sum asked to forward her the rest of the way was one hundred and seventy dollars, I think. The story was related to the group who had disembarked,

14*

when the two young Englishmen exclaimed, 'We'll go through the train.'

"No sooner said than done. Back and forth these gay young men went, representing the facts. A hundred dollars was soon collected, and with this sum the kind fellows hurried to the officers of the road.

"'No! it would not do;' they had no authority to pass any one with a corpse for a less amount than they had named.

"The youths were disheartened. Some one called out, 'Try the train again!' Again they went through it and collected a little more. Still the deficiency was great.

"In their dilemma, as they stood so sorry, so sympathetic, a voice was heard from a distant corner: 'Let her get on, I'll be responsible for the rest.'

"It was the brusque, crabbed Scotchman who spoke. There was a murmur of approbation, a fervent 'Thank God and you'—almost a cheer! went up. One young fellow ran to the office and then back again to explain to the woman that the fare was paid and she could go on; and the poor box was raised and carried to the baggage-car. The mother followed with her children, the kind young fellows on either side, but she was too dazed to understand or express her thanks. 'The Lord has indeed provided for us as Molly said He would,' she murmured, and being seated, the young gentlemen saw her lean her head down and burst into tears."

A pleasant anecdote is related of a well-to-do deacon in Connecticut who was one morning accosted by his pastor, who said, "Poor Widow Green's wood is out. Can you not take her a cord?

"Well," answered the deacon, "I have the wood, and I have the team; but who is to pay me for it?"

The pastor, somewhat vexed, replied, "I will pay you for it, on the condition that you read the first three verses of the forty-first Psalm before you go to bed to night."

The deacon consented, delivered the wood, and at night opened the Bible and read the passage: "Blessed is he that considereth the poor; the Lord will deliver him in time of trouble. The Lord will preserve him and keep him alive, and he shall be blessed upon the earth; and thou wilt not deliver him unto the will of his enemies. The Lord will strengthen him upon the bed of languishing; thou wilt make his bed in his sickness."

A few days afterwards the pastor met him again. "How much do I owe you, deacon, for that cord of wood?"

"Oh!" said the now enlightened man, "do not speak of payment: I did not know those promises were in the Bible. I would not take money for supplying the old widow's wants."

There are some persons who are deficient in those qualities which would enable them successfully to compete with others in the struggles of business. It is undoubtedly the duty of such to do the best they can in the effort to maintain themselves, and to endeavor as far as practicable to limit their wants by the means at their command. Yet it is a duty also on the part of those of more ability to feel for these and to be willing to aid them when necessary. "In every community," says a recent writer, "there are always a few, who, in common speech, 'have no faculty' to get along. They are deficient in judgment, in foresight, in ambition and enterprise, and everything else which goes to make success in life; and they must be helped by their more fortunate fellow-beings or drop hopelessly in the race. My dear sister, saving, prudent, thrifty, patterned after Solomon's virtuous woman, don't despise your weaker sister, but bear her burdens—for they are heavy, heavier than you can know unless with Christ-like sympathy you put yourself in her place.

"And brother A, don't think it hard when you are called upon to help brother B, who has had a constant run of ill-luck, though you feel sure that in his place you would have avoided it all. As you have just what he lacks, thrift, shrewdness, brains, this is very probable. But the glory of

Christ's religion is that the infirmities of the weak are the opportunities of the strong. Throw loving arms around your weak brothers, and lift them over life's hard places. These foolish, thriftless ones, on whom the battle presses so hard, bear God's divining rod to point out the hearts, in which are the holy wells of a pure and living charity."

The *Christian Observer* tells of a village carpenter, of whom his neighbor said that he "has done more good, I really believe, in this community, than any other person who ever lived in it. He isn't worth two thousand dollars, and it's very little that he can put down on subscription papers for any object. But a new family never moves into the village that he does not find them out, to give them a neighborly welcome, and offer any little service he can render. He is always ready to watch with a sick neighbor, and look after his affairs for him ; and I've sometimes thought he and his wife kept house-plants in winter just for the sake of being able to send little bouquets to invalids. He finds time for a pleasant word for every child he meets, and you'll always see them climbing into his one-horse wagon when he has no other load. He really seems to have a genius for helping folks in all sorts of common ways, and it does me good every day just to meet him on the streets."

In the days when Abraham Lincoln, as an Illinois lawyer, "rode the circuit" of the district in which he practised, an amusing incident occurred in connection with one of those journeys, which gives a pleasant glimpse into the honest lawyer's heart. He was riding by a deep slough, in which, to his exceeding pain, he saw a pig struggling, and with such faint efforts, that it was evident he could not extricate himself from the mud. Lincoln looked at the pig and the mud which enveloped him, and then looked at some new clothes with which he had but a short time before enveloped himself. Deciding against the claim of the pig, he rode on, but he could not get rid of sympathy with the poor brute; and, at last, after riding two miles, he turned back, determined to rescue the animal at the expense of his new clothes.

Arrived at the spot, he tied his horse, and coolly went to work to build of old rails a passage to the bottom of the hole. Descending on these rails, he seized the pig and dragged him out, but not without serious damage to the clothes he wore. Washing his hands in the nearest brook, and wiping them on the grass, he mounted his gig and rode along. He then fell to examining the motive that sent him back to the release of the pig. At the first thought, it seemed to be pure benevolence; but at length he came to the conclusion that it was selfishness, for he certainly went to the pig's relief in order (as he said to the friend to whom he related the incident,) "to take a pain out of his own mind."

Abraham Lincoln's friendly feelings towards all were such, that he never made much money in his business. An unfortunate man was a subject of his sympathy, no matter what his business relations to him might be. A man named Cogdal, who related the incident to Lincoln's biographer, met with a financial wreck in 1843. He employed Lincoln as his lawyer, and at the close of the business, gave him a note to cover the regular lawyer's fees. He was soon afterwards injured by an accidental discharge of powder, and lost his hand. Meeting Lincoln some time after the accident, on the steps of the State-house, the kind lawyer asked him how he was getting along. "Badly enough," replied Cogdal, "I am both broken up in business, and crippled. Then," he added, "I have been thinking about that note of yours." Lincoln, who had probably known all about Cogdal's troubles, and had prepared himself for the meeting, took out his pocket-book, and saying, with a laugh, "Well, you needn't think any more about it," handed him the note. Cogdal protesting, Lincoln said, "If you had the money I would not take it, and hurried away. At the same date, he was frankly writing about his poverty to his friends, as a reason for not making them a visit, and probably found it no easy task to take care of his family, even when board at the Globe Tavern was only "four dollars a week."

This incident brings to remembrance a similar circumstance recorded in "Lindley Murray's Introduction." As the younger generation of the present day are but little acquainted with the book, the anecdote may here be quoted.

Joseph Rachel, a respectable negro, resided in the Island of Barbadoes, where he kept a retail store. As he was obliging and honest, his business prospered. In 1756, a fire happened which burned down a part of the town in which were houses belonging to a man of his acquaintance, to whose family he had in early life been under some obligations. The man was entirely ruined by the losses occasioned by the fire.

Joseph had his bond for sixty pounds sterling. " Unfortunate man," said he, "this debt shall never come against thee. I sincerely wish thou could'st settle all thy other affairs as easily. But how am I sure I shall keep in this mind? May not the love of gain, especially when, by length of time, thy misfortune shall become familiar to me, return with too strong a current, and bear down my fellow-feeling before it? But for this I have a remedy. Never shalt thou apply for the assistance of any friend against my avarice."

He arose, ordered a large account that the man had with him to be drawn out ; and in a whim that might have called up a smile on the face of charity, filled his pipe, sat down again, twisted the bond, and lighted his pipe with it. While the account was drawing out, he continued smoking, in a state of mind that a monarch might envy. When it was finished, he went in search of his friend, with the discharged account, and the mutilated bond in his hand. These he presented to him with the assurance that he was overpaid in the satisfaction he felt from having done what he believed to be his duty.

Many interesting anecdotes are related of the benevolence of "Billy Bray,"* the Cornish miner. He says: "At one time I had been at work the whole of the month, but had no wages to take up when pay-day came : and, as we had no bread in the house, ' Joey,' [his wife] advised me to go up and ask the ' captain,' to lend me a few shillings, which

---

* A resident in Cornwall, England, noted for his zeal and originality. A local preacher, and a pious man. See *Life*.

I did, and he let me have ten shillings. On my way home I called to see a family, and found they were worse off than myself; for though we had no bread, we had bacon and potatoes, but they had neither. So I gave them five shillings, and went towards home. Then I called on another family, and found them, if possible, in greater distress than the former. I thought I could not give them less than I had given the others; so I gave them the other five shillings, and went home. And Joey said—

"'Well, William, have you seen the captain?'

"'Yes.'

"'Did you ask him for any money?'

"'Yes; he let me have ten shillings.'

"'Where is it?'

"'I have given it away.'

"'I never saw the fellow to you in my life. You are enough to try any one.'

"'The Lord isn't going to stay in my debt very long,' and I then went out. For two or three days after this, Joey was mighty down; but about the middle of the week, when I came home from the mine, Joey was looking mighty smiling, so I thought there was something up. Presently Joey said—

"'Mrs. So-and-so has been here to-day.'

"'Oh!'

"'And she gave me a sovereign.'

"'There, I told you the Lord wasn't going to stay in my debt very long; for there's the ten shillings, and ten shillings interest.'"

The incidents which from time to time are brought to notice of that benevolent feeling which lead persons to do good to others without any prospect of pecuniary reward to themselves, find an answering chord in the hearts of nearly all.

The *Chicago Herald* gives the following anecdote related by one whom it calls a "kind-faced old gentleman," who had for a tenant a child not more than ten years old.

"A few years ago I got a chance to buy a piece of land

over on the West Side, and I did so. · I noticed there was an old coop of a house on it, but paid no attention to it.   After awhile a man came to meet me and wanted to know if I would rent it to him.

"'What do you want it for?' said I.

"'To live in,' he replied.

"'Well,' said I, 'you can have it.   Pay me what you think it is worth to you.'

"The first month he brought two dollars, and the second month a little boy who said he was the man's son, came with three dollars.   After that I saw the man once in a while, but in a course of time the boy paid the rent regularly, sometimes two dollars and sometimes three dollars. One day I asked the boy what had·become of his father.

"'He's dead, sir,' was the reply.

"'Is that so?' said I.   'How long since?'

"'More'n a year,' he answered.

"I took his money, but I made up my mind that I would go over and investigate, and the next day I drove over there.   The old shed looked quite decent.   I knocked at the door and a little girl let me in.   I asked for her mother. She said she didn't have any.

"'Where is she?' I said.

"'We don't know, sir.   She went away after my father died, and we've never seen her since.'

"Just then a little girl about three years old came in, and I learned that these three children had been keeping house together for a year and a half, the boy supporting his two little sisters by blacking boots and selling newspapers, and the elder girl managing the house and taking care of the baby.   Well, I just had my daughter call on them, and we keep an eye on them now.   I thought I wouldn't disturb them while they are getting along.   The next time the boy came with the rent I talked with him a little and then I said :   .

"'My boy, you keep right on as you have begun, and you will never be sorry.   Keep your little sisters together and never leave them.   Now look at this.'

"I showed him a ledger in which I had entered up all the money that he had paid me for rent, and told him it was all his with interest. ' You keep right on,' says I, ' and I'll be your banker, and when this amounts to a little more I'll see that you get a house somewhere of your own.' "

The following simple incident told by a writer in the *Sunday Magazine*, confirms the truth of the poet's words, that kindness

"Is never
Without its excellent reward,"

even if that reward is only the feeling of comfort which it gives to him who does a kind act.

I remember once going with two young companions through a wildly romantic Scottish glen. Suddenly we came upon a broken bit in the road ; it had been torn up somehow, and was full of great holes, sufficient to throw a horse or turn a wheel. " An ugly place in the dark," said one of us as we stood looking at it. " Whose business is it to mend that?" asked another. " Let us do it ourselves!" cried the third. And so we set to the task. There were plenty of stones not far off, and as we had no tools we had to use the more ingenuity in the selection of shape and size. It did not take us three-quarters of an hour to make the road safe, if not neat.

" Now, we shall not be responsible for any accident there," we said, as we straightened our aching backs, " for there will be no accident for anybody to be responsible for ! "

What a light lay on the hills as we lifted our glowing faces towards them ! We seemed no longer strangers there ; we had made for ourselves a share in it all. What an appetite we had for the milk and bannocks we got at the nearest cottage ! And how distinctly we can all remember that ramble, though many another, under as fair a sky, and amid scenery equally grand, has faded behind the mists of memory.

Precious also is that feeling of love and respect which attaches to the memory of those who have been just and kind in their dealings with others. This is well shown by

15

a notice published in the *Messenger of Peace* by John Hem-menway, of Jeremiah Chaplin,* a Baptist minister, and the first President of Waterville College in Maine.

When Dr. Chaplin lived in Waterville, as President of the college, he bought his fire-wood, not a small quantity, for one year or more, of a poor man in Fairfield, about four miles off. Now all Maine wood-cutters and haulers know to their sorrow, that cutting and hauling green, heavy, hard wood with an ox team is very hard work for both man and oxen ; and when sold, as it was in Waterville more than fifty years ago, for two dollars a cord or less, it was a very small paying business. But this was not all the trouble of the poor hardworking wood seller. He was often dissatisfied with the measure given him by the wood buyer for his loads of wood.

Now as the poor man in Fairfield sent his youngest son down, day after day, with a load of wood, with one pair of oxen, to Dr. Chaplin's door, the doctor would step out and measure the load. Well, the poor man's son, the friend of mine, said to me, when speaking of Dr. Chaplin as President of Waterville College, "Dr. Chaplin was a fair man to measure wood. *He would make the loads measure more than I could !*" I do not know how this act, in the life of this great man will strike others, but it affects me very tenderly, so much so that my eyes grow wet as I write. Dear, good man! he well knew that he was making large measure in the loads of wood, and that was just what he intended to do. He meant to be *sure* not to wrong the poor man, and meant to give a larger measure than justice required.

Robert Moffatt,† in his account of his missionary travels in South Africa, relates the following occurrence :

In one of my early journeys, I came with my companion to a heathen village, on the banks of the Orange River. We had travelled far and were hungry, thirsty and fatigued;

---

* Born in Massachusetts in 1813. Author of *Evenings of Life*, etc.
† A native of Scotland, and for many years a missionary among the natives of South Africa. Born 1796. Died 1883.

but the people of the village rather roughly directed us to halt at a distance. We asked for water but they would not supply it. I offered the three or four buttons left on my jacket for a little milk, and was refused. We had the prospect of another bungry night, at a distance from water, though within sight of the river.

When twilight drew on, a woman approached from the height beyond which the village lay. She bore on her head a bundle of wood, and had a vessel of milk in her hand. The latter, without opening her lips, she handed to us; laid down the wood and returned to the village. A second time she approached with a cooking vessel on her head, and a leg of mutton in one hand and water in the other. She sat down without saying a word, prepared the fire and put on the meat. We asked her again and again who she was. She remained silent until affectionately entreated to give us a reason for such unlooked-for kindness to strangers. Then the tears stole down her sable cheeks, and she replied " I love Him whose servants you are; and surely it is my duty to give you a cup of cold water in his name. My heart is full; therefore I cannot speak the joy I feel to see you in this out-of-the-world place."

Further conversation showed that years before, she had attended a school, and had received a copy of a Dutch New Testament, which she drew from her bosom. The reading of this in measure supplied the place of that outward communion with fellow believers, which is often so helpful to the Christian; and He who has promised never to leave nor forsake his devoted followers, we may assuredly believe, had preserved her spiritual life amid her unfavorable surroundings, and enabled her to prove her faith by her works.

The sublimest proof of love is the willingness it has sometimes wrought to sacrifice one's own life for the sake of another—our blessed Saviour declared that the Good Shepherd laid down his life for the sheep. The Apostle Paul refers to this as a proof of the marvellous loving kindness of the Almighty, when he suggests that, " Peradventure for a good man some would even dare to die ; " and adds that, " while we were yet sinners, Christ died for the ungodly."

A striking instance, in which compassion overpowered the love of life, is the following taken from the *Sunday Magazine:*

A few years ago a sailing ship left Australia for England. One of the passengers was a gentleman who had recently gone to Australia for his health, but the place had not suited him ; his bad health became worse. So he immediately took his passage back, and was now returning. The ship had made more than half her homeward voyage, when she was caught in a storm, which lasted day after day and night after night in greatest fury. Winds fell upon her, tore her sails away, and snapped off and blew overboard her masts. Waves leaped upon the deck, tore coverings from over the stairways and ladders leading into the hold and cabins, and poured themselves down in tons of water, until the cook's fires were put out, the births and cabins were flooded, and all the miserable passengers were driven up to the deck, which, you may imagine, was a scene of danger and confusion.

· The ship was now sailless and mastless, and full of water, and rolling helplessly. All hands worked the pumps, but the water gained on them, and the ship sunk deeper and deeper into the sea, and long before the storm had abated it became quite clear that it must be abandoned if a single life was to be saved. So the captain gave orders to launch the boats which had not yet been swept overboard by the sea. These were only two, not half enough for the number of souls on board. The brave sailors obeyed as best they could, and while the boats were being got ready, the captain ordered that lots be cast as to who should go in the boats.

The people gathered under the shelter of some of the ruins of the masts. It was a deeply solemn time. Only one-half at most could be saved, the rest in a few hours, perhaps moments, must be drowned in the swirl of the ship going down ; they all stood in the presence of death. Each name was written on a separate slip of paper; then the papers were mixed up in a box; the captain inserted his hand, drew out a name, and read it aloud. It was a dreadful moment to many of them as one by one they heard the names read, yet still theirs had not come, and now the last is being drawn. The captain lifts it to the flickering light of his lantern and reads. The very storm seems silent. The name is read, the suspense is over, and all know their fate. "Range yourselves in line," cried the captain to the fortunate ones, "and move one by one to the boats." And they filed off as ordered, while the doomed ones gathered in lines on either side to watch them go.

The dark day had settled into darker night; the air was black. The vessel rolled terribly, and the little boats, now lowered to the water, leaped and plunged in the blackness below. A lantern swung at the point where the men were to leave the ship to light them down. One by one the procession disappeared over the gunwale, hung on to the ship's side till the boat was thrown near, and then leaped into it.

The young man I have named was one of the procession, for his name had been among the names drawn. At length he was the next man to go. As he waited till the man before him had leaped, suddenly his eyes fell upon a pale, wan face close to him. He remembered it, and its story flashed upon him. He had talked with that young man in sunny days, and learned from him that three years ago, with but a small chance of life, he had left behind him in England his wife, a child, and a child since born, and now full of health, he was on his way home again. Three years had they been parted, and there he stood among the doomed. He thought of the wife's hopes, the children's bright talk about him, and after all he was to be lost! He could not bear it. In an instant, and without a word, he seized the man, forced him over the gunwale and stepped aside into the man's place. It was the work of a second; there was no chance to demur. In a few moments more all was over. The ship had gone down, carrying with it a heart lost to itself, even to the value of life, in the thought of the miseries of others.

Some glorious deeds move us to clap our hands and shout. This moves us to tears and silence. It was the act

15*

of the the utmost tenderness and beauty; and such a heart is like Christ's.

One of the forms in which the love of mankind which flows from love to God, will manifest itself, is the desire to promote the reign of "peace on earth and good will to men." Our Saviour pronounced a special blessing on the *peace-makers*, even that they "shall be called the children of God."

Those who are turned in heart to the Lord, will assuredly be led to love their brethren also, and to desire to be reconciled to those with whom they have been at enmity. A pleasant, and to me, a *touching* illustration of this, is furnished by two anecdotes of Thomas H. Benton,* of Missouri, related in "Harvey's Reminiscences of Daniel Webster.†

The circumstances were narrated to Harvey by Webster himself, and present the two distinguished personages principally referred to, in an amiable light.

"We had had," said Webster, "a great many political controversies; we were hardly on bowing terms. For many years we had been members of the same body, and passed in and out at the same door without even bowing to each other, and without the slightest mutual recognition; and we never had any intercourse except such as was official, and where it could not be avoided. There were no social relations whatever between us.

"At the time of the terrible gun explosion on board the 'Princeton,' during Tyler's adminstration, T. H. Benton was on board; and he related to me with tears this incident. He said he was standing near the gun, in the very best position to see the experiment. The deck of the steamer was crowded; and, with the scramble for places to witness the discharge of the gun, his position perhaps was the most favorable on the deck. Suddenly he felt a hand laid upon

---

* See note, p. 75.

† A native of New Hampshire. Senator in U. S. Congress from Massachusetts. A distinguished orator and statesman. Born 1782. Died 1852. Several biographies of him have been published.

his shoulder, and turned; some one wished to speak to him, and he was elbowed out of his place and another person took it, very much to his annoyance. The person who took his place was ex-Governor Gilmer, of Virginia, then Secretary of the Navy. Just at that instant the gun was fired, and the explosion took place. Governor Gilmer was killed instantly. — Upshur, then Secretary of State, was also killed, as was one other man of considerable prominence. Colonel Benton, in relating this circumstance, said: 'It seemed to me,—Webster, as if that touch on my shoulder was the hand of the Almighty stretched down there, drawing me away from what otherwise would have been instantaneous death. I was merely prostrated on the deck and recovered in a very short time. That one circumstance has changed the whole current of my thoughts and life. I feel that I am a different man, and I want in the first place to be at peace with all those with whom I have been so sharply at variance. And so I have come to you. Let us bury the hatchet—Webster.' 'Nothing,' replied I, 'could be more in accordance with my own feelings.' We shook hands, and agreed to let the past be past; and from that time our intercourse was pleasant and cordial. After this time, there was no person in the Senate of the United States of whom I would have asked a favor, any reasonable and proper thing, with more assurance of obtaining it, than of T. H. Benton."

One day as Webster was seated in his library, he was waited upon by John Wilson, a lawyer of St. Louis, between whom and Benton had long existed an opposition so bitter and malignant as to be matter of public notoriety. Often in public debates they had abused each other in most virulent terms. Wilson was now a broken down man, prematurely old and wrecked in fortune; and he had determined to emigrate to California, then but recently conquered from Mexico by Fremont, T. H. Benton's son-in-law. He had called on Webster to request a letter of recommendation to some one in California, certifying that he was a respectable character and worthy of confidence. The kind feelings of the statesman were awakened, and after thinking over the case a few minutes, he suggested that a letter from Benton to Fremont would be of greater service than anything he could write. What followed shall be told in his own words, as related by his biographer.

"He looked me in the face, and half astonished, half inquiringly, as much as to say: 'Can it be possible that you are ignorant of the relations between Colonel Benton and myself?'

"I said: 'I understand what you mean; I am perfectly well aware of the past difficulties between you and Colonel Benton, and the bitter hostility that has existed. But I want to say to you that a great change has come over Colonel Benton since you knew him. His feelings and sentiments are softened. We are all getting older. Our fiery hot blood is getting cooled and changed. It is hardly worth while for men, when they are getting up pretty near the maximum of human life, to indulge in these feelings of enmity and ill-will. It is a thing that we ought to rid ourselves of. Colonel Benton and I have been engaged in a war of words, as you and he have; and, up to two or three years ago, we went out of the same door for years, without so much as saying 'Good morning' to one another. Now, I do not know a man in the Senate to whom I would go with more certainty of having a favor granted than to Colonel Benton. He feels that age is coming upon him, and he is reconciled to many of his bitterest opponents.'

"'Is thy servant a dog,' replied Wilson, 'that he should do this thing? I would not have a letter from him, I would not speak to him, I would not be beholden to him for a favor,—not to save the life of every member of my family! No sir! The thought of it makes me shudder. I feel indignant at the mention of it. I take a letter from Benton? I—'

"'Stop, stop!' said I; 'that is the old man speaking in you. This is not the spirit in which to indulge. I know how you feel.' And while he was raving and protesting and delaring, by all the saints in the calendar, his purpose to accept no favor from Colonel Benton, I turned round to my desk, and addressed a note to Benton, something like this:

"DEAR SIR:—I am well aware of the disputes, personal and political, which have taken place between yourself and the bearer of this note, John Wilson. But the old gentleman is now poor, and is going to California, and needs a letter of recommendation. I know nobody in California to whom I could address a letter that would be of any service to him. You know everybody, and a letter from you would do him a great deal of good. I have assured J. Wilson that it will give you more pleasure to forget what has passed between you and him, and to give him a letter that will do him good, than it will him to receive it. I am going to persuade him to carry you this note, and I know you will be glad to see him."

"Wilson got through protesting, and I read him the note. Then I said:—

"'I want you to carry it to Benton.'

"'I won't!' he replied.

"I coaxed and scolded and reasoned, and brought every consideration—death, eternity, and everything else,—to bear, but it seemed to be of no use. Said I:—

"'Wilson, you will regret it.'

"After awhile he got a little softened, and some tears flowed: and at last I made him promise, rather reluctantly, that he would deliver the note at Colonel Benton's door if he did not do any more. He told me afterwards that it was the bitterest pill that he ever swallowed. Colonel Benton's house was not far from mine. Wilson took the note, and, as he afterwards told me, went up with trembling hands, put the note, with his own card, into the hand of the girl who came to the door, and ran away to his lodgings. He had been scarcely half an hour in his room, trembling to think what he had done, when a note came from Colonel Benton, saying he had received the card and note, and that Mrs. Benton and himself would have much pleasure in receiving J. Wilson at breakfast at nine o'clock the next morning. They would wait breakfast for him and no answer was expected! 'The idea!' said he to himself, 'that I am going to breakfast with Tom Benton! John Wilson! what will people say; and what shall I say? The thing is not to be thought of. And yet I must. I have delivered the note and sent my card; if I don't go now, it will be rude. I wish I had not taken it. It doesn't seem to me as if I could go and sit there at that table.' 'I lay awake,' said he afterwards to me, 'that night, thinking of it; and in the morning I felt as a man might feel who had had sentence of death passed upon him, and was called by the turnkey to get up for his last breakfast. I rose, however, made my toilet, and, after hesitating a great deal, went to Colonel Benton's house. My hands trembled as I rang the bell. Instead of the servant, the colonel himself came to the door. He took me cordially by both hands, and said: "Wilson, I am delighted to see you; this is the happiest meeting I have had for twenty years. Give me your hand. Webster has done the kindest thing he ever did in his life." Leading me directly to the dining-room, he presented me to Mrs. Benton. and then we sat down to breakfast. After inquiring kindly about my family, he said: "You and I, Wilson, have been quarrelling on the stump for twenty-five years. We have been calling each other hard names, but really with no want of mutual respect and confidence. It has been a mere foolish political fight, and let's wipe it out of mind. Everything that I have said about you I ask your pardon for." We both cried a little, and I asked his pardon, and we were good friends. ' We talked over old matters, and spent the morning till twelve o'clock in pleasant conversation. Nothing was said of the letter, until just as I was about departing. He turned to his desk, and said: " I have prepared some letters for you to my son-in-law and other friends in California; and he handed out *nine sheets* of foolscap.

" ' It was not a letter, but a ukase; a command to "every person to whom these presents shall come greeting;" it was to the effect that whosoever received them must give special attention to the wants of his particular friend, Colonel John Wilson, of Saint Louis. Everything was to give way to that. He put them into my hands, and I thanked him, and left.' "

D. Webster continued : " Colonel Benton afterwards came to me and said : 'Webster, that was the kindest thing you ever did. God bless you for sending John Wilson to me! That is one troublesome thing off my mind. That was kind, Webster. Let us get these things off our minds as fast as we can; we have not much longer to stay; we have got pretty near the end; we want to go into the presence of our Maker with as little of enmity in our hearts as possible.' "

If those who promote peace are to be " called the children of God," does it not follow, that those who promote war, are acting under the influence of the spirit of evil? War and the religion of Christ are as opposite as light and darkness. The early Christians refused to fight, and the fact that so many who profess to be Christians have dropped this testimony, is one of the most striking examples of that spiritual blindness which has spread over Christendom. Assuredly, the same Holy Spirit which leads the converted man in private life to love his enemies, " and to pray for him who injures him," will never lead him to devise the destruction of multitudes, with whom he has no personal quarrel.

The Earl of Shaftesbury* related the following incident, which shows how one of the most celebrated generals of modern times, looked upon warfare.

" He once travelled to Hatfield with the Duke of Wellington,† who, as they passed through a lovely country, turned to him, after a long silence, and said, 'Can you guess what I have been thinking of?' Being answered in the negative, he said: 'I have been looking at this country, where every thing is beautiful and fills the heart with joy; and I was thinking that, if I had to take military possession of it, I should have to lay waste that beauty and dispel that joy, and produce instead nothing but devastation and misery.' Then the Duke added with a depth of feeling he should never forget, 'If you had seen but one day of war in the course of your life, you would pray before God that you might

* The seventh earl of same name. Distinguished for his zeal for philanthropy, morals and religion. Born 1801. Died 1885.
† Born in Ireland in 1767. Nearly all his life connected with military affairs. Defeated Napoleon at Waterloo in 1815. Died in 1852.

never see another.'"   In giving his reasons for conceding Catholic Emancipation, he said (Third Month 21, 1829): "My Lords, I have passed more of my life in war than most men, and I may say in civil war, and if I could avoid by any sacrifice whatever—if I could avoid, even for one month, a civil war, in a country to which I am attached, I would sacrifice my life to do it."

This testimony from a military man is strengthened by the record of a soldier in regard to his experience in battle.

In the wild exhilaration of the fight he was utterly insensible to the fact that his shots were carrying death to men. This was not thought of once in the mad intoxication of the storm of shot and shell.   But when the surge of battle brought him to the place where the wounded enemy lay dying, then the awful reality came over him.   "I had loaded and fired for hours," he said, "without compunction.   But when I saw a dying soldier whom my shot had pierced, and when I beheld his life-blood ebbing out, I was utterly overcome, and fell at his feet and wept like a child."

Another of "the fruits of the Spirit" is humility.   The true Christian knows that it was through the strivings of the Lord's Spirit, he was awakened from a state of sin, and through the power derived from the same unfailing fountain, that he was strengthened to forsake it.   He feels that he has nothing to boast of, but that all is of mercy.   He knows also that without the continued care and help of the Almighty, he cannot withstand the various temptations that assail him; and therefore he needs continually to heed the command of the Saviour, to "watch and pray."

There is much food for profitable reflection in the exhortation, "Let him that thinketh he standeth take heed lest he fall."   There are few or perhaps none of those who have attained to a good degree of religious stability, that, in reviewing their life, cannot recall seasons when through unwatchfulness and neglect of daily seeking for communion with God, their spiritual affections were in measure benumbed and their thoughts too much occupied with other lovers. Had it not been for the continued love and mercy of our gracious Lord, who afresh extended his visitations to their souls, and aroused them from spiritual slumber, they would have become more and more negligent of their eternal interests.

If the holy watch is not maintained, any of the varied engagements that claim a share of our time and thoughts may become a snare, however proper or allowable they may be when kept in due subjection to the cross of Christ.

John Churchman* mentions having a meeting among some tender-spirited people in Massachusetts, towards whom the doctrine of truth flowed freely. He says, " When the meeting was over, I felt an uncommon freedom to leave them, for they began to show their satisfaction with the opportunity in many words ; so speaking to the Friend who went with me, we withdrew and went to our horses. On mounting, I beheld the man of the house where the meeting was held, running to me, who taking hold of the bridle, told me I must not go away without dining with them. I looked steadfastly on him and told him, that I did believe this was a visitation for their good, but I was fearful that by talking too freely and too much, they would be in danger of losing the benefit thereof, and miss of the good the Lord intended for them ; and my going away was in order to example them to go home to their own houses, and turn inward and retire to the Divine Witness in their own hearts, which was the only way to grow in religion."

Anna Shipton† mentions meeting with a woman on the continent of Europe, who had been a Christian, but had become miserably entangled in the snares of the world. She says of her, " She had rambled from one country to another, devoted to art and enthralled by the beauty of nature, which she strove to justify as tastes given by God to be

* See note, p. 14.
† See note, p. 15.

16

cultivated. Her days were passed in sight-seeing, in churches, galleries, studios and antiquities; her ear and mind were filled with masses and music; until the natural vision of the natural mind came between the eye of faith and its heavenly vision, and destroyed the happy sense of adoption.

"She sought in vain to deaden her sense of desertion and lost peace, by the passing interests of the hour. She mourned to look back; she feared to look forward.

"Like a poor bird under the deadly fascination of the snake, she seemed unable to flee from the enchantment of sense that spread its web covertly around her.

"Late one night, she came to bid me farewell; and this was our saddest meeting of all—it was our last.

"'Pray for me,' she repeated, as she hung upon my neck. 'Pray that anyhow I may be taken out of all this. Ask that I may be stopped, for I am going downwards, downward!'"

"I heard of her again; she lay prostrate with the fever of the country. During her last illness she. expressed a wish to see me. It was delayed from fear of agitating her. And so she died."

"Bitterly mourning, as I know she did, her forfeited peace, her wasted time, her lost blessing, what availed her those purple mountains, and cloudless skies and sunny shores, in which her natural taste delighted, and where she found a foreign grave? What availed her art's multiplied forms of beauty, or the sweet sounds in which she vainly strove to forget her loneliness? Death, the grave, eternity, swallowed up the heart's false idols!

"The child of faith needs to be assured of the will of the Lord before he goes forth on foreign travel, aimless in all but the gratification of what is called the natural taste. The continual change of scene, the contact with what at first he would gladly avoid, will otherwise humble or depress him. It may possibly end by his looking more leniently on what first filled him with dismay. The lovely scenes and the enervating climate may weaken the life of faith by giving a preponderance to that of sense. Thus his own fair inheritance and the eternal glory, will wane paler and paler to the spiritual eye.   Things that cease to be desired are no longer realized, and this world's idols take possession of the mind. With Christ as our companion, our Shepherd and our Light, we may sojourn safely in the stranger's land, as elsewhere. Without Him there is danger everywhere; perhaps in no position so insidiously as in foreign travel."

A writer in the *Earnest Christian* mentions meeting with a woman at a meeting in Chicago, whose sorrowful countenance betokened sadness of heart.   In a conversation which followed, she said that she had once been a happy, earnest Christian, but had married a man who was not a religious person.   He did not like to see her reading the Bible, or to hear her conversing on religious subjects, and soon began to object to her going to meetings for worship, and would seem angry or displeased when she returned from them.   To please her husband, she gave up all these things; and in thus yielding her own convictions of what was right, she lost her own peace of mind and happiness.   "And now," she said, "five weeks ago, I left my home to visit friends in this city, and I have received a letter from my husband, saying he has no affection for me, and hopes I shall not come back again."   And she added, "O, if I had only been faithful unto God, I should have been happy myself, and I believe before now he would have been converted too."

Many have known what it is to suffer great loss and to be involved in serious difficulties from a neglect of the holy watchfulness enjoined by our Saviour.

John Richardson* in his journal mentions his return home from a religious visit to America, and says; "And now I was under a thoughtfulness how to walk and demean myself so as that I might be preserved near the Lord, and in due reverence and true fear before Him; that, inasmuch as I found there was something of 'Holiness unto the Lord,' imprinted or engraven upon the fleshly table of my heart, that now, in this time, when I was not so particularly and immediately concerned in the like daily travel on Truth's account, I might not lose the savor, relish and sensation of

* See note, p. 77.

heavenly things. * * * Now in this careful and watchful frame of mind, I have found preservation from time to time to this day, by retaining the salt of the kingdom in the soul of the inward man, which is of a preserving quality; with which the vessel is and can only be kept fit for the Master's use."

In another place, he pens this caution : "Now, my tender and well beloved Friends, watch against and strive to keep out the enemy that he enter not; for what way soever he enters and gets footing, he defiles God's temple; and before thou witnesses the Lord to destroy him and cast him out again, thou must have many a sore combat and some warfare (perhaps more than thou art aware ·of) before thou gainest all the ground thou hast lost, by giving way to the adversary of thy soul; therefore keep upon thy watch-tower, watch unto the end, watch and pray continually, that ye enter not into temptation, said our great Lord unto his followers."

This watchful care is as essential for those who minister unto others as it is for their hearers ; indeed, there are peculiar dangers in the path of those who are eminently gifted, and who attract the admiration of others. Rutty, in his History of Friends in Ireland, relates the case of Abigail Bowles, afterwards Smith, who was convinced about the year 1675, and about eight years afterwards came forth as a minister. He says :—

"She was an eloquent woman, of a majestic presence, much admired and followed. She travelled on truth's account both in Ireland and England, had acceptable service in many places, and several persons were convinced by her ministry. She was greatly applauded by many, and, not being strong enough to bear praise, was transported into pride thereby, lost her gift and fellowship with Friends, and from the highest pitch of applause fell into as low a degree of contempt. It is certain, however, that she became sensible of the fall, and suffered many bitter agonies on that account, passing the latter years of her life in retirement, great sorrow and mortification. She has left behind her a pathetic paper of self-condemnation, as a caution to all who think they stand, although in the highest station, to take heed lest they fall."

In a paper which she prepared, she "warned those concerned in the ministry to watch against that Luciferian spirit which would deck and adorn itself with the gifts and graces of the Holy Spirit, and not to value themselves upon any gift which God bestows on them; because that opens a wide door for temptation."

One of the most successful stratagems of the enemy of all righteousness, is to delude mankind with the idea that if they yield to the temptation which is presented it will matter little, for it is a small thing, a very slight departure from the right way, and that they need go no further than they choose in the path of self-indulgence. But it is by Grace only that we are able to stand, and he who leaves his only sure Helper, and follows the enemy, has no power of his own to return to the fold from which he has wandered. It can only be through the fresh extension of that Divine love, whose pleadings he has rejected.

It is recorded of a man who was confined in prison under sentence of death for murder, that he was visited there by two young men who manifested an interest in his condition, one of whom asked him how the sad occurrence happened.

"It did not all happen at once, young man," was the slow reply. "Sit down in that chair, and I'll tell you about it. It did not all happen at once," he repeated' "it did not all happen in a day or a month, or even in a year. It was true that I sent an axe crushing into the brains of a fellow man —that happened in a moment of time, but I was long years in getting to that moment. Once, young man," and here the speaker's voice trembled. "I was as pure as you are— vice had not then left its fearful stain upon my face; and I would not then have harmed the meanest of God's creatures. But the tempter whispered to me, just as he does to all, and I unconsciously yielded. He whispered again and again,

16*

and I yielded, each time resolving in my heart never to yield again. But I trusted in my own strength, so that when temptation came again, I was like a reed shaken in the wind. Little by little I gave up the contested ground to my enemy, and little by little I drifted away from right and truth—away from honor and manhood—away from God and heaven. The tempter whispered in louder tones, until he shrieked in awful tones, 'Murder that man,' and I did the awful deed. Young man, in God's name, don't yield to the first temptation. If an evil thought comes to you, crush it as you would a viper —turn away the very first suggestion of the tempter and then you are safe."

The rough-looking prisoner was trembling like a leaf when he ceased speaking, and the two young men were almost as deeply agitated. It was a lesson that they never forgot.

A boy from the country obtained a position in a banking-house in a city. Before leaving him in the counting-room, his father took him aside, and gave him this advice: "My son, be obedient, obliging, civil and respectful; be attentive to business, be honest, be trustworthy. Above all, remember the motto, 'Thou, God, seest me.'"

He promised he would, and kept his pledge for a time. He followed as closely as possible his father's advice, and gained the esteem of his equals and the confidence of his superiors. He rose step by step till he occupied one of the most responsible positions in the place.

But he was not to live always a stranger to temptation. At any moment he might have laid his hand on hundreds or thousands of dollars, and walked away with the money. At first he reproached himself for permitting the thought of such covetousness to enter his mind; but the temptation grew stronger, and he grew weaker. The plans by which the wicked act could be carried out opened before him. Everything arranged itself with the nicest harmony and precision. The evening was set, the money was where he could lay his hand on it in a moment. Through all the preceding day he was fearfully tried. At last the fearful moment came. All the others had left. He remained, under the pretence of finishing some business. He walked to the vault and swung open the heavy door. As he reached out his hand to grasp the money, it fell from his fingers as if it had been a bar of red hot iron. He trembled as if in convulsions, for then the burning thought flashed across his excited mind, "Thou, God, seest me." He felt the eye of God gazing upon him, and, with a reproving glance warning him of his guilt. He fell upon the floor and groaned aloud. The money he had dropped seemed to answer, "Thou, God, seest him." He cried out aloud, "O God of my mother, save me from this crime!"

And God did save him. In uttering the prayer he had passed the crisis. He replaced the package of money, closed the vault, and repairing at once to the house of the president of the bank, related to him all that had transpired, and begged to be dismissed from his position. The president was a good and wise man, and promised that he would keep the matter secret, assured him that his confidence in him was not destroyed, and that he would keep him in his place. But he advised him to retire for a month from the bank to recover his shattered energies, and to reflect upon the past and prepare himself for the future.

At the end of that time he came back, with a deep sense of his own weakness, but with a firm reliance on the grace of God as his only true safeguard, and with a more abiding sense than ever of the great truth, "Thou, God, seest me."

It is many years since this occurred. It is a lesson from the life of an experienced banker; but, with some modifications, it is a history of the temptations that beset scores of boys and young men in city life. May the result be also the history of every one that is tempted to do what is not right in the sight of God!

In one of the Methodist journals I find a narrative written by R. H. Howard, which illustrates the danger there is of going backward in religious condition, if the holy watch against evil is not maintained. The person of whom he speaks was the son of a wealthy and influential physician in Connecticut. When about twenty-two years of age he united himself with the Methodist Episcopal Church and became a zealous worker in that denomination. But a fondness for the wine-cup led him astray, as it has many others. Through neglect of the warnings of Divine Grace in his own heart, which would have preserved him from this snare, he became finally so enslaved by his passion for strong drink that he lost property and friends, and, sinking from one degradation to another, at length father and brothers cast him off, and finally his wife felt compelled to abandon him and seek a refuge in her own father's home.

Rendered reckless and desperate by the depths to which this habit had brought him, he enlisted in the United States army, then engaged in subduing the Indian tribes of Florida and the Western frontier. For eight years thereafter he continued to lead that half-civilized life that soldiers then led amid the Florida swamps and the Western prairies. Meantime, surrounded by the hardships and privations of such a life, he learned to prize the home he had so recklessly broken up, and to curse the habit which had caused all his bitter woe.

With the breaking, however, of the chain that bound him, strange to say, came no revival of his olden love to God. On the contrary, he seemed, rather, only to harden his heart and to sear his conscience by adopting every infidel doctrine he had ever known. The consequence was, that when his term of service was completed, and he had returned to home and friends, and had become a temperate man, and so a kind husband and father, and a respected citizen once more, he had also become a confirmed infidel —a bitter contemner and opposer of every thing connected with God and religion. The very talent which had once made him an effective worker in a good cause now made him no less successful in a bad one; and he who had once written of a Saviour's love, now not only utterly denied his divinity, but gave himself, with pestilent activity, to the destruction of the faith of others in that Saviour's Lordship and Godhead.

Some twelve years after his return his wife died. It was a terrible blow to him, for notwithstanding his previous faults, they were devotedly attached to each other. This affliction, however, severe as it was, did not yet seem in any degree to soften his heart. Instead, indeed, he seemed only the more rabidly to rebel against the hand that had chastened him.

Two years later consumption laid its remorseless hand upon him. Slowly he failed, until at length he knew he must die. At first he gave no signs of relenting. About two weeks, however, before his death, his stubborn heart, his pride of intellect that had so long upheld him, utterly gave away, and, like a poor, broken-hearted child, he came back to the foot of the cross, supplicating with a truly despairing earnestness and energy for the peace and pardon he had once enjoyed. He was one of the saddest, the most wretched, heart-broken of human beings. " I have sinned against such light!" he would say: " I have crucified the Saviour afresh —counted the blood of the covenant wherewith I was sanctified an unholy thing; there remains for me, therefore, no more atonement for sin."

He conversed freely about his former Christian experience, always closing with remarks like these: " I am worse than Judas. I sold my master for nothing. Like Peter, I denied Him but, unlike Peter, I did it without provocation. Like Saul of Tarsus, I persecuted Him, but, unlike Saul, I did it," he said bitterly, " with a full knowledge that he was the Messiah."

In this despairing frame of mind he remained until his death, earnestly entreating every one around him to pray for him, and with the publican's prayer ever upon his lips.

The last words he ever uttered were, " Lord Jesus have mercy! "

Whatever hopes we may entertain, that this prayer was heard and answered, yet the narrative is one that strongly enforces the need of obeying the command of our Saviour —" Watch and pray lest ye enter into temptation;" and of following the example of the Apostle Paul, who said, " I keep my body under and bring it into subjection, lest by any means, after I have preached to others, I myself should be a castaway."

Closely connected with humility and watchfulness, is that submissive spirit manifested by the Patriarch Job, who was grieviously afflicted, yet replied to the suggestion of his wife—"What! shall we receive good at the hand of God, and shall we not receive evil?" The submissive spirit which breathed in this answer is acceptable in the Divine sight, and ought ever to animate him who loves the Lord and desires to walk in obedience to his will. Indeed, hard as at times it may be to attain to this condition, yet there is great encouragement to strive for it, when we remember the declaration, that *all things* work together for good to them that fear God. The very trials which now seem grievous may be the channel through which greater blessings will flow; and are sure to yield "peaceable fruits of righteousness" to them who bear them in a proper spirit.

Want of submission really implies a rebellious spirit—not willing to trust the government of ourselves and of all that concerns us in the hands of the Ruler of the Universe. Hence, where it is indulged, it tends to bring a cloud over the mind, and to prevent the clear shining of the Son of righteousness into the heart.

It is recorded of a minister of the Gospel, whose labors had been blessed to his hearers, that he lost a young daughter whom he greatly loved, and grieved immoderately for her loss. He became sensible that the Divine Power which had once attended him, was no longer to be felt in his ministrations; and he sought out an aged woman, who was one of his hearers, and inquired of her, if she still received benefit from his teaching. She replied that now she could gain nothing from his ministry. A week after, he repeated the inquiry; and the faithful woman told him, that his discourse lacked unction, and that his words were nothing to her; that she had prayed for him, and the feeling that impressed her mind was—"he is joined to his idols." The admonition was not unheeded. He drew from his breast a portrait of the child he had so lamented, and broke it to pieces under his feet; and, it is to be hoped, bowed in submission to the dispensation allotted, in accordance with the prayer of our Holy Redeemer, "not my will, but thine be done."

One of the most touching instances of submission based on childlike faith and trust, that we have ever met with, is that narrated in the *Sunday School Times* of a tender-hearted, loving child in a New England home. The narrative says:

He loved as he was loved, and he was worthy of all the love which was given to him. One day, as he was starting out for a ride with his parents, he asked them where they were going; and they told him that they were going to take him up to the new cemetery, a beautiful city of the dead by the river's bank, beyond the town. His bright face grew shadowed, and his little lips quivered, so that his father asked him, "Why, Willie, don't you want to go there?" Quietly the trustful answer came back, "Yes, if you think it best, papa." And they rode on silently, in through the broad gateway; on, along the tree-shaded and turf-bordered avenues. The child seemed strangely quiet, clinging in love to his mother's side, and looking up from time to time with a face that seemed never so beautiful in its restful confidence. As they finally passed out again from the gateway they had entered, the dear child drew a breath of relief, and looking up in new surprise asked: "Why, am I going back with you again?" "Of course, you are. Why should you doubt it?" "Why, I thought that when they took little children to the cemetery, they left them there," said that hero-child. And then it was found that with a child's imperfect knowledge, that dear boy had supposed he was being taken, at the call of God, and by the parents whom he loved and trusted, to be buried in the place which he had heard of only as a place of burial. And all by himself he had had the struggle with himself, and had proved the victor. "Yes, yes," you say; "but that was a child's foolish fancy, a mere fear of his imaginings." Ay, and the most desperate of all struggles are our struggles with dangers that are unreal. The sorest conflicts for which we must make preparation are conflicts which do not occur; and the battles which we anticipate with direst dread are battles which are never fought. In all the course of life,

"Present fears
Are less than horrible imaginings."

When danger or disease comes upon those who are most dear to us, it is often very hard to bow in submission to the will of Him who doeth all things well. And yet He only knoweth what the end shall be, and what will most effectually promote the real welfare of his children. It has sometimes happened that those who have been raised from the bed of sickness, have become alienated from God, and a source of trouble and distress to their friends.

Many years ago, one who was a valued member of the Society of Friends, had a son who was highly esteemed and whom he greatly loved; and who, when about nineteen years of age, was very ill, apparently nigh unto· death. Anxious that he should not be taken away, the father knelt by his bedside and prayed that the life of his son might be spared. The son did recover from his sickness, but afterwards fell into evil courses.

About the time referred to, a merchant residing at Wheeling, Va., fitted out a boat with store-goods, and made a trading voyage down the river. In the neighborhood of Salina, the boat was observed by two men in a situation which awakened their suspicions. They obtained a small boat and crossed the Ohio to the opposite shore where it was lying. On inquiring of the crew for the captain, they were told that he had gone overboard in the night, and was missing. The men gave them his name, and said he came from Wheeling. On being further questioned, the boat hands slipped away; leaving the boat deserted. Not long after, a body was discovered, with marks of violence upon it, which was supposed to be that of the captain, as he was never heard of afterwards.

Under the circumstances, the two men at Salina thought it best to sell the boat and its contents. This they did, and wrote to the family, telling them the money would be delivered to the person they should send for it. The young man who had then recently recovered from his illness, was requested to go to Salina; the money was paid to him, but he never made a return of it to the family. It was supposed that he was enticed by some gamblers, and lost that with which he had been entrusted.

This incident was related to a friend of the writer by one of the members of the family of the missing merchant. It ought to teach us the need of a submissive spirit, even when the life of a beloved relative is at stake; for only He who knoweth the end from the beginning, can tell whether life or death will be the greatest blessing.

That submission which we owe in the first place to the great Ruler of the Universe, extends also in degree to those who are placed over us by his authority. Children must obey their parents, pupils their teachers, and citizens the magistrates. And in the church there is a deference due from the younger and less experienced to those who are further advanced. This is included in the Apostle's advice, "All of you be subject one to another, and be clothed with humility." In accordance with this principle, Isaac Penington says: "It is the ordinance of the Lord for the weak to receive counsel and help from the strong, and for the lesser to be watched over and blessed by the greater,—by such as more grown in the life and into the power."

This submissive spirit, of which I have been speaking, is shown in the patient endurance of those seasons of the withholding of spiritual comfort, which the Lord dispenses to his servants, as part of their necessary discipline.

The late James Emlen,* when speaking of his early re-

* An elder in the Society of Friends. Died at West Chester, Pa., in 1866, in the seventy-fifth year of his age. See *Memorials of Deceased Friends*, p. 390.

ligious life, said that for a considerable time after he had yielded to the work of the Spirit in his heart, he was favored with almost uninterrupted tenderness and peace—but as he progressed in religious experience, he found that he had seasons of desertion and conflict to pass through, as has always been the case with the Lord's servants. I remember hearing him remark to a young person who was in a tender state of mind, and enjoying the lively narratives of their religious exercises left on record by worthies who have passed away: "Ah! this is *bounty* money. The time will come in which thou wilt have to work for thy wages."

That worthy elder, Abraham Shackleton,* in a letter written to a grand-child in 1770, says of himself: "My mind is mostly centered among those who are begging their bread, and had rather be honestly poor, than filled with unwholesome food, and lose my appetite for that which nourishes the soul up to eternal life. At times I thankfully acknowledge, to the praise of the bountiful hand that satisfies the hungry babes with proper sustenance, I have partaken with the poor of the flock, of what keeps me from fainting."

His son Richard Shackleton,† in 1784, expressed himself as follows: "My heart is never so comfortable, and I am never so well satisfied with myself, as when I am in the deeps, with the billows passing over my head, engaged in a travail of spirit for the promotion of Christianity, and the welfare of mankind."

Some writer mentions meeting with an aged colored man, a sexton, who was sitting on the step of a small meeting-house, and with whom he entered into conversation. The old man told him that the greater part of his life had been spent in sin and folly; and though he had changed his course of life some years before, yet he had only just

---

* A prominent Friend in Ireland. Died in 1771, aged seventy-four years. The celebrated Edmund Burke was one of his pupils.

† Son of Abraham Shackleton, whom he succeeded in his school at Ballitore, Ireland. An intimate friend of Edmund Burke, and a most worthy and pious man. See *Memoirs* by his daughter, Mary Leadbeater.

learned how to *chew crusts.* When asked for an explanation, he replied, that when he gave up his heart to the Lord, for a long time he thought the Lord must feed him with "pie and cake and all good things. I was not pleased if He didn't, but now I'm satisfied any way. I can take a crust from his hand as well as any thing."

This old colored man appears to have learned the lesson of the apostle, to be content in whatever state he was; and to be satisfied with whatever food his Heavenly Father saw to be "convenient for him."

PART III.

THE LORD'S CARE OVER HIS PEOPLE.

CHAPTER VII.

Divine Help. Healing and Protection. Thomas Story and Drinking Healths. John Richardson Healed. Joseph Hoag and the Woman in Despair. Joseph Hoag's Injury. Endre Dahl Shipwrecked. The Highland Weaver. The Railroad Engineer. John Wesley's Prayer. Providential Preservation. Daniel Stanton in a Storm. Vessel on the Coast of Norway. The Poor Schoolmaster. Unexpected Relief. The Honest Costermonger. The Conscientious Mechanic. Bishop Gobat and the Hyena. Catharine Phillips and the Hostile Fleet. The Convicted Colonel. The Uneasy Captain. Trusting in God. Support under Suffering. William Leddra. James Renwick. Dying Grace for Dying Hours. The Resigned Cripple. "Couple Heaven with it." John Churchman in the Dead Timber. Old David's Weapons. Nicholas Waln. Thomas Story. Friends during Indian Wars.

THE illustrations in the preceding part of this volume have chiefly referred to the manner in which Divine Grace operates upon the heart of man; and to the blessed fruits brought forth in those who yield to its influence, and become branches of the True Vine. But the Saviour, who promised to be with his disciples even unto the end of the world, does not forsake his children, when their feet have been turned into the narrow way of self-denial, which leads to the Heavenly City; but goes with them on their journey; guiding, preserving and helping them, and enabling them to trust in his watchful care. In the present section, it is proposed to insert some illustrations of this branch of our subject.

The Psalmist, speaking in the name of the Most High, uses this encouraging exhortation, " Call upon me in the day of trouble; I will deliver thee and thou shalt glorify me." Many of the servants of the Lord since that day, have experienced the fulfilment of this precious promise; and some of them have left on record their testimony to His goodness, and the gracious manner in which He has appeared for their help in times of trial and perplexity.

When Thomas Story* was a young man, and had submitted to the visitation of Divine Grace with which he was favored; and had set his face in earnest to seek for treasures in Heaven; his father was greatly distressed at his son's conduct, which he feared would destroy the hopes and plans he had formed for his worldly success and prosperity; and he used many efforts to turn him aside from the path he had chosen. On one occasion, some of his friends, and his father among them, being at a tavern, they sent for Thomas to join them; thinking, that by the exhilarating effects of spirits, they might change the current of his thoughts. He says:—

"While they were contriving this scheme, I was retired alone in my chamber, and favored with a sense of the good and soul-nourishing presence of the Lord; but, after some time, a concern came upon me, which gave me to expect something was in agitation concerning me; and, soon after, an attorney-at-law of my acquaintance, came from the company to me, and mentioned certain gentlemen who desired to see me at the tavern." * * " When we came there, the company all arose from their seats, and seeming generally glad, put on airs of pleasantness.

* See note, p. 111.
17*

" In seating themselves again, they placed me so as that I was in the midst, environed by them, and then they put the glass round ; and to relish it the more, they began a health to King William. But the secret presence of the Lord being with me, though hid from them, it affected them all in a way they did not expect; for scarce had two of them drank, till their countenances changed, and all were silenced. The glass, nevertheless, went forward till it came to me, and then I told them, I wished both the king and them well, and if I could drink to the health of any at all, I should more especially to the king's, but should drink no health any more; and so refused it : And the glass never went round, for several of them fell a-weeping, and were much broken, and all of them silenced for a time ; which, when over, some of them said, they believed I intended well in what I did, and that every man must be left to proceed in the way he thinks right in the sight of God : and so we parted in solid friendship. It was the secret grace of God which wrought this ; and to Him, the Lord alone, did I impute it. And, the company dispersing, I returned to my chamber in Divine peace, and true tranquillity of mind ; with which I was favored for many days."

Many have had cause to bear witness to the goodness of the Lord in helping them in outward matters; and some to praise Him for the healing of their diseases, or the removal of their infirmities.

John Richardson* relates that in his youth he was much afflicted with lameness, caused by 'a disease in one of his limbs, which had resisted all the efforts and skill used to heal it ; and with a stammering tongue, which was a discouragement to him in yielding to the duty which he felt to be laid upon him to speak to the people as a Gospel minister. Soon after he gave up freely and cheerfully to answer the Lord's requirings, he says : "The Lord healed me of my lameness, and then I cried unto Him, that He would also heal my tongue of its stammering, believing that the Lord was as able to take away the impediment of my

* See note, p. 77.

tongue, as He was to stop the violence of that humor which had attended my body, and had a recourse to my leg, and made it sore from above the ankle to the knee: and notwithstanding several men had given their advice and had showed their skill, it all proved ineffectual, until I came to believe in Jesus Christ, and to press through all to Him, and to touch the skirt or lowest appearance of his blessed truth and power, in which I found true healing virtue to my soul, and also to my body, and to my tongue, even to my admiration; so that I did not only speak plain in the testimony the Lord gave me to bear, but also spoke plain in my intercourse with men."

When he had taken cold, it often caused sore throat, which so affected his voice that he could scarcely speak so as to be heard. On one of his religious journeys, he found himself in this condition, and sat in a meeting under great exercise of mind. "Having," he says, "left all, as I believed, to do what the Lord required of me, and yet I apprehended myself, by means of this affliction not likely to be of any service; and after some reasonings, and a fervent seeking to the Lord to know the cause of this great trouble, and withal to bring my mind to a true resignation to the will of God in this, and in all the trials the Lord might see good in his wisdom to exercise me in; I had not been long brought into this devoted and resigned state to be and to do what the Lord would have me do; but oh! I felt of the virtue of Christ as a sweet and living spring, *by which I was healed:* I was, and am to this day (when I remember the Lord's kind dealings with me) very thankful to Him."

When John Richardson visited the West Indies, he landed at Barbadoes on a Sixth-day of the week, so ill of a violent fever, that his life was considered in danger. The next day but one, he went to a meeting, though with great difficulty, being very weak. During his sitting there, he says: "Under much weakness of body, yet quiet in mind, the living virtue or heavenly power of Christ sprang up in my inward man, like healing and suppling oil, which so effectually helped me every way, that I could say feelingly and experimentally, miracles are not ceased; for I was raised beyond my own expectation, and all others who knew my weak state, to give testimony to the glorious coming and manifestation of Christ in power, spirit, life, light and grace, for the help, health and salvation of all the children of men who receive, believe in and obey his spiritual knocks, reproofs and heavenly calls in the soul, without any lessening to his humanity. Great cause have I, with all the living, to love, value, honor and reverence the great and mighty name of Him who hath helped and healed, by sending his eternal Word of living power into our hearts."

The goodness of the Lord is often manifested in the healing of our spiritual and mental diseases, as well as of those more purely physical. Joseph Hoag* mentions visiting a sick woman, who had long been a sufferer. He says:—

" I had not been long in the house, before it opened in my mind, that the sick woman was in despair,—wearing out in a decline, under the affliction of all the terrifying ideas that the human mind was capable of realizing. I was led to state her condition to her, and how she came into it, and that if she labored to get into the quiet, and then turn her attention to the Lord, and pour forth to Him her prayers, they would be heard, and she would experience reconciliation with her God, and her peace to be made, witnessing the seals of redeeming love, before she went hence to be seen of men no more. * * I was informed afterwards by her sister that nursed her, that she soon became very quiet; and sometime before she died, she expressed that she had become reconciled to her Maker, and was willing to die; feeling that peace and love that was an evidence to her that her sins were forgiven, and she should be happy."

Joseph Hoag in one instance, in his own case, experienced the power of the Lord both to wound and to heal. He was visiting meetings in New York State at the time. He says:

" While at Smith's Clove meeting, the last I expected to attend in this vicinity, except one in course next day, near

* See note, p. 100.

the close of the meeting it came over my mind with weight, to appoint three more meetings before I left. I exclaimed in my mind, I can not, for I have been five months from home, spring work is coming on, and I am in low circumstances and must go home. I broke up the meeting—a Friend came to me at the door, and expressed that his feelings were such that he wanted me to have three more meetings, and named the places that had opened to me. I told him bluntly, 'I have set my face homeward, I do not intend to turn to the right or left;' feeling determined that home I would go. I had not rode far, before my horse in a brisk trot, fell through the frost and threw me over his head with such force, that I dropped on my head. A Friend riding behind, said he heard my neck snap like a dry stick—I suppose it parted one joint; I rose upon my feet with a smile as was observed, then fell on the ground, remaining unconscious until I found myself sitting up, being supported, feeling as though I had awoke out of sleep. My neck and head soon commenced paining me very severely: it seemed almost insupportable. I was taken by short stages to the Friend's house, where the meeting was held that I expected to attend, which I think was the next day. I kept my bed mostly that and the following day until meeting-time; my neck being swollen with a hard ring around it, that felt more like a bone than flesh, and looked nearly black, so that my case was thought dangerous; but through divine mercy I had a number of hours for reflection, in which my feelings were solemn. When meeting-time came, I was placed on a bed in the room where the meeting was held, it being my desire. In the early part of the meeting a voice spoke to me, as intelligibly as ever I heard a vocal sound, 'If thou wilt go back and have the meetings, I, the Lord, that have wounded thee, and stopped thee in thy course, will enable to perform all I require of thee; and this shall be an evidence to thee, that I, the Lord, speak to thee—thou shalt be enabled to bear a testimony for me in this meeting.' Under the impressions of this voice, my mind was brought into a calm, and I was led to view, why it was, that I was brought into this situation; and also that it was offensive to the Almighty, and dangerous for man who knew the Lord's will, stubbornly to disobey. My mind was seriously humbled, my spirit contrited before the Lord, and glad to feel the smiles of forgiving mercy once more, being made willing to give up all to his disposal. Towards the close of the meeting, with the help of my companion, unexpectedly to my friends, I rose on my feet, and was enabled, I believe, to bear an acceptable testimony to my friends, and felt great peace of mind for the obedience; my pains also were much mitigated.

"At the close of the meeting I called a Friend to me, agreeably to the opening of the light on my mind, and desired him to go to the nearest place, and give notice of a meeting for the next day; and word was sent to the other two places, one in the day, and the other in the evening. He answered me, 'I have not faith to believe thou canst possibly do it.' I answered, 'My faith is enough for both of us—the meeting must be appointed.'

"He went and did accordingly. Next day I rode twelve miles, reached the place in good season, and had a satisfactory meeting. The following day and evening, attended the other two, to the relief of my mind—having to endure considerable pain, which I endeavored to bear with cheerfulness, as I brought it upon myself. I had thought to omit this event; but finding an uneasy feeling to pervade my mind, therefore I have recorded it, much desiring that when my young Friends read these lines, they may pause a little, and behold the tender mercy of Jehovah, when we are brought under the chastening rod, to spare life, even when apparently in the jaws of death; and when rightly sought unto, equally tender to forgive, heal, and give ability to do all He requires of us; and then richly to reward the obedient with heavenly peace. Adored forever be his holy name!"

There are many remarkable instances on record of the care which He, without whose notice not a sparrow falls to the ground, extends for the help and preservation of those who place their trust in Him.

William Tallack of London, relates of the late Endre Dahl, a well-known and greatly respected Norwegian Friend, that when a young man, he came to England in 1843.

After a considerable stay at Newcastle, he took passage in a small vessel bound for Norway, and found that he had a very ungodly and scoffing band of companions on board. In crossing the German Ocean, they were run down in the night by a much larger ship on her way to England. The smaller vessel began to sink, and, but for the vigorous assistance furnished by young Dahl, the little company on board must have gone with her, as the captain of the other ship pitilessly pursued his course and left them to their fate. They managed, however, to get into their boat, which was a leaky one. They had only one oar to row with, and a pair of boots to bail out the water. E. Dahl in this extremity was able to maintain a confident trust in God, and a profound peace. His companions who had previously ridiculed him, now relied upon him for comfort and guidance. He exhorted them to turn to the Lord.

When morning broke, the ship which had run them down was a mere speck on the distant horizon, and quite beyond the reach of any such poor signals of distress as the men in the boat could make. But as the day passed on it became evident that the ship had completely reversed her course, and was again approaching them. By-and-by she came up to them, and took them all on board, shortly after which the little leaky boat sunk beneath the waters. Endre Dahl could not refrain from expressing to the captain of the ship his sense of the cruelty he had at first shown in sailing away, and leaving them to their fate; but he also asked him why, after proceeding so long on his way, he had at length come back to their rescue. The captain confessed that he hardly knew why he had returned, for he had fully resolved to take no further trouble in the matter. But a mysterious impulse to rescue them had, after all, come upon him so strongly that he felt impelled to yield to it, and accordingly did so. The earnest prayers in the boat, and the strong faith reposed in God by the leader of the little party, had been responded to by the Highest.

.An interesting incident is related in the *S. S. Classmate*, that occurred in the Highlands of Scotland years ago, when inns were not numerous, and wayfarers were accustomed to ask lodgings at the houses by the wayside. At a lonely part of a highland road a weaver had his home. He was a very good man, and one who had real faith in God. He was poor, but hospitable, and kindly entertained belated strangers who asked to tarry for the night. But he was sometimes imposed upon by worthless characters, who rose early and made their escape with what they could most readily carry off.

His wife frequently said to him, that if he took in people he knew nothing of after the way he had been doing, they would be ruined by their depredations; but he felt the necessity laid upon him, in his circumstances, to fulfill the Scripture command, "to entertain strangers," and, although he wished to discriminate, he could not think of giving up the practice.

A person presented himself at his door shortly after he had suffered at the hands of dishonest guests: and he, wishing to satisfy himself and his wife of the man's goodness of character, said, "Well, now, you are a stranger to me; what security do you give that you are such a person as I ought to entertain?" Without a moment's hesitation the man answered, "The Lord." "That's quite enough," said the good man, opening the door wide to the wall. "Come in, come in. I receive you in the name of the Lord." And so the stranger admitted was hospitably treated, and, after worship, was shown to bed; but he was a thorough rogue, and before the day dawned, he had left the house with a web the weaver had got ready on the previous evening to carry to his employer.

When the weaver and his wife got up the next morning, and found the fellow gone, his wife was in great perplexity, and, in her anxiety, gave way to upbraiding her husband, saying, "Now you see, it is just as I said; we shall certainly be ruined by this foolish practice of yours. What are we now to do? The web's away, and how are we to live until you weave another?"

It was a dark day to her, but not so to him; for he said, "I got a good security, and I keep the security, and I am sure it will be all for the best. It was for the Lord's sake I received him; and although he has proved himself unworthy of our hospitality, yet Jesus is worthy, and we shall yet lose nothing by it."

As the thief was crossing a hill, shunning the usual road, God enveloped him in a misty covering. He wandered long upon the hillside, this way and that, and at last got to the foot of the hill, and, knocking at a cottage, he asked if they would keep him for the night. The good man of the house recognized the voice, and said to him at once, "Come in, and down with the web!" The thief was thunderstruck, while the man said, "When you next intend to play similar pranks, mind not to give your security!" Down fell the web, and the thief in consternation, took to his heels.

The explanation of the matter is, that the thief got bewildered in the mist, and instead of going down the farther side of the hill, he came down the same side, and knocked at the very cottage door from which he had set out in the morning with the poor man's web.

The *Rochester Democrat* describes as follows, a remarkable occurrence on a New York express train, that was running west from Albany :—

The engine's headlight threw a strong reflection in advance, but the storm was so blinding it was almost impossible to distinguish anything even at a short distance. Under such circumstances instinct necessarily takes the place of sight. All seemed to be going well, when, in an instant, the engineer reversed his engine, applied the air brakes, and came to a full stop. Why he did so, he could not tell any more than any of us can account for the dread of coming disaster and death, and to the wondering inquiry of his fireman, he simply said: "I feel that something's wrong." Seizing a lantern, he swung himself down from the cab and went forward to investigate. Everything appeared to be right, and he was about to return to his engine, when his eye caught sight of a peculiar appearance at the joint of the rail next to him. Brushing the accumulated snow away, he looked a moment, and then uttered an exclamation of horror. The rails on both sides had been unspiked and would have turned over the instant the engine touched them. What inspired this attempt at train wrecking is

18

unknown, but it was presumed the confederates of some prisoners who were on the train, hoped, in the confusion of an accident, to deliver their friends.

The engineer, to whose instinct was due the safety of the train, when asked why he stopped his engine, said:

"I can't tell why, I only know I *felt* something was wrong."

An interesting incident is related by Adam Clarke* of John Wesley,† who had taken passage for Bristol in an English brig, which had touched at Guernsey on its voyage from France. They left Guernsey with a fine fair breeze; but in a short time it died away, and a contrary wind arose and blew with great force. John Wesley, who was in the cabin, broke forth in fervent supplication, which seemed, says A. Clarke, more the offspring of strong *faith* than mere *desire*. He said : "Almighty and everlasting God, thou hast thy say everywhere, and all things serve the purposes of thy will; thou holdest the winds in thy fists, and sittest upon the water floods, and reignest a King forever; command these winds and these waves that they obey THEE, and take us speedily and safely to the haven whither we would be," &c. The power of the petition was felt by all present. A. Clarke went on deck and found the wind changed, and the vessel standing on her course with a steady breeze, which did not abate, but carried them at the rate of nine or ten knots an hour, until they were safely anchored at their desired port.

The following incident was related to the writer, by the person who was so remarkably preserved from a sudden death. He was, at the time it happened, a member of the Virginia Legislature, but felt conscientiously bound to always attend his week-day meeting for public worship.

The room at Richmond, immediately over that in which

, *A distinguished Methodist scholar and writer. Born in Ireland in 1762. Died in 1832. Author of *Clarke's Commentary on the Scriptures*, and other works.

† A clergyman of the Church of England, and founder of the Methodist Society. Died in 1791 in his eighty-eighth year. He is said to have preached more than 40,000 sermons.

the legislature met, was occupied as a Court-room; and an unusual concourse of people was drawn there by a case before the court which had excited the public interest. The weight was so heavy that the floor gave way, at a time when the Friend was at his meeting, and some sixty persons were killed. On returning from meeting, he found the desk at which he sat crushed to splinters by the fallen timbers; and if he had been there, there is little doubt that he would have been among the killed.

In the beginning of the year 1749, Daniel Stanton* in the course of a religious visit, sailed for England. As they approached the British coasts, they encountered a storm, and the vessel having received some damage, the captain determined to alter his course, and take refuge in the harbor of Kinsale, in Ireland. D. S. says:—

"We got in sight of the harbor; but night coming on, and being fearful of rocks and shoals, they put off to sea, and the weather being moderate the fore part of the night, the seamen were too careless, and did not keep so strict a watch as they ought; but the captain, as he lay in his cabin, had so great an uneasiness on his mind, that he could not lay still any longer, and went towards the head of the vessel, and found that, instead of being out at sea, we were near striking on the land; whereupon he immediately awaked the sailors, and they tacked the vessel about, and were very watchful until morning; thus we escaped that danger.

"In the morning it was very foggy and a storm arose, and we could not discover the harbor, but were driven about for a considerable time. They threw overboard one anchor, but the storm continuing, and the weather distressing, we were drove towards the land, and the seamen being almost wearied out, apprehended we could not keep off much longer. Thus we were in great distress, expecting the vessel would be wrecked; and the captain being much surprised, came to my companion and me, telling us he would do what he could to save our lives, but that we were in great danger of being lost, and he expected we would be drove on shore in

* See note, p. 34.

the night if we kept off in the day; and was desirous to know our minds, what he had best to do, whether to run the ship aground while we had daylight, that if any of our lives were spared, we could the better see how to help ourselves. We, not knowing what to advise him for the best, only to trust in the good providence of God, the captain concluded to steer towards the land. The cries and lamentations of the people were great for mercy to their souls, apprehending the vessel might soon be dashed to pieces and we might suddenly lose our lives; but I had reason to believe that the gracious and merciful Being was pleased to hear our cries; for the nearer we came to land the fog cleared away, and they espied a vessel, which as we approached nearer, we discovered was lying at anchor, at the mouth of Kinsale harbor, where we wanted to be; and as we came on our way the harbor appeared plain. Thus through the great deliverance of the Almighty, we arrived there safe and dropped anchor; for which merciful preservation our hearts had great cause to be humbly bowed before Him. The captain came to me, saying, 'Now, if you have it in your heart to return God thanks, I will join with you on my bare knees; and if it had not been for your prayers, we should all have been lost;' but I ascribed this great deliverance to the kind mercy of Divine Providence to us all; although I can truly say, my soul was earnest in supplication before the Lord at times on this trying passage; and at one particular season, as I lay in my cabin, not knowing but that we might be swallowed up in the mighty ocean, the spirit of prayer came on me, and I was raised on my knees to make intercession with the All-powerful Being; after which I went upon the deck, and the captain, seeing me, expressed in a very loving manner, his unity and satisfaction; and I thought that the same good power and presence which attended my mind, had some reach upon his heart."

When in England during this visit, D. Stanton met with one "professing the truth," who did not manifest a trusting confidence in the care and protection of the Ruler of the universe, but pleaded for carnal defence, and asked what defence people had in the province of Pennsylvania. Daniel says :—

"I told him that Providence was our defence; yet he pleaded for carnal defence in such a manner that gave me much pain of mind, and I told him that I had no unity with his principles, and bore my testimony against his unprofitable discourse."

The Leominster Tract Association has published an account of a remarkable deliverance of the crew of the "Providence," a vessel that sailed from Sunderland, and was overtaken in a storm on her voyage home from the White Sea. The crew were at the pumps when the deck was swept by a large wave. In reply to the captain's question, "Are you all there?" he was answered, "All here, but the ship is a mere wreck." The cabin being filled, all the provisions were spoiled, and the water on deck was gone, all they had left being a cask in the forecastle and a few biscuits for a crew of seven or eight men. In this great trouble the master went below, and fell on his knees in his cabin, to ask the Lord to show him what he was to do. On rising from his knees, he fell into a kind of trance, in which it was clearly shown him what kind of coast they would approach, and the creek into which they would find an entrance. He saw a high bold shore with a sugarloaf cliff and a long low reef beyond, and three men in a boat coming towards the ship. He went on deck and ordered the foresail to be loosened and set, which after much difficulty was done. The mate asked him what they were going to do, he replied, "We must get the ship before the wind, and make for some place where we may obtain water and provisions." They had made an observation that day, and found that they were a hundred miles from the coast of Norway. The captain, after watching most of the night, lay down to rest, and after a time was awoke by the mate, saying, "Here is a high bold shore ahead, sir!" On going on deck, Captain H. knew it was the shore he had seen in his cabin the day before, and went aloft on the cross-trees, telling the mate to steer according to his orders.

They sailed along the coast all that day, the snow often
18*

falling heavily; sometimes the ship was so near the rocks that the mate was alarmed. They passed two or three openings in the shore, and felt inclined to put into one or other of them, but as neither of them was the place the captain had seen, they sailed on; but by and by he told the mate that he would soon see a sugarloaf rock and then a long low reef, and inside that a sloop's mast at the end of the reef, and a boat would come out with three men in it. All this soon came in view, greatly to the mate's astonishment. When they got to the end of the reef the boat came alongside the "Providence," and the captain asked the men if they could take him to an anchorage. One of them came on board and asked the captain if he had not had a pilot, and when he was told he had not, he put his hands together and exclaimed, "Then how have you got in here? you must be a good man, God has been your Pilot." They brought the ship to anchor by the fishing craft, and the men soon supplied the strangers with water, bread and fish. The fisherman took the captain to his home, and when he told the wonderful facts to his wife, she also exclaimed, "You must be a good man, God has been your Pilot!" In the morning the pilot took Captain H. to the top of a mountain, from which he could see several creeks, and asked him, pointing to some of them, if he came in by any of those? And when, after hearing it was none of those, he showed him the right one, and was told that was the one he had entered by, he told him it was the only one by which it was possible to gain an entrance to that coast, again exclaiming, "You must be a good man, for God has been your Pilot."

After a good deal of delay, during which time the "Providence" had been given up as lost at home, she was put into the best sea trim possible, and sailed for England, where she arrived in safety, to the joy and satisfaction of all connected with her heaven-preserved and now restored crew.

Captain H. could indeed say, "This poor man cried, and the Lord heard him, and saved him out of all his troubles."

The following narrative furnishes an example of those remarkable co-incidences in which the Christian loves to recognize the hand of his Heavenly Father. It was related in my hearing by a valuable friend:—

At one time he chanced to be walking in the outskirts of Camden, New Jersey, and fell into conversation with a man there who kept a small grocery or provision store. The conversation assumed a somewhat serious tone, and the grocer narrated to my friend an incident of his early life. He was then very poor, and endeavoring to support his small family by teaching a few scholars at Berlin, N. J. His income was small, and it was with much difficulty that he could meet his necessary expenses. One day there was a vendue in the neighborhood, at which he was present. A horse was offered for sale on which few seemed disposed to bid. Tempted by the low price at which the animal could be bought, and by the long credit offered by the auctioneer; and having little doubt of being able soon to sell at an advance, and thus make some profit by the transaction, he bid thirty dollars, and became its owner. He found a purchaser, as he had anticipated at a considerably higher sum, and might have done well pecuniarily, only that the man to whom he sold failed to pay and it was all lost.

When the time approached for the payment of his note to the auctioneer, he was short about ten dollars, which he seemed entirely unable to raise, and in his humble way of business was as much perplexed as many a man would be to procure one thousand times that amount. He was greatly disturbed and distressed at his situation, and often pondered it over, but without seeing any source of relief. Finally, he felt ability to pour forth his needs in the ears of that Heavenly Helper who regards the cries of his distressed children. This brought to his mind a sweet feeling of composure and relief. He knew not how the debt would be paid, but this no longer distressed him.

Shortly after this, perhaps the same day, he heard the sound of wheels passing over a small bridge near his house, and looking out saw that it was one of his neighbors, a man of infidel principles who was very fond of arguing on religious subjects. One of his children was among the scholars of our friend's little school: and a shade of fear crossed the

teacher's mind lest the visit might be to find some fault respecting the child's progress. On coming up the visitor
addressed him about as follows.

"Well, P——, how are you getting along?"

"Oh, tolerably well, I guess."

"Here, take this,"—handing him an envelope which contained ten dollars—the sum he was in need of.

"Why! you don't owe me this money."

"That's all right, put it in your pocket," and then he
rode away.

Some time after, as the same parties were conversing,
P—— asked his benefactor how he came to give him that
money in the time of his distress, for he knew nothing of
his peculiar need. The man replied that he had been to
Philadelphia to collect some dividends, and as he was riding along thinking of how differently persons were situated
as to money matters, he remembered the poor teacher who
had but little, and the thought came into his mind to give
him ten dollars, and so he did.

There are many testimonies to the watchful care of our
Heavenly Father, and many proofs that his ear is open to
the cries and prayers of his people who look to Him in the
day of distress even as to outward things. The ancient
declaration, "This poor man cried and the Lord heard him,
and saved him out of all his troubles," is applicable to many
in the present day.

This is illustrated by the following incident related not
long since at a meeting, I believe in New York:

A friend in business in this city told me a few days ago
of an answer to prayer in his own case. Said he: "I had
certain bills to meet, and tried every resource I had, but
could not get the money. As the time approached, and my
ability to meet my obligations seemed out of the question,
I went to God with my troubles, and poured out my soul in
earnest prayer to Him to send me help. The morning of
the day when my obligation became due arrived, but the
help had not come. I went to my store, and soon after a

gentleman came in whom I had known for some years, but not intimately. He greeted me kindly, and then asked after my business, and if I had plenty of funds, &c. I frankly told him the truth, and that I was quite short of funds for that day. He asked me how much I needed, and I told him. Without another word he drew a blank check from his pocket and filled it out for the sum I had named, and handed it to me, saying I could repay it when I became easy again."

In the latter part of last century a Friend belonging to Wilmington Monthly Meeting, Delaware, was appointed on a committee set apart to pay a religious visit to its families. In reference to this he has left the following memorandum :—

I believe it right to mention a circumstance that occurred some days before we set out on this family visit, and which brought me into deep concern, so that I thought I could not go. Being called upon for a sum of money very unexpectedly, I knew not where to obtain it, (although I made many efforts,) and to take it out of our small stock, would prevent us from going on with our business to much purpose. While I was under great concern and anxiety about it, a stranger who was not a member, spoke to me at the close of our meeting on this wise: "I want you to come to my house in the morning about ten o'clock." I accordingly went, when he said to me, "I have a sum of money which I have a mind you should have on loan, and that without interest." I was filled with admiration and gratitude, and could but look upon this as a providential act of favor to me. Surely I have cause reverently to bow before God; his continued care and kindness toward me are great. He casts up a way, even marvellously so, where no way appeared. Surely there is no occasion to distrust his all-sufficiency; for He will not leave nor forsake those that put their trust in Him. My mind being thus relieved, I felt perfect liberty to proceed on the visit."

The Christian must be prepared to sacrifice all his wordly

prospects for the sake of peace of mind and the favor of his Creator ; and be willing to give up even life itself if the sacrifice is called for ; knowing assuredly that the joys of Heaven will abundantly compensate for all the trials he may meet with here. Yet the Lord is often pleased to open the way before his faithful children, even in worldly matters, to their comfort and rejoicing. At a meeting in England Dr. Bernardo* related the following incident as an illustration of the effect of religion :

A costermonger, who used to sell shrimps and periwinkles and whatever was in season, came to me and brought his three tin measures, and said : " I can't sell any more with these." Then he showed how each of them had a false bottom, so as not to hold more than half a measure. He said : " I don't know what to do. I can't use these ; and I can't make a living by giving honest measure." I thought it over, and said to him, " Put up this card :" " I have got religion, and I give honest measure ; but I charge more for it." So he did. For a few days, it went very hard ; but presently the women found out that it was better to buy of him and get honest measure ; and now he has a cart and a little shop of his own, and is doing very well.

A laborer, who believed it wrong for him to work on the First-day of the week, was told by his employer on a Seventh-day evening, when he received his week's wages, that he must be on hand the next morning to push forward some machinery that was to be sent to South America by a given time. He replied that he could not conscientiously work on that day.

" That is nothing to me," said his employer. " You may stick to your principles, but my work must be done, and if you cannot do it I do not need your services any longer."

" This blow," said the workman, " came upon me in the

* A philanthropist of London, who has devoted his life principally to the education and care of the neglected children of that city.

dullest season of the year, and my wife and children were sick; the shops were everywhere discharging their men. But I went out, and for eleven days diligently sought for work. On the evening of the last day, while crossing the ferry, I lifted my heart to God in prayer, saying, 'Now, Lord I have done all I can; thou hast promised that my bread should be given to me, and that my water should be sure.' I went home and told my wife. The next morning came. After working-hours began, who should enter my home but my old employer, asking if I had any work yet. I answered, 'No. But I do not suppose you want me?' 'Well,' said he, 'I think you were very stiff in your opinions, but I want you to take up that job where you left it.' I went to work, and discovered that he had placed a man in my position who had damaged the work, and set it back two full weeks. He was a drunkard and wholly unreliable." The account was written five years after this occurrence, and during that interval, he had had constant employment, and had not been asked to work on the First-day of the week.

It is a very comforting and soul-sustaining assurance which the true Christian is at times permitted to feel, that all things are under the control of his Heavenly Father; and that whatever trials and afflictions may await him, yet the Lord can sustain him through them all; and even make them conduce to his highest welfare. A feeling of this kind animated the apostle when he queried, "Who can harm you, if ye be followers of that which is good?" So, also, in another place, the same apostle expresses his confident conviction that neither heights nor depths, things present nor to come, shall ever be able to separate from the love of God which is in Christ Jesus, our Lord.

He who is possessed with this holy faith can meet the difficulties of life with quiet confidence; being mainly concerned lest in anything he should depart from the Divine guidance, and thus bring loss and suffering on himself; for he is assured that all things will work together for good to them that fear God. Though he has no reason to expect entire exemption from the ordinary accidents of life,—for one event happeneth to the righteous and to the wicked— yet there are many instances of preservation from danger, seen and unseen, in which the devout mind delights to trace the protecting hand of Him without whose notice not a sparrow falls to the ground.

It is related of Bishop Gobat of Jerusalem, when engaged as a missionary to Abyssinia, that on one occasion, in a season of deep spiritual depression and gloom, he retired to a cavern and there poured out his heart in earnest supplication to the Lord. He remained in the cavern for some time. When he rose from his knees his eyes had been accustomed to the darkness, and he saw that he had been there with a hyena and her cubs, which yet had not been suffered to attack him.

On another occasion this animal was made the instrument of his deliverance from a violent death. While laboring among the wild tribes of the Druses, a messenger was sent from one of their chiefs, whose influence it was important to secure, with a message entreating Gobat to visit him. The latter, however, was unable to do so in consequence of indisposition. A second messenger repeated the invitation, but still Gobat was unable to comply with the chief's wishes. A third messenger prevailed on him to set out, by the assurance that if he went at once he might spend the night with the chief and be ready to return in the morning, so as to join a ship about to sail for Malta, in which he was anxious to embark. On their journey the guides lost themselves in the mountain paths. Having at last, with some difficulty regained their route, they suddenly saw by the light of the moon that a hyena had laid itself down across the path exactly in their way. They threw stones to frighten it, when the animal sprang up and ran along the path which the party were to travel. The superstition of the natives, as well as their fear of the animal, prevented them from pursuing their journey, and saved Gobat from falling into the hands of those who had intended his destruction.

In the journal of that eminent minister, Catharine Phillips,* who then resided in Cornwall, England, the following circumstance is related—at that time the English nation was at war with France and Spain. She says:

Our quiet was disturbed in the Eighth Month, 1779, by an alarm of the French and Spanish fleets being off Falmouth Harbor. What the design was could not be known, but there they lay for some days, the wind not permitting them to go up the channel; and, as they did not land, it was conjectured that their hostile views were turned towards Plymouth and the king's dock near that place.

Soon after they had sailed up the Channel, being in a week-day meeting, with my mind retired to the Lord, under an exercise on account of the intended mischief, it run through it, "He sent forth lightning and scattered them." I think as we returned home from meeting the wind was rising; the sky soon lowered, and a terrible storm gathered, and discharged itself with fierce lightning, and tremendous thunder, and violent rain; which continued through the greater part of the night, and indeed, the thunder continued until the next evening. The fleets had, by the time the storm began, got near Plymouth; and we heard that the commanders had deliberated about the business they had in view; but the Lord, who holdeth the winds in his fists, discharged against them his terrible artillery so powerfully as to prevent their designs, and obliged them to sheer off from our coasts in a shattered state.

He who turneth the hearts of men as a man turneth his water-course in the field, often effects his gracious designs by the secret but powerful impressions made by his Spirit on the minds, even of the rebellious. An interesting illustration of this is mentioned by Robert Sutcliffe in his travels in America:

*See note, p. 44.

19

During the revolutionary war in America, a part of the American army lay near Gunpowder Falls Meeting-house, which, however, did not prevent Friends from holding their meetings for worship.   Amongst the troops there was a colonel of dragoons whose hatred of Friends was raised to such a pitch of malice, that one day when traversing the country, he came to the most cruel and extraordinary resolution of putting to the sword the Friends who were then collected at their place of worship, considering them as no better than a company of traitors.

Drawing up his men near the spot, he ordered them to halt, in order to make arrangements for the execution of his dreadful purpose.

At this moment an awful silent pause took place, in which he felt his mind so powerfully smitten with conviction, that he not only drew off his men, but conceived very favorable sentiments of the Society; and continuing to yield to his convictions, he afterwards joined in communion with Friends, and continued faithful to the principles of truth professed by them.

The same author mentions that when in Philadelphia, he was entertained at the house of a Captain H., whom he had seen at Liverpool.   He had been for some time commander of a ship in the East Indian trade, and had acquitted himself so much to the satisfaction of his employers, that he was engaged to go out again, as commander of the Hindostan, in which very large property was embarked.   The whole management of the outfit had been committed to his care, and everything having been made ready for the voyage, the vessel was on the point of sailing.   At this period he found his mind so oppressed at the prospect of the voyage, that he requested the owners of the ship to liberate him from his engagement of taking the command; but could assign no other reason than the oppression of his mind at the prospect of the voyage before him.

The owners at first seemed disposed to enforce his compliance; yet after a little reflection they gave up the point, there being several well qualified captains to supply his place.   The command of an Indiaman is a situation eagerly sought after, being considered the most profitable of any in the commercial line, as it affords opportunities of making larger profits than any other trade. Another captain was accordingly appointed, and the Hindostan left Philadelphia, in appearance as fine a ship as had of late sailed from that port ; but she was never heard of after she left the Delaware River.

The quietness and composure with which the trusting follower of his Lord is often favored in times of danger, flows from his confidence in the Divine power and goodness. It is related of a pious man, who was at sea in a violent storm with his wife and children, that he seemed calm and composed amid the alarm which prevailed on board the vessel. His wife upbraided him with not manifesting that concern for his family which affection would lead to. He immediately left the cabin and returned in a short time with a drawn sword, and with a stern countenance pointed it at her breast; but she, smiling, did not appear at all disconcerted or afraid. "What!" said he, "are you not afraid when a drawn sword is at your breast?" "No!" she replied, "not when I know it is in the hand of one who loves me." "And would you have me," he answered, "to be afraid of this storm and tempest, when I know it to be in the hand of my Heavenly Father, who loves me?"

Though the Lord often delivers those who trust in Him from dangers, seen and unseen, yet at times He permits them to partake of the cup of suffering.

There is something very animating and encouraging in the records which have been preserved of his supporting presence with his faithful servants at such seasons, enabling them to bear with fortitude the trials to which they were subjected, and oftentimes filling their souls with holy joy. William Dewsbury,* who was imprisoned for many years

---

*A native of Yorkshire, England. A zealous minister among Friends who spent many years in prison for his religion. Died, 1688. See *Life in Friends' Library*, vol. 5, p. 213, etc.

for his religious testimony, says, that he entered prisons as joyfully as palaces, and esteemed the bolts and bars of his prison-houses as jewels.

How powerless are the efforts of persecutors against those who are so clothed with the armor of Heaven! These know that the Lord is able to make their sufferings the means of spreading his kingdom in the earth; and that if their outward lives are taken, He can raise up many more witnesses to his blessed truth, They are made to rejoice in the feeling of the love of God, and to triumph in the glorious prospect of the crown immortal which awaits them. How beautifully does William Leddra* show forth the peace and comfort which he enjoyed, when under sentence of death at Boston, for going there in the service of his Lord, contrary to the orders of those in authority! The day before his execution, he wrote a letter to his friends in which he says:—

" The sweet influences of the morning star, like a flood distilling into my innocent habitation, hath so filled me with the joy of the Lord in the beauty of holiness, that my spirit is as if it did not inhabit a tabernacle of clay, but is wholly swallowed up in the bosom of eternity, from whence it had its being.

" Alas, alas, what can the wrath and spirit of man, that lusteth to envy, aggravated by the heat and strength of the king of the locusts, which came out of the pit, do unto one that is hid in the secret places of the Almighty? or unto them that are gathered under the healing wings of the Prince of Peace? under whose armor of light they shall be able to stand in the day of trial. I have waited as a dove at the windows of the ark, and have stood still in that watch, which the Master (without whom I could do nothing) did at his coming reward with fulness of his love, wherein my heart did rejoice, that I might in the love and light of

---

* An inhabitant of Barbadoes. Put to death at Boston for his religion in 1661. See Sewel's *History of the Quakers.* Evans' *Friends in the Seventeenth Century,* etc.

God, speak a few words to you, sealed with the spirit of promise."

James Renwick*, one of the Scottish martyrs, speaking of his sufferings for conscience' sake, says: "Enemies think themselves satisfied that we are put to wander in mosses and upon mountains; but even amidst the storms of these last three nights, I cannot express what sweet times I have had when I had no covering but the dark curtains of night. Yea, in the silent watch, my mind was let out to admire the deep and inexpressible ocean of joy, wherein the whole family of Heaven swim. Each star led me to wonder what He must be who is the Star of Jacob."

But though the Lord thus lovingly watches over his children and supports them in their distresses, yet the sensible evidence of his love is not always felt. The promise is, "as thy day, so shall thy strength be," and though He extends help in the time of need, yet He is often pleased to hide his face, so that we may clearly see and feel how helpless we are in ourselves, and how entirely dependent on the supplies of Grace.

In *The Secret of the Lord*, written by Anna Shipton†, we find an illustration of this. She visited a rudely constructed cabin by the road side, where she saw an aged woman peeling potatoes, with an open Bible before her, into which she glanced from time to time as she proceeded with her work. After some conversation, the visitor spoke to a little grandchild, a girl of about eight years of age, and said to her, "Do you know that your grandmother is the daughter of a king?" and added, "The royal family are poor here." "No," was the reply of the old woman, "We are rich now, rich now. My Father owns the cattle on a thousand hills, and every beast of the forest is his." But though then rejoicing in faith, it was not always so; for at a subsequent

*One of the Scotch "Covenanters." Born 1662. Executed 1688, for denying the King's authority, &c. "The last of the Covenanters who sealed his testimony on the scaffold."
† See note, p. 15.

19*

visit the old woman was depressed in spirits. She had been ill, and in the time thus given for thinking, had come to the conclusion that she was not a child of grace; not at all like the good old martyrs. "I said to myself last night, when I could not sleep, 'would I die for God? Would I be sawed in two, or burnt on a gridiron, or with fagots in the market-place, or be torn in pieces, for the faith that's in me?' No!" repeated the old woman sorrowfully. Her visitor replied, "Has the Lord called on you to be burnt in the market-place, or to be torn in pieces? If so, be sure that He will give to you, as He did to his martyrs of old grace to witness for Him. Dying grace for dying hours. 'Without Me, ye can do nothing.'" This view of the subject calmed her tossed mind.

Dr. Gregory* relates that at the request of a poor but benevolent woman, he went to visit an indigent man in his neighborhood, who was greatly afflicted. On entering his cottage he found him alone, a pale, emaciated man, fastened in his chair by a rude mechanism of cords and belts. He was totally unable to move either hand or foot, having been for more than four years deprived of the use of his limbs, and suffering extremely from swellings at his joints. Dr. Gregory says, "As soon as I had recovered a little from my surprise at seeing so pitiable an object, I asked, 'Are you left alone my friend in this deplorable situation?' He replied in a feeble tone of mild resignation, 'I am not alone for God is with me!' I found that his wife had left on his knees, propped with a cushion formed for the purpose, a Bible lying open at a favorite portion of the Psalms of David. I sat down and conversed with him. On ascertaining that he had but a small weekly allowance certain, I inquired how the remainder of his wants were supplied? 'Why, sir,' said he, ''tis true as you say, seven shillings a week would never support us, but when it is gone, I rely upon the promise I find in this book; 'Bread shall be given and his water shall be sure.' I asked him

*Probably George Gregory, who was born in Ireland in 1754, and settled at first in London and afterwards in Essex, as a clergyman of the Church of England. He was the author of several theological and literary works, and died in 1808.

if he ever felt tempted to repine under the pressure of so long continued and heavy a calamity? 'Not for the last three years,' said he, 'Blessed be God for it! for I have learned in this book in whom to believe; and though I am aware of my weakness and unworthiness, I am persuaded He will never leave me nor forsake me. And so it is, that often when my lips are closed with lock-jaw, and I cannot speak to the glory of God, He enables me to sing his praises in my heart.'

"This and much more did I hear during my first visit, and in my subsequent visits, I uniformly witnessed the like resignation. He died with a hope full of immortality. And gladly would I sink into the obscurity of the same cottage, gladly even would I languish in the same chair, could I but enjoy the same uninterrupted communion with God, be always filled with the same strong consolation, and always behold with equally vivid perception, sparkling before me, the same celestial crown."

Ah! this "hope full of immortality," how it sweetens the bitter cups of life, and gives the weary pilgrim courage to press on through all difficulties—nay, even enables him to rejoice in tribulation, and to reckon as a blessing everything that may help him to win the crown at the end of the race.

An aged Christian had paused to rest himself as he trudged along under a heavy load on a warm summer day. An acquaintance had just accosted him, when a splendid carriage rolled past, in which a haughty man rode, whose whole appearance bespoke a life of luxurious ease. "What do you think of the Providence of which you sometimes speak?" said the acquaintance. "You know that that is a wicked man; yet he spreads himself like a green bay tree. His eyes stand out with fatness; he is not plagued as other men; while you, believing that all the silver and gold is the Lord's, serving Him and trusting in his providence, and toiling and sweating in your old age, get little more than bread and water. How can you reconcile this with Providence."

The aged saint looked at the questioner in amazement,

and, with the greatest earnestness, replied: " *Couple Heaven with it!* couple Heaven with it, and then !" Yes, that addition sweetens many a bitter cup, and enriches many a poor lot. " For our light affliction, which is but for a moment, worketh for us far more exceeding and eternal weight of glory ; while we look not at the things which are seen ; for the things that are seen are temporal, but the things that are not seen are eternal."

It is one of the many privileges of those who are honestly endeavoring to serve their Heavenly Father, that in times of perplexity and danger, they can appeal to Him for guidance and help ; and they are often favored at such times with a degree of confidence in the Lord, which calms the mind and frees it from that timidity or those anxious forebodings which would naturally arise.

John Churchman* relates that when he was about eight years old his father sent him about three miles from home on an errand.   He says:—" On my return, the colt which accompanied the mare I rode, ran away to a company of wild horses, which were feeding not far from the path I was in. My father bid me go back to the place with speed, that it might follow the mare home.   I went, and found the horses feeding on a piece of ground where the timber trees had been killed perhaps about two or three years.   Before I went among the dead trees, a mighty wind arose, which blew some down, and many limbs flew about.   I stood still with my mind turned inward to the Lord, who I believed was able to preserve me from hurt ; and passed among the trees *without fear*, save the fear of the Lord which fills the hearts of his humble, depending children with love that is stronger than death.   I found the colt, and returned home with great bowedness of heart, and thankfulness to the Lord, for his mercy and goodness to me."

Some years ago a citizen of western North Carolina, who was called " Old David," was travelling along the borders of Missouri and Nebraska, at that time but thinly peopled,

* See note p. 14.

and infested with highway robbers. He was urged by his neighbors to procure a couple of revolvers to protect himself, but he declined and went on his perilous journey, trusting to the Lord for protection. He had passed some dangerous places on the northern borders of Missouri, and was nearing the resort of one of the most formidable of the marauding gangs, headed by a notorious desperado named Stevens, when he met a man heavily armed. The first question he propounded to Old David was, "Are you armed?" "Yes," was the aged Christian's reply, as he produced a pocket Bible. The man laughed outright at what he considered the old man's folly, and with considerable ridicule in his tone, remarked, "If that is all the weapon you have, you had better be saying your prayers. The den of Jim Stevens is about ten miles further on, just where you will get by night, and he cares as little for bibles as a rattlesnake." They exchanged names, and each went his own way.

Night had thrown her dark mantle around the earth, and the chilling blasts had begun to pierce the somewhat feeble frame of Old David, when he descried a light far down in a glen a short distance from the road. He was sure that it proceeded from a robber-den, but he must have shelter, and impelled by almost boundless faith, he directed his course thither. He halted when within a few paces of the door, and, being coarsely greeted by some uncouth, mean-looking men, was invited to alight. When he entered the humble habitation he saw significant looks pass between the inmates, and each chuckled to himself; and he knew that he was among a desperate, relentless and murderous clan of banditti. Nothing daunted, he occupied the proffered seat. Having partaken of a rough meal, which they furnished him at his request, he began conversation, which was continued till far in the night, when it was interrupted by the return of the captain Jim Stevens, and a couple of his comrades in crime, from a plundering raid. Stevens, advancing within a few feet of him, asked jeeringly, "Old man, aren't you afraid to travel in this section among the robbers, alone and unarmed?" "No," was Old David's bold and fearless reply, as he again produced his Bible, continuing: "This is my weapon of defence. I always read a chapter before I retire.

I know you are robbers, but I shall read and pray here to-night, and you must join with me." The roof of the shabby hut shook with loud, taunting peals of laughter at this expression of the old man; but nothing dismayed, he began. Gradually all became silent. When he had finished, he was conducted to a hard pallet, where he slept the live-long night undisturbed, and even free from haunting fears. When he arose in the morning, his hosts refused to receive aught for his entertainment during the night, and, instead, cordially thanked him for the interest he had manifested in their behalf.

At the next settlement he learned of the death of the man that he had met on the road, who ridiculed his Bible as a weapon of defence. Old David prosecuted his journey successfully, and returned home safely.

Though outward peril may seem very great, yet the Lord often enables his servants to adopt the language of the Psalmist, "The Lord is my light and my salvation; whom shall I fear? The Lord is the strength of my life; of whom shall I be afraid?" He who can truly say, "One thing have I desired of the Lord; that will I seek after; that I may dwell in the house of the Lord all the days of my life, to behold the beauty of the Lord and to inquire in his temple;" will have ground to hope for the fulfilment of the declaration, "In the time of trouble He shall hide me in his pavilion; in the secret of his tabernacle, shall He hide me."

When Nicholas Waln* and David Bacon, of Philadelphia, were crossing the ocean to England on a religious visit, a violent storm arose, so that the captain thought they must inevitably perish. After exerting himself to the best of his ability to save the ship, he thought it best to inform the

*Born near Philadelphia in 1742. Practised law for some years, but resigned the profession and became a preacher in the Society of Friends. Went to England in 1783 and 1795 on religious visits. Died in 1813. See *Eminent Philadelphians* and N. Kite's *Biographical Sketches of Friends.*

passengers of their perilous situation, and of the fate which he thought awaited them. On entering the cabin, he found the two Friends engaged in pleasant converse. When he had communicated his message, his passengers remained composed and placid ; and Nicholas remarked, that he supposed it was as easy to travel to Heaven by water as by land.

The vessel weathered the storm, the visit was paid, and they returned in safety to their native land ; but the quiet resignation to the Divine will of these good men made a strong impression on the mind of the captain.

Thomas Story* mentions in his journal that when travelling on a religious visit in the Southern States of America, —" The company was taken with the greatest storm of lightning, thunder and rain, that ever I remember I had been in before ; insomuch that the fire and water seemed to be commixed in their descending upon us, and the thunder so sharp and sonorous, and so near, as if it had been bombs splitting among us ; so that I, being the second in the company, looked back several times to see if any were slain behind ; and it was attended with a stifling smell of sulphur. The storm abating a little, it was quickly renewed with equal show of terror ; so that we had it along for the space of about eight miles in the first, and three in the latter, in a very dreadful manner ; but the Lord preserved us from all harm. And though I was a little concerned at the first approaches of so terrible threatenings by an irresistible power, though from natural causes ; yet feeling the Creator near, who ordains it, and that His all-ruling authority was above and over it and all things, I was much comforted in Him, in the time of the most apparent danger : For which I was greatly thankful to the Lord, and for our preservation ; for we observed that several great trees had been shattered to pieces by it ; and so we got safe to Robert Jordan's that evening. But another storm, with much thunder and rain, coming on in the night, awakened the family, and some of them were much terrified, the thunder breaking out near the house ; but upon my retiring inward, I had great

*See note, p. 111.

peace in the good presence of the Lord, and His holy love ejected all fears."

John Richardson,* in the course of his many travels by sea and land, was several times exposed to great danger; but preserved his presence of mind in a remarkable degree. He thus relates one peril which he encountered when crossing the James' River in Virginia

Now we came to the ferry over the river, being, as I remember, five horses and nine people; there was Jane Pleasants a public Friend, and her man servant who rid before her upon a great horse, and high in flesh; and about the midst of the river, it being two miles over, he rose upon his hind feet, and flung himself upon the edge or gunnel of the boat, half into the river; the fall of the horse, and the motion of the other horses thereupon, caused the boat to make such sallies that it took in water, and was very likely to sink: But before he could have time to rise again, or to make any more springs, I took several young men by the shoulders, and flung them upon his neck to keep him down, and told them, as fast as I could, why I did so. Now I had to deal with the ferryman, who was about to strip for swimming, and said we should all be drowned; but for his part he could swim; and was about to leap into the river, for he said, the boat would either break or sink. I told him, it was soon enough for him to swim, when he saw the boat either break or sink, and if he would not row, then I would. With much entreaty he took the oar again, and rowed us to the shore. But in our imminent danger, I looked over my tender friends (for so they appeared to me), and thought in my heart, what a pity it would be, if all these were drowned! Yet the thought of my own drowning never entered my mind, until I was got over the river, which was a mercy to me, and a great means to keep out disorder and confusion, which commonly attend sudden surprises and frights, or else they make people dead-hearted and almost senseless." On this occurrence, he makes these judicious comments: "As I had now an occasion to observe, as well as in some

* See note, p. 77.

imminent dangers I had seen before, where I happened to be, I find it an excellent thing to be, as much as we can, always ready; and by being frequently thinking upon death, it is not so surprising when it does come."

In 1704 Thomas Story visited New England, at a time of great distress from the Indian war then raging. He says: "It was a dismal time indeed in those parts; for no man knew in an ordinary way, when the sun set that ever it should arise upon him any more; or, lying down to sleep, but his first waking might be in eternity, by a salutation in the face with a hatchet, or a bullet from the gun of a merciless savage; who, from wrongs received, as they too justly say, from the professors of Christ in New England, are to this day enraged, as bears bereaved of their cubs, sparing neither age nor sex." Yet the faithful members of the Society of Friends, "trusting in the Lord, neither used gun nor garrison, sword, buckler nor spears; the Lord alone being their strong tower and place of refuge and defence; *and great was their peace, safety and comfort in Him.*"

After a meeting at Salisbury, he lodged at Henry Dow's on the edge of a great swamp or thicket, "where," he says, "there was neither gun, nor sword, nor any weapon of war, but truth, faith, the fear of God, and love, in a humble and resigned mind; and there I rested with consolation."

This family had recently met with a severe affliction, which is thus related. "The mother of Henry Dow's wife, being a Friend of a blameless life, and living in this same house with them, let in reasonings against their continuing in a place of so much apparent danger, and frequently urged them to remove into the town, where the garrison was, that they might lodge there in the night for safety, as many others, and some Friends did; which, her daughter could never be free to do, believing, that if they let in any slavish fear, or distrust in the arm and protection of the Lord, some very hard things would befal them; till at length her mother said to her, that if she could say she had the mind of the Lord against it (being a minister, though young), she would rest satisfied; but nothing less than that could balance so rational fears in so obvious danger. But the young woman

20

being modest, cautious and prudent, durst not assume positively to place her aversion to their removal so high; but at length she and her husband complied with the mother, and they removed to the town, to a house near the garrison; where the young woman was constantly troubled with frightful surprising fears of the Indians; though, while at the house by the swamp, she was free from it and quiet.

"But the mother, having left some small things in the house by the swamp, was going early in the morning to fetch them, and, by some Indians in ambush near the town in her way, was killed. And the same morning a young man, a Friend, and tanner by trade, going from the town to his work, with a gun in his hand, and another with him without any, the Indians shot him who had the gun, but hurt not the other; and when they knew the young man they had killed was a Friend, they seemed to be sorry for it, but blamed him for carrying a gun: For they knew the Quakers would not fight, nor do them any harm; and therefore by carrying a gun, they took him for an enemy.

"When the town was alarmed, the young woman concluded her mother was slain (but it was not by shot, but a blow on the head), but did not go into the garrison, but took one of her children in each hand, and went with them into a swamp or thicket, full of reeds, near the place; where all her tormenting fear left her, and she was then greatly comforted and strengthened in the presence of the Lord, and confirmed in her thoughts, that they should not have left their house for her mother's fears, though reasonable in human view.

"The loss of the mother was much lamented by the son and daughter, and others; but as soon as her body was ininterred, they went back with their little children to the same place by the swamp; where I lodged with them and they gave me this relation."

CHAPTER VIII.

Faith. William Bray. The Crippled Man. The Timid Slave. Abraham Lincoln's Trust in God. Emancipation Proclamation. The Doctor taken at his Word. Divine Guidance. David Sands and Remington Hobby. George Withy's Impression to go Home. John Knox Saved from being Shot. Matthew Warren's Wife. Elizabeth L. Redman and the Escaped Prisoner. Prepare for Death. A Lantern for the Footstep. Joseph Lybrand and his Stolen Child. Healing a Breach. Thomas Waring. R. Bourdman Saved from Drowning. Dr. Guthrie and the Paralytic. Daily Bread. Widow Safford. Changing Residence. John Richardson. Joseph Hoag. The Decayed Meeting House. Joseph Hoag and Slave Holders. Thomas Story and the Practice of Law. John Richardson and his Step-father. Frederick Smith and his Wife.

THE apostle Paul describes Faith as "the evidence of things not seen." By which description he may well be understood to refer to that conviction of the truth of the openings of the Holy Spirit in the heart of man, which gives him as positive an assurance of the certainty and reality of things yet distant and unseen, as if they were actually present and visible. The great object of the saints' faith is and always has been, as Robert Barclay shows in his "Apology," the voice of God speaking in the soul. That voice we are bound to listen to and obey in all things; whether it warns us against danger, points out the way in which we should walk, reproves us for our sins, or leads us to seek forgiveness for our past transgressions through the mercy of God manifested in the atoning sacrifice of the Saviour of mankind.

If we obey this voice of God, which teacheth as never man taught, then we show our faith by our works. But we may hear it, and be convinced of its Divine authority, and yet refuse to submit to its directions; thus manifesting that

our faith is a "dead faith," which doth not profit us. By that.
living faith which is inseparably connected with obedience,
the apostle assures us the saints. of old wrought many
mighty works; and the same principle operates in man to
the present day, producing the fruits of righteousness in all
in whom they are brought forth.

A striking example of this faith is found in the life of a
poor Cornish miner named William Bray,* but in his neighborhood familiarly called Billy Bray. He had been a reckless,
profane, drunken man for many years; but was converted
to righteousness without much outward help, by yielding to
the visitation of Divine Grace. He became as conspicuous
for his piety and devotion to the cause of Christ, as he had
before been for his service to the world, the flesh and the
devil. He was a man of much originality of mind, quickness of wit, and decidedly eccentric. Many amusing incidents are preserved which illustrate these traits; but with
them all, there was a sincerity and earnestness in his
devotion to religion, which made him useful in the circle
in which he moved.

The following anecdotes show the undoubting faith with
which he relied on the Divine openings in his mind. He
says:—

"There was Justin T——, who was with me in Devon-
shire; we were companions in drunkenness and came home
to Cornwall at the same time. I was converted before he
was; and when I told my comrades what danger the wicked
were in, and where they would go if they died in sin, they
would persecute me and call me a fool. But J. T. used to
say, 'You shall leave that man alone and say nothing to
him, for I knew him when he was a drunkard, and now he
is a good man; I wish I was like him.' Then my heart
went out after J. T. One day when at work in the field,
I knelt down to pray for him. *The Lord spoke to my mind,*

* See note, p. 166.

'I will save him soon.' When I next saw him I told him I had good news for him, for while I was out in the field praying for him, the Lord told me he should be converted soon. And so he was. Shortly after his conversion he was taken ill. I saw him many times in his illness, and he told me he was happy in Jesus, and going to heaven to praise God forever."

On one occasion, in his capacity as captain-dresser, William Bray engaged to dress a quantity of ore, and had to employ a number of young persons. But the general opinion was, that the lot was all but worthless, and for a time it was a great trial to Billy as there would be nothing for him, and worse still, nothing for those under him. " Why, the people will say, there's that ould Billy Bray, an ould Bryanite, an ould rogue, he has cheated the boys and maidens of their wages. A pretty Christian he !" But Billy wrestled and labored in prayer, until he got the assurance that the Lord was on his way. (Dan. x. 9.) " I will bring thee through," the Lord said to him one day while he was praying; to which gracious word he at once answered, " I believe it, Lord, I know Thee wost (Thou wilt); praise the Lord, amen, glory. I don't care now what the devil says. If Thou tell me, that Thou wilt bring me through, I believe Thou wilt." And his foot once placed upon the rock, he was not to be moved. The struggle was again and again renewed, but to all suggestions, from whatever quarter they came, his answer was, " I don't care whether the stuff is worth anything or not. The Lord hath told me He will bring me through, and I believe Him." And did the Lord disappoint His servant? or leave " him at last in trouble to sink?" No, no! On the " sampling " day the " stuff" was found to be more valuable than any person expected, enabling Billy to pay the boys and girls their wages, his own, and then have five-pounds left for himself.

At one time he had a child seriously ill, and his wife feared it would die. She wished Billy to go to the doctor, and get some medicine. He took eighteenpence in his pocket, all the money there was in the house. On the road he met a man who had lost a cow, and was then out beg-

20*

ging for money to buy another, whose story touched Billy's heart, and to him the money was at once given. He said afterwards, " I felt after I had given away the money that it was no use to go to the doctor, for I could not have medicine without money, so I thought I would tell Father about it. I jumped over a hedge, and while telling the Lord all about it, I felt sure the ' cheeld ' would live. I then went home, and as I entered the door, said to my wife, ' Joey, the cheeld's better, isn't it?' ' Yes,' she said. ' The cheeld will live, the Lord has told me so,' " was his answer, and the child soon got well.

During his wife's long illness, which ended in death, he "had many blessed seasons while praying with her, and promises from the dear Lord." At one time the words were so deeply impressed on his mind, "She is mine forever," that tears came into his eyes. At another time he was greatly comforted by the conviction, inwrought into his heart by the power of the Holy Ghost, that he himself, his wife and family, should be saved. Therefore he said, " I had no reason to doubt of my wife's going to heaven ; nevertheless the devil often tempted me that, because I was not home with her when she died, it was not well with her. But the devil could not make me believe it. Since the dear Lord has settled the matter, *the old king of the blacks* does not tempt me that she is not in heaven. When the dear Lord speaks to His children's hearts, He speaks the truth; He is a God of truth, and all who love Him are children of the truth."

The editor of the *Earnest Christian* mentions meeting with a friend who had been an active, stirring man, but who had lost one foot and part of the other, and was then on his way to a place where he could be provided with artificial limbs. He had gone to see him with some anxiety as to how the misfortune was being endured. But the greeting of the patient was cordial and pleasant, and his tone full of peace and joy. During a two hours' visit, he conversed not on the affliction but the blessings that had come from this visitation of Providence—though he was in the prime of life and had a family to support. Faith in the goodness and care of a Heavenly Father was sufficient to keep the mind quiet and peaceful.

G. M. Howe relates the following incident, which he heard from the lips of an eye witness.

Some years ago, while travelling upon a steamer on one of the Southern rivers, the captain stopped at a landing to receive a score or more of slaves who were to be shipped down the river. When the poor, frightened crèatures were all gathered upon the deck the captain opened a trap door and ordered them all to descend. The less timid ones at once obeyed, but presently a middle aged negress was led to the ladder and told to follow her companions below. She gazed shrinkingly for a moment down into the darkness, and then starting back exclaimed, "Oh, massa, I can't go down there, it's *so* dark!" The more they urged her to descend the more reluctant she seemed to be to go. And to their solicitations, commands and threats would reply, "I can't go, it's so dark down there." So genuine was her grief and fear that many hearts were touched with sympathy for her. After standing with her hands folded meekly over her breast for a few minutes, her lips moving as if in prayer, she looked up and said, "Yes, I'll go; there is no place too dark for the Lord Jesus," and suiting the action to the words she stepped cheerfully down the ladder into the dense darkness.

Somewhere this poor slave woman had learned to love and trust the blessed Saviour, and when her faith in Him had gained the mastery over her physical fear, a sweet calm filled her troubled heart, and she was willing to go anywhere, even into this dark hold of the steamer that was to bear her far away from all she held dear in life, because she felt that Jesus would be present with her.

This dependence on a Higher Power appears to have been a prominent trait in the character of Abraham Lincoln, President of the United States. His biographer says of him:—

He believed in God, and in his personal supervision of the affairs of men. He believed himself to be under his control and guidance. He believed in the power and ultimate triumph of the right, through his belief in God. This unwavering faith in a Divine Providence began at his mother's knee, and ran like a thread of gold through all the inner experiences of his life. His constant sense of human duty was one of the forms by which his faith manifested itself. He recognized an immediate relation between God and himself in all the actions and passions of his life.

This constant reference to the Divine will, and dependance on an overruling Providence, is well illustrated by a conversation which took place during the interval between his nomination for the office of President of the United States and his election. Abraham Lincoln was well known to be opposed to slavery, and to any extension of the system. Its advocates were greatly excited, and were then plotting those treasonable measures which involved this country in a costly and bloody war. Lincoln knew he was entering upon a path full of danger, overshadowed with doubt and fear; and he deeply felt the burthen. But he believed that he was an instrument in the hands of God for the accomplishment of a great purpose. He felt that in the struggle before him he ought to be supported by the Christian sentiment and the Christian influence of the nation.

Newton Bateman, Superintendent of Public Instruction for the State of Illinois, occupied a room adjoining and opening into the Executive Chamber. Frequently this door was open during Lincoln's receptions; and throughout the seven months or more of his occupation, Bateman saw him nearly every day. Often when Lincoln was tired, he closed his door against all intrusion, and called Bateman into his room for a quiet talk.

On one of these occasions, in the course of the conversation, he dwelt much upon the necessity of faith in the Christian's God, as an element of successful statesmanship, especially in times like those which were upon him, and said that it gave that calmness and tranquillity of mind, that assurance of ultimate success, which made a man firm and immovable amid the wildest excitements. After further reference to a belief in Divine providence, and the fact of God in history, the conversation turned upon prayer. He freely stated his belief in the duty, privilege and efficacy of prayer, and intimated, in no unmistakable terms, that he had sought in that way the Divine guidance and favor.

The effect of this conversation upon the mind of Bateman, a Christian gentleman whom Lincoln profoundly respected, was to convince him that Lincoln had, in his quiet way, found a path to the Christian standpoint—that he found God, and rested on the eternal truth of God. As the two men were about to separate, Bateman remarked: " I have not supposed that you were accustomed to think so much upon this class of subjects. Certainly your friends generally are ignorant of the sentiments you have expressed to me." He replied quickly: " I know they are. I am obliged to appear different to them; but I think more on these subjects than upon all others, and I· have done so for years; and I am willing that *you* should know it."

His biographer makes this comment. " This remarkable conversation furnishes a golden link in the chain of Lincoln's history. It flashes a strong light upon the path he had already trod, and illuminates every page of his subsequent record. Men have wondered at his abounding charity, his love of men, his equanimity under the most distressing circumstances, his patience under insult and misrepresentation, his delicate consideration of the feelings of the humble, his apparent incapacity of resentment, his love of justice, his transparent simplicity, his truthfulness, his good will toward his enemies, his beautiful and unshaken faith in the triumph of the right. There was undoubtedly something in his natural constitution that favored the development of these qualities; but those best acquainted with human nature will . hardly attribute the combination of excellencies which were exhibited in his character and life to the unaided forces of his constitution. The man who prayed, who thought more of religious subjects than of all others, who had an undying faith in the providence of God, drew his life from the highest fountains."

The dependence for success on Divine help which has been referred to, as an important element in the character of Abraham Lincoln, is further illustrated after his election, by the touching remarks he made to his fellow-citizens of Springfield, Illinois, who collected at the railroad station as he was leaving home to enter on the duties of President of the United States.

"My friends," said he, "no one not in my position, can appreciate the sadness I feel at this parting. To this people I owe all that I am. Here I have lived more than a quarter of a century. Here my children were born, and here one of them lies buried. I know not how soon I shall see you again. A duty devolves upon me which is greater, perhaps, than that which has devolved upon any other man since the days of Washington. He never would have succeeded, except for the aid of Divine Providence, upon which he at all times relied. I feel that I cannot succeed without the same Divine aid which sustained him; and on the same Almighty Being I place my reliance for support; and I hope you, my friends, will pray that I may receive that Divine assistance, without which I cannot succeed, but with which success is certain."

This was so unlike the usual language of a politician, that those who knew not the simple and earnest truthfulness of the man, knew not how to understand it.

His biographer says his religion "was one which sympathized with all human sorrow; which lifted, so far as it had the power, the burden from the oppressed; which let the prisoner go free; and which called daily for supplies of strength and wisdom from the Divine fountains. He grew more religious with every passing year of his official life. The tender piety that breathed in some of his later state papers is unexampled in any of the utterances of his predecessors. In all great emergencies of his closing years, his reliance upon Divine guidance and assistance was often extremely touching. ' I have been driven many times to my knees,' he once remarked, ' by the overwhelming conviction that I had no where else to go. My own wisdom and that of all about me seemed insufficient for that day.' On another occasion, when told that he was daily remembered in the prayers of those who prayed, he said that he had been a good deal helped by the thought ; and then he added with much solemnity : ' I should be the most presumptuous blockhead upon this footstool, if I for one day thought that I could discharge the duties which have come upon me since I came into this place, without the aid and enlightenment of One who is wiser and stronger than all others.' "

When the time came for issuing the Emancipation Proclamation, which converted millions of slaves into freemen, and Abraham Lincoln was detailing to his Cabinet, the reasons which influenced him in believing that to be the right time, he added in a low and reverent tone, " I have promised my God that I will do it." These last words were hardly heard by any but Salmon P. Chase,* who sat nearest to him. He inquired, " Did I understand you correctly, Mr. President?" Lincoln replied : " I made a solemn vow before God that, if General Lee should be driven back from Pennsylvania, I would crown the result by the declaration of freedom to the slaves."

The Second Inaugural Address of Abraham Lincoln is a remarkable document. It thus refers to the two parties in the war then raging,—

" Both read the same Bible and pray to the same God,

*Afterwards appointed Chief Justice of the Supreme Court of the United States. Died in 1873.

and each invokes his aid against the other. It may seem strange that any men should dare to ask a just God's assistance in wringing their bread from the sweat of other men's faces; but let us judge not, that we be not judged. The prayers of both could not be answered. That of neither has been answered fully. The Almighty has his own purposes. 'Woe unto the world because of offences, for it must needs be that offences come : but woe to that man by whom the offence cometh.' If we shall suppose that American slavery is one of these offences, which in the providence of God must needs come, but which, having continued through his appointed time, He now wills to remove, and that He gives to both North and South this terrible war as the woe due to those by whom the offence came, shall we discern therein any departure from those Divine attributes which the believers in a living God always ascribe to Him? Fondly do we hope, fervently do we pray, that this mighty scourge of war may soon pass away. Yet, if God wills that it continue until all the wealth piled by the bondmen's two hundred and fifty years of unrequited toil shall be sunk, and until every drop of blood drawn with the lash shall be paid with another drawn with the sword ; as was said three thousand years ago, so still it must be said, 'The judgments of the Lord are true and righteous altogether.'"

The *Parlor Magazine* relates a pleasant anecdote in which the unhesitating trust of a child opened the heart of the man on whose word he relied.

When Doctor Byron was one day passing into the house, he was accosted by a very little boy, who asked him if he wanted any sauce, meaning vegetables. The doctor inquired if such a little thing was a market man. "No, sir ; my father is," was the prompt answer. The doctor said, "Bring me some squashes," and paid him the money. In a few moments the child returned with the change. The doctor told him he was welcome to it, but the child would not keep it, saying his father would blame him. Such singular manners in a child attracted his attention, and he began to examine the child attentively. He was evidently poor ;

for his jacket was patched with almost every kind of cloth, and his trowsers darned with so many colors it was difficult to tell the original fabric, but very neat and clean withal. The boy quietly endured the scrutiny of the doctor while examining his face. At length he said, "You seem a nice little boy; won't you come and live with me, and be a doctor?"

"Yes, sir," said the child.

"Spoken like a man," said the doctor, dismissing him.

A few weeks passed on, when one day Jim came to say there was a little boy with a bundle down stairs, waiting to see the doctor, and would not tell his business to any one else.

"Send him up," was the answer, and in a few moments he recognized the boy who sold him the squashes. He was dressed in a new, though coarse, suit of clothes, his hair nicely combed, shining shoes, and a little bundle under his arm. Deliberately taking off his hat, and laying it down with his bundle, he walked up to the doctor, saying, "I have come, sir."

"Come for what, my child?"

"To live with you, and be a doctor," said the child with the utmost naiveté.

The first impulse of the doctor was to laugh immoderately; but the imperturbable gravity of the little fellow rather sobered him as he recalled, too, his former conversation; and he silently felt he needed no addition to his family.

"Did your father consent to your coming?" he asked.

"Yes, sir."

"What did he say?"

"I told him you wanted me to come and live with you and be a doctor, and he said you were a very good man, and I might come as soon as my clothes were ready."

"And your mother, what did she say?"

"She said Doctor Byron would do what he said he would, and God had provided for me. And," said he, "I have on a new suit of clothes," surveying himself, "and here is another in the bundle," undoing the kerchief and displaying them, with two little shirts white as snow, and a couple of neat checked aprons so carefully folded it was plain none

21

but a mother would have done it.   The doctor's sensibilities
were awakened to see the undoubting trust with which that
poor couple had bestowed their child upon him, and such
a child!   His cogitations were not long.   He thought of
Moses in the bulrushes, abandoned to Providence, and
above all he thought of the child that was carried into
Egypt; and that Divine Saviour had said, "Blessed be little
children;" and he called for his wife, saying, "Susan, dear,
I think we pray in church that God will have mercy upon
all young children."

"To be sure we do," said the wondering wife: "and what
then?"

"And the Saviour said, 'Whoever receiveth one such little child in my name, receiveth me.'   Take this child in his
name, and take care of him."

From this hour the good couple received him to their
hearts and home.   It did not then occur to them that one
of the most eminent physicians and best men of the age
stood before them in the person of that child, nor that he
was destined to be their staff and stay in declining age,—
a protector to their daughter, and more than a son to themselves.   All this was at that time unrevealed; but they
cheerfully received the child they believed Providence had
committed to their care, and if ever beneficence was rewarded, it was in this case.

There is no more certain truth, or of more practical importance in our course through life, than that "The Spirit
of the Almighty giveth understanding."   Especially is this
important as it refers to the enlightening influence of the
Spirit of Christ, graciously bestowed on all who will receive
and obey it, to guide them into and in the way of peace,
and out of spiritual darkness.   Some may be disposed to
question its universal extension, when they see so many of
mankind walking in the way of evil, and apparently destitute
of any conviction that they are doing wrong; but these
cases are only illustrations of the truth of the scripture de-

claration: "Light has come into the world, but men loved darkness rather than light, because their deeds were evil."

This Divine guidance in the way they should go, through the impressions on the mind of the Holy Spirit, is the experience of every true Christian of all religious denominations; and is continually known by those who are walking in that highway cast up for the ransomed and redeemed of the Lord. It was the experience of the patriarchs, prophets and saints of olden times; and it is the especial mark of the more perfect dispensation under which we live; for it was prophesied of it, that the Lord would pour out his Spirit on all flesh.

Besides this general guidance, which all continually need, there is abundant evidence that the Lord at times gives to his servants such an insight into the thoughts of others, and such impressions as to the path that He would have them pursue as may be needful to enable them to perform the services which He requires of them.

Among the anecdotes of David Sands,* is one recorded in his journal which shows that the thoughts of others are at times revealed to the Lord's servants.

Many years ago, David and a companion were visiting in Maine, then a newly settled country, and remained for several days at one place. A man of some note in that place, named Remington Hobby, remarked to his wife, "These Quakers seem to be respectable people, and I do not think they are very well accommodated where they are staying; I have a mind to invite them to our house." She approved of it, and he accordingly gave them an invitation, which was accepted. On arriving at his house, instead of entering into familiar conversation, the Friends were drawn

---

* A minister in the Society of Friends, residing at Cornwall, New York, who labored extensively in the Gospel in various parts of the United States, in Great Britain, France, Germany, and other parts of Europe. Died in 1818, aged seventy-two years.

into silence.   This being new to their host, he did not understand it, and at length concluded it must be because they did not like their entertainment in being received in the kitchen.   He thought, perhaps if I make a fire in the best room, and take them there, they will like it better and be more sociable.   Accordingly he did so; and still David was drawn into silence, and not disposed to enter into conversation, to the great disappointment of Remington, who began to feel sorry that he had taken so much pains to accommodate them, saying to himself, "Either they are fools, or else they think I am one."

As this thought was passing through his mind, David turned to him and said, "Art thou willing to be a fool; art thou willing to be a fool for Christ's sake?" and went on preaching to him until he was so fully convinced, that he joined himself to David and his companion, going with and assisting them in their journey; and was soon brought forth as a fellow laborer with them in the work of the ministry. So devoted in spirit did he become, and so diligent in his labors for the Master, that, in after years, he said, his own house was but as an inn, in which he might rest himself occasionally.

The closer our communion with our Heavenly Father, and the more attentively we watch to know the revelations of his will, the more quick we will become in seeing the path in which He designs that we should walk.   While careful to avoid mistaking the mere suggestions of the imagination for the pointings of duty, we may, through faithfulness, become "quick of discernment in the fear of the Lord." These pointings will often be found to direct us to things from which we naturally shrink; but the experience of the willing-hearted is in accordance with what William Penn* says: "Christ's cross is Christ's way to Christ's crown;"

---

*Eminent as a minister, statesman and author. The founder of Pennsylvania.   Born 1644, died 1718.   See *Life in Friends' Library*, vol. 5, p. 23, etc.

and that which is done from a sense of duty is often followed by a sweet and peaceful feeling.

There are many instances of the safety and comfort to be found in following the pointings of the Divine finger. When George Withy,* of England, was in this country, he was accompanied in a part of his travels by the late Thomas Evans, to whom he related the following incident:

He was travelling alone, paying a religious visit in Wales. He had been at a meeting in the morning, and was going to another to be held in the afternoon. As he was riding along, he felt a sudden impression that it would be right to turn round and go directly home. So unexpected and sudden an impression caused some hesitation; and he stopped and weighed the thing in the best manner he could. The result was, that he must go home, and as quickly as he could. He did so, and travelled all night, reaching home in the morning. Here he found that a niece had been drowned about the time the impression was made on his mind. His wife had a family of children; and his presence and assistance were almost indispensable.

John Knox,† the Scottish reformer, is said to have been saved from death by attending to an internal admonition. He was accustomed to sit at the head of his table with his back towards a window. One evening, in obedience to a feeling which covered his mind, he would neither take that seat himself, nor suffer any of his family to do so. Whilst they were sitting round the table, a bullet, evidently fired with the intention of killing him, passed through the window, grazed the back of the unoccupied chair, and buried itself in the foot of the candlestick.

Matthew Warren, a pious man, was exposed to persecution during the reigns of Charles II. and James II., of Eng-

---

* An English minister, who travelled in America on a religious visit and died in 1837, aged seventy-four years.

† A noted Scoth Reformer. Born 1505. Died 1572. A man of great zeal, fervor and courage. It was said over his grave, "Here lies he who never feared the face of man."

land, on account of his religious principles. At one time he was remarkably preserved from the hands of those who sought to seize him, by a strong impression made on the mind of his wife, that unless he left the house in which he was then sheltered before a particular hour, he would be taken prisoner. Under this feeling, she sent a messenger to him with a letter, stating her desire that he would be at his own house at the hour specified, or else he might never see her more. Supposing her to be ill, he immediately took leave of his friend, and set homewards.

From the summit of the first ascent, he looked back towards the house he had left, and found it surrounded by the persons who were seeking him.

In a letter written by the late Joseph Kite, in 1852, I find the following anecdotes of Elizabeth L. Redman,* of Haddonfield, which furnish additional illustrations of the safety and importance of walking in the *light:*

" On the 24th (of Tenth Month) our dear, innocent and loving friend, Elizabeth L. Redman, departed this life in her sixty-seventh year. She appeared much in the simplicity in her ministerial labors; yet she was often very remarkably led in humble obedience to heavenly monitions, where human reasoning would have led astray. Dost thou remember the case of Clough the murderer, who was confined in Mount Holly jail? After he was condemned, a concern came upon Elizabeth's mind to visit him; and she laid the prospect before Friends at Haddonfield, who encouraged her to attend to her concern, and nominated two individuals to accompany her. When they came to take her, the prospect had been suddenly closed, and she dared not move. A few days after, the concern clearly revived, and the Friends were sent for and the visit paid; which was relieving to her own mind, and tendering to that of the convict. The remarkable part of it was, that when the concern passed from her view, the prisoner had broken jail and escaped; and

---

* A minister in the Society of Friends, who resided at Haddonfield, N. J. Born 1785. Died 1852. See *Memorials of Deceased Friends* of Philadelphia Yearly Meeting.

when it recurred, he had just been retaken and confined. Had she moved on in the dark, the visit to Mount Holly would have been fruitless, and cavillers might have had room to say, she was under a delusion. Poor Clough said, that if any one had exhibited such a religious concern for his soul's welfare before, he had not been in that condition.

"Somewhat similar in regard to the necessity of attending to the pointings of the finger of Truth, was a circumstance Sarah Hillman related at our house. Elizabeth L. Redman, when on a visit in Bucks County, was passing along the road to meeting, when she felt a warning given her to a man who was working by the road-side. She put it by for the present, under the impression that she should be late at meeting. The message to him was, 'Prepare for death.' After meeting she went to Ruth Ely's to dine, with the omission of duty pressing hard on her. She asked one of the domestics if she knew such a man describing him. But she did not. Elizabeth then went into the kitchen to inquire of the cook, who, from the description, remembered the man. Elizabeth then bid her to tell him from her, to prepare himself for death for his days were nearly numbered. The cook probably promised, but failed to deliver the message; and the man shortly after was thrown from a load of boards, and his neck broken! How important that we do our individual duty, nor trust to others to do it for us."

A little incident related by the wife of a sea captain illustrates the manner in which the Almighty often leads his children, showing his obedient followers each successive step which they are to take, and enabling them to pass in safety over many dangers.

"We were on shipboard," said she, "lying in a Southern harbor, and we were obliged, first, to make our way ashore. The waves were rolling heavily. I became frightened at the thought of attempting it, when one came to me saying, 'Do not be afraid: I will take care of you.' He bore a peculiarly shaped dark-lantern, only a single ray of light being emitted from a small, circular aperature. 'Now,' he said, ' take my hand ; hold fast, do not fear. Do not look about you, or on either side of you, only on the little spot lighted by my lantern, and place your footsteps firmly *right there.*' I heard the rushing of the waters, and was still conscious of fear ; but by looking steadily only where the light fell, and planting my footsteps just there, not turning either to the right or the left, clasping firmly the strong hand, the danger was overcome and the shore reached in safety. The next day, my kind guide said, ' Would you like to see the way by which you came last night ? ' Then he showed me where our vessel had been lying, and the very narrow plank (just a single one) by which we had reached the shore. He knew that, had I turned either to the right or to the left, I should in all probability have lost my balance, and gone over into those dark waters ; but by ' holding fast,' and treading just where the light fell, all danger would be averted."

One of the most blessed promises from the Lord to his people in ancient times, is that in which it is declared that He would put his law into their minds and write it on their hearts. The pure law of the Lord condemning all iniquity is written on the hearts of all through the inshining of the Light of Christ, so that if man will sincerely and humbly wait for, observe and follow its teachings, he may be led out of all sin, and enabled to walk acceptably before God. This communion with his Creator is a blessed reality ; and is as an anchor to the soul of the Christian in times of trial. As he grows in religious experience, he learns to depend more and more fully on the teaching of the Spirit, and becomes more quick of discernment ; so that he is less likely to be led astray by the suggestions of his own imagination, which he might be in danger of mistaking for the leadings of the Spirit.

These Divine intimations are often extended for the guidance and help of the Lord's children even in their outward affairs. A striking instance of this is seen in the following narrative of Joseph Lybrand.

Jospeph Lybrand* was a minister of the Methodist Episcopal Church, and in the summer of 18—, had charge of a congregation in the upper part of the city of Philadelphia, his home being in Crown Street, above Race Street. On a certain First-day morning, he crossed the river to Camden, N. J., having engaged to preach both morning and evening to a Methodist congregation there, intending to spend the time between the two services at the house of one of his brethren in that town.

. Shortly after dinner he told his host that he must return to Philadelphia. On being asked why? he answered that he did not know why, only that he must return. His friend was quite grieved to hear him say so, and expostulated with him, urging that he had promised to preach at both the services; that the congregation that would meet in the evening would be greatly disappointed, and that he would be ashamed to tell the people that the minister felt that he must return to the city, but could give no reason for his conduct.

By this time the sense of duty had become clearer, and J. Lybrand answered that though he knew not the object of his return, he was well satisfied it was a Divine intimation that he must not, and could not, resist.

Leaving the house of his friend, he directed his steps towards the Market Street Ferry, for by it he was accustomed to cross the river. Soon he found that that was not the right path, but that he must walk a long distance, exposed to the scorching rays of the sun, to the Cooper's Point Ferry, which would land him at Callowhill Street. Wondering, but satisfied to follow Divine leading, wheresoever it might carry him, in due time he stepped ashore at Callowhill Street wharf, and walking up the hill, as he crossed Water Street, the cries of a little child fell on his ear.

---

* A Methodist minister. Born in Philadelphia in 1793, and died in 1845. The notice of him in the *Cyclopedia of Methodism* says, "His name will remain a sweet savor to thousands of our Israel throughout the States of New Jersey, Delaware, Maryland and Pennsylvania." His last words were, "Last year I had such a sweet and precious communion with God; and now I close my eyes to sleep, hoping that sleeping or waking, my thoughts will be of Him and with Him."

Musing upon the wondrous way in which God was leading him, he was so absorbed in contemplation that for a moment he gave no heed to the cry, 'twas but for a moment, the next instant the earnest sympathy of his nature, and his intense love for little children, were fully aroused by the piteous crying that plainly told of no common sorrow. Turning quickly to learn the cause, he saw a great rough man leading, or rather dragging, a little boy of about three years of age, who was crying bitterly, and exerting his puny strength to retard his steps. On asking why the child was in such distress, the man let go of him and ran away, and then J. Lybrand, to his horror and to his great joy, saw that the wretched looking little creature, so begrimed in person and clothing, was his own son, whom till this moment he had failed to recognize. The leading was now plain, and the blessing of obedience manifest.

As to how the little fellow came to be in the street—it seems that early in the afternoon his mother went up stairs, leaving him to play below, and finding the gate unfastened he went out. How far he went before he was kidnapped was never known, but he could not have been long away, for his mother had missed him but a little while before his father brought him home.

The whole life of the Christian is a continued experience of Divine guidance; for it is by the Light of Christ that he is enabled to distinguish good from evil, and know how to choose the one and reject the other. And this Light not only points out the evil, and warns man to forsake it, but it guides his steps in the accomplishment of those services and duties which he is called upon to perform. This is illustrated in a narrative which a person gave of the manner in which he was helped to heal a breach of friendship which had greatly troubled him. He said:—

One day I had some difficulty with one of my neighbors, and he let in hardness towards me, so that he would not speak when we met, and he would not shake hands with me. I felt very much cast down and distressed in my mind both day and night; so I cried inwardly to the Lord for deliverance out of this state, and that the unity and good feeling between us might be restored. One day, as I was sitting in meeting, waiting in silence on the Lord, He put it into my heart to go to the man as soon as meeting ended; so, before I had spoken to any one, or had eaten or drank, I went in the faith, and found my neighbor alone in the barn, threshing. He threw down his flail and looked very much surprised. We both stood still for some time, until tears began to run down my face; he then shed tears also. I told him of the great distress I had felt day and night. He said it had been the case with him too. So we made friends, and the unity was never again broken, for afterwards, when we met, we always had good feelings.

The following incident in the experience of Thos. Waring, a Friend of Leominster, England, was related by a clergyman of the Church of England, who had a high respect for the character of the good old man. As he sat one afternoon, in his shop, among his work people, it was strongly impressed on his mind that he must set off directly to the neighboring town of Ross. It was winter time; the days were short, and the weather none of the best. The idea seemed so strange to him that he tried to get rid of it, but he could not free his mind of what appeared to be his duty. It was impressed upon him like a mission, and he was one of those pure, simple and obedient spirits, that once knowing the will of God, he must implicitly obey it.

He rose from the seat where he was at work, and gave orders that his horse should be immediately saddled. It was four o'clock in the afternoon, and thirty miles to Ross. He stopped at Hereford to bait his horse, and, in order to lose no time, fed it with oatmeal mash, and resumed his journey. Is was late in the night when he approached Ross, and still his business there remained unknown to him. In passing over the Wye, however, as he entered the town, he cast his eyes upward, and saw in the darkness of the night, and amid the tall, dark houses, a light in an attic window, and immediately it was revealed to him that there lay his mission, and that in going there all would be made plain.

He lost not a moment, but riding directly up to the door, knocked loudly. No one came, and while waiting, he gave his horse in charge to a boy in the street, bidding him take it to a brother Quaker's, one George Dow, and say that the owner of the horse would sleep at his house that night. Any one but a simple man full of faith, as old Thomas Waring was, would have feared lest the boy should run off with the horse, but the boy conveyed both the horse and the message faithfully.

After waiting long at the door of the house, a young woman opened it, and timidly asked, "what he pleased to want?" He told her in all simplicity that he did not know, but that if she would listen for a few moments to what he had to say, perhaps she herself might explain it. She invited him in, and he related to her the way his mind had been impressed, remarking in conclusion, "And having told this, I can only repeat that I do not know for what I am come."

The young woman was much affected, and wept bitterly. "Sir," said she, "I can tell you for what you are come; it is to save me. I was gone into that upper room with a firm intention of putting an end to my life, which has become very miserable. Nothing would have prevented me from committing suicide had you not come. God has sent you. I now see that I am not altogether forsaken or abandoned by Him." "Thou art not forsaken of God, indeed," said the good man, himself deeply affected, as he went on to pour hope and consolation into her sorrowful spirit.

Many are the remarkable incidents recorded, where the impressions fastened on the minds of individuals have been instrumental in saving themselves or others from impending dangers. One of these refers to R. Bourdman, who was travelling from Mould to Parkgate in Flintshire, Wales.

After riding some miles, he asked a man if he was on the road to that place, who replied, "Yes, but you will have sands to pass over, and unless you ride fast you will be in danger of being enclosed by the tide." It then began to snow so fast that he could hardly see his way. He, however, got to the sands, and pursued his journey over them, till the tide came in and surrounded him on every side, so that he could neither proceed nor turn back; and to ascend the perpendicular rocks was impossible. In this situation, he says—"I commended my soul to God, not having the least expectation of escaping death. In a little time I perceived two men running down a hill on the other side of the water; and by some means they got into a boat and came to my relief, just as the sea had reached my knee as I sat on my saddle.

"They took me into the boat, the mare swimming by our side till we reached land. While we were in the boat, one of the men said, 'Surely, sir, God is with you.' I answered, 'I trust He is.' The man replied, 'I know He is,' and then, related the following circumstance: 'Last night I dreamed that I must go to the top of the hill. When I awoke, the dream made such an impression on my mind that I could not rest. I therefore went and called on this man to accompany me. When we came to the place, we saw nothing more than usual. However, I begged him to go with me to another at a small distance, and there we saw your distressed situation.' "

I find in a manuscript volume of a friend, an account given by E. J. Way, of his own narrow escape from injury or death. He had been in attendance at a camp-meeting, and left it on the morning of the last day. He says: "About two miles out from the ground I met the stage which was going up to the camp for persons who were to leave. Having been up all the preceding night, and laboring hard for several days, I was both tired and sleepy. As the horse was going along steadily, I fell into a doze. How long I slept I know not, but I was greatly oppressed with a sense of danger. Rousing from sleep, I discovered myself in a narrow piece of road, with a high embankment on each side; but everything was safe. I looked to see what had so strongly excited my fears, but found nothing. Happening to look behind me, I saw the stage which had passed awhile before, coming back. The vehicle was empty, and

22

the horses were running furiously.   The road was too narrow for them to pass without tearing my sulky to pieces. Escape seemed impossible, but suddenly turning my horse, I drove him up the steep bank just in time to save my life. I could not but lift up my heart in gratitude to God, who had so strangely warned and timely delivered me."

Dr. Guthrie* narrates an experience of his own which furnishes an additional illustration of this subject.   He was in the habit of occasionally calling upon a poor widow, who was helpless from paralysis, and was tended by a very dutiful daughter who worked in a neighboring flax mill, toiled hard and lived sparingly, that she might help to maintain her mother.   Before leaving the cottage for her work, she was in the habit of heaping up the refuse of the mill in the grate and kindling it.   She placed her helpless mother in a chair before the fire, and as this fuel burned slowly away, the old women was kept comfortable till her return.   Dr. Guthrie says :—

"It happened one day I took my way down the winding dell to the cottage of the old woman, which stood in its garden embowered among trees.   But having met a parishioner with whom I had some subject of interest to talk about, I called a halt, and sitting on a bank of thyme, we entered into conversation.   Ere the subject was half exhausted, the widow rose to my recollection.   I felt somehow I must cut it short and hasten on my visit.   But the idea was dismissed and the conversation continued.   However, it occurred again and again, till, with a feeling that I was neglecting a call of duty, as by an uncontrollable impulse I rose to my feet and made haste to the cottage. Opening the door a sight met my view that for a moment nailed me to the spot.

"The erection of mill refuse which had been built from the hearth some feet up the open wide chimney, having its

* Probably Thomas Guthrie, a distinguished minister of the Free Church of Scotland. Born 1800.

foundation eaten away, had fallen, and precipitating itself forward, surrounded the helpless paralytic with a circle of fire. The accident took place some minutes before I entered. She had cried out, but no ear was there to hear her, nor hand to help. Catching the loose refuse about her, on and on, nearer and nearer the flames crept. By the time I had entered it had almost reached her, where she sat motionless, speechless, pale as death, looking down on the fire as it was about to seize her clothes and burn her to a cinder. Ere it caught I had time, and no more, to make one bound from the door to the hearth-stone, and seizing her chair and all in my arms, to pluck her from the jaws of a cruel fiery death."

To his narrative, Dr. Guthrie appends the following reflections: "By what law of nature, when I lingered on the road, was I moved, without the remotest idea of her danger, to cut short against all my inclinations, an interesting conversation, and hurry on to the house, which I reached just in the nick of time? One or two minutes later, the flames had caught her clothes and I had found her in a blaze of fire. Be it mine to live and die in the belief of a present and presiding God!"

In the winter of 1845, in one of the towns of New England, a youthful mother and her little children were brought into great straits. The husband and father was from home, and their stock of food was nearly exhausted, but a few ounces of Indian meal being left. The night was dark, the snow deep, and the paths unbroken. In her distress the poor woman offered to God the prayer for "daily bread," which our Saviour taught his disciples."

In another part of the city a young lawyer of pious character was sitting in his room. His mind seemed to be brought into sympathy with those in distress, and his thoughts turned to the dwellers in the cottage of this praying mother. He knew nothing of their special needs, and he had never spoken with them, but their case seemed to lie upon his heart, and a secret impulse urged him to go to their relief. He sallied out into the snow, purchased five loaves of bread at a baker's, and, making his way to their house, knocked at the door. It was opened by the woman, to whom he handed the loaves, and then departed, with a peaceful mind.

Not only were her present wants thus relieved, but the remembrance of this deliverance often acted as a stimulus to her faith in subsequent times of trial, strengthening her to believe that the Lord would still be mindful of her, hear her petitions, and send help in his own time and way.

A somewhat similar instance is related of a widow woman named Safford, residing in the town of Mercer, Maine, who was left, in the year 1832, with three children to provide for, by the death of her husband, without other means of support than the labor of her own hands. Of course she had the ordinary trials and privations of poverty to endure. When winter came, a severe storm, occurring near the close of a week accompanied with bitter cold, prevented her from securing her usual store of supplies; and First-day morning found her with only wood enough to make a single fire. When the fire was nearly burned out, the daughter asked her mother if they should not bury in the ashes the last remaining brand, and so preserve it for a little while. The mother said "no;" and expressed her belief that the Lord would certainly supply their needs.

That same morning, a Christian woman, the wife of a Methodist minister, who lived not far distant, retired alone in her room to hold communion with the Lord. As she endeavored to draw near to Him in spirit, her mind turned towards her neighbor Safford, with a feeling to send her some wood. It seemed so strange to be hauling wood on that day, that she dismissed the thought as a freak of her imagination, and sat down to read the Bible. But she found no life or comfort in its perusal, and the inward monitor still seemed to direct her to send some wood to the widow Safford. She hesitated no longer, but directed the boys to load the hand sled with wood and drag it through the snow to her neighbor's, saying, "I don't know as she wants any, but I must send it." Before the last stick was consumed on the widow's hearth, the boys arrived with their load, bringing enough to last them until more could be procured.

The Psalmist, in referring to the superintending care which the Lord exercises over his trusting children, makes this encouraging assertion : " In all thy ways acknowledge Him, and He shall direct thy steps." This is applicable to all our movements, both in temporal and spiritual matters. As to the latter, we all admit it, and generally in some degree attempt to act upon it; but in our outward affairs we are far more deficient in faith, and less disposed to submit them to the Divine judgment and disposal; and hence we often become involved in difficulties, which might have been avoided if there had been less self-will and self-confidence, and more of a humble seeking to the Lord for counsel.

These thoughts are connected at the present time, in the mind of the writer, with the removal of residence from one neighborhood to another—a matter in which serious mistakes are sometimes made. Some years ago a valuable friend lived in the compass of a country meeting, where he was esteemed by his friends, and was useful both as a citizen and as a member of religious society. In these respects, probably few in his own vicinity excelled him. Some family changes presented an inducement to move away from this sphere of usefulness, and he parted with his farm and took his family to reside in another neighborhood. The meeting he had left sustained a loss by his removal, but that to which he went was not benefited by his coming.

This case was an illustration of what Grattan,* the Irish orator meant, when he said that an oak at fifty ought not to be transplanted. He retained the esteem of his friends as a worthy man, but for many years, and in successive removals, he did not *take root* in the different meetings and

An Irish statesman. Born 1750. Died 1820. Distinguished for purity of life, and eloquent advocacy of the rights of his country.

22*

circles where he went.   Thus what ought to have been the
most useful period of his life, was comparatively wasted;
and he could scarcely be considered as having been har-
nessed again into religious service till the decline of life,
when strength and vigor were failing.

His example has often been remembered as showing the
need there is to consider well, before leaving the field of
usefulness in which any have been placed.

Yet there are cases, where the way clearly opens for
change, and where it is plainly the duty of individuals to
follow on in the way cast up before them, relying on that
Divine Power which can enrich them both with outward
and with spiritual blessings.

There are many who can bear witness as to the reality of
the guidance furnished by a wisdom higher than that of
man, to those who sincerely seek it, and follow its directions
even when they lead (as is often the case), in a way contrary to the natural inclinations.

John Richardson,* relates, that when about twenty-seven
years old, having for a time some release from the active
religious service in which he had been engaged, he wished
to settle more closely to business.   He says: "Upon seeking unto the Lord to know what place I might now settle
in, though my great inclination was for Whitby, yet it
sounded as in my ear, Bridlington, Bridlington is the place
to settle in; and in the cross, I repaired thither, and settled
for some time, keeping a little shop, and mended clocks and
watches, as I had done for several years past at times.   It
was of good service my settling there, for the Lord began
to work mightily, especially amongst the young Friends, so
that in a few years many had their mouths opened in testimony for the Lord, and a fine spring of heavenly ministry
was in that Monthly Meeting, the like I have not known
in the like bounds (for it is but a small Monthly Meeting,
and hath been so ever since I knew it).   For Truth did so

* See note, p. 77.

mightily prosper, and Friends grew so in the ministry, that it became a proverb, that Bridlington *was become a school of prophets.*"

When Joseph Hoag* was about to settle in life his mind was turned towards the small meeting in Little Nine Partners, in New York ; but he yielded to the suggestion that if he went there he would not prosper in business, and so took a farm in another neighborhood.   For several years he met with much trouble, and little success, though he labored hard.   At length, he says: "After living through many and varied trials, with an almost constant scene of conflict, and being permitted to get my mind into the quiet, I entered into deep searching of heart, to know the cause of all these troubles so continually coming upon me.   The Lord in his own time gave me to see, that if I had sought to Him for directions, instead of listening to others' contrivings, I might have been settled in Little Nine Partners for many years, and been in my right place, where the Lord's blessing would have been upon me; but as I had neglected his pointings therein, He had withheld his blessing.

"Having striven so long that I had neither money nor friends to help me, it now appeared clear that if I would give up and go into the new country, I would then be blessed.   It so settled on my mind that I told it to my wife, and opened my prospect to my own and my wife's relatives. Keeping steadily to the prospect, it brought my wife under deep concern.   It was not long before she told me, that she saw clearly there was a good farm for us in that country, and was willing to go with me, ever after remaining steady in the prospect; and I now believe we are on the very spot presented to her view.   When I opened it to my friends for their consent, they utterly denied me any liberty to move. In this situation they kept me for more than two years, which did not jostle or move me, feeling easy as having done all on my part, without feeling hard towards my friends; fully believing they would have to give it up. The Lord had shown me that I had much to suffer for my own neglect, so that I dared not murmur."

*See note, p. 100.

After a time, the way opened for them to move, and they settled in Vermont, where they witnessed a prosperous change, and soon became comfortably established.

It requires care that people do not imagine that every idea that may be suggested to their mind is a Divine impression; and, on the other hand, that they do not reject those feelings which are mercifully given for their guidance and help. Even the humble and sincere soul may for a time be in doubt what step to take where there is danger in either course; and this very doubt, and the conflict of mind it involves, may be part of that humbling discipline which our Father in Heaven sees to be good for it to pass through; but in due time it will experience the fulfilment of the promise, " Light is sown for the righteous, and gladness for the upright in heart."

That the Lord's servants are sometimes led in a manner for which they do not see an adequate reason, is shown in an anecdote preserved of George Richardson and Solomon Chapman. When they were engaged in a religious visit in Ireland, George felt a strong impression that it would not be best to hold a meeting in the meeting-house in a certain neighborhood, but that he must visit Friends in their families, going from house to house. As there was no known reason why a meeting should not be held, Solomon rather objected to its omission, because then other persons not members would be passed by, who often attended the meetings of Friends. But George's judgment was clear, and Solomon yielded. It was believed afterwards, that if the meeting had been held, the house could not have borne the pressure of the people, but would have fallen upon them. The roof was very heavy, and some of the timber much decayed, so that it fell on the evening of a Seventh-day, when there was no unusual wind or other exciting cause, the evening before the time when Friends were expecting to meet in it, to hold their usual First-day meeting.

The following incident is told by J. D. Hampton, who

listened to Joseph Hoag's relation of it, in his father's house in 1841.

When Joseph Hoag* was on a religious visit in the Southern States, he felt it right to have a meeting in a neighborhood where he was a stranger and Friends were not very well known. A full and attentive audience assembled.

When the meeting had settled into stillness, it was soon made manifest to him that he should speak of slavery and the evils thereof. At this he was almost ready to flinch, as he had good reason to believe that most of his audience were slaveholders.

While thus pondering the subject, and knowing the magnitude of it, he had some misgivings whether he should be able to treat the subject as it should be treated, and asked his Lord and Master to excuse him from speaking on that subject, lest he might not be able to do it justice, and the truth suffer by it. But the query came immediately, " have I ever required anything at thy hands that I did not enable thee to perform ; " to this he could not say nay. So he concluded that it would be safest for him to watch the pointings of his Master in this matter, as on other occasions. At the proper time he arose to his feet and took the subject of "Slavery and the Evils thereof" as his text. After the meeting closed, many of the slaveholders gathered about him, giving him an invitation, here and there, to dine with them ; and, as he could not go with them all, he accepted the hospitality of one, to whose home the others followed to the number of twelve or fifteen. After they were all seated in his stately parlor, Joseph began to talk upon the subject on which he had preached, continuing his conversation for about thirty minutes, not giving any one an opportunity to say anything ; and, just as be closed, the landlord made his appearance and announced that dinner was ready. All repaired to the dining room save one, a lawyer. The landlord gave him a pressing invitation, saying there was provision for all now in waiting. The lawyer replied: "I can't eat with that preacher." "Why?" asked the landlord. The lawyer said there was something about him that he couldn't

*See note, p. 100.

comprehend. " I was at his meeting, as you know, and did not like his subject, nor the manner in which he treated it, and so I concluded I would trap the old man by watching his discourse and taking note of such points as I thought he would not be able to answer. I followed him here for that purpose. To make it more effectual I have made known my intentions to no one. Here I have twelve questions arranged respecting his sermon, and while we were all in this room he has answered them. I can't eat with him; there is something about him I cannot comprehend."

There are many evidences that the Almighty does condescend to influence the minds of his children so as to guide them even as to the outward business in which they shall engage. Thomas Story* relates that he was educated for the practice of law, but after he had been divinely visited, and taken up a fixed resolution to seek first the kingdom of Heaven and the righteousness thereof, he says :

" I clearly perceived the practice of the law, and to be frequently in the suits and contests of the world, would be inconsistent with Divine peace in my own mind, expose me to many tempations, and confine me so as that I could not follow the Lord in that way wherein I understood He was leading me, and proposed to bring me forward ; that is, not only in sanctification and justification for my own salvation, but also in a public ministry of that holy and powerful Word of life ; by which the Lord of his own free will and grace had called me; and to that end, I knew was working in me qualifications suiting his own purpose thereby : And therefore my secret concern was how to get rid of that great and dangerous obstruction; well knowing it would very much oppose my father's views.

" Duty to the Almighty, and the will and terrene views of my natural parents becoming opposite, I remained not long in suspense what to do; for, as through grace I had been enabled to take up the cross of Christ in confessing his holy name, in the dispensation of God to his people at that time ;

* See note, p. 111.

so, by the same grace, I was likewise enabled to undergo the displeasure of my father, to close my eyes from all wordly views, and to stop my ears forever from hearkening to any preferments there; and being furnished with a full resolution in my mind to decline the practice of the law, though the only thing designed as a means of life, accordingly the next persons who came to employ me in business of that kind, I refused in my father's presence; and told them in his hearing, that I should not undertake business of that kind any more."

Thomas Story's subsequent experience justified his trust in his Heavenly Father; for in the intervals between the journeys which he performed in spreading the gospel tidings of salvation, he found such openings for business as appear to have supplied his needs.

There are few subjects on which people are more disposed to indulge in pleasantry with one another than that of marriage; and yet there is perhaps none more serious and important in its results, reaching through time and even into eternity; none in which there is greater need to know that we have Divine guidance and sanction.

John Richardson's* father died when he was quite young and his mother inclining to marry again with one who was of a different religious persuasion and was considered to be wealthy, John felt uneasy with the prospect, and told her, "he was afraid she had too much of an eye to what he had," "but if she thought to augment our portion in so marrying, the hand of the Lord would be against her, and a blasting or mildew would come upon even that which we had got through industry and hard labor, and what the Lord had intended to have blessed to us, if we kept faithful to the Truth, and contented ourselves with our present conditions."

Notwithstanding John's caution, the marriage took place, and the result was as he had foreseen. The difference in their religious views was destructive to the family har-

* See note, p. 77.

mony; and his father-in-law would not permit him to remain in the house, unless he would give up the attendance of his religious meetings and conform to his own manner of worship. John had been very faithful and diligent in his attention to business, and appears to have received no wages for his labor, being still a minor; but this availed not. He thus describes his expulsion from home:

"Notwithstanding I pleaded with my father to let me stay until I could hear of a place, he would not, though I was scarce fit for service, being almost like an anatomy (as the saying is), so that most who knew me said I would pine away in a consumption; but turn out I must, and did, though I was weak, poor and low in body, mind, pocket and clothes; for I think I had but twelve pence in my pocket, and very ordinary clothes upon my back. Thus I took my solemn leave of the family, with my heart full, but I kept inward to the Lord, and under Truth's government; many tears were shed in the family, especially by my poor mother, when I left them; my father said little, but appeared like one struck with wonder, to see so much love manifested toward me by the family, and so much wishing that I might not go away. But out I came on the great common, where I had had many solitary walks, but none like this, for this reason, that I knew not where to go."

When his step-father died, he left by his will five shillings to John, which was all the share he received of the family estate; confirming his prediction, that the marriage would bring a blasting and mildew upon even that which they had gotten through hard labor. John Richardson makes the following judicious comments upon these occurrences:

"I write this partly, that all who do marry, may take special heed that it be done with great caution, and under due consideration, and the Lord sought to in it, that it may be done in his counsel, and not only nominally but truly in his fear; and then no doubt but it will be well with both husband and wife; and being equally yoked, such will not only be meet and true helpers in all things belonging to this life, but more especially in things appertaining to the world that is to come, and the good of the immortal soul, which to the faithful people of the Lord is of great value.

Oh, how happily and peaceably do such live together in the Lord, as they keep to that which thus joined them."

Frederick Smith* relates in his autobiography, that he married young in life, when he was far from living in obedience to the Divine will. As years passed on, he was brought to submit himself to the Grace of God; and feeling drawn towards the Society of Friends, joined with them in religious fellowship. This was very distasteful to his wife, who seemed much alienated from him and carried her opposition so far as to threaten to leave him altogether. His prudent behavior in some degree softened her feelings, though it failed to bring about that unity which was desirable. Whilst matters remained in this state, his wife was compelled on account of her health to take lodgings out of London, and Frederick remained in town to attend to his business. He says: "One day, while serving a customer in the shop, I felt the sweet influence of heavenly love in a remarkable degree, and, at the same time, such a powerful union with my dear wife, that I was overcome with the sensation; and having dismissed the customer as speedily as I could, I went up stairs to give vent to my feelings, where I continued the greater part of the day. Under this influence I felt an inclination either to speak or write to her, on the subject of a nearer religious fellowship. I was not however in haste to put it in practice, but waited till the next day, that I might, when my mind became more settled, judge of the propriety of such a step. The next day, on sitting down before Him by whom I wished to be rightly instructed, I again felt the same sweet impression; when, without hesitation, I wrote a few lines to her, expressive of what I felt. I took the letter that evening, and soon found that the Master had been there before me. She read what I had written several times over, but said nothing. After a time, I ventured to begin the conversation, though in much fear and brokenness, and I told her all that I had felt. She was much affected at the relation, and asked me at what time of the preceding day it was, that I felt the impression I spoke of; I replied that the clock struck

---

* Born in London 1757. Died 1823. A minister in the Society of Friends. See T. Chalk's *Autobiographical Narrations.*

23

eleven as I was going up stairs, on leaving the shop. She said it was very remarkable, for just at that time she felt the same impression towards me, which had continued with her ever since, much to her comfort and consolation. We now mingled our tears of real joy together, under a sense of the gracious dealings of our Heavenly Father to our poor souls; and we had to admire that our present union had not been effected by any human means, but by the power of the Lord alone, *He having given my wife to me.* Great, I believe, were our desires that we might in no respect know a separation from each other, but that we might so walk before Him as to experience a continuance of his love and regard. I believe we both considered this extraordinary manifestation of Divine love, through which we were so sweetly united, as our spiritual marriage; for what we had before known of love, fell far short of that which we now felt towards each other—nay, appeared as nothing in comparison of it."

PART IV.

SERVICES TO BE PERFORMED BY THE FOLLOWERS OF CHRIST.

CHAPTER IX.

Concern for Others. Restore thy Brother. John Churchman and his Drowsy Friend. William Baily. Elizabeth Bathurst. Job Scott. Christian Woman and her Drunken Brother. Joseph Hoag and the Elder. Reproof for Swearing. The Moorish King and the Sack of Earth. Frederick of Prussia and the Mill. James Naylor. Andrew Fuller. The Swiss Colporteur. Mary Swett. John Wesley and the Swearers. Satan's Hook. A Box on the Ear. The Motion was in Himself. Bishop Simpson and Brother Swank. Illustrations. The Two Mines. The Queen Has Sent for Him. Geraldine Hooper and the Dress. The Soldier who Did Not Intend to Fight. The Drowsy Committee Woman. The Remedy that Cures. John Churchman and the Watch. Food in Winter. The Potter's Care. The Polished Clam Shell. Rowland Hill and the Pigs. The Snuffers. The Pilot.

WHEN the Divine power and spirit of Christ has been allowed to operate on the mind, and to turn the sinner from darkness to light, and from the power of Satan to God, not only do there appear in him the fruits of repentance, conscientiousness, self-denial, loving-kindness, humility, and other Christian graces and qualities; but he finds duties to perform and services to be done for Him, under whose government he has now come. So closely connected are these subjects—of character and of labor—that a separation between them may be regarded as only theoretical; and they might have been grouped together under the *Second* Division of these illustrations—many of the incidents in which indeed apply to both,—but as a matter of convenience it is proposed to introduce here some additional illustrations.

One of the fruits which soon becomes apparent, is an increased love and concern for others, which seeks their welfare both in outward and in spiritual things; and enables man to enter into feeling with those in distress.

An illustration of this occurs in the life of "Billy Bray,"* of Cornwall, England. He says: "At the time I was building Bethel Chapel, I knew a very good man, but who had a very wicked woman for his wife. She persecuted him in various ways; sometimes by throwing water in his face. One day she provoked him so much that he swore. He at once keenly felt that he had grievously sinned. Very earnestly did he ask the Lord to have mercy on him, Satan busily telling him all the while that it was no use to pray, for no one would believe in him again. When I was working about the chapel the Lord spoke to me and said: 'Go up and restore thy brother.' So I threw down the shovel that I was working with, and away I went to his house. When I got there his wife began to curse him, and to tell me what her husband had said. When she had done I asked the husband to walk out with me. I then said, 'Is not the devil telling you that it is no use to pray, and that nobody will believe in you any more? 'Yes,' he said. Then I told him that the dear Lord had sent me to him, and that He was on his side, and that I was on his side; and while I was talking to him, the dear Lord sent another brother to encourage him. And on the following Sunday the darkness was all dispersed, he regained the blessing he had lost, lived and died trusting in the Saviour; while his wife, continuing to harden her heart, and make the path of her husband rough and difficult, was soon removed by death,

* See note, p. 166.

to answer at the judgment-seat of Christ for all that she had done."

The testimony given to the disciple of the Lord to deliver, is sometimes one of rebuke, which may not be pleasant to those to whom it is addressed, and which the servant would gladly feel excused from uttering. But if it is faithfully proclaimed, the obedience will receive its reward.

John Churchman* mentions in his Journal, that when a young man he was brought under great concern on account of a Friend who gave way to sleeping in meetings for Divine worship. He says: "I knew not what was best to do, and reasoned after this manner: Lord, thou knowest that I am young, and he an elderly man; he will not take it well that I should speak to him, and, perhaps, I may yet fall; and, if so, the more I take upon me the greater my fall will be; besides, though I have spoken in meetings for discipline, when Truth hath been strong upon me, yet out of meetings, I am not fit to reprove, or speak to particulars. I was cautious, indeed, in those days, of talking about religion, or good things, from a fear I should get a habit thereof, and so not know the true motion; which I thought I had observed to be the failing of some. In this strait it came into my mind to go to the person in the night, as the most private time and manner; for if I took him aside before or after a meeting, others might wonder for what, and I might betray my weakness, and reproach the good cause, and do no good; and if the Friend should be displeased with me, he might publicly show, what otherwise he would conceal after private deliberation. So, in the evening I went, desiring the Lord to go with and guide me, if it was a motion from Him. When I came to the house, I called and the Friend came out to see who was there, and invited me in. I told him I was in haste to go home, but wanted to speak with him if he pleased, and so passed quietly toward home, to draw him from the door, and then told him my concern for him, in a close, honest, plain manner; and without staying to reason much, left him in a tender, loving disposition, as I believe,

*See note, p. 14.

23*

and returned home with great peace.   When thou doest or givest alms, let not thy left hand know what thy right hand doeth, is an excellent precept."

This feeling of love and sympathy in the Lord's servants, —the fruit of that love which He first showed towards them —extends even towards those who have proved unkind to them or rebellious to their Lord.

William Baily,* who was an earnest minister in the early days of the Society of Friends, published "A Warning" to all persecutors. In the preface he speaks of being haled out of the meeting-houses at the town of Pool, and denied entrance when he desired to communicate to them the message with which he believed he was commissioned of his Divine Master. "Yet," he says, "notwithstanding all this their rebellion, bath the Lord in mercy laid it upon me (whether they will hear or forbear) to write a few words even in tender compassion, with bowels and tears of love, to their captivated souls, if happily they might return unto Him that often smiteth them, before the things of the eternal peace be hid from their eyes."

Another tract by the same author, entitled "The blood of righteous Abel crying from the ground," commences in this pathetic strain : " My heart within me is broken because of the false prophets and persecuting rulers, who are found fighting against the Lamb of God and his followers. Alas, alas? woe is me because of the misery that is coming upon you ; my heart is filled with sorrow and mine eyes with tears, and my bowels are turned within me, to consider the day of your desolation and destruction."

After Elizabeth Bathurst† had been convinced of the

---

*One of the early ministers and writers of the Society of Friends. He was a mariner, and died at sea in 1675. See his collected *Works*, also Sewell's *History of the Quakers.*

† Elizabeth Bathurst was a young woman, a resident of London, of unusual intellectual ability, and much religious experience, who died about the year 1691. During her short life she labored both as a preacher and a writer to spread a knowledge of the principles of Christianity ; and suffered imprisonment for her religious principles.

principles held by Friends, and through faithful obedience to the Light of Christ in her heart, had attained a degree of religious settlement and stability; she wrote an epistle to some of her former acquaintance, inviting them to come and partake of the blessings she had experienced. She says: "The constraint which [the Lord] hath laid upon me hath been so powerful, that my heart hath been pained in me, and my soul hath been distressed for you, and often have I been bowed down in spirit, yea, till I could hardly stand upon my feet, until the Lord who bowed me down raised me up, and set before me a door of hope, whereat his prisoner in you might be brought forth, which is that for which God's seed in me hath travelled through many tribulations; and now having delivered me from that cruel bondage of corruption which I once groaned under, this makes me restless in my spirit, that others may believe in that inward power that is able to rescue from the fury of their soul's oppressor."

In the year 1784 Job Scott* paid a religious visit to some parts of New York State and adjacent places. At the conclusion of this, when he set forward for home, he says: "My mind was much affected at and after parting with Friends; with great tenderness and tears of joy, which, for a considerable space of time flowed copiously from mine eyes. I suppose I rode more than a dozen miles under this sensation, being altogether indisposed for conversation. My mind was carried back to view the places where we had visited; and my soul was melted into ardent mental supplication for the preservation of Friends in general, and many individuals in particular; attended with such endeared affection and brokenness of spirit, as has rarely been my lot to witness for so long a time together. Oh! with what heart-felt fervency did I intercede for the help and preservation of the little flock and family up and down in the world! Oh! the earnest requests that I was enabled to put up for the instruction and Divine assistance of the many messengers of the Lord, who are running to and fro in the earth among the people: that their labors may prove successful, and benefit

* See note, p. 14.

the souls of mankind. Indeed, the language of solemn supplication ran powerfully through my mind, with a melting sensibility for all; that the dead might be raised, quickened and made alive in that life which is hid with Christ in God. Many individuals of my acquaintance, both in places where I had visited abroad, and also at home in our own and neighboring Monthly Meetings, came fresh into my remembrance, with such ardency of desire, and breathings of soul for their growth, preservation and improvement, as will not readily be conceived by such as have not felt the same. Yea, my desires for them were conceived in intelligent language in the secret of my soul, in a number of little, short, though sweet and melting requests for one after another as the Father of Spirits brought them to my remembrance. Oh! how often did it flow through me as a stream of life on this wise; 'O most mighty and omnipotent Lord God! commissionate thine holy angels to attend and guard thy exercised pilgrims through this vale of tears. Let cherubim and seraphim encamp about and surround the little host of militants, thy wrestling seed, while here on earth, and forever more.'"

In her *Wayside Service*, Anna Shipton* relates a remarkable instance of loving and long-suffering service on the part of a Christian woman, who though living in affluence and having many friends, devoted herself to the care of an only brother, who was a confirmed drunkard.

"This affectionate and intelligent woman, strong in Him who is able to subdue all things unto Himself, left her own pleasant home, and took up her abode in the poor drunkard's dwelling. Years passed by, but they wrought no change in him. Day after day on the borders of the lake where they dwelt, she might be seen in the summer twilight following at a distance the unsteady steps of the wanderer, as a mother would watch her child.

"The position which she voluntarily accepted sundered her even from Christian relationship. In the minds of others all expectation of any favorable results from her self-denying service had failed long since. Not so in the mind of a

* See note, p. 15.

faithful disciple of Him who came to seek and to save. When urged to leave the wretched man to his fate, and to bestow her time and abilities on more fruitful sources of service, her reply was always the same, 'The Lord has called me to *this* work; there is no one else to do it. God will give me my brother's soul.'

"After a few days sudden illness, the Lord of seed time and harvest called home his faithful laborer. And some who had known her faith, and the patient, watchful care bestowed upon one who disregarded it, said, 'It has been all in vain! Who will watch him now! who will care for him now?'

"The grass was not green upon her grave not far from the shore of the lake where the faithful woman trod so often in faith, when the brother so long sought is found! Behold him clothed and in his right mind sitting at the feet of Jesus, a living testimony to the power of believing prayer."

It has often been the case, that one who is living in a state of watchful obedience to the light of Christ in his soul, has been made sensible of the condition of a fellow servant, and enabled to be truly helpful to him. This is peculiarly the case with rightly-anointed elders in the Church, who through Divine help have been instrumental in encouraging and cheering the drooping spirits of those who are laden with a burthen of the Word, as well as of cautioning them against dangers to which they are exposed.

Joseph Hoag* mentions attending a meeting where his line of service was so close, that the members were offended, and after meeting refused to shake hands with him. He says, "It took such hold of me, that I took my bed as soon as I arrived at my stopping place. I had parted with my pilot, an elder from a neighboring meeting, expecting never to see him again; but while they were at dinner, this Friend came and said, 'Where is Joseph?' They replied, 'He is in the other room very sick.' He came in and said, 'Get up and

---

*See note, p. 100.

go to dinner.' I replied, 'I cannot, I am very sick; I cannot eat or drink, very likely by to-morrow I shall be in another world.' He replied, 'Thou art not so near dead as thou thinkest for; come get up,' and added, 'I saw how thou wast treated to-day. When I parted with thee, I never expected to see thee again, and expected to sleep with my family; but after riding a few miles, something spoke to me and said, 'Joseph is sinking, for he is letting in the reasoner; thou must return and let him know the matter in the meeting—some of the occurrences that have transpired in it, and the exercise that meeting has caused the Quarterly Meeting.' I have been on a committee from the Quarter three times with others to try to settle matters. Thou charged it on the leaders of the people, which many knew to be the case, so that by their conduct, they had led the young people astray, and become a proverb among the people. They knew all this to be the truth. Come, get up now and go to dinner.' By this time I began to conclude, if it was really so, and I had not hurt the cause of Truth, nor offended the great Master, I mattered not the rest My headache soon ceased, the swelling of my chest went down, and the fever left me. I sat down and ate my dinner, and rode fifteen miles that afternoon."

The feeling of Christian love often prompts to the administering of reproof to those who have gone astray: In this service there is often room for the exercise of skill in conveying it, in such a manner as not to close up the way for its reception. Of this a pleasant illustration was given by an aged man who was remarkable for the kindliness of his manner.

He was one day a passenger in one of the Firth and Clyde canal boats, in company with a number of soldiers, who shocked him exceedingly with their profane swearing. Fearing that an abrupt reproof might only provoke to an aggravation of the crime, he entered into a familiar conversation with them; and, seizing a proper opportunity, inquired, if any of them could tell him what that sin was, in the commission of which men exceeded the devils in wickedness?

As he anticipated, the singularity of the question arrested their attention, and engaged them in an unsuccessful attempt to point out the character of the sin. Having thus excited their curiosity, he quoted the passage, "Art thou come hither to torment us before the time?" in which the devils addressed our Saviour; and remarked that when men wantonly call upon God to damn their souls, they are worse than the devils, who, knowing by experience how dreadful it is to suffer under the wrath of the Almighty, earnestly entreated our Saviour not to add to their torments.

Such was the awe produced on the minds of the soldiers by this remark, that not an oath was uttered during the rest of the passage; and at parting the sergeant in charge of the company shook hands with him, and cordially thanked him for his kind admonition and advice.

It is said that one of the Moorish kings of Spain wished to build a pavilion on a field near his garden; and offered to purchase it of the woman to whom it belonged; but she would not consent to part with the inheritance of her fathers. The field however was seized, and the building erected. The poor woman complained to a cadi, who promised to do all in his power to serve her.

One day while the king was in the field, the cadi came with an empty sack and asked permission to fill it with the earth on which he was treading. He obtained leave, and when the sack was filled, he requested the king to complete his kindness by assisting him to load his ass with it. The monarch laughed and tried to lift it, but soon let it fall complaining of its enormous weight. "It is, however," said the cadi, "only a small part of the ground which thou hast wrested from one of thy subjects. How then wilt thou bear the weight of the whole field, when thou shalt appear before the Great Judge, laden with this iniquity?" The king thanked him for his reproof; and not only restored the field to its owner, but gave her the building which he had erected, and all the wealth it contained.

This case reminds one of the windmill near Potsdam, in

Prussia, which interfered with the symmetry of the grounds of the Sans Souci palace. Frederick the Second resolved to buy and demolish it; the miller, however, would not sell it. It had been his father's and his grandfather's, and he wished to die, as they had died, owner of the mill. The king raised his offer and still failed of success. He then threatened to take the mill without paying for it. "Well, you might," said the miller, "if we had not the Supreme Court at Berlin." The king laughed on finding, somewhat unexpectedly, that in his realm there was so much confidence in the integrity of the judiciary. He made no further attempt to obtain the mill. The late king of Prussia, finding the mill in a state of decay, and the miller's descendants poor, rebuilt it at his expense, and secured it to them. The mill is still standing.

Though the proper administration of reproof is often a matter requiring skill and prudence, yet there are cases which require great plainness and openness—and what may seem to be severe may really proceed from a true feeling of love. This is pointed out by James Naylor* in his *Love to the Lost*, where he says:

That was the great love Christ showed to the Jews, when He told them they were hypocrites, blind guides, liars; and said, 'Woe unto you, ye serpents, ye generation of vipers, how can ye escape the damnation of hell?' And many such plain, true words, He spake in *love* to them. And that was the love of God in Paul, which said to Elymas, 'O full of all subtilty and all mischief, thou child of the devil, thou enemy of all righteousness, wilt thou not cease to pervert the right ways of the Lord?' For all the love that can be showed to any creature, is to deal faithfully and truly with them, as they are seen in the Light.

In this connection, I remember the case of one who was a member of the Society of Friends, at Wilmington, Ohio, whose death was caused by his drinking habits. On his

* See note, p. 109.

death-bed, he said the discipline ought to have been honestly enforced against him, and this might have aroused him to a sense of his danger. He evidently felt that it had been a mistaken kindness that allowed him to go on in his downward course.

"Let the righteous smite me; it shall be a kindness: and let him reprove me; it shall be an excellent oil, which shall not break my head."

This text may have been in the remembrance of Dr. Ryland,* when he gave the following hint to Andrew Fuller.† It was difficult for Andrew to be faithful without being severe; and in giving reproof he was often betrayed into intemperate zeal. Once, at a meeting of ministers, he took occasion to correct an erroneous opinion, delivered by one of his brethren, and he laid on his censure so heavily, that Dr. Ryland called out vehemently, "Brother Fuller, brother Fuller, you can never admonish a mistaken friend but you must take up a sledge-hammer and knock his brains out."

A very effective reproof was that given by a colporteur in Berne, Switzerland, who was offering Bibles for sale. At one place the man of the house replied to him with abuse, and a positive order to leave instantaneously. He however stayed, urging them to buy a book. The man then rose in a violent rage and struck him a severe blow on the cheek. Up to this moment the colporteur had stood quietly with his knapsack on his back. He now deliberately unstrapped it, laid it on the table, and turned up the sleeves of his right arm, all the while steadily looking his opponent in the face. The colporteur was a very strong man. Addressing his opponent he said:

"Look at my hand, its furrows show that I have worked;

* A Baptist minister and writer. Born 1753. Died 1825.
† An eminent English Baptist minister and writer. Born in 1754. Died 1815.

24

feel my muscles they show that I am fit for work. Look
me straight in the face, do I quail before you? Judge then
for yourself if it is fear that moves me to do what I am about
to do. In this book my Master says 'when they smite
you on one cheek, turn to them the other also.' You have
smitten me on one cheek, here is the other! Smite! I
will not return the blow." The man was thunderstruck.
He did not smite; but bought the book.

An aged friend once related in my hearing an exhortation delivered by Mary Swett, a minister among Friends,
in one of her sermons, which from its brevity and quaint-
ness, probably long adhered to the memory of many of her
hearers. In rebuking a fault-finding disposition, she said
"Friends, I want you to turn the wallet about. Put your
own faults before your face, and your neighbors'' behind
your backs."

John Wesley* when advanced in years, was once riding
in a stage-coach with a young man who swore a great deal.
When they stopped to change horses, he said to his young
companion, "I perceive by the registry books, that you and
I are going to travel together a long distance in this coach.
I have a favor to ask of you, I am getting to be an old man,
and if I should so far forget myself as to *swear*, you will
oblige me if you will caution me about it." The young
man instantly apologized, and there was no more swearing
heard from him during that journey.

At another time, he went into a coffee-house in London,
for some refreshments. There were several gentlemen at
the other end of the room, and an army officer who swore
outrageously. Wesley saw he could not address him a
reproof without much effort and difficulty. He asked the
waiter to bring him a glass of water. When it was brought
he said aloud, "Now carry it to yon officer in the red coat,
and ask him to wash his mouth after his oaths." The officer rose up in great fury and threatened an assault, but the
by-standers laid hold of him saying very decidedly; "Nay
colonel, you gave the first offence; it is an affront to swear

*See note, p. 206.

in his presence." They restrained the enraged officer and permitted Wesley to depart. Years after he was walking in St. James' Park. A gentleman approached, and after some quiet conversation, enquired if he had any recollection of meeting him before. "No, sir." "Well I am the officer you met with a stinging rebuke in the coffee-house. Since that time, sir, I thank God I have feared an oath ; and as I have never forgotten you, I rejoice at seeing you, and cannot refrain from expressing my deep gratitude to you and to God."

The following is taken from the *New York Observer*.

I was some time since walking upon the wharf where a fishing boat lay, writes a Christian traveller, and as I was passing and re-passing, the master was uttering tremendous oaths. At length I turned to him, and, standing beside his boat, said:—

"Sir, I am unacquainted with your business. What kind of fish are these ?"

"They are codfish," replied he.

"How long are you usually out in order to obtain your load !"

"Two or three weeks," he answered.

"At what price do you sell them ?"

He informed me.

"Well, have you had hard work to obtain a living in this way ?"

"Yes, hard work," said he.

"With what do you bait these fish ?"

"With clams."

"Did you ever catch mackerel ?"

"Yes."

"Well, now, did you ever catch a fish without bait ?"

"Yes," said he, "I was out last year, and one day when I was fixin' my line the bare hook fell into the water, and the fool took hold of it, and I drew him in."

"Now, sir," said I, "I have often thought that Satan was very much like a fisherman. He always baits his hook with that kind of bait which different sorts of sinners like best; but when he would catch a profane swearer, he does not take the trouble to put on bait at all, for the fool will always bite at the bare hook."

He was silent. His countenance was solemn; and after a pause, as I turned to go away, I heard him say to one standing by him, "I guess that's a minister."

The following anecdote, taken from the *Cincinnati Gazette*, shows the good effect produced by an earnest reproof.

In one of the most important commercial cities of North Germany, there lived a merchant named Muller, who, in his walks about the city, often encountered a bright-faced, well-dressed young man, who always took off his hat, and bowed to him in the most deferential manner.

The young fellow was an entire stranger to the merchant, but the latter always returned his greeting with a friendly nod, supposing himself to be mistaken by the young man for some one whom he probably resembled.

One day Muller was invited to the country seat of a friend, and, arriving there at the appointed time, he noticed this young man walking up and down the shady paths of the garden, engaged in earnest conversation with the host.

"Now I shall know who this young gentleman is," thought he; and hastily approached them.

"Allow me," said the host, after exchanging greetings with his friend, "to introduce—

"It is not necessary, I assure you," interrupted the young man eagerly, "we have known each other for many years!"

"You must be mistaken," said Muller, "for though, in answer to your greetings, I have repeatedly bowed to you, still you are entirely unknown to me!"

"And yet I insist," replied the young man, "that I have been acquainted with you for a long time, and am delighted to have the opportunity of meeting you here and to present my most heartfelt thanks for a service you once did me!"

"You speak in riddles," said Muller; "how can you be under obligations to me, when I do not even know you?"

"It does seem a little mysterious," laughingly answered the young man, "but let us sit down here on the piazza, while I throw a little light on the statement.

"Seventeen years ago, when I was a lad of nine, I started for school one morning, with my books under one arm and my lunch of bread and butter under the other. I was a poor boy with a big appetite. My luncheon seemed never enough for my hungry stomach, and I used often to envy boys whose mothers could afford to give them choice fruit with their dinner.

"This morning I had been especially dissatisfied. 'If I only had an apple with my bread,' I thought, 'how nice it would be!'

"My way to school was through the market place, and as I arrived there it seemed to me the fruit had never looked half so beautiful or desirable. I stood there several moments gazing at the abundant supply, instead of hastening away from the temptation as I should have done.

"Suddenly an old market woman, who superintended large rosy-streaked apples, turned her back on her wares to gossip with a neighbor.

"'Such lots and lots,' I thought to myself, 'surely one from so many would never be missed, yet would do me so much good.'

"Quick as a flash I stretched my hand out, and was just about to thrust an apple into my pocket, when a sharp box on the ear caused me to drop the fruit in an agony of terror.

"'Youngster,' said an earnest voice close to my burning ear, 'have you forgotten the ten commandments? Now, I hope this is the first time that you have ever stretched out your hand after goods that are not your own, let it be the last time also.'

"I hung down my head for shame, and only for an instant lifted my eyes from the ground to see who my reprover was.

"When I reached school the words I heard were still sounding in my ear. My heart was so full I could scarcely keep from crying. 'Let it be the last time also,' 'let it be the last time also,' again and again confronted me. Bowing my head on the desk, I then resolved that indeed it should be the last time, even as it had been the first; that never as long as I lived would I covet what belonged to another, or strive to gain unlawful possession of it.

24*

"After a few years I left school and became a clerk in my uncle's counting-room. From there a year or two later I went to South America. You will readily believe me when I tell you that there the temptations to a young merchant are not few. I repeatedly had opportunities, which acquaintances of mine did not hesitate to improve, to benefit myself at the expense of others, but every time these presented themselves, that ringing blow on the ear, and those words, ' Let it be the last time also,' reminded me of my duty, and helped me to distinguish between right and wrong.

"I have been back in my native country about five months. I have come back possessed of considerable wealth —but money earned squarely and honestly! Never have I knowingly reached out this hand and taken a penny even that did not rightfully belong to me!"

The young man remained silent for a few moments, overcome with emotion, then, reaching forth his hand, he took that of Muller, and exclaimed :

"Allow me to gratefully grasp the hand that once did me such a service!"

"And permit me," said Muller, embracing him, while the tears came into his eyes, " to love the man who is capable of such gratitude, and who in later life so faithfully keeps the resolve made in boyhood days."

That favored minister of the gospel, Richard Jordan,* of New Jersey, knew how to administer a gentle caution in a skilful manner.

A young man called upon him, who thought he had been unfairly treated by the members or officers of the meeting to which he belonged. He poured his complaints into Richard's ear, who patiently heard the whole story, and formed his judgment of the merits of the case. He then told the young man that he was reminded of his own experience, when he landed in Liverpool after a rough voyage

* An eminent minister among Friends. Born in North Carolina, and afterwards removed to New Jersey. Visited Europe in the service of the Gospel. Died in 1826.

across the ocean. His head was so unsteady, that as he passed up the street, all the houses seemed to him to be vibrating as if shaken by an earthquake. They were very high, and the prospect was so dangerous that he sat down on a step to consider what it was best for him to do. Then he found that *the motion was in himself.* What further advice, if any, he gave to the young man is not mentioned; but doubtless he felt, that if the distubance in his own mind was quieted by the influence of Grace, the imagined harshness of his friends would disappear from view.

The *St. Louis Evangelist* relates the following anecdote of the late Methodist Bishop Simpson.*

When he was President of Indiana Asbury University, he occasionally preached in the adjoining towns and villages. Upon one occasion he visited a neighborhood where a number of Methodists had settled, and was the guest of a brother named Swank. He had immigrated from Kentucky, and had brought with him the means of purchasing a fine estate, and at the time of which I write was very prominent as a citizen, a man of wealth, and a church-member.

After dinner, Swank invited the bishop to walk out and look at his improvements and lands. They looked at his glossy imported cattle, at his numerous beautiful horses, and his flocks of sheep, over his wide meadows, and luxuriant fields of corn and wheat.

In the presence of these broad acres, where every clod blessed its owner, and where every creature was basking in the sunshine of the highest enjoyment of which its nature was capable, the bishop expressed the greatest pleasure.

"Brother Swank," said he, "you ought to be one of the most grateful of men. God has filled with all good things your basket and store. Where did you obtain the means for all these improvements and purchases? Did you not tell me that you sold land in Kentucky?"

"Oh yes, all I had there I sold before I left," he replied.

"Had you negroes, Brother Swank?"

* Born at Cadiz, Ohio, in 1811, died in 1884. A Bishop in the Methodist Episcopal Church.

"Oh yes," he answered. "I sold them all; I could not bring them here."

"And you sold your negroes; and some of them members of the same church with yourself, were they not?"

"Oh yes," replied Swank; "how could I do otherwise? Everybody, members of all churches, sold their slaves; what else could I do with them?"

"You could have emancipated them, Brother Swank; taken them, if necessary, to a free State, bought land for them, and paid them back something of what they earned for you. Brother Swank," said the bishop, stopping and looking most earnestly into his face, "you want to be saved don't you?"

"Certainly I do," replied Swank, rather crustily.

"Then," said the bishop, "go and find those negroes and buy them back; for in selling them you sold Jesus Christ, your Lord; for what you did to the least of his brethren, you did to Him."

Swank made no reply, walked home in silence, did not attend the evening meeting, and never entered the church again.

When our Blessed Lord was personally on earth, He often explained and enforced his teachings by parables and illustrations which were drawn from customs or objects familiar to his hearers—such as his comparison of himself to a vine, of which his disciples were the branches. His servants have often been led to follow his example in this respect.

The biographer of William Bray* mentions that he once heard him address a large congregation of miners in Cornwall, England. In that neighborhood there were two mines, one very prosperous, and the other quite the reverse, for the work was hard and the wages low. He represented himself as working at *that* mine, but on the "pay-day" going to the prosperous one for his wages. But had he not been at work at the other mine? the manager inquired. He had, but he

* See note, p. 166.

liked the wages at the good mine the best. He pleaded very earnestly, but in vain. He was dismissed at last with the remark, from which there was no appeal, that he must come there to work, if he came there for his wages. And then he turned upon the congregation, and the effect was almost irresistible, that they must serve Christ here if they would share his glory hereafter; but if they would serve the devil now, to him they must go for their wages by and by.

On another occasion, William visited an invalid; and the sick man expressed a hope that the Lord would take him to heaven, there and then, as he felt quite ready for the change, and he should not then grieve his best Friend again by carelessness or unbelief. His wife, who was standing by the side of the bed, turned away, her eyes filled with tears. To her Billy immediately turned and said, "So you would not like to have your husband promoted then?" And then he took up his parable: "Don't you think that your eye ought to be as much upon the Lord Jesus Christ, as the eye of the wordly woman is upon the Queen? Now if the Queen were to send for the brother, or son, or husband of any such woman, would not she say, 'I am sorry to part with him, but it may be the making of him, I must let him go. *It is the Queen who has sent for him.*' And yet you know," he continued, "that it might be a great expense to prepare him to go; or the Queen might soon die, or he offend her, and then he would be as bad off as ever. But the Lord Jesus Christ is at all the expense of the '*fit out.*' He provides the robe in which your husband will be clothed, the crown that he will wear, the palm that he will wave; the Lord Jesus Christ will never die, and your husband wants to go because he knows he shall never offend him again: *now ought you not to be willing?*" The distressed wife, who was now smiling through her tears, said she was willing, but she did not want to lose him just yet. "And do you think," said Billy, "that you will ever be willing. If my 'Joey' lives, and if I am to wait until she is willing for me to go to heaven, I shall never get there. The fact is, the Lord has a right to take your husband, or me, or any of his children whenever He pleases."

There are many pleasing illustrations of the Heavenly skill, with which the Christian warrior is sometimes enabled to shoot an arrow into the heart of careless or apparently hardened sinners, and through Divine help awaken in them the earnest inquiry, " What shall I do to be saved ? "

On one occasion, Geraldine Hooper* went into a shop at Norwich to buy a dress, and made use of the opportunity thus afforded to give a lesson of instruction to the young woman who waited on her. After she had selected a dress and was paying for it, they entered into conversation, which she thus narrates: " Now you'll be sure and send me this dress ? " " Oh, yes, ma'am." " You'll send it me now, at once, to-day ? " " Certainly ma'am." " You won't take it and *wear it out first*, and then send it to me when it's worn out, will you ? " The young woman seemed quite hurt and offended. " Why, you surely don't know our house, ma'am ; this is one of the first houses in Norwich : of course we should not dream of such disgraceful conduct! I never heard of such a thing ! " " My dear young friend," said I, " are you not wearing out your precious life, which He bought and paid for with His own priceless, precious blood, in the service of the world, and self, sin and Satan ? Have you given Him what is his own by right of purchase ? You are not your own ; *you* are bought with a price ! Have you given yourself, body, soul, and spirit to God ? " The young woman burst into tears."

Whatever may have been the future history of this person, whether the impression made on her heart was abiding in its character, or whether it was like the early dew and the morning cloud that passeth away ; the appeal to her conscience was skilfully made, and we may hope that it was inspired by that wisdom which is profitable to direct.

When travelling once with an old general, she entered into conversation with him about his soul, and he asserted that he was all right, because he had been made a Christian

* An English writer.

when he was baptized in his infancy. She asked him if he was doing or had done anything for Christ. "Oh, no!" he replied. "Now, what would you think, general, of a soldier who, when the order to charge was given on a field of battle, should turn round and say, 'It is true I am a soldier—I was made one when I enlisted, but I never intended to fight!' What would you do with such a one, General?" "Tie him up to the cannon's mouth, as an example to the rest, to be sure!" "And that is what the Lord will do with you," she solemnly replied, "He will drive you forever from His presence, unless you get a new heart, and lead a new life, through the Grace of God! You say you are a Christian, and yet by your own confession you have never used your time or talents in the service of Jesus Christ." He was not offended; but looking seriously at her said, "I never thought of it in that light, my young friend, but I will not forget your words." The train stopped, and as he left the carriage he thanked her for her faithfulness.

It is related that Bishop Kavanagh was one day walking when he met a prominent physician, who offered him a seat in his carriage. The physician was an infidel, and the conversation turned upon religion.

"I am surprised," said the doctor, "that such an intelligent man as you should believe such an old fable as that."

The Bishop said, "Doctor, suppose years ago some one had recommended to you a prescription for pulmonary consumption, and you had procured the prescription and taken it according to order, and had been cured of that terrible disease, what would you say of the man who would not try your prescription?"

"I should say he was a fool."

"Twenty-five years ago," said Kavanagh, "I tried the power of God's grace. It made a different man of me. All these years I have preached salvation, and wherever accepted have never known it to fail."

The following is an interesting illustration of the manner in which those who are called upon to advise others, may be helped by passing through similar trials and temptations.

It was furnished to the writer by a descendant of the person referred to, who was a valued Friend, residing in Chester County, Pennsylvania.

The Monthly Meeting of which she was a member, at one time appointed a committee to visit the delinquent members, and also those who were troubled with sleeping or drowsiness in meeting.

The committee (of whom our friend was one) were united in believing it the right time to enter on the duties of their appointment, after a meeting for worship on a certain Fifth-day. Never having been troubled with drowsiness, she was surprised soon after taking her seat at the head of a large meeting, (on the day mentioned), to be beset with a strong temptation to fall asleep, and her conflict to keep from yielding was painful in the extreme. So alive was she to her condition, and the necessity of struggling, as for her best life, not only on her own account, but for the sake of others, and for the cause she loved, lest it suffer through her weakness, that every effort was used by her to resist the temptation, and so little did it seem to avail that she almost despaired; when with great power the words of the dear Saviour were brought to her remembrance, " Without me ye can do nothing," relief came, the tendency to sleep almost instantly vanished, and she could humbly and gratefully acknowledge the One who had given this never to be forgotten lesson of instruction; had also in mercy extended to her the hand of deliverance in a time of sore need.

The effect of this experience was to imbue her with a spirit of charity which she had not before felt for those who are tried with drowsy feelings; and to prepare her for entering upon the service to which she had been appointed, with greater sympathy for the weakness of others. The experience told of human frailty; and how, in our own strength alone, we cannot overcome temptation; and the effect of the wisdom thus gained was the uplifting of the finite to the Infinite, in the full assurance, " there is balm in Gilead and a healing Physician there."

When John Churchman* was in England, in the course

* See note, p. 14.

of his religious visit, he came to Kendal, in Westmoreland.
In speaking of that town, he says:—

In the course of our visiting families here, during our
silent sitting in one of them, my mind was much taken up
in thinking of a watch, and the several wheels and movements thereof; until I was grieved at such trifling thoughts,
as I esteemed them, when suddenly there appeared something instructive therein, and I had a freedom to say, the
several parts thereof seemed to represent the excellent
faculties and gifts bestowed on man. Though the wheels,
&c., of a watch were truly made, and placed in their proper
order, yet there must be a main-spring to give them motion;
so the gifts and faculties of men must have their main-spring
and cause of motion to every good work, a zeal to the honor
of the Lord, their Creator, and a fervent holy desire to
answer the end of their creation; and as there is a regula-
ting spring to a watch, so also there should be the true
knowledge of God and of themselves experienced in his
light, to preserve from going too fast, knowing by his heavenly instruction, that no wisdom, zeal, strength or ability,
will enable to do the Lord's work to his honor and the good
of man, but that which God giveth. In order that a watch
may answer the end intended by its maker, there is a visible
face and hands to discover the inward motion, thereby
showing time; so it is needful that a man should be a co-
worker with the spirit and gift of grace in his heart, that
others beholding the light thereof might be taught to glorify
God, and in his light so to number his days and walk in
his fear, as to die in his favor. As a zeal for the cause of
truth and a fear of falling short of duty, may at times prompt
man to rush on too fast, it is needful that he should wait in
humble reverence to feel the love of God, and the influence
of that knowledge and wisdom which is from above, and
experienced by those who are spiritual, that the end of all
their labor may be in the spirit of meekness to restore those
who are overtaken in error. In order that men may dwell
in that which gives ability to labor with success in the church
of Christ, it is needful that their minds should be enclosed
in the bosom of truth, in humble retirement, to be preserved

25

from the various tumults, cumbers, cares and temptations of the world, which would otherwise clog their minds and deprive them of their true spiritual sense and motion. So in a watch it is needful that all the inward parts, which are so curious, should be enclosed from damps, vapors, motes and dust, otherwise it would thereby be deprived of its motion and become useless for keeping time.

My intent in this relation is to show the infinite conde-scension of Him whose mercy is over all his works, to instruct the children of men, each as it were, in his own tongue or language, suitable to his understanding; the man being by trade a watch-maker. He seemed to be tenderly reached, and we parted in a degree of sweetness; it was the Lord's doing and marvellous to me, praised be his holy name for-ever!

The Journal of this valuable Friend contains several examples of the skilful manner in which, by comparisons drawn from the outward world, he explained or enforced the spiritual truths he wished to convey. In the winter of 1738, he visited some of the meetings in Philadelphia and Chester Counties, Pennsylvania. He says:

"The weather was very cold, being about the middle of the Tenth Month when I set out, and in my journey I went to visit a worthy Friend who was indisposed, and as we sat together in the evening, he asked me why I chose the win-ter season to visit my friends, for many infirm folks could hardly attend meetings; and said he was sometimes ready to query, whether public Friends do not take that time to serve their Master, because they could do but little for themselves. I was thoughtful and low in my mind before, and had some reasoning whether it had not been better that I had staid at home, than ventured out on the service at that time of the year. Though I thought I had an engage-ment sufficient when I set out, his query made me more thoughtful and added to my reasoning. But I soon recov-ered strength, and it came into my mind to ask him whether Friends could eat to supply and sustain their bodies in the summer, and partake also of spiritual food for their souls in that season, so as not to labor in the winter, and care for the sustenance of their bodies, or assemble and attend meetings to worship and wait upon God for spiritual food for their souls? He acknowledged I had by this query satisfied him to the full, and said he was glad of my visit, and hoped his talking as he did, would not discourage me, for I believe he saw it brought a damp over me at first."

In a meeting that he attended while in England, he was lead to treat of the transforming power of Christ, the Word of God, in changing the mind, will and affections, and placing them on heavenly objects. In illustration of this, he referred to the comparison of the potter:

When an earthly potter hath formed a vessel for use, he carefully setteth it aside, until it be prepared to bear a further operation, to harden. and glaze it for the use for which it is made; if man should put even water into an earthen vessel formed for that use, before it is hardened and prepared by fire, he would both mar the vessel and expose that which was put therein. Let not such therefore who have known the Heavenly hand so to prepare them, that they are willing to be whatsoever the Lord would make of them, marvel if the Lord should be pleased to set them by awhile for the trial of their faith. If the earthly potter's vessel should crack in drying, it would be marred, so if these vessels of the heavenly Potter keep not the word of his patience in this their drying season, to prepare them for the operation of the heavenly fire and furnace, in which the Lord will sanctify and fit his vessels for the use of his holy sanctuary, they will also be marred; but otherwise they will come forth vessels of honor in his house.

There are very few persons that do not appreciate and enjoy an apt comparison; and indeed instruction often penetrates in this way the mind that seems nearly impervious to more didactic teaching. A pleasing illustration of this is contained in some reminiscences of the late E. R. Beadle,* published by one of his friends.   He says:

There was a mission-school in Hartford, in a garret room of a rickety building, in the earlier days of such schools in this country.   It was what the English would call a " ragged school," made up of boys and girls of the very lowest class in the community, out of homes of squalor and of vice along the river-banks in one of the poorer quarters of that city. It was not an easy matter to catch and hold .the attention of that motley assemblage.   There was rarely a visitor who was equal to the emergency.   But E. R. Beadle won the eyes and ears of all who were there when first he came to that school.   Standing in front of the superintendent's desk before the school closed for the day, he held up a common fresh-water clam-shell, and called out : " Boys, what is that?" "A clam-shell," cried a hundred voices.   " Yes, it's a clam-shell—a rough, coarse clam-shell ; just such a shell as you could pick up any day by the bank of the river, or back in the country by a brook in the woods."   Then, turning the shell quickly in his hand, he showed the other valve, beautifully polished, its irridescent colors reflecting the light attractively.   " And what is *that*, boys?" he said.   " That's a clam-shell, too," was the answer.   " Yes; but see how much prettier this side is.   What makes the difference?" " It's been rubbed down," said one.   " It's been smoothed off," said another.   " It's been polished up," said a third. " Yes, that's it.   And boys, do you know that's just what we are trying to do with you in this Sunday-school ?   We've brought some of you in here as rough as the other side of the clam-shell ; and now we are trying to rub you down, to smooth you off, to polish you up, so that you'll shine like this side of the shell.   This polishing business is hard work, boys, and it takes time ; but it pays."   Then he pressed home the need of soul-polishing in words which were never forgotten in that room.   E. R. Beadle was thenceforward

* A Presbyterian clergyman and a scientist. Born in New York State in 1812. At one time a missionary in Mt. Lebanon, and afterwards pastor to several congregations in America. He died in Philadelphia in 1879.

known by those boys as "the clam-shell man;" and they always gave him a hearty welcome in their school-room, or as they met him from time to time in the street.   Many of them were more willing to be rubbed down and smoothed off in consequence of his suggestive words of then and later; and some of them came finally to have a character which reflected beautifully the rays of the Sun of Righteousness.

In teaching his disciples, our blessed Saviour frequently resorted to parables; and to this day lively comparisons between things natural and things spiritual, such as He uttered 1800 years ago, are a means of instruction, which his disciples often make use of.

A young man, who had not been fully brought under the influence of religion, was about to go from England to India. A pious friend, who was very anxious that he should not leave the country in that state of mind, induced him to stay a week with him in London, and took him to hear a minister of much repute—a very able man—a man of sound argument and solid thought, in the hope that perhaps something which he said would lead to his friend's conversion.   The youth listened to the sermon, pronounced it an excellent discourse, and there was an end of it.   He was taken to hear another earnest preacher, but no result came of the service.   When the last night came, the godly friend, in a sort of desperation, ventured with much trembling to lead his companion to hear Rowland Hill,* earnestly praying that he might not say any funny things, that he might preach a very solemn sermon.   To his horror, Rowland Hill that night said many quaint things, among the rest he said that he had seen a number of pigs following a butcher in the street, at which he marvelled, inasmuch as swine usually have a will of their own, and that will is not often according to their driver's mind.   Upon inquiring he found that the pigs followed the leader because he had peas in his pocket, and every now and then he dropped a few

*An eminent and somewhat eccentric preacher in England, attached to the doctrines of the Calvinist Methodists. Born 1744. Died 1833. A man of great benevolence, piety and zeal.

before them, thus overcoming their scruples and propensities.
Even so, said the preacher, does the devil lead ungodly men
captives to his will, and conduct them into the slaughter-
house of everlasting destruction, by indulging them in the
pleasures of the world.

The sober man who had brought his friend to the chapel,
was greatly shocked at such a grovelling simile, and grieved
to think of the mirth which his young friend would find in
the comparison. They reached the door, and to his surprise the youth observed: "I shall never forget this service.
That story about the pigs has deeply impressed me, for I fear
it is my case." The critic could only retract his criticism,
in the silence of his own grateful heart.

When Rachel Wilson, a ministering Friend of England,
was in this country in 1760, she attended Philadelphia
Yearly Meeting, and in the concluding sitting of the select
meeting, she imparted much solid advice, particularly to
the elders, whom she compared to the golden snuffers under
the law, that were made of the same beaten gold with the
lamps. She remarked that if a proper use was made of
the snuffers, by taking away that which dimmed the lustre
and was superfluous, the light would burn and shine clearer
and brighter. But some were so fond of snuffing, that they
at length waste the life of the candle and put it out; and it
was much easier to take away the light than to give it.

The force and appropriateness of this comparison are very
clear to those who have been familiar with candles as their
principal dependence for artificial light; but in these days
of gas and kerosene and electric currents, there may be
some who do not know how greatly the light of the candle
is dimmed by the excrescences which form on the top of the
wick, and which it is the ofhee of the snuffers to remove.

At a meeting in New England, in 1850, Mary Davis, of
Dartmouth, delivered an interesting communication. She
lived in a seafaring neighborhood, so that it is not surprising
that the lesson she wished to convey should be couched in

terms familiar to sea-going people. The subject that came before her mind was a ship, tossed with contrary winds, and a *head-beat* sea, that yet neared the desired spot, almost without being conscious of it. The reckoning might be outrun, but she thought it high time to take a pilot on board. When a ship is nearing port, the mariners look anxiously for the pilot; and he, knowing their wants, will come a long distance to meet them. But it is not enough merely to take a pilot on board, we must give up the whole government of the ship to him, and obey his commands, if we expect to be brought safely in. Unless we are thus obedient and submissive, we may be shipwrecked and cast away at last, after safely voyaging a long distance.

CHAPTER X.

Prayer. Thomas Chalkley and the Privateer. The Religious Wife. Prayer for Bread. Ministry. Thomas Story and America. John Churchman and Great Britain. Job Scott's Prospect. Job Scott Shut Up. Willing to be Silent. Resolved to do Better. The Emptied Pitcher. Burning the Bad Bushel. Waiting on the Lord. Robert Barclay's Testimony. Tennent's Extremity. The Norfolk Preacher. Women Preachers. Mary Collet. Mary Brantingham and the Preacher. George Withy and the Unitarian Minister. James Naylor's Preaching. The Trumpeter. Conscientiousness in Small Things. Thomas Willis. Elizabeth L. Redman and the Slave Dealer. "Ephraim is a Cake not Turned." "Quench not the Spirit." How to Listen to Preaching. John Finch Marsh. Richard Jordan at Richmond. Barbara Everard. Job Scott's Care. Thomas Wilson. Isaac Penington.

THERE are many experiences of the righteous which confirm the truth of those promises of Scripture which assure us that our Father in Heaven listens to the cries of his children, and answers them; not always in the way that they may look for, but in that manner which is consistent with his holy will. Without Divine help we know not what we should ask for, for we cannot see the far-reaching consequences which might follow the indulgence of our wishes; but the Spirit itself maketh intercession for us in accordance with the Divine will. It is only as we are brought under the influence of this Spirit, and put up our petitions through its aid and prompting, that our prayers are true and living, and effectual in drawing a blessing upon us. Yet it is our duty to live in habitual communion with God, with the mind often turned to Him the fountain of all spiritual strength, so that we may be preserved from evil, and be made quick of understanding to know his will. This is in accordance with the exhortation of the apostle, to pray without ceasing, which cannot mean that we are to be always uttering words of prayer.

That the servants of the Lord are sometimes led to pray for outward blessings and preservations as well as for spiritual ones, is interestingly shown by an experience of Thomas Chalkley,* related in his journal, under date of 1707. He says:

On our way to Jamaica, we saw a small privateer, that gave us chase, and it being calm, she rowed up towards us. The master prepared the vessel for fight, hoisting up the mainsail and putting on our colors; some were bold and some were sorrowful. One, coming to me, asked what I thought of it, and what I thought of the Quakers' principles; I told him I thought I was as willing to go to Heaven as himself was; to which he said nothing, but turned away from me.

Another asked me, what I would do now; I told him I would pray that they might be made fit to die. Then in the midst of their noise and hurry, in secret, I begged of the

---

* See note, p. 156.

Almighty, in the name and for the sake of his dear Son, that He would be pleased to cause a fresh gale of wind to spring up, that we might be delivered from the enemy without shedding blood (well knowing that few of them were fit to die), and even while I was thus concerned, the Lord answered my desire and prayer; for in a few minutes the wind sprang up, and we soon left them out of sight, our vessel sailing extraordinarily well. The next day we went to Jamaica and had divers meetings.

A striking incident is related of a seriously minded young girl of sixteen years of age, who was imprudent enough to enter into marriage with an ungodly man; and thus involved herself in many deep trials. Her husband opposed her going to a place of worship, and for a time she yielded to his wishes in this respect. But finding that her compliance produced no good effect upon him, she obeyed what she believed to be the will of her Heavenly Father, and resumed her attendance of religious meetings. The rage of her husband was hard to bear, but, sustained by the Grace of God, she patiently persevered in the path of duty.

This continued for several years, and her husband in the meantime fell into drunken habits, and treated her with increased cruelty, threatening to burn her clothes, break her head, and turn her out of doors. One day, as she was combing her hair, his behavior was so bad as to seem no longer to be endured. She laid aside her comb, and falling on her knees in the presence of the astonished man, she poured out her soul to her Father in Heaven, earnestly pleading for the salvation of her husband. This completely silenced him; and during the remainder of the day, he went about the house as quiet as a lamb. That night to her surprise and joy, he said, "Oh, Mary, what a wicked man I am! How dreadfully I have treated you! Can you forgive me? If you can forgive, I know God can!" "I forgive you with all my heart," was the sincere reply.

The account states that he became a changed character, and was enabled to lead a consistent Christian life.

As a family were about sitting down to breakfast one

morning a strong impression rested on the mind of the mistress, that she must carry a loaf of bread immediately to a poor man who lived about half a mile from her house, by the side of a common. Her husband wished her to postpone taking it till after breakfast, or to send it by a servant; but she chose to take it herself and without delay. As she approached the hut, she heard the sound of a human voice, and coming to the door unperceived, found the poor man was praying for relief. Among other things, he said, " Oh, Lord, help me! Lord, thou wilt help me! thy promise cannot fail: although my wife, myself and children have no bread to eat, and it is now a whole day since we had any, I know thou wilt supply me, though thou shouldst again rain down manna from heaven." At these words, the listener could wait no longer, but opening the door, " Yes," she replied, "God has sent you relief; take this loaf and be encouraged to cast your care upon Him who cares for you; and, whenever you want a loaf of bread come to my house."

There are many such instances on record, in which the prayer of faith has been answered. ˙Indeed he who lives in communion with the Spirit of God, and recognizes the Divine government in the moral as well as the material world, has an habitual feeling of his dependence on the Lord for all his blessings, both inward and outward. This dependence will not lead such an one to slothfulness, or carelessness in his outward business; as if he might idly spend his time, and expect to be fed by some miraculous means. The same grace which leads him to trust in the Lord, will lead him to be diligent in business, and to labor to provide for his own wants and the wants of those dependent on him.

When our Saviour commissioned and sent forth his chosen disciples to proclaim the glorious Gospel message to the people, He commanded them to go into all the world, and preach the Gospel to every creature. Down to the present day, He continues to prepare some of his servants for a like service, and still sends them forth to various parts of his footstool, to invite the sons and daughters of men to come unto Him and be saved. It has often been a matter of interest to notice the unfoldings of the Divine will; and the pointings to duty, sometimes in distant parts of the world; as they are related by those, who have been under the preparing hand of the Lord for his work.

Thomas Story* thus describes his own experience: " In the year 1693, towards the latter end of autumn, as I was riding alone in an evening, in Cumberland, the power of Divine Truth moved upon my mind, and my heart was greatly tendered before the Lord; and the Word of the Lord opened in me, saying: ' Behold, my visitation cometh over the western parts of the world, towards the sun-setting in the time of winter.' And I was greatly comforted in the words of his holiness.

" From henceforth I was often tendered in spirit, in remembrance of the western world, in a sense of the love and visitation of God to a people there, whom I had never seen; which was more and more renewed and settled upon my mind, in frequent tenderings and brokenness of heart, under the holy influence of the Divine presence, until the year 1695; when, at the house of our friend, John Whiting, at Wrenton, in the county of Somerset, upon a visit to Friends in those parts, with Aaron Atkinson, looking occasionally upon a map of the world, especially upon the southwesterly parts from England, the power of the Lord suddenly seized my soul, and his love melted me into a flood of tender tears. But hitherto I knew not that the call of the Lord was to me to visit those parts; though, from henceforth, I began to be afraid of it.

" And in the time of the Yearly Meeting at London, in the Bull and Mouth, Aaron Atkinson being concerned in prayer, among other petitions to the Lord, prayed for the western countries and places beyond the seas, ' That the Lord would please to send forth his ministers in the power of his Word, to publish the day of glad tidings more and

* See note, p. 111.

more among them. Upon which the power of Divine life
moved sensibly in my heart; and the concern, secretly begotten in my soul, now began to answer and appear; and,
after that, great heaviness and fear came over me.

"The same day after the meeting, several Cumberland
Friends and others being together after dinner, upon occasion of mentioning some of those countries by one of the
company, the Word of life moved powerfully in my soul,
with open assurance of the call of the Lord to me to visit
some of the American countries; but, though I was exceedingly broken, to the tendering also of most of the Friends
there, yet I was silent as to the particular matter, being
willing to conceal it as long as I could, since no time was
then prefixed when I should move forward therein. And
being young and weak in the exercise of the ministry; and
having no opinion of my own abilities of any kind, I urged
it before the Lord as a reasonable plea, as I thought, against
it at that time.

"At London I remained for some time, and entered into
some writing business for necessary subsistence; but, before
the year ended, I suffered much in spirit by reason of my
confinement thereby; since this calling of God cannot be
answered by any one too much entangled in other affairs,
though the employment in itself be very lawful, and, to the
reason of man, seeming needful; but, though loth to leave
all, (for it was no less than life, and all that was near and
dear in the world), yet, finding my concern remain and
increase, I yielded at length, in the secret of my mind, to
answer the call of the Lord to that part of the world."

John Churchman* relates, that after returning from a
visit to Friends in New Jersey, "I felt such an inward
silence for about two or three weeks, that I thought I had
done with the world, and also any further service in the
church, and the preparing hint† was brought to my mind,

* See note, p. 14.
† This alludes to a caution received some months before, and which
is thus narrated: "As I sat in a week-day meeting, in the winter of
1748, I felt great weakness and poverty attending my mind, which occasioned a deep inquiry into the cause. After a time of inward waiting, the humbling Divine presence was felt in reverent profound

with thankfulness that I had endeavored in good degree to practise it. One day, walking alone, I felt myself so weak and feeble, that I stood still, and by the reverence that covered my mind, I knew that the hand of the Lord was on me, and his presence round about; the earth was silent and all flesh brought into stillness, and light went forth with brightness, and shone on Great Britain, Ireland and Holland, and my mind felt the gentle, yet strongly drawing cords of that love which is stronger than death, which made me say, Lord! go before and strengthen me, and I will follow whithersoever thou leads. I had seen this journey nearly fifteen years in a very plain manner, and at times for ten years thought the concern so strong upon me that I must lay it before my friends for their advice, but was secretly restrained; being made to believe that an exercise of that sort would ripen best to be kept quiet in my own heart to know the right time, by no means desiring to run without being sent. To see a thing is not a commission to do it; the time when, and judgment to know the acceptable time are the gifts of God."

Job Scott,* at one time was brought so low with sickness, that many of his friends thought he would not recover. He says of this period, " I was, after a season of deep exercise and probation, enabled to resign up life and all into the hands of Him who made me, and to say in sincerity, thy will be done in life or death. And as I lay one night in great distress of body, and deep thoughtfulness of mind, I was drawn into an awful view of death, eternity, and eternal judgment, in a manner that I never had before; but feeling my mind perfectly resigned to depart this life, and launch into an endless eternity, if so the Lord my God

silence, yet the gentle operation of the Divine power caused an inward trembling, and the following was uttered in a language intelligible to the inward man: ' Gather thyself from all the cumbers of the world, and be thou weaned from the popularity, love and friendship thereof.' I believed this to be the voice of the Holy One of Israel, as a merciful warning to prepare for my final change, or to stand ready for some service which would separate me from temporal business and the nearest connections in life ; and from that time I endeavored to settle my affairs, and contract my little business as well as I could."
* See note, p. 14.

26

should please to order it, and finding all pain of body and anxiety of mind removed, I lay still some time, thinking probably I might ere long be released from all the pangs and toils of time, into the glorious rejoicings of eternal life. But after a considerable length of time had passed in inward and profound stillness and adoration, large fields of labor were opened, and I saw that I must travel from place to place in this and distant lands, in the Lord's commission and service. From this time I never entertained a doubt of my recovery, although I had afterward a return or two of the disorder, more severe than before; for these openings were in the fresh evidence of Divine life, which never deceived me."

The exercise of true Gospel ministry is always in the ability which is received from a fresh extension of Divine help; and without the sensible evidence of that help, the true minister will not venture to enter upon this sacred work, however much he may have been favored in his communications at other times. Hence there are many such ministers who often pass the time of meetings for worship in a silent wrestling for the arising of Divine life; or, it may be, in the enjoyment of a sense of the Lord's goodness and mercy. And this has often been the case with those who are travelling on the Gospel errand. When the Lord withholds his command, they dare not speak to the people, lest the reproving language should be sounded in their spiritual ears, "Who hath required this at thy hands."

When Job Scott was visiting the churches in Pennsylvania and adjacent parts, in the year 1786, he passed through such an experience, which he relates to his wife in a letter written from Philadelphia. In this he mentions that he had been out in the country, and that at the first *eleven* meetings after leaving the city, he was shut up in profound silence, except a very few words at the close of the first; and he makes the following comments: "I now know that when [the Lord] shuts none can open. I read it and believed it, and in good degree felt and experienced it before; but now I know it in the deeps, in a manner past all human penetration or natural apprehension; and what is more than all that, I rejoice in it too; yea, I greatly rejoice that it is so, and that I have thus exercisingly found it so. For, by thus fully learning this part of the lesson, I have been led feelingly, and to my great admiration, to dip far deeper than ever into a clear experience of the other part, that "when He opens none can shut." And blessed be his holy name, after I gave all up, and, not daring to shrink back, concluded to go on, and be a fool, a spectacle and a sign in dumbness and silence, or whatever He pleased, I felt the word of his power, and the eternal influence of his Divine life to arise in my soul, in majesty and mighty dominion: and in the fresh openings of the vision of light, my trumpet was prepared to sound; and the openings being indisputably clear, great was my confirmation; yea, and consolation also; for it was like a resurrection from the dead. And, indeed, a good, honest old woman said to me after meeting, ' I am glad I was at thy resurrection to-day.'

"Many, my dear love, were the kind Friends that sympathized with me in my baptism unto death; and how could they but rejoice with me in the aboundings of that which was evidently felt to be 'the resurrection and the life?' My way has been opened and good ability given in every meeting since, save one."

The experience of Job Scott as above related, that after he had submitted to appear as a fool, he felt the influence of the Divine life to arise in his soul, brings to mind the relation made by another minister. As he approached a house where many persons were collected, in the expectation of hearing him preach, when he saw the number who had assembled, an earnest desire sprang up that they might not be disappointed. As he sat in the meeting under this feeling, many texts passed before his mind, but he could feel no spiritual life accompanying any of them. Finally, he was enabled to settle down with this conclusion—that if the Lord had any service for him to perform in that company, He would show him what it was; and if He had nothing for him to do, he would remain quiet.   After arriving at this state an exercise spread over his mind, under which he was enabled to minister to the congregation.

One of the great objects of true ministry is to turn the attention of people to the Light of Christ in their own hearts, the great Teacher, to guide them in the way of salvation; and as the apostle says, " to stir up the pure mind in them." This purpose may be effected and substantial benefit derived by the hearer who yet may sometimes be unable to retain in his memory anything that the preacher has said, or even the subject on which he spoke.   Bishop Hoskyn of old times, says:

I have heard of one who returning from an affecting sermon, highly commended it to some; and being demanded what he remembered of it, answered: "Truly, I remember nothing of it at all; but only while I heard it, it made me resolve to live better; and so, by God's grace, I will."

There is a story to the same purpose of one who complained to a holy aged man that he was discouraged from reading the Scriptures because he could fasten nothing upon his memory.   The hermit bade him take an earthen pitcher and fill it with water.   He then bade him empty it again and wipe it clean, that nothing should remain in it.   This being done, "Now," said he, "though there be nothing of the water remaining in it, yet the pitcher is cleaner than it was before; so though thy memory retain nothing of the word thou readest, yet thy heart is cleaner for its very passage through."

To the above may be added the following of a later date:

" What a sermon we had last Sunday!" said a poor woman, who kept a small shop, to a neighbor.

" What was it about?" asked her friend.

" I don't remember," she replied.

" What was the text?" she was then asked.

" I cannot quite think," she replied; "but I know that when I got home, I took and burned up my bad bushel."

The spiritual benefit to be derived from reading the Scriptures, or from hearing the gospel preached, depends on the willingness wrought in the reader or hearer to yield himself to the convictions of Divine Grace which may accompany these outward ministrations; and to co-operate therewith. Without this religious exercise, the mere listening to a sermon or reading a portion of Scripture, will not profit. Yet to the humble, submissive, seeking soul, a blessing is often extended in connection therewith.

The exercise of soul, which sometimes covers the mind when seated in silent meetings for Divine worship, is attended with a similar blessing. If the mind is brought to feel the good presence of the Lord and to partake of spiritual refreshment from his heavenly table, it matters not whether the blessing is *immediately* communicated, or through an anointed instrument. In either case the hungry soul is satisfied. That experienced Christian, Richard Shackleton,* in writing to one of his daughters, says: "I seldom find any opportunities, of a religious kind, more deeply and solidly beneficial to my spirit, than those which I meet with in my seasons of private retirement at home. To this assiduous, diligent waiting for, and seeking after, the resurrection of a Divine life, inwardly stirring in their own minds, I, above all things, recommend my dear children, as the surest way to be preserved, as well as to grow and thrive in religious experience."

Robert Barclay† says in his *Apology:* "It was not by strength of argument or by a particular disquisition of each doctrine, and convincement of my understanding thereby, I came to receive and bear witness of the truth, but by being secretly reached by this *life;* for when I came into

---

*See note, p. 194.

† See note, p. 39.

26*

the *silent assemblies* of God's people, I felt a secret power among them, which touched my heart, and as I gave way unto it, I found the evil weakening in me, and the good raised up, and so I became thus knit and united unto them, hungering more and more after the increase of this power and life, whereby I might feel myself perfectly redeemed. And indeed this is the surest way to become a Christian, to whom afterwards the knowledge and understanding of principles will not be wanting, but will grow up so much as is needful, as the natural fruit of this good root."

The records which have been preserved of some of those who have been engaged in the work of the ministry, of the manner in which they have been led in the exercise of the gifts and calling bestowed upon them, contain much that is interesting and instructive.

It is recorded of one of the Tennents,* that when meditating on a subject for a discourse which he was expected to deliver at a meeting for public worship, he was assaulted with the temptation, that the Bible was not of Divine authority, but the invention of man. All efforts to repel the temptation seemed unavailing, and his mind became so agitated and distressed that all the thoughts which he had collected in connection with his proposed sermon disappeared, nor could he think of any subject on which to speak.

In this tried condition he went to the place of assembling where he found a large congregation collected; waiting to hear him. He was now more distressed than ever, especially for the dishonor which he feared would fall upon religion through him that day. When the usual time for prayer arrived, he arose, as one in a most painful and perilous situation, and with arms extended to heaven exclaimed, "Lord, have mercy upon me!" In the utterance of this heart-felt petition, the cloud broke away, and light shone upon his soul. A deep solemnity spread over the people,

* See note, p. 57.

heavenly help seemed administered to him, and the opportunity was so blessed to his audience, that he ever afterwards spoke of it as "the harvest day."

His experience was similar to that of a colored Methodist minister in Norfolk, Virginia, with whom the writer of these articles met a few years since. Whilst visiting among some of the sick and afflicted in that city, reference was made to a sermon which had produced an unusual impression on the people. My curiosity was awakened, and I inquired of the minister what there was about it which was out of the usual course. He replied in substance, that his feelings on that occasion were not like what he usually experienced. He had gone to the meeting with a sermon prepared to deliver according to his general custom. But on taking his place before the audience, he felt a Divine command not to preach the sermon which he had brought with him. This prohibition was so clear and positive, that he did not dare to disobey it; yet no other subject presented to his mind, and he sat there humbled and helpless. In accordance with the custom among the Methodists, a portion of Scripture was read, and a word or expression in that fastened upon his mind. With this he arose, and as he kept close to the Divine Guide he was led on from one thing to another, till a degree of tenderness and brokenness was manifested among the people, such as he had never before witnessed.

Perhaps there are none who have been rightly exercised in this service, but have been conscious of a marked difference in the degree of Divine help afforded them at different times; and have been sensible that any spiritual benefit to the people must depend on the Lord's blessing. One who ministers at stated times recently remarked to one of my friends, that he sometimes felt that a measure of life and unction attended his sermons which was not perceptible on other occasions. The same idea was expressed by another such minister, who said that sometimes he *preached* but often he only *talked*. These experiences are a confirmation of the doctrine that all true gospel ministry must come from the Head of the Church, who alone can confer the gift, and instruct his servants when and how to exercise it.

The experience of the Society of Friends as to the exercise of ministry by women as well as by men, has verified the truth of the prophetical declaration : " I will pour out my spirit on all flesh, and your sons and your daughters shall prophesy." They can testify that the Divine Gift is bestowed without distinction of sex. Among some other religious denominations a degree of liberty is given for women to engage in this service. Among the Wesleyans in England, women have often spoken in religious meetings. Among others a very excellent woman named Mary Collet, a Wesleyan, believed she was called of the Lord to preach, and frequently did so. The Wesleyan Superintendent of the district in which she resided, was only half-satisfied with women's preaching ; and on one occasion gave notice that he would himself conduct the services at a time and place where in regular course Mary Collet would have spoken. Accordingly he came, and when the time came, stood up and gave out the text on which he designed founding his discourse. But he was utterly unable to go on. Every appropriate idea disappeared, and after struggling in vain to find something to say, he was compelled to call on Mary Collet, who was seated among the audience, to come and take his place. Her mind was under exercise for the people, and she was able to obtain relief for herself.

An illustration of the need of being careful how we judge of religious services by outward appearances alone, is given in an anecdote related of Mary Brantingham, a valuable minister, who resided near Stocton-on-Tees, England.

At a meeting at Helmsley, in Yorkshire, she spoke to an individual, whom she addressed as a poacher, a smuggler and exceedingly immoral; calling him in a moving manner to repentance and amendment of life, with gracious offers of pardon and mercy. Friends thought that her remarks would not apply to any individual in the room, and it is probable that some of them felt considerably uneasy at the time. The meeting was held in a large upper room, with the door and stairs open to the street; and it was afterwards found that a man was accidently passing, to whom Mary's address was very appropriate, and who, hearing the sound of her voice, had stopped to listen.

A similar incident is recorded of the late George Withy,* of England. He was at a week-day meeting at Frenchay, which was small, owing to many members being absent attending the Quarterly Meeting. He spoke on the divinity of Christ in a close and searching manner, as though some present did not believe in it. The few friends present were so well acquainted with one another, that they became uneasy, about such a sermon having been preached at that time and place, as not being applicable to any of the auditors.

In the evening of the same day George Withy called on a Unitarian minister with whom he was well acquainted, and found him suffering severely with pains in his head and face. In reply to an inquiry as to his health, the minister said, I was passing your meeting-house to-day when I heard your voice, and stopped through all the cold and rain to hear what you had to say." "Well," said George, "and what did'st thou hear? for listeners seldom hear any good of themselves." "Why, sir, you said, that at the name of Jesus Christ every knee shall bow." "Yes, I did say, that at the name of Jesus Christ every knee shall bow, and every tongue confess: and at the name of Jesus, thy knee shall bow either in mercy or in judgment."

The searching manner in which George Withy applied this truth, may well be connected with what is told of an individual who was not remarkable for his piety. As he was walking near a meeting-house to which Friends were gathering,

* See note, p. 245.

he saw one of them with whom he was on intimate terms, and feeling disposed to enter, he asked his acquaintance when proceedings would commence. The Friend, pointing him to a convenient seat, replied in a whisper, " If thou sits down there, and looks back over the bad actions thou hast committed, preaching will begin with thee directly."

In the Journal of James Gough,* there is mentioned an interesting incident which illustrates the remarkable power that attended the ministry of some of the early members of the Society of Friends. A person of some note, who had been an officer under Oliver Cromwell, related the anecdote as follows, to some people at an inn, among whom was James Wilson, who thereby became more favorably disposed towards Friends, and willing to attend their meetings, he having been, before that time much prejudiced against them.

" After the battle of Dunbar, as I was riding in Scotland, at the head of my troop, I observed at some distance from the road, a crowd of people, and one higher than the rest; upon which, I sent one of my men to see and bring me word what was the meaning of the gathering; and seeing him ride up and stay there without returning according to my order, I sent a second, who stayed in like manner; and then I determined to go myself.

" When I came thither, I found it was James Naylor† preaching to the people, but with such power and reaching energy, as I had not till then been witness of. I could not keep from staying a little, although I was afraid to stay; for I was made a Quaker, being forced to tremble at the sight of myself. I was struck with more terror by the preaching of James Naylor than I was at the battle of Dunbar, where we had nothing else to expect but to fall a prey to the swords of our enemies. I clearly saw the cross of Christ

---

* Born in Westmoreland, England, in 1712; removed to Ireland in 1738, and died in 1780. A minister among Friends. See *Journal.*

† See note, p. 109.

was to be submitted to, so I durst stay no longer, but got off and carried with me condemnation, for it was in my own breast. The people there, in the clear and powerful opening of their states, cried out against themselves, imploring mercy, a thorough change, and the whole work of salvation to be effected in them. Ever since, I have thought myself obliged to acknowledge on their behalf, as I have now done."

The "power and reaching energy" of which this military officer was a witness, were due to the Divine authority which accompanied the message of salvation delivered by James Naylor; and they could not be derived from any other source. Some men are gifted with great natural eloquence, and a wonderful ability in swaying the feelings and passions of men by their oratory, and such men may undertake to preach the Gospel, and may produce much excitement for a time by appeals to the feelings of their auditors; but it is the Lord's power alone that can seal conviction on the heart, and bring into a willingness to bear the cross by bringing all to the Light of Christ that everything may be judged, and that only embraced which is in accordance with the will of God.

William Sewel,* in his *History of the Quakers*, mentions the case of an evilly-disposed trumpeter, who, coming into a meeting of Friends, began in an insolent manner to sound his trumpet, thereby to drown the voice of him that was preaching. This stirred up the zeal of the preacher the more, so that he went on as if none disturbed him. The trumpeter at length to recover his breath, was fain to cease blowing; but being still governed by an evil spirit, after some intermission began to sound again: but whatever he did, he was not able to divert the preacher from his course, though he might hinder the auditory from hearing what was spoken. Thus he wearied himself so much, that he

* Historian of the early Quakers, and author of an English and Dutch dictionary, and other works. Born in Amsterdam, Holland, in 1650. Died about 1725.

was forced to rest again for respiration, whereby, in spite of his evil will, he came to hear what the preacher spoke, which was so piercing that the trumpeter came to be deeply affected with it, and burst into tears, confessed his crime, and came to be a true penitent.

Some years ago, there appeared in the *Vermont Courier* an interesting relation of the effect produced by a practical sermon, from the text, "He that is unjust in the least, is unjust also in much." The preacher stated that men who take advantage of others in small things, have the element of character which would lead them to wrong the community and individuals in great things, when detection or censure is as little to be dreaded. He pointed out various ways by which people wrong others; such as borrowing improperly; by mistake in charge; by error in accounts; by escaping taxes and custom-house duties; by managing to escape postage; by finding articles and never seeking owners; by injuring articles borrowed and not making the fact known to the owner when they were returned, &c.

"One lady met the minister the next day, and said, 'I have been up to Mr.——— to rectify a mistake he made in giving me change a few weeks ago, for I felt bitterly your reproof yesterday.' Another individual went to Boston to pay for an article not in her bill, which she had noticed was not charged when she had paid it. A man going home from meeting said to his companion, 'I do not believe there was a man in the meeting to-day who did not feel condemned.' After applying the sermon to a score or more of his acquaintances, he continued, 'Did not the pastor utter something about finding a pair of wheels?' 'I believe not, neighbor A. He spoke of keeping little things which had been found.' 'Well, I thought he said two or three times something about finding a pair of wheels, and really supposed he meant me; I found a pair down in my lot some time ago.' 'Do you know,' said his companion. 'whom they belong to?' 'Mr. B——— lost them a short time ago.' The owner was soon in possession of his wheels."

Though all spiritual good comes from God, the source

and fountain of all our blessings, yet He is often pleased to bless the services of those whom He calls to teach the glad tidings of salvation to others, and to cause the word spoken to profit in that whereunto He directs it.

It is related that Thomas Willis, of Cornwall, was once preaching from the passage, "My grace is sufficient for thee," and mentioned the following circumstance. A serious young woman was laboring under a strong temptation to drown herself. The enemy so far succeeded, as to prevail on her to go to the river to put the plan in execution, but as she was adjusting her clothes to prevent her from floating, she felt something in her pocket; it was her Bible, and she thought she would take it out and look in it for the last time; she did so, and the above mentioned text caught her eye. It was, under the Divine blessing, applied with energy to her soul; the snare was broken, the temptation was removed, and she returned praising Him who had given her the victory.

The relation of this incident by the preacher proved the means of the conversion of a man and his wife then present, and of effecting a similar deliverance. These persons had been living in a state of almost continued enmity; and their home exhibited a scene of discord and confusion. In one of these unhappy seasons, the wife came to the dreadful determination to drown herself; she accordingly left her house for the purpose, and came near the river, but it being too light, she feared on that account she should he detected. Seeing the place of worship open, she thought she would go in; and when the services were over, it would be sufficiently dark to accomplish her purpose. When she entered, Thomas Willis was preaching, and the striking incident described by him so affected her mind, that through mercy, she returned to her home with changed feelings. When she entered the house, her husband looked at her with surprise; her countenance had lost its malevolent expression, and indicated meekness and gentleness. Struck with her appearance, he asked her where she had been, she told him. "And did you," said he, "see me there?" "No," she replied; "but I

27

was, and blessed be God, I found his grace sufficient for me
also." The reality of the change thus begun was shown by
their future lives, which were such as became the Gospel of
Christ.

An interesting illustration of the goodness of the Lord,
who sometimes commissions his ministers to extend the offers
of mercy to those who have long lived in rebellion to Him,
is furnished by an anecdote told of Elizabeth L. Redman,*
of Haddonfield, N. J. In 1833 she was liberated by her
Monthly Meeting to attend the Yearly Meeting of Balti-
more. While there she was introduced into much exercise
on account of an individual whom, three years previously,
she had observed at an inn a few miles from that city.
Feeling that she could not with an easy mind proceed homeward, without endeavoring to see him, she mentioned the
subject to her companion, 'who inquired his name. She
replied, "I know not his name nor his home; I can only
say that I saw him not far from this place; but whether he
is a traveller or a resident here, I am unable to tell. But
I believe if we can see him, we shall find him in affliction."

It being thought right to make the effort to discover him,
it was mentioned to a friend, with her description of the
appearance of the individual, which was so striking that it
was immediately believed to be that of a person known as
a slave-dealer, noted for great inhumanity. Inquiry was
made for the man, and after much search it was ascertained
that he resided near where she was then lodging. Elizabeth
with her companion went to see him. He was confined to
his chamber by indisposition, she at once recognized him;
and taking a seat by him, sat for some time in profound
silence. He also sat with his eyes fixed upon her in apparent amazement. She then addressed him in close but kind

* See note, p. 246.

language, describing his condition as being desperate in the extreme; but said she believed the door of mercy was now open to him, if he would submit to the terms of salvation. After this she knelt and supplicated in a remarkable manner, interceding with the Father of mercies, that in the day of final retribution, the blood of none might be found upon him unrepented of. He was greatly broken by this appeal to the Throne of Grace, and tears flowed down his face abundantly. She then took a kind leave of him, much to the relief of her own mind. He did not recover from this sickness, but after this interview became greatly humbled and changed.

Many and interesting are the anecdotes related of the manner in which the truly anointed ministers of the Lord have been led to open to individuals or to meetings their real condition.

When Christopher Healy* was in England on a religious visit, more than fifty years ago, he attended Kendal Meeting. Soon after taking his seat, he saw in mental vision a fire almost as clearly as if it had been visibly before his eyes; and he saw that the people were going round it and round it, but none of them would venture through it. He stood up with the text, "Ephraim is a cake, not turned." He described what he had seen—that the people were going round the fire of the Lord, which, if submitted to, would burn up their corruptions; and that they were turning, as it were, only one side to it, and letting that get a little scorched; and trying to make that answer instead of fully submitting to the refining operations of the Lord's hand.

This was close doctrine; and probably would apply to the people in many other localities than Kendal, for it is a

* A valuable minister among Friends. Born in Rhode Island in 1773. Died at his home in Bucks County, Pennsylvania, in 1851. He travelled extensively in the United States and Canada, and in Great Britain and Ireland. See his *Journal.*

common weakness to try and find some easier way into the kingdom of heaven than the narrow path of self-denial, and the bearing of the cross, although our Saviour has declared that without these, we cannot be his disciples.   But it was probably a comfort to Christopher to be told afterwards by a minister belonging to Kendal Meeting, that some time before, Jonathan Taylor, a minister from Mt. Pleasant, Ohio, had been there, and had commenced with the same text, which he applied in much the same way.

A somewhat similar unity of exercise in two ministers, was witnessed by the writer.   At Birmingham Monthly Meeting, held, I think, on that occasion, at West Chester, Chester County, Pennnsylvania, about the beginning of the year 1845, Samuel Cope* was present and spoke, commencing his sermon with the Apostle Paul's exhortation to the Thessalonians, "Quench not the Spirit, despise not prophesying," &c.—quoting several verses.   This was on the Fourthday of the week.   Rebecca Kite, who was then a teacher at Westtown Boarding School, and was present at the meeting, mentioned the presence of Samuel Cope, in a letter which she wrote to the family in Philadelphia, but purposely refrained from giving the text on which he spoke, lest it might embarrass her father in his ministerial services, as she knew that he would probably be at West Chester Meeting in a few days.   Thomas Kite did attend that meeting on the following First-day.   I was there and was interested, perhaps rather startled, when he arose with the same passage which Samuel Cope had used four days before.

"Words fitly spoken" are compared to "apples of gold in pictures of silver."   Where the language and delivery of a minister are dignified and graceful, they may be compared to the "silver" framing in which the "golden" apples of truth are presented; and their beauty is admitted by all.

---

* A minister among Friends, who resided in Chester County, Pennsylvania.   Born in 1789.   Died in 1871.   A man of decided character and convictions, and firm in upholding what he believed to be right.

Yet it pleases the Head of the Church to call into his service as ministers of the Gospel, many on whom these qualities have been bestowed only in small measure. If these "preach the preaching" which He bids them, the Divine blessing may make their unpolished sentences as fruitful in good results, as the utterances of those who are more eminently gifted with oratorical powers.

Cowper speaks of the fashionable world as drawing gross sensuality through the golden tube of refinement, "The neat conveyance hiding all the offence;" but there are some fastidious people who seem scarcely willing to receive the most important spiritual truths unless they are conveyed to them through a similar tube. Such unwise ones may find instruction in an anecdote of Rowland Hill.*

In advanced life he made a tour in Yorkshire, in the course of which he paid a visit to an old friend of his, who said to him: "Mr. Hill, it is just sixty-five years since I first heard you preach, and I remember your text, and part of your sermon." "T'is more than I do," was the reply. "You told us," his friend proceeded, "that some people were very squeamish about the delivery of different ministers, who preached the same Gospel. You said, 'Suppose, you were attending to hear a will read, where you expected a legacy to be left to you, would you employ the time when it was reading in criticising the manner in which the lawyer read it? No, you would not; you would be giving all ear to hear if anything was *left to you*, and how much it was. That is the way I would advise you to hear the Gospel."

A writer in *The British Friend,* among some memoranda of his early life, describes a visit to his father's house, paid by the late John Finch Marsh,* of Croydon, England. He says:

He was then a saintly-looking elderly man, evidently

* See note, p. 293.
* Died in 1873, aged eighty-four years. See *Letters.*

27*

weighted with a load of real humility and a deep sense of
the sacredness and responsibility of his calling. After he
had addressed my father and mother, a pause ensued. Believing that he had been really sent by his Divine Master,
and being at that time specially depressed by a feeling
almost of hopelessness as to realizing the state to which I so
earnestly aspired, I put up a silent prayer that he might be
commissioned to help me. Immediately he turned towards
me and told me that although I was a perfect stranger to
him, a feeling of strong and loving encouragement arose in
his mind for me. He bade me be patient and trustful and
faithful; and then he assured me that I should be brought
out into a large place, and find freedom and strength beyond
what I could at that time imagine. When the opportunity
was over he was very affectionate to me, and we were both
deeply touched with a sense of the loving-kindness of the
Lord, and of his special condescension and guidance on that
occasion.

Precious indeed is the feeling of reverence and solemnity
which the Lord is pleased at times to spread over the minds
of those who are assembled to wait upon and worship Him.
It is an evidence of the fresh extension of his goodness and
mercy. A remarkable instance of this is mentioned in connection with a meeting appointed many years since, at Richmond, Virginia, for Richard Jordan,* who was then travelling in that State. It was designed for the members of the
Legislature which was then in session, and was held in the
Legislative hall. The meeting was well attended, and Richard was engaged in ministerial labor, in so powerful a manner that the company was much melted into tears. After
he had finished his service, and when it seemed seasonable
for the meeting to separate, Richard arose and said he
thought it a suitable time for those present to withdraw.
No one moved. Richard repeated the words, still all remained seated. He then left the house, but having forgot-

*See note, p. 282.

ten his overcoat went back to procure it, and found the company still sitting under a solemn covering which they seemed unwilling to dissipate, and so he left them.

In the exercise of the ministry, as in other things of a spiritual nature, the Lord is often pleased to make use of instruments that seem weak and even contemptible to the wise and prudent of this world. Barbara Everard, who lived at Ashwell in England, was an example of this, of whom Joseph Oxley* says in his journal:

In this place lives Barbara Everard, a poor, honest, decrepid creature, apparently convulsed all over, by which her speech is much affected, and understanding also. Yet the Lord has been pleased to make use of this young woman in an extraordinary manner, having bestowed on her a gift in the ministry; in which office she appears above many of far more natural talents. In common conversation she is difficult to be understood, being of a stammering tongue; but very clear in utterance in her ministry, her matter very correct and sound, opens the Scriptures very clearly, and preaches the Gospel with great power and authority, and is of singular service in this place: she had at this meeting good service.

In a letter to Joseph Oxley, dated 9th of Seventh Month, 1760, Barbara speaks of herself and of one of her engagements as follows:

I believe the Lord will have a people to bear testimony to his great name and truth in the earth, for He is sometimes pleased to make use of mean and contemptible instruments, to bear testimony to his great name, of which number I am one, as thou knowest very well. Yet the Lord doth not forsake me, for He is near to help all those that put their trust in Him.

For some time I had a concern upon my mind to go to a

---

* A minister among Friends in England. Born 1715. Died 1775. Came to America on a religious visit. See *Life in Friends' Library*, vol. 2, p. 415, etc.

place called Weson, about two miles from Baldock, to have a meeting, where there had not been a meeting held for about twenty years before, which made me loth to give up to it. But when the mighty power of God arose in me, I was made willing; and my uncle and one of our young Friends went with me; and the meeting was very large, there being as was supposed two hundred people at it; and I had a good open time among them, and they behaved soberly, so that I came away with a reward of peace in my own bosom: for the Lord is a rich rewarder of all them that faithfully serve Him.

Barbara's expression, "When the mighty power of God arose in me, I was made willing," reminds one of the similar language of the Apostle, "I can do all things through Christ, who strengtheneth me." It is this Divine power and wisdom which comes from on High that gives all its authority to Gospel ministry. As people come to feel after and trust to this, they will be preserved from placing their confidence in anything which man can do in his own unassisted strength. The Apostle Paul reminds the Corinthians that his speech and his preaching among them had not been with enticing words of man's wisdom, but in demonstration of the Spirit and of power, so that their faith should not stand in the wisdom of men, but in the power of God. Yet Paul was brought up at the feet of Gamaliel, and was well versed in the learning of the Jews. Rutty, in his account of Friends in Ireland, makes a similar statement in regard to Alexander Seaton, one of the early ministers among Friends; that although he was a scholar, he was not much known to be such in his services for the Lord, not esteeming that learning in comparison to the gift of God, and the operation of his Holy Spirit.

Job Scott* was a man of unusual powers of mind; but it

* See note, p. 14.

is recorded of him, that in the exercise of his gift he was "circumspect not to minister without fresh anointing; and careful in attending to the turnings of the key of David; well knowing that when that shuts none can open: and therefore when he perceived his subject to close and the life withdraw, however clear his opening, and free the spring of life had been at his beginning, he would suddenly sit down, however, in the cross; for he had a testimony to bear against all superficial and lifeless ministry, and very exemplarily avoided it."

The same care was exercised by Thomas Wilson,* one of those dignified laborers in the Gospel, whom the Lord raised up in the early days of the Society of Friends. When on a religious visit in Ireland, he says, "The motion of life in me for travelling ceased, and I durst not then go further, but returned back to the County of Wexford, and wrought harvest-work at Lambstown for some time." James Dickinson coming over from Cumberland, "the Lord was pleased to open my way to go with him, and we travelled together in true brotherly love, and had a prosperous journey." After a time, "I was afraid of running before my true Guide (because they who run and are not sent of God can neither profit the people nor themselves) and so I staid at work in the City of Waterford about sixteen weeks."

Isaac Penington,† in describing his own experience gives an interesting account of the effect upon him of that Divine power which accompanied the ministry of George Fox.

He had before met with Friends, but, he says, "the more I conversed with them, the more I seemed in my understanding and reason to get over them, and to trample them under

* See note, p. 46.

† A deeply spiritual minister and writer among early Friends. The father-in-law of William Penn. Died 1679. His works have been several times reprinted.

my feet, as a poor, weak, silly, contemptible generation. After a long time I was invited to hear one of them (as I had been often, they in tender love pitying me, and feeling my want of that which they possessed): and there was an answer in my heart, and I went with fear and trembling, with desires to the Most High, who was over all, and knew all, that I might not receive anything for truth which was not of Him, nor withstand anything which was of Him; but might bow before the appearance of the Lord, my God, and none other. And indeed, when I came, I felt the presence and power of the Most High among them, and words of truth from the Spirit of truth reaching to my heart and conscience, opening my state as in the presence of the Lord. Yea, I did not only feel words and demonstrations from without, but I felt the dead quickened, the seed raised; insomuch that my heart (in the certainty of light, and clearness of true sense) said, ' This is He, this is He, there is no other; this is He whom I have waited for and sought after from my childhood; who was always near me, and had often begotten life in my heart; but I knew Him not distinctly, nor how to receive Him, or dwell with Him.'"

His own convincement having been effected, not by the wisdom of man but by the power of God, when he was called unto the ministry, he was careful that his own labors and those of others should be under the same Divine anointing. William Penn, his son-in-law, testifies of him, that "He was very urgent that all those who knew anything of the heavenly gift of ministry unto others, would always wait in their several exercises to be indued with matter and power from on high, before they opened their mouths in a testimony for the Lord."

CHAPTER XI.

Ministry continued. Prophetic Visions. John Richardson. Joseph Hoag. Peter Gardiner. Miles Halhead. John Roberts. Dr. Leifchild's Sermon. James Simpson's Sermons. James Simpson and the Deist. Maintenance of Ministers. Remarks of John Richardson. Of Thomas Story. Joseph Hoag's Experience. Industry. Daniel Stanton. John Parker. John Banks. John Simpson. When to be Silent. Thomas Story. Joseph Hoag. William Bray. John Churchman. Without Outward Information. Joseph Hoag. John Churchman. Communion of Spirits. Thomas Story. Robert Scotton and the Indian Woman. Richard Shackleton's Advice.

It is an opiniou prevalent in the Christian world, that the prophetic visions with which holy men were favored in former ages are no longer vouchsafed; and that in these days we are not to expect manifestations of Divine power, such as the healing of the sick, which was practised by the Apostles, and which no doubt aided them in convincing the people of the Divine origin of the religion they preached to the world. The testimony of scripture does not seem to sanction this opinion, for it was foretold by the prophet Joel, as one of the features of the Christian dispensation, that the Lord would pour out his Spirit upon all flesh, and the sons and daughters should prophesy, the old men should dream dreams, and the young men should see visions. There are many proofs that the spirit of prophecy, in the sense of foretelling future events, as well as of preaching the gospel to the people, is not wholly withdrawn from the Church.

John Richardson* mentions that as he was walking in a field with his soul in deep concern, meditating on the things of God, and fervently praying to Him for preservation, his mind was brought into an heavenly frame as in the presence of the Lord, and covered with fear and reverence before the

*See note, p. 77.

Majesty of heaven. In this condition the language was presented to his mind, " The people are too many, I will thin them, I will thin them, I will thin them." In a re- ligious visit, which he paid soon after, this prophetic vision was published, at such places as he felt called upon to do so. At Kilmouck, in Scotland, he was concerned to tell Friends, " that the Lord would take many of them away ; which in a short time came to pass, for many died before that time twelve month, it being the time of scarcity of corn ; and it was thought many died for want of bread the year ensuing my being there."

John Richardson, in his account of this matter, gives a wise caution to all who may apprehend that they have re- ceived similar openings, to be. careful, that " nothing of the warmth of their own spirits be stirred up," but that the mind may be purged from its own workings and be fitted to receive the gift.

When the same Friend was about to embark for America, he went aboard a ship in the river Thames. He says: " We had not been long there, and having considered our free- dom about going in the ship, it opened clearly in my mind, in the Light, that I must not go in that vessel ; and I said to the Friends, I could not go in her, for I saw nothing but death and darkness there. The account of what afterwards happened to the ship I had from two particular friends, in two several letters from London into America, wherein they expressed a thankfulness for our deliverance, and magnified that Hand which wrought it, and preserved us from going in that ship, which was lost near the islands of either Jer- sey or Guernsey, and, as it was said, about seventy people were drowned."

At a meeting in Acushnet, Massachusetts, nearly eighty years ago, Joseph Hoag* arose, and uttered these solemn words of warning :

" Friends I have a message to deliver, and I want you

* See note, p. 100.

individually to turn your attention to your own feelings, for if you do, doubtless the one to whom it belongs will feel the force and evidence of it. It has appeared as plain to my mind, as a plain printed book, so that I neither doubt nor scruple, that there is one in this meeting, who has lived a good moral life, been a good companion, a good parent, a good neighbor, and an honest dealer, but has settled down at ease, thinking this was enough; yet thou hast not made thy peace with thy God, and not a moment to spare, for thy time is very short; thou must go home to be seen of men no more. O! let not sleep rest upon thine eyes, nor slumber upon thine eyelids, until this work is done; for thou shalt have no time upon a languishing bed; for when thy change comes, in the language of the apostle,—it shall be in an instant, at the twinkling of an eye; for the mouth of the Lord hath spoken it."

It may well be imagined that this message, accompanied with a measure of Divine authority, must have produced a great effect upon those assembled. Some time after a Friend about sixty years of age, who belonged to Acushnet Meeting, and was present on this occasion, went to the barn near night to milk his cow a little earlier than usual, as it seemed likely to rain. While he was milking, he was struck with lightning and instantly killed.

When the same minister was in Nova Scotia in 1801, he had a meeting at Digby. In the course of his communication, he says, "I was led to address the mother of a family, that mourned with heart-rending grief for a drunken husband, that was spending his property at taverns in drunkenness, so that she greatly feared her children would come to poverty and want. I had to speak to her thus: 'Hold up thy head in hope, for thou shalt soon be relieved of thy burthen; thy husband shall be taken away and laid beneath the turf, and not suffered to deprive thee of a living, nor thy children of a home. When this takes place, see that thou art a mother to thy children, bringing them up in

28

the fear of the Lord, that He may be a husband to thee, and a father to thy children, and may bless you.'

"After meeting there came in several where I was; one man looked on me and said: 'According to your preaching, such a man is going to die soon, and you pictured him out exactly.' I asked if he was at meeting? He answered, 'Yes, and his wife too.' Before I got away from the place, there came a man into the house where I was, and said, such a man is dead, just as the minister said. He died drunk, and now we want to get the minister to stay and preach the funeral sermon. I thought it best to pass away as quickly as I could."

When Joseph Hoag was travelling in the Southern States, he attended a Monthly Meeting at Springfield, where, he says, "I felt my mind drawn to make a visit to the women's meeting. I opened it to the men, had their consent, and a Friend was named to go in with me. Soon after I got there, it was opened to me that there was one in the meeting who was accused of stealing, and who was entirely innocent of the crime. I sat under the exercise until my Master showed me how and in what manner to take hold of the subject. I then rose and said, 'Had I in the men's meeting met with what I have here, I should not have been so much surprised, for men engaged in the business of the world, will sometimes run across and spot each other; but to find amongst the other sex, where we look for the finest feelings of sympathy, an accusing of an innocent sister of taking property which is not her own, and keeping it for her own use, who is as innocent of any such crime as a child unborn; and not only accusing, but whispering and spreading it abroad to the great injury of the credit of the innocent; and what is worse, for those who sit in high stations to sanction these reports, and to give them force, is cruel; and that this should be found among them, I am surprised; but rest assured, that the Lord will overturn all this, and the day will come that it will be known who is innocent. The Lord will plead the cause of suffering innocence; and if thou who art the sufferer keeps in the quiet, abiding in patience, the day shall come that thou shalt be carried over the heads of thy accusers.'

"I passed on, and no one said anything to me on the subject. I heard nothing of it for years, but when I did, it was said that two members of that meeting, with their children, had accused a daughter-in-law, a widow, of taking and secreting several hundred dollars in money, that was not her own. Several years passed. At length the man who had the money came forward and let it be known that he had it, and that the widow's husband had paid the money to him a few days before his death, for land that he gave a deed for. The deed was found, which agreed with the man's testimony. Thus I was credibly informed, the poor widow was cleared. I leave this with a hope it may be a caution to others, how they accuse on suspicion, and give pain to suffering innocence."

Many years ago, Peter Gardiner,* a Friend who lived in Essex, England, on a religious visit to Scotland, came to the house of John Richardson, who then dwelt at Bridlington, in Yorkshire. "In the evening the doors being shut, Peter asked him if any Friend lived that way, pointing with his finger; John told him he pointed towards the sea, which was not far from thence. He said he believed he must go and see somebody that way in the morning. John asked him if he should go with him? he said he believed it would not be best, and so went to bed.

"In the morning when John's wife had prepared breakfast, he thought he would go and see if the Friend was well, but found that he was gone; at which John Richardson wondered. Soon after, Peter came in, to whom John said, Thou hast taken a morning walk, come to breakfast. Before they had done eating, a Friend from the quay, or harbor, which lay in the direction that Peter Gardiner pointed to over night, came in, and said, 'I wonder at thee, John, to send this man with such a message to my house; and related as follows, viz: That he came to him as he was standing at the fish-market-place, looking on the sea, to observe the wind, and he asked him if he would walk into his house? To which Peter answered that he came for that

---

* Died at Carlisle in 1695. See *Account in Friends' Library*, vol. 6, p. 237, etc.

purpose; this was in the twilight of the morning. When
we went into the house, Peter inquired whether his wife was
well; to which the man answered, that she was sick in bed,
and invited him to go in and see her; he said he came so to
do. Being conducted into the chamber where the sick woman was, he sat down by her; and after a short time told
her, that the resignation of her mind was accepted instead
of the deed, and that she was excused from the journey
which had been before her, and should die in peace with
God and men. Then turning to the man, her husband, he
said, Thy wife had a concern to visit the churches in another country beyond the sea, but thou wouldst not give her
leave, so she shall be taken from thee; and behold, the
Lord's hand is against thee, and thou shalt be blasted in
whatsoever thou doest, and reduced to want thy bread."
The man seemed angry with John Richardson, who said to
him, "Be still, and weigh the matter, for I knew not of
the Friend's going to thy house; but thought he was in
bed, and did not inform him about thee nor thy wife;" at
which he went away.

"In about two weeks afterwards the man's wife, before
mentioned, died, as Peter had foretold. At that time, the
man had three ships at sea; his son was master of one, and
a second son was on board of another, and in their voyages
they were all wrecked, or foundered, and their cargoes
chiefly lost; his two sons and several of the hands being
drowned. The man soon after broke and could not pay
his debts, but came to want bread before he died, though
he had been in good circumstances, if not very rich."

On Peter Gardiner's return from this visit to Scotland,
he was taken sick at Carlisle and there died. Whilst on
his death-bed, John Bowstead relates, that "there came into
the room one that was not a Friend, but under convictions
in his heart; Peter Gardiner asked me, as I sat upon the
bedside by him, Who that was that came into the room?
There being many, and most of them Friends, I said, This
is a Friend. Ah! said he, it is no Friend; is it not such a
one? so called him near,—and it was so. Peter Gardiner
was so full of the small-pox, that he could not see at that

time. He then spoke to the young man, and said, Thou hast no peace in thy lying down, nor in thy uprising; therefore, I charge and warn thee in the name of the Lord my God, that thou speedily return, and draw near unto the Lord, whilst thou hast a day afforded thee. For now is the day of thy visitation, and the Lord is still striving with thee; and if thou dost not return, thou wilt repent, when time will be too late with thee. I tell thee, thou wouldst be heir of two kingdoms, but wilt never obtain them both."

A very striking illustration of the continuance in modern times of Divine revelation, is furnished by the case of Miles Halhead,* a minister among early Friends, who was committed to prison by the Mayor of Berwick, for exhorting him in his own shop to desist from persecution. When brought before the court, the chief priest of the town desired permission of the court to ask him a question. To this Miles replied:

"The Lord knows thy heart, O man! and at this present has revealed thy thoughts to his servant; and therefore now I know thy heart also thou high priest, and the question thou wouldst ask me; and if thou wilt promise me before the court, that if I tell thee the question thou wouldst ask me, thou wilt deal plainly with me, I will not only tell thee thy query, but I will answer it." The priest said he would, and then Miles proceeded :—" The question is this: thou wouldst know whether I own that Christ that died at Jerusalem, or not." To this the priest, wondering, said, "Truly, that is the question." Then Miles said; "According to my promise I will answer it before the court. In the presence of the Lord God of Heaven, I own no other Christ than Him that died at Jerusalem, and made a good confession before Pontius Pilate, to be the Light and Way that leads fallen man out of sin and evil, up to God, eternal, blessed for evermore."

* For further particulars concerning this faithful servant of the Lord, see Sewel's *History of the Quakers.*

28*

In the lively Memoirs of John Roberts,* another of the early Friends, who was willing to endure suffering for the Truth's sake, there is preserved an account of some interviews which he had with the Bishop of Gloucester, a man who appears to have appreciated John's honest boldness and sincerity of character. At the last of these conferences the Bishop asked what it was that opened the heart of Lydia when she heard the preaching of Paul. John replied that it was the Spirit of our Lord Jesus Christ, the same spiritual key that opened the hearts of all the holy patriarchs, prophets and apostles, in ages past, and "the same that must open thy heart, if ever thou comest to have it truly opened." The Bishop evidently felt the force of these remarks, for he replied:—"It is the truth, the very truth, I never heard it so defined before. John I have done you much wrong, I desire you to forgive me, and I'll never wrong you more." To this John replied, " I do heartily forgive thee, as far as it is in my power, and I truly pray the Father of mercies may forgive thee and make thee his. As to the latter part, that thou wilt never wrong me more, I am of the same mind with thee; for it is in my heart to tell thee; I shall never see thy face any more."

The Bishop died soon after.

This incident is the more striking from the fact that in the same conversation reference was made to the case of the jailor of Gloucester Castle, who had been very cruel to Friends, and illegally kept them in prison by not sending up their names for trial at the assizes. When at length this was discovered, the judge discharged the prisoners and very severely reprimanded him; and the jailer was overheard to say that if John Roberts ever came into the castle again he should never go out alive. The turnkey meeting with John begged him, if he could possibly avoid it not to come to the castle a prisoner whilst his master was jailer—

---

* A native of Gloucestershire, England. Died 1683. A man of a fearless disposition, quick of understanding, and of a devout spirit. See *Memoir*, written by his son Daniel Roberts.

and John sent this message to him, "Tell him from me, I shall never see his face any more." Soon after, the narrative says, it pleased God to take him away by death.

In these instances, it pleased the Lord to give to his faithful servant a sight of things which were shortly to come to pass. And such cases are more frequent than a sceptical generation are willing to admit. It is very needful to be on our guard that we do not mistake the excited imaginations of our own minds for Divine impressions; yet the Christian would lose one of his great sources of comfort and hope, if he were deprived of his belief in the immediate communication of the Divine will to him; and of his confidence in a perceptible communion with his Creator and Redeemer.

It has often happened that religiously-minded men, even among those who do not fully hold the doctrine of the necessity of experiencing the immediate guidance of the Holy Spirit in the exercise of the ministry of the Gospel, have been sensible on especial occasions of its extension leading them into a line of service quite different from that for which they had prepared, and in which they had expected to labor.

In the life of Dr. Leifchild*, it is related, that when he arose from sleep one First-day morning, he could not recollect any portion of the discourse which he had prepared the day before, nor even the text on which it was founded. He says: "I was perplexed, and walked before breakfast in Kensington Gardens, and there a particular text occurred to my mind, and my thoughts seemed to dwell so much upon it, that I resolved to preach from it, without further attempting to remember what I had prepared, a thing which I had never attempted to do in all my ministry. From this text I preached, and it was, 'Weeping may endure for a night, but joy cometh in the morning.' I preached with great

* An independent minister in London. A popular preacher, and author of several religious works.

liberty, and in the course of the sermon, I quoted the following lines :

'Beware of desperate steps : the darkest day—
Live till to-morrow, will have passed away.'

I afterwards learned that a man in despair, had that very
morning gone to the Serpentine to drown himself in it.
Some passengers, however, disturbed him on the brink, and
he returned to Kensington, intending to drown himself in
the dusk of the evening.   On passing the chapel, he saw a
number of people crowding into it, and thought he would
join them in order to pass away the time.   His attention
was riveted to the sermon, which seemed to be in part composed for him, and when he heard me quote the lines alluded
to, he resolved to abandon his suicidal intentions."

The following incident has reached me through two separate channels.   It illustrates the peculiar manner in which
the ministers of the Lord are sometimes led in the performance of their duty ; and also the weakness of the instrument when passing through those humbling seasons which
often seem needful to prepare for service.

Many years ago James Simpson visited a meeting in
Chester County, Pennsylvania.   He arrived at the house of
a Friend named Eldridge, in the evening before.   In the
morning James did not make an appearance.   When the
Friend went to his room, he found him much discouraged
(as was frequently the case with James Simpson), so that
he thought he was too unwell to get up and eat his breakfast.   After much persuasion his host succeeded in getting
him down stairs, telling him it would soon be time to start
for meeting.   James replied that it was not worth while to
talk of that, as he could not go to the meeting.   The Friend
said, he must go, for the people had been invited to be present, and it would not do to disappoint them.   On arriving
at the house they found a large congregation gathered.
After taking his seat, James' head soon dropped low, a position he was apt to assume when under much exercise of
mind.   At length he raised it, and startled the people by

calling out in a loud voice, "How is butter going, and what is the price of eggs to-day?" From this he enlarged, saying he feared some of them were more engaged in thinking of these things, and of their worldly concerns than of the things which pertain to their eternal welfare; and spoke powerfully of the danger of being too much taken up with temporal business.

The person who described the scene said, that by the time the discourse was ended he did not believe there was a dry eye in the house.

The people in the neighborhood were at that time much in the way of attending markets in Philadelphia, with the produce of their farms; and the question so startlingly uttered in their hearing by James Simpson, would naturally be very frequently in their minds and on their lips.

James Simpson was an eminent minister of a past generation, who resided a few miles north of Philadelphia. The nervousness and eccentricity of his temperament, are kept in remembrance by many amusing anecdotes, which are still narrated in social gatherings; but notwithstanding these weaknesses, he was often greatly favored with Divine help in his labors, to the comfort and refreshment of his friends. Joseph Kite says of him, in the *Arm Chair*,—

"Filled by his Master, wondrously he shone:
The emptied vessel scarce could stand alone."

A few months before his decease, which occurred in the year 1811, he delivered a sermon at Frankford, which was somewhat peculiar in its style, and yet contained much instruction. The following account of it has been preserved:

"What I am now going to relate is but a simple story, and it is probable some of you may have heard me tell it before, but it has taken such possession of my mind, that I thought I would just drop it for your consideration. When I was a young man, there lived in our neighborhood a

Presbyterian, who was universally reported to be a very liberal man, and uncommonly upright in his dealings. When he had any of the produce of his farm to dispose of, he made it an invariable rule to give good measure, over-good, rather more than could be required of him. One of his friends, observing his frequently doing so, questioned him why he did it, told him he gave too much, and said it could not be to his own advantage. Now, my friends, mark the answer of this Presbyterian—'God Almighty has permitted me but one journey through the world; and when gone, I cannot return to rectify mistakes.' Think of this, friends! 'But one journey through the world;' the hours that are past are gone forever, and the actions of those hours can never be recalled. I do not throw it out as a charge, or mean to imply that any of you are dishonest; but the words of this good Presbyterian have often impressed my mind, and I think in an instructive manner. ' But one journey,' we are allowed but one journey through the world; therefore let none of us say, ' My tongue is my own, I'll talk what I please. My time is my own, I'll go where I please; I can go to meetings, or if the world calls me, I'll stay at home, it's all my own.' Now, this won't do, friends, it is as impossible for us to live as we list, and then come here to worship, as it is for a lamp to burn without oil. It is utterly impossible. And I was thinking what a droll composition man is. He is a compound of bank-notes, dollars, cents and newspapers; and, bringing as it were the world on his back, he comes here to perform worship, or at least would have it appear so. Now, friends, I just drop it before we part for your consideration. Let each one try himself, and see how it is with his own soul."

While speaking of James Simpson, the following circumstance may be introduced, which was related by him after his return from a religious visit in New England. It occurred whilst he was travelling in Rhode Island.

"I was with a young doctor, whom I took to be a deist. I asked him if he was not a deist, and he frankly acknowledged that he was. I then told him, that I supposed it was of no use to talk with him about the Scriptures, for he did not believe in them. His answer was, 'No sir, I do not.' 'Well,' replied I, 'as it is reason thou buildest upon, render me a reason for thy disbelief.' That he could readily do; 'for,' said he, 'there are so many foolish, nonsensical passages in them, that it is beneath a man of good understanding to believe them.' I then requested him to single out one of those foolish passages; and the one he fixed on, was the woman being cured of a grievous disease by touching the hem of our Saviour's garment, which he considered foolish nonsense. I then told him, that I supposed he was well acquainted with the power of electricity. 'Yes,' he said, he was. 'Well,' said I, 'supposing thou had never seen or heard tell of it, and a stranger as I am should come from another country, and tell thee that he could·fill thee so full of fire, that another touching thy garment, the fire would fly out of thee into him; wouldst thou not think it a foolish tale, that was not worth thy notice?' After some pause, he said he thought he should. I then replied, 'If a man can be filled so full of fire, that another touching his garment, the fire will go into him, as this we know to be the case, why not admit the Saviour of the world to be so filled with virtue, that another touching his garment, virtue should go out of Him into them?'—at which he sat a considerable time silent. Finding he was in a better state to hear me, I asked him if he had never been sitting in his room, thinking little or nothing, not nothing, because thoughts are never quite still; and all at once something alarms thee, perhaps it is a gun shot off out yonder, and so soon as that sound strikes thy ear, thy eye is turned to see, and when thy eye discovers it, thy nerves and members are at command to start up and go! now, as thou art a physician and pretends to understand the human frame, render me a reason (as it is reason thou buildest upon) of this intelligence from the ear to the eye, and so on to thy other faculties. His answer was, 'O, sir, that is out of my reach;' and finding him in a better state to hear than to talk, I went on from one thing to another, till I beat him as effectually out of his deism, I believe, as ever a man was beaten out of anything; and I thought he loved me as well as ever he loved any man, for he followed me several hundred miles, assisting me in appointing meetings where there were no Friends."

There has been in the Christian world much conflict of opinion on the subject of proper maintenance of those who are called to labor as ministers of the Gospel. The Scriptures declare that a laborer is worthy of his hire; and speak of those who sow spiritual things partaking of carnal things; yet the command of our Saviour to those whom He sent forth to preach was imperative, "Freely ye have received, freely give."

John Richardson* remarks that the outward maintenance of ministers, so far as depends on their hearers, is showed by Christ, who directed that where they were received, they should eat such things as were set before them. When the disciples returned from their mission, and were asked whether they had lacked anything, they answered "nothing." The effect of their ministry among their hearers had been such, that those who had been convinced by their doctrine, and turned to the effectual power of Christ in themselves, had from thence known their hearts so opened, as to administer to all their immediate necessities; and these, thus sent, had only eaten such things as were set before them, as they were appointed.

In a conversation on this subject, it was urged, " that if the maintenance of the priests was to be wholly withdrawn, or left to the freedom and generosity of the people, many of them would want and come to poverty, and be forced to labor with their hands, which would distract or at least impede, their studies." To this, John Richardson replied:

"That with such ministers as they were, this might be the case: but if all would come truly and rightly to wait on the great Teacher, the Anointing in themselves, it would

* See note, p. 77.

greatly tend to the advantage of Christendom; for the Almighty, who by his good Spirit is alone able to raise up and qualify Gospel ministers, as He knows the wants of his people and their faith and trust in Him, would no doubt raise up from among them faithful ministers; such, who being humble, meek and low in heart, like Him of whom they had learned, would be content to live in moderation on a little, and to labor in their respective callings, like the Apostle Paul, that great minister of the Gentiles, working with their hands that their ministry might not be chargeable, such as fishermen, collectors of customs, &c., whose ministry being not their own, but received immediately from the great Shepherd of the sheep, would not require much time and study to pen down, but coming from the Spirit of truth immediately moving upon the minister's heart, would be more effectual to reach the Witness of truth in the hearts of their hearers than all the labored discourses of the most subtle priest, though the produce of much pains and study. Neither have I found in all my travels from any observation I have made, that ever the faithful ministers of Christ became any great burden or charge to the churches; for I have seen the Divine Providence attend the Lord's faithful servants, who thereby have been enabled to order their affairs with discretion, so as to want little."

T. Story* relates a conversation with one who had made this remark, "No doubt but you have a good intent in what you do, in travelling so 'in the world; but you must have some good considerations for it, as our priests have gold and silver;" and mentioned about 300 guineas for that time. He says, "I told him, 'No; we whom God had raised up, and qualified in some degree, in this age, to that service, were advanced above any such mean, base, and mercenary considerations, as to take anything from men for this labor; which we bestow freely in the love of God, and by his commandment, for the common good of men.' 'Why,' said he, 'the apostles were but poor men, and wanted necessaries, and must have received of the people, or wanted.' 'True,' said I, 'but then they say, Having food and raiment, let us

* See note, p. 111.

29

be therewith content; and where that is really the case, such as are poor among us we would not begrudges them that; 'but it is very seldom, or never so among u ; but rather, with Paul, we can generally say, These hands of mine have ministered to my necessities, having no desire that any such thing should be done unto us; and we generally have sufficient of our own."

"Then, said he, 'But in case your friends, after some very good sermon, that pleaseth a great congregation well and generally, should offer you a purse of 200 or 300 guineas, would not you accept it, being freely given?'

"I replied, 'No ; I hope it would be no temptation, if so it were; which never can be as long as they and I abide in the Truth we profess, either to give or receive that way. I should rather be greatly troubled to see so great a degeneracy, as to subject them to so great an evil.' "

In the year 1719 Thomas Story, in company with some other Friends, called on the Archbishop of Canterbury and other dignitaries, to solicit their favor in an application to Parliament for an amended form of affirmation to be used by Friends as a substitute for an oath. The maintenance of ministers coming up in their conversation, Thomas thus explained to him the practice of the Society of Friends.

"When at any time we are sitting together in silence, (as we usually do) waiting upon the Almighty for the influence of his Holy Spirit, that we may be comforted, refreshed and edified thereby ; if any one hath his understanding enlightened thereby into any edifying matter, and moved and enabled to speak, the rest have proper qualifications, by the same Spirit, to discern and judge, both of the soundness of his speech and matter, and also of the spirit and fountain from which his ministry doth arise ; and if from the Holy Spirit of Christ, who is Truth, it hath acceptance with the congregation, and though but in a few words, it is comfortable and edifying ; for as the palate tasteth meats, so the ear, or discerning faculties of an illuminated, sanctified mind, distinguisheth words, and the fountain from which they spring. And such a person thus appearing, may so appear at another time, and be enlarged in word and in power, and so on gradually, till he hath given proof of his ministry to his friends and brethren, among whom in the neighborhood, he hath been exercised therein, until he becomes a workman in the gospel, in some good degree fitted for the service ; and then it may so happen, as often it doth, that this person is moved or called by the Word of God, to travel in this service in some other places remote from his habitation, which will take him off from his business whereby he maintains himself, his wife and family ; and suppose him to be a cobbler of old shoes, a patcher or translator of old clothes, or the meanest mechanic that can be named, poor, and not able to fit himself with common necessaries for his journey, he wanteth a horse, (though some only walk,) clothing and the like ; in such a case the Friends of the meeting to which he belongs provide all such things and furnish him. And if in that service he is so long from home, as that his horse fails, and his clothes wear out, and necessaries are wanting unto him, then the Friends where he travels, where his service is acceptable, take care to furnish him till he returns to his family and business. And in the time of his absence from them, some Friend or Friends of the neighborhood visit his family, advise in his business, and charitably promote it till he return. But as to any other temporal advantages, or selfish motive of reward for such service, there is no such thing among us : for if our ministers had the least view that way, and insisted upon it, or our people were willing to gratify that desire, we should then conclude we were gone off from the true foundation of Christ and his apostles, and become apostates. But though our principles allow such assistance to our ministers as I have related ; yet I have not known any instance (save one) of any such help : for, by the good providence of God, our ministers have generally sufficient of their own to support the charge of their travels in that service, and are unwilling that the gospel should be chargeable to any ; only as their ministry makes way where they come, their company is acceptable to their friends, who afford them to eat and drink and lodge with them for a night or two, more or less, as there may be occasion."

It is often a trial of faith to those who are but poorly supplied with this world's goods, to be called upon to sacrifice of their time and means to the Lord's cause. But they who are in earnest in seeking *first* the kingdom of Heaven and the righteousness thereof, will be strengthened to obey the Divine requisitions, and be enriched with the reward of peace; whether their outward possessions increase or not.

The record which Joseph Hoag,* has left of his experience in his younger years, is instructive. He says:

" We were married when I was a little past twenty years of age, and the spring following commenced house-keeping; being poorly provided with things necessary for farming, which rendered my situation embarrassed. I often felt my mind drawn to visit neighboring meetings, and sometimes those more distant, which gave uneasiness to some who concluded that it could hardly be required of me to leave home so often, considering my limited circumstances; and that in so doing, instead of keeping more strictly to business in order to provide for my family, room would be given for others to fix the stigma upon me of being a forward person, which might be injurious to my services. These reasonings brought a great exercise of mind, and bore me down exceedingly, until the Lord helped me, and enabled me to see with clearness, that there was no room to scruple the manifestations with which He had favored me; speaking thus intelligibly to my spiritual ear: ' I, the Lord, hold all the treasures of the creation in my hand, and I can blast all the endeavors, contrivances and wisdom of man, and give bread to the hungry, and water to the needy. When didst thou ever see the righteous forsaken or his seed begging bread? Obey thou my voice, and not that of man, and thy bread and thy water shall be sure, thy family shall be fed of my bounty, and ta'en better care of than thou art able to take of them.' * * These openings in the Light revived me,

---

* See note, p. 100.

and encouraged me to press forward with renewed confidence in the Lord."

True religion not only preserves the mind from being swallowed up in outward cares, but it also leads to industry and a proper attention to the ordinary duties of life.

In the Memorial respecting that zealous minister of the Gospel, Daniel Stanton,* issued by the Monthly Meeting of Friends of Philadelphia, it is said: "He was very exemplary in his industry and diligence, in laboring faithfully at his trade, to provide for his own support, and, after he married and had children, for their maintenance; and was often concerned to advise others to the same necessary care; yet he continued fervent in spirit for the promotion of truth and righteousness."

Daniel himself says: "I wrought hard at my outward calling when at home, yet not so much confined but that I kept close to religious meetings; in which the good presence of Christ, our dear Lord, would many times overshadow them, and I have had to sit under the shadow thereof with great delight; and after such precious meetings with his people, I found my mind better qualified to attend to my necessary business and the affairs of life."

In another place, after describing a religious visit to New England, he adds: "After I came home I kept close to meetings, and faithfully labored in that ability God giveth, being much concerned for the prosperity of his glorious work amongst us; my outward endeavors were also blessed, as I kept to industry, and I always found it best to be diligent and not slothful in business, yet fervent in spirit, serving the Lord."

At another time, when travelling in the Southern States, he mentions being at a meeting at Dann's Creek, of which he remarks, "it was a laborious time, and I wish it may have a good effect on the minds of the people, for I trust

* See note, p. 34.

29*

they were faithfully warned both on account of their sloth-fulness in the things of God, and *the things of this world.*"

This hint of the nature of his concern for the people of Dann's Creek, brings to mind the remark made by John Parker,* of Chester County, Pa., after his return from a religious visit in a section of country where the people mani-fested too much slothfulness. The substance of it was, that usually he had felt a concern to labor with his hearers to bring them out of the earth, but on this visit he had been concerned to exhort them to enter into it.

In his diligence in business, Daniel Stanton followed the example of the great Apostle Paul, who, by the labor of his hands, ministered to his own necessities, and to those of his companions. The habit of industry is good for all, and it is especially valuable to those who are called to the work of the ministry. The restraints of outward business, when not carried to excess, tend to steady a man's course, and prevent him from falling in with every suggestion of the imagina-tion as to religious service. I remember hearing one, who had had much experience in the work of the ministry, say, that some of his precious seasons of Divine communion and of pointings to religious labor had been dispensed while he was following the plough.

Many of those who have been eminent as ministers, have been laborious in both spiritual and temporal things. Among these was John Banks,† one of the early Gospel laborers in the north of England. In his *Journal,* he says:—

"In my native county in Cumberland, and also in many places elsewhere, it is well known to Friends, with what diligence I labored among them in the work of the Gospel,

---

* A minister among Friends, who resided in Chester County, Penn-sylvania. Died in 1829, in the eighty-first year of his age. See *Memor-ials of deceased Friends* of Philadelphia Yearly Meeting.

† See *Friends' Library,* vol. 2, p. 1, etc.

early and late, far and near, to much hardship to my body, · in heat and cold; and yet, through the strength and ability given me of God, I was preserved in and through all, having faith therein. And with all diligence, when I was at home, I labored with my hands, with honest endeavors and lawful employments, for the maintenance of my family."

In another place, he says:—"In temporal things as well as spiritual, diligence must be used, with a Godly care and honest endeavors, with what labor and pains the body is able to answer; which always was my concern when at home; but still in and through all to have a true regard to God in our hearts; this is the way to bring a blessing and increase upon all our endeavors."

To the same purport is a letter of counsel to his wife, in which he thus advises:—"The Lord be with thee and thine, and comfort and refresh thy soul in the assemblies of his people; with whom meet as often as thou can'st, First-day and week-day, with the rest of the family, for thou knowest it was always my care when present; wherefore, I did rise early and sit up late, and worked and labored with all diligence, that the same might be effected according to the desire of my heart; and that through diligence in lawful business, with the blessing of the Lord, I might also provide for and maintain thee with the children in decent and comely order, according to truth and my ability." ·

The union of fervency of spirit with industry in business, indicated in some of the preceding passages, is shown in the memoranda of John Simpson,* a brother of James, and like him, a minister of the gospel. He says:

"Let us often retire into silent meditation, even when our hands are engaged in labor, this has been an unspeakable comfort to me, when I saw no other way to do justly, than to work harder than some might think right, rising early

* A minister among Friends. He removed from Bucks County, Pennsylvania, to Ohio, in 1810, and died there in 1811, aged seventy-two years. See *Memorials of Deceased Friends* of Philadelphia Yearly Meeting.

•and lying down late. But the Lord was my portion to whom I could appeal, "Thou knowest I wish to do right;" and though my slips were many, yet He who seeth not as man, often replenished my heart with a measure of his heavenly grace; and to this day, I am made thankful that I have been industrious."

In one of John Simpson's letters, this passage occurs:— "These long wilderness journeys have been trying in younger life, and in all probability will be more so when advanced in years. Yet this is trifling in comparison with life eternal and the good of souls, for which I have for the most part of thirty years labored diligently, during which time my own hands have ministered to my necessities, working day and night rather than to make the gospel chargeable; and the Lord has blessed me in basket and in store."

As the Lord only knoweth the hearts of men, and what will be useful to them in the way of doctrine, exhortation or reproof on any occasion, such as a gathering for Divine worship; it is unsafe for any to undertake to teach the people, except as their minds are illuminated by the heavenly gift, their spirits clothed with a true concern, and they made sensible of the call to service. Hence it has often happened that ministers have found the way closed for vocal service, even when the people have been called together at their request for the purpose of worship.

Thomas Story,* in his journal, mentions holding a " meeting at Bishops-town in a barn, where some of the town's people came in: but, to me," he says, " the meeting was very dull and dead a long time; and after some Friends had spoke what was in their minds, the meeting was silent awhile, and then I stood up and told them, ' That there had not been more mischief done among the children of men by any one thing, in most ages of the world, than by men's running in the name of God as his messengers; when He did not send them; who not only did not profit the people at all,

* See note, p. 111.

as set. forth in the twenty-third chapter of Jeremiah, but did much hurt by misguiding them; and though it might look strange to some, a meeting being appointed and the people invited, that I said nothing; yet as no consideration arising that way ought to prevail with me to run in my own will, to speak of the things of God among them; so it might be better both for them and me, I were silent than do it. For though the Apostle was come to so clear a distinction in himself, as to be able to say, " This say I, and not the Lord;" and again, " Thus saith the Lord, and not I;" this *I*, without the Lord, having in many others done so much hurt, I would rather at that time hazard their censure, and what might follow from thence, than be too busy with the things of God where He did not concern me. For though the day before, and many other times, I had been rightly concerned from the Lord; yet it did not follow that I might employ myself that day when the Lord did not fit me, and require it at my hand, lest instead of comfort I should procure reproof from Him; and, in seeking my own honor, dishonor the Lord, and so become a transgressor.' "

Joseph Hoag* relates that when he was about thirteen years old, he listened to a conversation between some old men about a Methodist minister that had recently visited them. They all agreed that he was an able minister, and believed that the Lord had sent him. In their neighborhood he said but little, and informed the audience that he could not preach any more, and dismissed them; which disappointed them very much, and they thought it was not right, and that he ought to be talked to.

As Joseph sat listening to them, a solemn feeling came over his mind, and, under an impression of Divine requiring he told them; that if the Lord sent the minister, the Lord knew best what He wanted him to preach, since He knew the state of the people. If the man preached any more than the Lord gave him, it would only be man's preaching, and might not be suitable to the states of any of the meeting; they ought to be careful therefore how they meddled with him, seeing it was his duty to mind the Lord who

* See note, p. 100.

sent him out. If, by their talking to him, he should preach more than the Lord gave him to preach, then he would turn from pleasing the Lord to pleasing man; this might offend the Lord, that He might take away the gift of the ministry from him.

The men were so impressed with the correctness of these sentiments that they concluded to withhold what they had intended saying to the minister.

In the life of William Bray,* a member of the Bible Christians in Cornwall, England, the following incident is related: "When I was in the St. Neot Circuit, I was on the plan; and I remember that one Sunday I was planned at Redgate, and there was a chapel full of people, and the Lord gave me great power and liberty in speaking; but all at once the Lord took away his Spirit from me, so that I could not speak a word: and this might have been the best sermon that some of them ever heard. 'What!' you say, 'and looking like a fool and not able to speak?' 'Yes,' for it was not long before I said, 'I am glad I am stopped, and that for *three* reasons. And the first is, To humble my soul and make me feel more dependent on my Lord, to think more fully of Him and less of myself. The next reason is, To convince you that you are ungodly, for you say we can speak what we have a mind to, without the Lord as well as with Him; but you cannot say so now, for you heard how I was speaking, but when the dear Lord took away his Spirit I could not say another word; without my Lord, I could do nothing."

John Churchman,† relates that in a meeting at Egg Harbor,—"I stood up with a large opening as I thought, but after a short introduction it closed up, and I sat down again, which was some mortification to me as a man, though very profitable."

Again, at the time of a Yearly Meeting at Flushing, Long Island, John Churchman remarks, "On First-day I thought I had an engagement to stand up, and considerable matter

* See note, p. 166.
† See note, p. 14.

before me, and after speaking three or four sentences which came with weight, all closed up, and I stood still and silent for several minutes, and saw nothing more, not one word to speak. I perceived the eyes of most of the people were upon me, they, as well as myself expecting more ; but nothing further appearing, I sat down, I think I may say in reverent fear and humble resignation, when that remarkable sentence of Job was presented to my mind, 'Naked came I out of my mother's womb, and naked shall I return ; the Lord gave, and the Lord hath taken away ; blessed be the name of the Lord.' I suppose for nearly a quarter of an hour I remained in a silent quiet; but afterwards let in great reasonings and fear lest I had not waited the right time to stand up, and so was suffered to fall into reproach ; for the adversary who is ever busy and unwearied in his attempts to devour, persuaded me to believe that the people would laugh me to scorn, and I might as well return home immediately and privately, as attempt any further visit on the island. After meeting I hid my inward exercise and distress as much as I could. I lodged that night with a sympathizing friend and experienced elder, who began to speak encouragingly to me, but I said to him that I hoped he would not take it amiss if I desired him to forbear saying anything ; for if he should say good things, I had no capacity to believe, and if otherwise, I could not then understand so as to be profitably corrected or instructed, and after some time I fell asleep. When I awoke, I remembered that the sentences I had delivered in the meeting, were truths which could not be wrested to the disadvantage of Friends, or dishonor of the cause of truth, though they might look like roots or something to paraphrase upon ; and although my standing some time silent before I sat down, might occasion the people to think me a silly fellow, yet they had no cause to blame me for delivering words without sense or life. Thus I became very quiet, and not much depressed, and was favored with an humble resignation of mind, and a desire that the Lord would be pleased to magnify his own name and truth, and preserve me from bringing any reproach thereon."

After attending some other meetings in that section of country, at most of which he says he had good satisfaction, John Churchman thus refers to his experience at Flushing:

"That humbling time I had at Flushing was of singular service to me, being thereby made willingly subject to the Divine openings of truth, the motion of the eternal Spirit and pure Word of life, in speaking to the several states of those who were present in the meetings, and life came into dominion, and the power thereof overshadowed at times, to my humble admiration; blessed be the name of the Lord, who is worthy for ever and ever!"

When ministers are travelling in religious service, it is often important that their minds should not be pre-occupied with information as to the state of things among those they are visiting. They are more likely to depend on the fresh openings of Truth, in their communications to the people; and the word spoken will have more place with the hearers than it would if they supposed it to be the result of previously formed impressions. An interesting illustration of this is furnished by Joseph Hoag's,* experience, when visiting in Canada, in 1807. At West Lake he says:

We put up at a Friend's house where a number soon came in. I felt that I could not stay in the house in peace. The sun being yet two hours high I walked into the woods, and did not return until after dark, when I found the house clear of its company. The next day at meeting, I was led in the course of my testimony to speak of high professors taking advantage of the necessities of the poor, screwing them down and grinding the faces of the needy. I had to make some close remarks on the subject; and not feeling easy nor clear of the place, we appointed a meeting in the afternoon. Many people came. There, I had to take up the subject at large, and show that the rich had it in their power to wipe the tear from the widow's eye, and make the

* See note, p. 100.

fatherless sing for joy, and their hearts to bless them; that the honest and industrious poor ought to be helped; that this would be acting as ministers for the Lord to the poor. But while the rich were taking the advantage of the poor to increase their hoards, they caused the poor to mourn, the widow to weep, and the fatherless to cry for want, by their adding grief to sorrow, and vexation to those already in trouble, so that in vain is the profession of such! The Lord will have no respect to your offering, until you can stretch out your hands to the poor, to relieve their woes. The word of Truth went forth in such authority, that all opposition fell before it; the meeting was broken into tenderness, and many to weeping—a solemn, humbling time. May the Lord bless it to the people, and to the praise of his own name!

After we left there, I was informed that those who were at the house where we first went, were gathered on account of an arbitration between a rich Friend and a poor man. They sat by and heard the investigation, and it was made to appear that the Friend had taken unjust advantage of him several ways, and screwed him down cruelly; and when the award was brought in, the Friend refused compliance, and went off offended. This was whilst I was in the woods. Both parties were at the meetings. It was said the Friend came forward the next day to settle the matter. Thus I had a hope that some good was done, and in humility admired the tender care of the Lord in leading me into the forest solitary and alone, so that I heard nothing of it until I got away from them."

When John Churchman* was travelling in the north of England, he joined with a committee of Pardsay Hall Monthly Meeting in a visit to their families. He says: " Before the service was much proceeded in, a heavy concern came upon me from a secret sense I had, that one of them was under the censure of some, by which I feared her service would be laid waste, unless it could be removed. Although I had no intimation of anything of the kind from any person, I became heavily exercised, and at length requested a

* See note, p. 14.

30

Friend to invite the man and his wife to dine with him, who I apprehended were uneasy with the woman, and I desired her and her husband to come to the same house in the afternoon, who accordingly came, and thus the parties met unexpectedly to each other. I was humbled under the weight attending my mind, and no others being present except the Friend and his wife at whose house we were, I ventured to let them know the exercise I had been under some days, from an apprehension of a difference or prejudice subsisting between them, which, if not removed, would devour like fire, by which I believed they were already much affected. As I had not received information, more or less, I might be mistaken, and did not desire they should say anything on the subject before me, but honestly confer on it between themselves first, and if it was so, remove the cause, and if nothing was amiss, then to let me know, that I might be warned to be more cautious in future. I then left them and walked by myself about an hour, when the man of the house called me in, and they told me I was not mistaken, for there had been an hardness subsisting for some time, which they hoped was now done away."

To these interesting illustrations of the clearness of that Divine guidance with which the attentive servant of the Lord is often favored in the performance of the services required of him, may be subjoined another drawn from the experience of the same Friend. When visiting families at Edenderry, in Ireland, he says:

I asked the Friend who accompanied us, whether there was any other Friend's house to which we had not been; he said he thought not. My mind had a draught to some house, and I pointed toward it, he then said he believed he knew where; so we went to the place, and the family being called together, I inquired whether there was not another belonging to the house, and was told there was. As soon as he came, I knew it was the man whom my mind was concerned to visit, and something I had to express reached and tendered him very much, he being exceedingly wild and fashionable, and did not love to attend religious meetings, but truth now reached him. On the First-day following I saw him at Edenderry meeting, where the visitation seemed to be renewed to him; I afterwards heard that he continued to be sober and thoughtful, and I was thankful to the Lord that He was pleased to condescend in mercy to gather the outcast of Israel.

The most cogent train of reasoning, and the most earnest appeals that a preacher can make will have little or no effect in awakening a sinner to true repentance, or in promoting the spiritual welfare of his hearers, unless it be accompanied by a measure of that Divine power which the Lord alone can dispense. Where the preacher is careful to minister only in the authority and under the direction of the Head of the Church, he may safely leave the results in his Master's hand, who has declared that his word shall accomplish that which He pleases, and shall prosper in the things whereto He sends it. We are prone to place too much reliance on words themselves and to look more to the preachers than to the quickening Spirit which must give force to their expressions. Yet there is a ministry without words—a communion of spirits in which refreshment and consolation spreads from one person to others, without anything being said. Thomas Story* describes an interesting occurrence of this kind, when speaking of the first meeting he attended among the Society of Friends. He says:—

"Not long after I had sat down among them, that heavenly and watery cloud overshadowing my mind, broke into a sweet, abounding shower of celestial rain, and the greatest part of the meeting was broken together, dissolved and comforted in the same divine and holy presence and influence of the true, holy and heavenly Lord; which was divers times repeated before the meeting ended. And in the same way, by the same divine and holy Power, I had

* See note, p. 111.

been often favored with before, when alone; and when no eye but that of Heaven, beheld, or any knew, but the Lord himself; who, in infinite mercy, had been pleased to bestow so great a favor.

"And as the many small springs and streams, descending into a proper place, and forming a river, become more deep and weighty; even so, thus meeting with a people gathered of the living God into a sense of the enjoyment of his divine and living presence, through that blessed and holy medium, the mind of Jesus Christ, the Son of God, and Saviour of the world, I felt an increase of the same joy of the salvation of God."

This spiritual communion may take place not only where individuals are gathered into solemn silence; but it may be experienced where the gospel is preached in a language unknown to the bearer, who yet may be made sensible of the gospel authority which accompanies the words spoken. Of the truth of this, there is abundant testimony.

When Thomas Story was in America, coming to Philadelphia, he had a meeting at Myrion (Merion) with the Welsh Friends who had settled there; among whom, he says, "I was much satisfied: For several of them appearing in testimony in the *British* tongue, which I did not understand; yet being from the Word of truth in them, as instruments moved thereby, *I was as much refreshed as if it had been in my own language;* which confirmed me in what I had thought before, that where the Spirit is the same in the preacher and hearer, and is the Truth, the refreshment is chiefly thereby, rather than by the form of words or language, to all that are in the same spirit at the same time. And this is the universal language of the Spirit, known and understood in all tongues and nations, to them that are born of Him."

Some years after this, when in Wales, he met with an old Friend, named John Bevan, whom he accompanied to a meeting at Pontapool. There, John Bevan spoke in *Welsh.* T. Story remarks :—

"Though I understood not the language, yet was much comforted in the Truth all the time; by which I perceived his ministry was from that ground. His speech flowed very free and smooth, carrying a proportion and satisfaction to the ear, not easily expressed: For though the languages of men differ very greatly, yet the language of Truth as to the comfort of it, is one in all nations; but the matters receive various forms as the languages differ."

The late Robert Scotton,* of Frankford, Philadelphia, spent several years among the Indians on the Allegheny Reservation in Western New York, laboring for their welfare. He was asked on one occasion as to the religious character of the Indians—whether any permanent spiritual results were to be expected among them. In his reply, he said that when he lived among them, it was his custom after breakfast on First-day morning to walk out for some distance from the house, and then return in time for a meeting; or, if alone, for a silent sitting by himself waiting on the Lord. In one of those early walks, as he passed an Indian cabin, he heard the voice of the woman who inhabited it, engaged in supplication. She knew not of his nearness, as she poured out her soul unto the Lord; nor did he know enough of the language to understand her petition: but he was seldom if ever more sensible of the spirit of prayer being perceptibly felt than on that occasion.

The incidents above related need not seem strange to us, if we reflect that words of themselves cannot furnish spiritual instruction and refreshment to the hearers, but that these depend on the Divine power that accompanies them.

It is the evidence of spiritual life, and not the eloquence of words, that satisfies the mind. For the arising of this Life in the heart, the experienced Christian longs and

*A minister among Friends, who resided at Frankford, Philadelphia. Died in 1860, in the seventy-ninth year of his age.

30*

waits; and to it, he calls the attention of those for whose welfare he is concerned. Richard Shackleton,* writing to his daughter Margaret in 1773, thus expresses his earnest desires:—

"Mayst thou, dear child, be preserved in simplicity and nothingness of self; in humility and lowliness of mind, seeking diligently after, and waiting steadily for, the inward experience of that which is unmixedly good. This is the way to be helped along from day to day, through one difficulty and proving after another, to the end of our wearisome pilgrimage; having recourse, like the hunted hart, to the brook by the way, when pressed by our spiritual enemies. By this, my dear child, the predecessors in our family, who lived in the truth, were enabled to wade through their afflictions, and knew that overcoming which entitles to the glorious, eternal rewards."

CHAPTER XII.

Religious Meetings. Individual Labor. Drowsiness. George Withy. William Hunt. Grace at Table. John Richardson. David Ferris. Meat *versus* Bones. Dr. Manton's Sermon. Balaam's Ministry. Religious Opportunities. John Richardson at Bermuda. Thomas Story at Bristol. Cuthbert Featherstone. Sarah Grubb and Ann Baker. Joseph Oxley. Religious Controversy. Thomas Story and Dr. Gilpin. Thomas Story and a Priest. Job Scott and a Baptist Preacher. Isaac Penington. A Crooked Spirit. Religious Conversation. William Lewis. Richard Shackleton. The Two Merchants. The Teacher's Influence.

THOUGH our Saviour has promised to be in the midst of those who are gathered in his name, yet it is not always that He *manifests* his presence in religious assemblies by the outpouring of comfort and sensible refreshment. For wise

* See note, p. 194.

purposes, no doubt, He sometimes permits even those who sincerely desire to worship Him, to wrestle long for a blessing; and the careless and indifferent are often "sent empty away." Thomas Story* says of a meeting he had in Virginia, that it was "very small, hard, dark and dull;" and he attributes it to the fact, that "the people were busy planting tobacco, and those that came to the meeting left their minds behind them in that business."

In the course of his American journey, he was at Salem, Massachusetts, in the year 1699, where, he says, "part of my testimony was against a sleepy state in some, and a wandering spirit in others; which I perceived infested and hurt that meeting, and hindered the growth of several. It was a tender, comfortable meeting; and I was told afterwards, there was great need of such a testimony: and one ancient Friend confessed, with tears, that he had received great hurt in meetings by a wandering spirit; which draws away the mind from a true and sincere waiting upon God, by insensible degrees, and hinders the progress of the mind in the Truth, and the true worship."

How many there are of us at the present day, who could (if we were so disposed) make the same confession as this aged Friend, and acknowledge, that *our* minds were often drawn away "from a true and sincere waiting upon God," by a wandering spirit! May we all heed the exhortation which T. S. was concerned to give at Hampton Meeting, where (as at Salem,) he bore testimony against a drowsy, lukewarm, and indifferent spirit. Here he exhorted, "The old convinced not to rest in that condition, lest they might lose their crowns, and become stumbling blocks in the way of the weak, then under convincement: And to the young, that they should mind the Lord alone; and that if they

*See note, p. 111.

should espy anything in any one, who had for a long or short time professed the truth, either in conversation or in meetings; whether in the vanity of the one, or indifference of the other; or in coming to meetings, or negligence when in them, they should not look out at the failings of others, but to the Lord for help; to whom we must all stand or fall, and answer for ourselves, and not for another."

The object of religious meetings is the performance of Divine worship, which, as our Saviour told the woman of Samaria, must be in spirit and in truth. It is not therefore at all essential that there should be anything uttered on such occasions; but the duty of those assembled is to turn their minds inward, and endeavor to feel the solemnizing presence of the Lord. In this way meetings may be profitably held, whether any ministers are present or not. Indeed, it has been a frequent experience, that where the expectation of the people is much turned to those who sometimes speak in the congregations, it has a tendency to close up the spring of true Gospel ministry.

The observation has sometimes been made, that meetings which contained a body of sound and religiously concerned members, but none in the station of minister, more frequently retained their place as vigorous branches of the Church; than those meetings which were favored with a lively gospel ministry. The reason given for this is, the tendency in the minds of the people to depend upon the labors of the minister for their spiritual comfort and refreshment, and thus gradually to slide away from a state of wrestling for the Heavenly blessing. The inevitable result of this is a dwindling in the life of religion. Gospel ministry is undoubtedly a great blessing to the Church, and is designed to instruct, edify and comfort the flock of Christ; but, like other blessings, we may fail to use it to the best advantage.

When assembled to wait upon and worship the Lord, if we are not careful to maintain a religious exercise of mind, and sincerely to wrestle in spirit for a blessing; the minds of some will wander off to the very ends of the earth; and others, whose constitutional temperament is different, will become drowsy. The two classes are equally deficient in the performance of the duty for which they were convened; but the neglect of the latter is the more conspicuous to observers. Many anecdotes are preserved of the cautions and rebukes extended to such; and some of them might indicate that the speakers had read the advice of Paul to Titus, to rebuke the Cretans *sharply*.

An anecdote of George Withy,* that has often been related in social circles, shows that he at times carried a keen-edged weapon. When in this country on a religious visit, he was at a meeting where a drowsy spirit was manifested. At last he arose and delivered an *awakening* sermon, substantially as follows: " If Friends would bring their pillows with them to meeting, they could sleep much more comfortably."

Somewhat different was the method adopted by William Hunt† to arouse a lethargic audience. He had risen to preach, but stopped, and stamped loudly on the floor three times. When the attention of the people was fully awakened by this unusual proceeding in a Friends' meeting, the preacher remarked, that when he saw people in danger of going to sleep, he felt himself justified in using any means to awaken them. He then went on with his discourse.

It is right to cultivate a thankful disposition, and to bear in mind how much we owe to the Lord who giveth us richly all things to enjoy. Hence the propriety of the practice of lifting up our hearts in gratitude to our heavenly Father,

* See note, p. 245.
† A minister among Friends from North Carolina. He died of small pox in 1772, while in England on a religious visit.

before partaking of the food set before us. From the frequent recurrence of these seasons there is danger of their degenerating into a mere form, in which a momentary outward silence is observed, but no effort used to place ourselves mentally in the presence of our Creator. There are many seriously minded persons who habitually make use of a form of prayer on such occasions, offering vocal thanks for the bounties set before them. To this practice, there is this serious objection, that true prayer can only be offered when the heart is prepared by the power of the Lord's spirit; and to offer it with the lip only, when the heart is not quickened by a fresh visitation of grace, is worse than useless.

When John Richardson* was still a boy, his mother married a man who was a zealous Presbyterian. He says in his journal: "The God of love and pity saw me and helped me in my distress, * * when I came to my father's house, he being a man much given to family duties of saying grace, &c., before and after meat, none of which I could comply with, except I felt evidently the Spirit of truth to attend therein, and open the heart and mouth into such duties. The first day I came to the house, being called to the table with all or most of our family, I thought, ' Is it now come to this? I must either displease my Heavenly or earthly father. But oh! the awfulness or deep exercise which was upon my spirit, and strong cries that ascended unto the Lord for my help and preservation, that I might not offend Him. My father-in-law sat with his hat partly on and partly off, with his eyes fixed on me, as likewise mine were on him in much fear; so we continued as long or longer than he used to be in saying grace, as they call it, but said nothing that we heard; so at length he put on his hat again, to the wonder of the family; neither did he then, or ever after, ask me why I did not put off my hat; neither did he perform that ceremony all the time I stayed with him, which was above one year. Thus the Lord

*See note, p. 77.

helped me, renowned be his great name now and forever. * * I saw clearly, that there could not be any true and acceptable worship performed to God, but what was in the Spirit and in the truth, neither could any pray aright, but as the Spirit helped them, which teacheth how to pray and what to pray for, and rightly prepares the mind and guides it in the performance of every service which the Lord calls for from his children."

In another part of his journal, John Richardson relates, that when on the Bermudas Islands, he was invited to dine at a Friend's house, and when they were seated at the table, "the woman of the house desired that one of us would say grace; from which I took an occasion to show her, and several more in the company, who appeared not much more grown in the Truth than she, that since we had been a people we had both believed (and accordingly practised) that true prayer was not performed without the help of the Holy Spirit of God; and no man could pray aright and acceptably without it; nor was it in man's power to have it when he pleased; therefore it is man's place to wait upon the Lord for the pouring forth of this gift upon him; and also to know whether it be required of him to pray, so as to be heard by man, or only to pray secretly, so as to be heard of God, as did Hannah, and many more have done; which, as they do aright, no doubt but as Christ said to his disciples, their Father will hear them in secret and reward them openly."

In connection with this subject may be quoted a remark made by David Ferris,* that in the early part of his religious experience he thought as a child and understood as a child respecting ministry and Divine worship. "I did not clearly perceive that all worship, performed in the will of the creature, and without the immediate assistance of the Holy Spirit, was truly will worship and idolatry. But in process of time I clearly perceived that this was the case."

The unsatisfying character of that ministry which does not proceed from the Source of all good, is illustrated by an

* See note, p. 49.

anecdote related of the Poet Cowper's friend, John Newton.* He once visited a minister who affected great accuracy in his discourses; and who, on that day, had occupied nearly an hour in insisting on several labored and nice distinctions made in his subject. As they walked home he asked Newton whether he thought the distinctions just insisted on were full and judicious. Newton said he thought them not *full*, as a very important one had been omitted. "What can that be?" said the minister, "for I have taken more than ordinary care to enumerate them fully." "I think not," replied John Newton, "for when many of your congregation have travelled several miles for a meal, I think you should not have forgotten the important distinction between *meat* and *bones*."

A similar lesson is taught by the case of Dr. Manton,† who, when preaching before the Lord Mayor and Aldermen of London, chose a subject in which he had an opportunity of displaying his learning and judgment. He was heard with admiration and applause by the intellectual part of his audience; but as he was returning from dinner with the Lord Mayor, a poor man following him pulled him by the sleeve of his gown and said: "I came with hopes of getting some good to my soul, but I was greatly disappointed, for I could not understand a great deal of what you said; you were quite above my comprehension." "Friend," said the doctor, "If I have not given you a sermon, you have given me one; by the grace of God, I will not play the fool in such a manner again."

The account of Balaam, who was sent for by Balak, King of Moab, to come and curse the children of Israel, is one that is full of interest and instruction. There can be no doubt that he was divinely visited and instructed, and enabled to foretell to others the Lord's purposes. But he

---

*Born 1705. Died 1807. A native of London. At one time engaged in African slave trade. Afterwards a minister in the Church of England, and a writer of religious works. See his *Autobiography*.

† An English Non-conformist clergyman. Born 1620. Died 1677. Distinguished as a preacher. See Neal's *Puritans*.

loved the wages of unrighteousness; and though, while the holy influence was upon him, he could utter the petition, "Let me die the death of the righteous," yet he was at last slain among the enemies of the Lord's people. Those who have known the Divine command to preach unto others, are by no means exempted from obedience to our Saviour's injunction, "Watch and pray lest ye enter into temptation;" if they neglect this they will assuredly fall away.

Balaam's experience shows also, that the Lord, in his wisdom, sometimes uses as his instruments, to accomplish particular purposes, those who are not fully brought into subjection to his government. Joseph Hoag* relates an incident of this kind in his own experience, which occurred when he was seventeen or eighteen years of age. He was then visiting a relative, in company with a cousin. He says:

It was a time of life when, at times, I indulged myself in such conversation as promoted merriment. In this way I entertained my cousin most of the way going; but on my return, we had not travelled far, before we were overtaken by a man, who soon fell upon me, cursing the Quakers in strong terms, because they would not fight. It was during the revolutionary war, and critical times in that part of the country. I heard him pretty much through, by which time I felt my mind closely arrested with an uneasy feeling, that the principles of Truth, and the people that I believed were faithful to them, should be so censured, though I felt conscious that I was not one of the faithful, which at times I forcibly felt; yet, notwithstanding my embarrassed state of mind, the Lord, I believed for the sake of his own name, and the tender regard He had for his faithful ones, touched my mind, though I was hardly sensible what it was that required me to speak, let the consequence be what it would. As I commenced, all fear departed, words flowed rapidly, and I was enabled to show the difference between the law

* See note, p. 100.

31

and the gospel—to open to him our principles, giving him our reasons for them, and to prove them by many Scripture passages; and, finally to show him it was impossible for a true Quaker, to be either whig or tory, for they implied opposite parties, and both believed in war, but Friends did not. The man became tender, and with tears running down his cheeks, acknowledged our reasons were good, and that our principles were right, and wished that Friends would keep to them; if they did, it would be a blessing to the world. This remark came home to my feelings. He added that he was fifty-five years of age, and never saw these things before, and that it was marvellous to him to believe. He said there must be great wisdom amongst the Quakers for so young a man to know so much. He urged me to go home with him; I informed him I could not. When we parted with him, he gave me his hand, wished me well, desiring me to remember him, and to pray for him. This thought went through me like a sword; "How can I pray for thee, when I neglect to pray for myself."

As I turned from this man, I discovered a man that had been riding behind us several miles unperceived by me. He suddenly rode up and said: "I was glad to hear you bang off that old whig, for he is an old rebel, an enemy to his king, and it is good enough for him." I turned and looked him full in the face; it came forcibly into my mind, "Thou art one of the vilest of men." I soon replied, "I believe thou art mistaken in me, for I can no more be a tory than I can be a whig." He said, "Whig?" I replied that before the war our country got much filled up with a sort of men that hung about the taverns, practiced card-playing, cock-fighting, horse-racing, and getting drunk, and then would go home and abuse their families; they were in the service of the devil, and of course were his children. The Lord had suffered an evil spirit to divide them; for they corrupted the land—one part had taken side for the king, and the other for the country. Both parties were still in the same practices. For these reasons I cannot be tory nor whig." He went off whistling and left us. My cousin then rode up, and with a serious look, said in substance: "Joseph, all the way going to uncle's thou kept me laughing with thy nonsense, and now thou canst talk like an angel;—set the first man a crying, and the last one thou hast pictured out as correctly as I could, that have lived by him all my days. He is a neighbor to father, and is called many things but good, and thou hast been talking to him like a minister; what can I think of thee?" Her simple remarks went through me like an arrow thrown at venture. It cut me so close that I had to sink down, reasoning with myself, "Sure enough, what am I?" And as I sank down in my mind, I felt the weight of my folly; then after a while it was opened to me in the Light, and with such clearness that I had no power to disbelieve, that the Lord put a word in Balaam's mouth to deliver to the Midianites and Moabites, though his heart was not right before the Lord; and though he was highly favored, yet he did not give up to cleave to the Lord with all his heart, and keep to the word he had spoken to the people, therefore the Lord cut him off. And now the Lord had put a word in my mouth for those men, and for the upholding of the Truth in the earth, though my heart was not right before Him, and if I did not cleave to the Lord with my whole heart, and keep to the word spoken, the time was coming that I should be cut off as Balaam was.

The force of this solemn subject turned my jesting into heaviness of heart. I marvelled at the wisdom, goodness and tender mercy of the Almighty towards me, in awakening and instructing me in such a wonderful manner. Adored and praised forever be his holy name!"

Among the pleasant things to which the mind reverts with grateful feeling, as the occurrences of former years pass in review before it, are some of those seasons of spiritual refreshment, which are often spoken of in the Society of Friends as "religious opportunities." When friends and relatives are gathered in social circle, and passing the time in conversation, a feeling of silent solemnity sometimes spreads over the little company. One after another yields to the quieting influence, till without a word being said, all are found waiting in silence on the Lord, and gathered into a sense of His holy presence. The silence is sometimes broken by the voice of supplication, or the word of exhortation; and sometimes it continues unbroken till a liberty is felt again to resume the social converse. We doubt not most of our readers can recall such seasons, in which their hearts have been melted before the Lord, and earnest desires raised to run with patience in the heavenly path set before them.

John Richardson* relates that after landing on the Bermudas, he and his companion came after night to the house of Richard Stafford, an old man in the station of Judge, who was one of the leading men on the island. On reaching the house, his wife took them to the room where the Judge was. John says: "When we came to him he rose up, and took the candle in his hand and said, 'Are you the strangers that I have sent for?' I said, 'Who thou may'st expect I know not, but we are strangers.' When he had looked well in my face, he set down the candle and said, 'What a mercy is this, that the Lord should send men from I know not where, in his love to visit me!' and took me in his arms and kissed me; and I said to him, 'The Lord of heaven and earth bless thee;' and we shed many tears and wept together.

"As I entered the house, I felt the love of God; and his glory, I thought, shone in and filled every room as I passed through them; and I said, 'Peace be to this place,' and I felt it was so."

The next morning, "I was walking in our lodging-room early, and the Judge's wife came to the door and asked, if she might speak with us? I said she might; then she came in and said, she had a message from her husband to us. I queried what it was. She said, he desired we would come and pray for him before we went away. I desired she would favor us so much as to lay before her husband something which I had to say, and she promised she would: well then, tell the Judge, that if he will suffer us to come into

* See note, p. 77.

his room, and sit down and wait upon the Lord, as our manner is in such a case as this, if it please the Lord to move us by his Holy Spirit to pray, we may; but if not, let not the Judge take it amiss, for we are willing to be at the Lord's disposing in all things. She went, and I believe, as she said, laid the matter before him as I had delivered it to her; for she was a woman of a good understanding, and came back again to us in a very little time. I asked what the Judge said? She replied, he said, 'Let the men take their own way, and whether they pray for me or not, I believe they are men of God:' So after some little respite, we being brought to the Judge's bed-side, sat down and waited upon the Lord, who was pleased in his love and by his mighty power, to break in upon us, and also opened my mouth in his gift of grace and of supplication, in which gift, ardent and fervent cries went up to the Lord of heaven and earth that He would send health and salvation to the Judge, and also to all his family, and to all people far and near, that all every where might repent and come to the knowledge of the Truth and be saved. The Judge wept aloud, and a mighty visitation it was to his family, and especially to himself and his tender wife. We left the Judge in a fine frame of spirit, and no doubt near the kingdom."

Thomas Story* mentions, that in the course of one of his religious visits, he came to Bristol, " Where, lodging at our ancient and honorable friend, Richard Snead's, one morning the canopy of the Divine presence came over us in the family, and brought us all into right silence for a time; and then the holy spirit of prayer and supplication came upon us: And, while we were in that exercise, William Penn, who ever loved the Truth in the meanest, came into the room, and joined with us; and, after him, that ancient, able and eminent Friend and minister of the Lord Jesus, Roger Haydock, who joined in the same likewise; and some others following them, all coming to see us, were favored with the same visitation and good presence of the Lord our God, and the enjoyment of Him together

* See note, p. 111.

31*

in the Beloved, to our great and mutual refreshment, edification and consolation."

On another occasion, when at West Allandale, he says, "In the evening came to us several friends, and among others our ancient and honorable friend, Cuthbert Featherstone; and, as we were conversing together in that friendship which the Lord begets in those who are his, He drew our minds under the canopy of Divine silence; in which, remaining for a time, we had a heavenly visitation of his soul-melting goodness together; and I, observing the tears to trickle down from the eyes of our ancient friend, upon his clothes, was greatly affected with love towards him from the same cause; and had this hope and confidence upon that occasion, that as I then observed the Lord was as near his children in old age, who had served Him faithfully from the time of their visitation, as when He first revealed Himself through his Son, the Lord Jesus Christ in their own hearts, so He would be with me also in advanced years, if I proved faithful and true to the Lord, and attained that degree."

In 1698, when he was about to embark for America on a religious visit, several of his friends accompanied him on board the vessel in which he proposed to make the voyage. He says: " Being together in the great cabin, the good presence of the Lord commanded deep and inward silence before Him, and the Comforter of the just brake in upon us by his irresistible power, and greatly tendered us together in his heavenly love, whereby we were melted into many tears. Glorious was this appearance to the humbling of us all, and admiration of some there who did not understand it. And, in this condition, we remained for a considerable season; and then William Penn was concerned in prayer 'For the good and preservation of all, and more especially for us then about to leave them; with thanksgiving also for all the favors of God, and for that holy and precious enjoyment, as an addition to his many former blessings.' And when he had finished, the Lord repeated his own holy embraces of Divine soul-melting love upon the silent weeping assembly, to the full confirmation of us more immediately concerned, and further evidence to the brethren of the truth of our calling."

Sarah [Lynes] Grubb,* in one of her letters, after speaking of the marriage of her dear friend, Ann Baker, says: "We made an excursion to Malvern, eight miles distant from Worcester, where we were delighted with the admirable display of the beauties of nature in the country; but without attempting a task I am unequal to, that of describing the scene, I hasten to tell thee that I think we had a mark that this innocent gratification was not displeasing to our Heavenly Father; for, as we had descended a little below the summit of the highest hill, sitting down to rest on a bank, an uncommon degree of Divine light and sweetness spread over my mind, under which I recollected a dream I had in the winter, and felt the opening of life to tell it to my companions, and that the reality was then my experience. I dreamed I was on an eminence, surrounded by my fellow-creatures in their habitations, and under great exercise for myself and them, when serenity and sweetness preciously diffused itself into my soul, and my tongue was loosened to sing, 'Alleluia, Alleluia." The relating of it, together with enlargement through the gospel light vouchsafed at the time, broke us all into contrition. My dear Ann said a little matter, and supplication was poured forth, with thanksgiving and praise to Him who shuts and none can open, who opens and none can shut. We went home under the consoling persuasion that He mercifully cares for his little ones. I felt the incomes of love and life so strong, while thus, as it were, unbent with my dear Ann, that we reckoned it might be intended to answer the purpose of the forty days' food."

Joseph Oxley† mentions in his journal, that when his uncle Edmund Peckover was on his way to London in order to pay a religious visit to the churches in America,

---

* An eminent minister among Friends. Died in 1842, at Sudbury, England, aged sixty-nine years. See her *Letters.*

† See note, p. 319.

several friends being in company, a remarkable feeling of holy solemnity overspread them. He says:—

"In this manner we continued some time, and then dear uncle made a full stop, and so did all the rest, and alighted from our horses; uncle being filled with the power and love of God, kneeled down on the wide heath, and supplicated the Almighty with that fervency of spirit, and we were all so affected and reached by the power of Truth, which was over all, as was to our inexpressible joy, consolation and comfort. This was a renewed confirmation and opportunity to dear uncle and us, of his concern being grounded upon a right bottom. I never at any time felt and enjoyed anything to the like degree as this; it was to us at that time, even as if the very heavens were opened, the fragrancy thereof remains sweet in my remembrance to this day! In this heavenly frame, we saluted one another, whilst tears plentifully trickled down our cheeks—we knew not how to part, and yet it must be. Thus in much brokenness and contrition of soul and spirit, we took an affectionate leave one of another; but, indeed, we were so overcome as almost past utterance."

The caution which a true minister of the Gospel, should feel to know a right opening and commission from the Lord, before entering upon religious service, has been referred to in several of the incidents and experiences already related. A similar care is needed in entering upon religious controversy. The remarks upon this subject of Thomas Story* are very instructive.

He was a man of good education and much ability, and in his extensive travels in the service of the Gospel often met with opponents, and was drawn into public disputes with them. While still a young man, residing with his father at Carlisle in England, and soon after he had joined the Society of Friends, a certain Dr. Gilpin of his acquaintance invited him to his house, and desired to see some of

* See note, p. 111.

the writings of Friends. Thomas thereupon sent him all
that he had. His journal says:

"Soon after I had parted with these books, I observed a
cloud come over my mind, and an unusual concern; and
therein the two sacraments (commonly so termed) came
afresh into my remembrance, and divers scriptures and
arguments, *pro* and *con,* and then I was apprehensive the
Doctor was preparing something of that sort to discourse
me upon; and I began to search out some Scriptures in
defence of my own sentiments on those subjects; but as I
proceeded a little in that work, I became more uneasy and
clouded; upon which I laid aside the Scripture, and sat
still, looking toward the Lord for counsel; for I considered
the Doctor as a man of great learning, religious in his way,
an ancient preacher and writer too, famous in Oliver's time,
and a throne among his brethren; and that he might advance
such subtilities as I could not readily confute, nor would
concede to, as knowing them erroneous, though I might not
suddenly be furnished with arguments to demonstrate their
fallacy; and so might receive hurt.

"And then it was clear in my understanding that, as he
was in his own will and strength, though with a good intent
in his own sense, searching the letter, and depending upon
that and his own wisdom, acquirements and subtilty, lean-
ing to his own spirit and understanding, I must decline that
way, and trust in the Spirit of Christ, the Divine Author of
the Holy Scriptures. And as this caution was presented in
the life and virtue of Truth, I rested satisfied therein, and
searched no farther on that occasion. When I went to his
house, he entered into a discourse on those subjects; and
had such passages of Scripture folded down as he purposed
to use; and when I observed it, I was confirmed that my
sight of him, in my own chamber at Carlisle, and of his
work, some days before, was right; and my mind was strengthened thereby."

The conference between them was a friendly one, and
Thomas Story experienced the Spirit of the Almighty to
give him understanding, so that he was enabled to explain

to the Doctor the spiritual views he had embraced of true religion, and the outward and temporary nature of what is termed the Lord's Supper.   The Doctor heard without oppositiou and they parted in friendship.

"From henceforth," T. Story continues, "I was easy as to every thing any of that sort could say.   And divers disputes I have had with many of them since, in other parts of the world; but never began any controversy, being always on the defensive side; and rarely entered upon any point in question, with any sect, till I knew the Divine Truth over all in my own mind, and my will subjected by it.   And my next care usually was, not to provoke my opponent; for, by keeping him calm, I had his own understanding, and the measure of grace in him, for truth and my point, against the error he contended for; and my chief aim generally hath been to gain upon peoples' understanding for their own good. But when a man is put into a passion, he may be confounded but not convinced; for passion is as scorching fire without light; it suspends the understanding and obstructs the way to it, so that it cannot be gained upon or informed, which ought to be the true aim in all conferences and reasoning in matters of religion; else all will end in vain and unprofitable jangling, contrary to the nature of the thing they reason about, and displease the Holy One, and end in trouble. But two or three times at most, in the course of life, and occasional occurrences, in some low cases, with meaner opponeuts, in too hasty engagements in my own strength, and off my full guard, my mind hath been ruffled.   And though I have gained the point by force of argument, from the principle of reason only, and not from the principle of Divine Truth; yet have not had that peace and satisfaction of mind which is to be found in the virtue of Truth alone.   And this also taught me to be totally silent, and sometimes even insulted by ignorants as if I had nothing to say; till the power and virtue of Truth hath arisen in my mind, and then it hath never failed, by its own light and evidence, to support its own cause, and justify me."

On one occasion, when at London, visiting among his

relatives, T. Story accompanied his elder brother, who was Dean of Limerick in Ireland, to the house of Robert Constable, a Justice of the Peace, and a near relation. Among other company was a priest who was a stranger to him, and not knowing their relationship, thought Thomas fair game, and, as he says, " Began to peck at me by several sour hints, which showed his dislike of my company ; which, for conversation's sake, I passed by. · But my forbearance and silence encouraging him to be a little bolder, at length he moved a plain accusation, and said, " You deny the ordinances of Christ, Water Baptism, and the Lord's Supper."

· " I replied : 'Thou hast not heard me say anything on these subjects ; how dost thou therefore know what I deny or affirm ?' Then, said he, ' I perceive you are one of that sect that does deny them.' 'What authority hast thou, said I, for Water Baptism ?' He was ready with that much mistaken text, ' Go ye therefore and teach all nations, baptizing,' &c. ' This, said I, was a commandment given by Christ to his apostles ; but dost thou think this is a command to thee ; (for thou seems to be a teacher of the people), hast thou any authority by this text ?' Upon this he hesitated a little, and the Justice began to smile. The pause being over, the priest answered, ' Yes.' Then, said I, ' how many nations hast thou travelled through in this work ? how many taught and baptized ?' His countenance began a little to alter, and then he replied, ' I have never been out of England.' My next question was : 'How many counties of England hast thou travelled in this service ?' He answered he had not travelled in any on that account. ' Then, said I, thou wicked and unfaithful servant, out of thy own mouth shalt thou be judged : Thou hast here affirmed before these witnesses, that the Lord Jesus Christ hath commanded and sent thee to teach and baptize all nations, and thou art set down in a corner, and hast not baptized any one. For thou must understand, friend, that sprinkling an infant is no baptism, either in mode or subject.' Upon this the Counsellor laughed outright' (for so he was as well as a Justice), and the other priests smiled.   Then, said the Justice, 'Sir, this gentleman is my near relation, a cousin-german, you will get nothing by meddling with him on these subjects.'   And so the matter dropped, and we entered on such matters as occurred, and more natural for conversation among relations and acquaintance."

An incident related by Job Scott* in his journal, illustrates the importance of keeping close to our Heavenly Guide, especially when we are endeavoring to defend the cause of religious truth.

In the year 1784, he attended a meeting at Saratoga, of which he says, "It was to me a time of awful silent waiting; and though several subjects seemed to be opening on my mind, yet they all closed up, and I had no liberty to say any thing among them.

"Near the conclusion of the meeting it sprang a little in my view, and I thought likely I might have to mention it, that I had a little cabinet with me, that contained a valuable treasure; but that I was not the keeper of the key; that He kept the key, who, when He opens, none can shut; and, on the contrary, when He shuts, none can open; so as He did not open, I had nothing for the people.

"After meeting we went home with James Seal.   Here came a Baptist preacher who had been at the meeting. Soon after he came in he began to discourse, and seemed to manifest a disposition to dispute.   I felt a caution arise, not hastily to speak what was on my mind.   So keeping silence, I had an opportunity to hear him work around and try to get hold of something, as he conversed with Daniel Aldrich and the other Friends, till dinner was ready.   Also at the table he manifested the same disposition, and said he should like it better if Friends would state some propositions, and clearly illustrate them, than to dwell much on exhortations &c., meaning in public testimony, I suppose.

"I remained silent till dinner was over; and then, before we rose from the table, I felt an openness to speak.   First, I related the constrainings to silence which I had felt in the

* See note, p. 14.

meeting, and what sprang in my mind near the close of it, respecting the little cabinet I had, the key of which I was not the keeper of, &c. And then, enlarging a little, I added, that I had found by trying to open something myself, I had run into words, to the grief of my own mind, and not to the profit of the people. And further, that by endeavoring to be methodical, I had sometimes lost the life, in which the pure opening was, and so been confused and confounded. But that, by waiting in silence till the life hath arisen, and therein a living opening; and by carefully moving, as the true key opened things suitable to the states of the people, I had often known the power of Truth arise into great dominion; to the consolation of my own soul, the great tendering of the people, and, as I have no reason to doubt, to their real benefit and spiritual advantage.

" After thus expressing, as things opened in a good degree of the influence of truth, the poor man seemed to be entirely shut up; and without making a word of reply, arose from the table, took his stick in his hand and went away. He soon after returned again on some outward occasion, but did not come into our company, and said nothing about religious matters.

"Thus that spirit, wherein he appeared to think himself able to crush and confound us all, was overcome, and as it were chained and bound fast in silence. Let God have all the glory, as it is evidently due to Him. For by waiting his time, He gave us the victory, and that without many words; whereas, had we engaged this priest at a venture, and entered into a dispute with him, in our own creaturely ability, as if our time was always ready, it is very likely it might have led into a large field of words and arguments, without much satisfaction on either side."

On the subject of controversy, Isaac Penington* thus speaks in one of his letters : " As touching disputes, indeed, I have no love to them : Truth did not enter my heart that way; yet, sometimes a necessity is laid upon me, for the sake of others. And truly, when I do feel a necessity, I do it in great fear; not trusting in my spear or bow, I mean in

* See Note, p. 321.

32

strong arguments or wise considerations, which I (of myself) can gather or comprehend : but I look up to the Lord
for the guidance, help and demonstration of his Spirit, that
way may be made thereby in men's hearts for the pure seed
to be reached to, wherein the true conviction and thorough
conversion of the soul to God is witnessed."

This reaching to "the pure seed"—the gift of Divine
Grace—is the surest way to produce conviction.   Many
years ago, a Friend in the vicinity of Philadelphia committed some act against the good order and discipline of the
Society, and justified himself in his offence.   A committee
was appointed to wait upon him, but he was full of arguments in defence of his conduct.   A party was forming in
the Monthly Meeting, for he went about telling what he had
said, and what the committee had said ; and some thought
one thing, and some another.   A Friend, who felt his mind
drawn in love and life to go with the committee to see him,
knowing very well that he would fortify himself with arguments against everything that could be said to him, told his
companions that " we were going to meet with a crooked
spirit, that never could be overcome with words."   He thus
described the interview :

So we went to see him, and he invited us into a room ; and
we all sat in solemn silence together, until he became very
uneasy and restless.   We then conversed about other matters, and afterwards walked out, looked at his farm, and
talked friendly together.   So we came in and took tea ; and
after tea we sat in silence, in a feeling and tender state.
We then concluded to order our horses and go ; but he
said, "Friends, not so.   It is too late."   So we consented
and stayed all night, and in the morning, after breakfast,
we sat down again in solemn silence, and were all much
tendered together.   When we had bid the family farewell,
and had mounted our horses, he called us back and said,
" Friends, I am conquered ; for I could not sleep last night.

I had nothing but my conscience to war with, and it continually reproached me with having done wrong. Oh! Friends, I am willing to make any acknowledgment, if it will only atone for the evil I have done." I told him, he had not much acknowledgment to make to Friends; if he could only make peace with his Heavenly Father, a very little would satisfy Friends. So we went back again, and he wrote an acknowledgment which we thought was more than enough; and when it was made right, we parted in much tenderness, and he gave the paper to the Monthly Meeting. It was freely accepted, and peace and harmony were restored among Friends.

David Ferris,* in speaking of his spiritual progress, gives the following caution:

"Here I think proper to remark, that in one respect I was apt to err, until experience taught me better. This was talking too much about religion in my own will and time. At length I found it tended to poverty; and I learned, when in company, not to be forward to enter into any discourse concerning religion or any other subject; but to be content to keep silence and be esteemed a fool; until Truth arose, a subject clearly presented, and liberty was given for conversation. Then I found a qualification to speak to the edification of others, and my own peace and satisfaction. I mention this for the benefit of others; being convinced that many who have had experience of the Truth, and have in some degree witnessed a change of heart, have talked so much on religious subjects, that their souls have become barren; so as scarcely to know when good cometh."

In conversation on religious subjects, the mind is often influenced by a concealed self-love, which is gratified by the impression we think is made on others as to our own spiritual attainments. This disposition is one that will not bear the searching scrutiny of the Light of Christ to which all our words, as well as thoughts and actions, ought to be

* See Note, p. 49.

brought, to see whether they are "wrought in God." William Lewis,* a valuable minister who deceased at Bristol, England, has left us in his Memoirs, the following remarks on this subject:

"When I consider, and considering, feel, the depth and strength of self-love in the fallen soul of man, broken off from union with the perfect will of its glorious Creator; and the almost perpetual springing forth of vain-glorious desire, branching and spreading in some direction or other from this bitter root; writing, or even speaking of ourselves, appears to my view, an engagement requiring watchfulness and self-abasement; under this persuasion I have cautiously avoided epistolary correspondence on my own spiritual concerns, and have long believed it would be better for all religiously exercised persons (particularly those who are young) to be less employed in this way than is commonly the case. I remain fixed in the judgment, that (unless peculiar circumstances attach) *self* should not be our subject, when we write on spiritual matters; that the marvellous work of a gracious God in the depth of our hearts, should be gratefully acknowledged to *Him* in secret; our inward sorrows poured out *before Him;* that under the painful sense of our defilement, we should simply seek to that fountain which He hath provided, and which He alone opens, for the washing it away; and thus go with the confession of our sins to Him who is faithful and just to forgive them; and who (if we are 'workers together with Him') will assuredly 'cleanse us from all unrighteousness.'"

Just and valuable as are the above observations, they should not be so applied as to limit a *right* freedom of unfolding our exercises, in which there is sometimes a service for the good of others. It is recorded, "They that feared the Lord spake often one to another; and the Lord hearkened and heard it; and a book of remembrance was written

* A minister among Friends, who resided at Bristol, England. Died in 1816. See *Memoirs.*

before **Him** for them that feared the Lord and thought upon His name." If the heart is truly possessed with the love of God, the conversation will evince it, for " out of the abundance of the heart, the mouth speaketh." There is perhaps no safer rule to follow, than that pointed out in the petition of the Psalmist—" May the words of my mouth and the meditations of my heart, be acceptable in thy sight, **O** Lord, my strength and my Redeemer."

Richard Shackleton,* of Ballitore Ireland, in a letter to one of his daughters, after giving her some weighty counsel adds, " These things occurred, and I venture to pen them down, in a degree of freedom of mind. And indeed, without such freedom, we should be cautious of writing or speaking on the solemn subject of religion. Our own spirits, as human creatures, may agitate other matters; but the Spirit of Christ in us should more or less open our understandings, and give liberty, where we meddle with the things of his kingdom."

While there is need of care in this respect, there is also a danger to some, especially to those of a diffident disposition, and those who are not so thoroughly humbled under the Divine Power as to be willing to appear as fools for Christ's sake,— that they may withhold a testimony for their Master, when it is really called for. In the *Youth's Companion,* an instance is recorded, where a manifest blessing rested upon the faithful discharge of such a duty. After speaking of the wisdom needed in speaking to another person upon his religious welfare, and that personal allusions of the kind should be made modestly and quietly, the narrative says:

Two New York merchants lived near neighbors in the environs of the city, and rode to and from their business in the morning and evening trains. They saw each other every

* See Note, p. 194.

32*

day, but were not intimate friends, and were very seldom together.   One was a religious man and the other was not.

One day it happened that they occupied the same seat in the car.   They fell into talk on business matters, discussed the general conditions and prospects of trade, and then spoke of their personal successes.

" It has been a lucky year for me ;" said the elder of the two.   " I suppose I could retire with a hundred thousand dollars.   That certainly is a competence, and I don't know as I care for any more."

" Yes, that is enough," replied the younger.   " You are provided for."

" I suppose I am."

" For *this* life.   Excuse me, may I ask how about the next—the life beyond ?"

" Oh, I don't worry myself about that !"

" But wouldn't it be wise now to give serious thought to what comes after death ?"

" I can see no use in it.   These matters are beyond our control.   I've no fears but it will all come out right."

" But isn't that a rather uncertain trust?   I would not risk it without inquiry and study.   Here, if anywhere, we want things plain, and the words of Christ have made them so."

The merchants parted, to all appearances as totally different men as when they met ; the one with a Divine love in his heart ; the other taken up with the present life, and with no thoughts for the life of eternal future.

No opportunity occurred to renew their conversation. Months passed—and not many—before the elder was taken ill.   His neighbor missed him from the daily trains.   He inquired after ·him, but learned of no alarming disease or danger.   At length, one day while he was in the city, a telegram, sent at the sick man's request, was handed to him in his office, " A. is dying, and wishes to see you."·   The merchant hurried away and at the earliest possible moment stood by his neighbor's bedside.

" I could not die," the sick man whispered, " till I had seen you and thanked you.   What you said that morning on the cars, came up to me since I have been confined at home. I've looked into it, thought over it and prayed over it. I'm going now, but going in peace. Christ is my Saviour. My trust and hope are in Him."

The power for good of a "word fitly spoken," when impressed on the heart by the Spirit of Christ, is shown by the following incident:—

Many years ago, a child was leaving the junior department of a city school for a new home in the country. As he left, his old teacher put her hand upon his head, and in a single, simple sentence, commended him to God and to good. Years passed, and the child grew up, and read books, English, French, German, Greek, on ethics, and listened to lectures on the same subject, by famous professors in a venerable university. But no word which he read in the pages of ancient philosophers, or listened to from the lips of living teachers, ever proved to him a beacon-light like the simple words of his old school-mistress. In the time of temptation, the learned discussions of the philosophers were forgotten, or were remembered only to cause bewilderment as to the basis of right and duty; but the lesson of childhood shone then the most clearly in the secret chamber of the soul and neither time nor doubt had power to dim its radiance.

That eminent minister, Richard Jordan,* who died in 1826, is said to have been one who was "apt to teach" in social conversation. He remarked of himself, that he sometimes felt himself as much under the Divine anointing when engaged in serious conversation, or relating religious anecdotes, as when pleading the cause of his Saviour in the public assemblies of his people. On one such occasion, when visiting at the house of a friend in New Jersey, during the evening, he addressed each of the four sons in the family where he was staying, in a conversational way. One he

* See Note, p. 282.

cautioned against the use of tobacco; another against excess in eating; another he warned against too much laughter; and the fourth against talking too much.

What effect attended the admonitions we are not informed; but they were probably all judicious, and no one of that four addressed could evade the application to himself of the advice, on the plea that it was intended for others.

PART V.

REWARDS OF FAITHFULNESS.

CHAPTER XIII.

Joy, Hope, Peace. Job Scott. Thomas Wilson. Thomas Thompson. William Hornold. Thomas Camm. Samuel Bownas. A. F. Priscilla Richardson. Epidemic in Philadelphia in 1699. John Fletcher. Peter Gardiner. John Churchman. Death of a Sceptic. Mary Griffin. Comfort Collins.

THERE is a satisfaction in being brought under religious exercise, and in the performance of the Lord's will, which is truly comforting to the sincere Christian, being an evidence to him of a degree of unity with his Divine Master. Yet in addition to this, our Heavenly Father is sometimes pleased to fill the souls of his faithful servants with a fulness of rejoicing, that there is scarce room to receive.

In a letter of Job Scott,* he thus refers to a religious visit he had paid: "After all my painful conflicts in your land, the satisfaction I felt the day I bent my course for home, on looking back and over the visit made, was truly beyond my present ability to describe, and, I trust, will leave a lasting seal on my mind. It seemed as if the heavenly hosts hovered over me, for many miles on the way, so that tears of joy flowed irresistibly, like a river. I was not fit for any conversation for a dozen miles, but rode alone, mostly behind. And oh! the heart-heaving emotions which I felt towards many whom I had seen in your western world! Oh! the cries which ascended for your preservation! How

* See note, p. 14.

often did this language run powerfully through my mind:
'Ye that keep watch in Heaven watch over them.'   But I
must not lavish away too much of that ecstatic, rapturous
enjoyment, I then felt."

Many are the records preserved which show the comfort
and satisfaction which the Lord pours into the hearts of
those who have been faithfully engaged in his service.
When Thomas Wilson,* who had long labored for the good
of others, was enduring the last conflicts of nature, he was
asked—"If he would have anything to wet his mouth;" to
which he replied, "The Lord hath taken away all my pain,
and given me the bread of life and the water of life, and
quenched my thirst, which hath been great; the will of the
Lord be done."   And again said, "The Lord's goodness
fills my heart, which gives me the evidence and assurance
of my everlasting peace in his kingdom, with my ancient
friends that are gone before me, with whom I had sweet
comfort in the work of the gospel."   "The Lord visited me
in my young years, and I felt his power, which hath been
with me all along, and I am assured He will never leave
me, which is my comfort."

The true Christian will be preserved from placing any
dependence for salvation on his works or merits, and will
unfeignedly acknowledge that he is an "unprofitable servant," having done no more than was his duty to do; and
this, no matter how earnestly and zealously he may have
labored in the Master's cause.   As he nears the close of
life, it is often the case that such an one is made strongly to
feel that his hopes must rest on the mercy of God in Christ
Jesus our Lord; and yet the remembrance of the labors and
exercises undergone for the sake of his Redeemer, are attended with great comfort and satisfaction, as evidences of
that Divine love and help which enabled him to perform
them.

* See note, p. 46.

It is recorded of Thomas Thompson,* one of the early Friends, that he was convinced by William Dewsbury, in the year 1652, and soon afterwards received a gift in the ministry, which he exercised faithfully during a period of about fifty years. When on his death-bed, and previous to a very triumphant transit from time to eternity, he was enabled to make this remarkable acknowledgment: "Since the day that the Word of the Lord came to me saying, ' As thou art converted, strengthen thy brethren ; and, if thou lovest me, feed my lambs,' I have spared no pains, neither in body nor spirit, neither am I conscious of slipping one opportunity of being serviceable to Truth and Friends ; but have gone through what was before me with all willingness possible ; and now I feel the love of God and the returns of peace in my bosom." Yet he did not fail to ascribe all to the efficacy of redeeming love and mercy, saying, "The Lord Jesus Christ has shed his precious blood for us, and laid down his life, and become sin for us, that we might be made the righteousness of God in Him."

William Hornold,† whose residence was in Middlesex, England, and who died whilst absent from home in the service of the Gospel, was a faithful laborer. Among his dying sayings, the following have been preserved.

" I thank the Lord my God, who hath kept and preserved me ever since He made me sensible of his everlasting Truth ; and through the help of the Lord my God, I have labored faithfully, according to the ability the Lord hath given. Yea, I can say, I have labored freely in the service of the Lord, that He called me to, for the promotion of his everlasting Truth on earth, and for the gathering of the people to the holy way of the Lord. And I have not sought myself, but served my God in truth and faithfulness, according to that ability the Lord gave me, praised be his holy name forever, for all honor and glory, thanksgiving and everlasting praises shall be given, attributed and ascribed to the Lord my God ; for it is his due, and He is everlastingly worthy of it."

* Died 1704. See notice of him in *Friends' Library*. vol- 1, p. 191.

† A resident of Middlesex, England. Died in 1710. See notice in Evans' edition of *Piety Promoted*, vol. 2, p. 43.

The memoir of Thomas Camm,* manifests the same ascription of all to the mercy of God, mingled with rejoicing that he had been enabled to fight a good fight, and keep the faith.   As he was sitting in his chamber, during the time of weakness that preceded his removal from this stage of existence, when asked how he did? he replied: "I am but weakly in body, but strong in the inner man, blessed be the Lord, who hath been my support and strength hitherto." And he then farther said, "I have been pondering in my mind, and meditating of the wonderful and unspeakable mercies and loving kindnesses of God, to me extended all my life long, even to this very day; that I, such a poor, weak, feeble creature, should be enabled to hold out and go through those many trials, travels, sufferings and exercises, both inward and outward of various kinds, that have fallen to my lot.   It has indeed been the Lord's doings, who is and has been all along my buckler and my shield; He shall have the praise and the glory of all, for He alone is worthy of it, forever and forevermore."

In the cases of some who have been greatly blessed as laborers in the Lord's vineyard, there has been in old age a decay of the mental powers, which has precluded such expressions of the spiritual feelings as are shown in the instances already referred to.   Such an one was Samuel Bownas,† whom Samuel Neale visited in 1752, and of whom he says: "My heart was made sensible of the necessity we have, while day and capacity are afforded, to work in the vineyard into which we are called, by seeing this laborer in a decaying, drooping way, by a failure of those faculties that were once so bright, fertile and fruitful.   But still he maintains that innocency and sweetness which Truth gives, and leaves the savor of, to all who are faithful to its manifestations, which remark may my soul treasure up; so that I may make right use of my day and time, and ardently preserve the one thing needful, that leads to eternal repose,

* A minister of Westmoreland, England. Died in 1707, in his sixty-seventh year. See notice in Evans' edition of *Piety Promoted*, vol. 1, p. 396.

† A native of Westmoreland, England. Twice came to America on religious visits. Died 1753. See *Life in Friends' Library*, vol. 3. p. 1, etc.

where the wicked cease from troubling and the weary are at rest."

With Samuel Bownas, spiritual greenness was preserved amid mental decay. But how affectingly contrasts with this another case also mentioned by Samuel Neale, who attended the funeral of the man in 1769. He says:

"This man, A. F., was well gifted, well accoutred, and a serviceable man in his younger days; but by being too much made use of by Friends, in the several offices of the church, he took too much upon him, became rather exalted, and did not abide enough in the lowly self-denying life of truth; by which his spirit became too sufficient of himself, and his sufficiency was not enough of God, and the spirit of his Son. The fall of man is by little and little, not all at once; his departure is established as he forgets the rock from whence he was hewn, and the hole of the pit from whence he was digged; wrong is substituted for right, and error for truth; a lording spirit prevails, and so the poor creature falls into delusion, even to believe a lie!

"A. F. was a man of good capacity, good natured to a large degree, and was very compliant and obliging, which made him much beloved by those of others as well as our own Society. An inclination to gratify a passion which has overthrown many was his foible: and though it began by a seeming temperance, yet habit confirmed a love for it, and so little by little the passion strengthened as it was gratified and became master of the man; which increased so powerfully, as to weaken and enfeeble his love for God and man. The good cause he once delighted in, and was an advocate for, he neglected, and so was bound to his Delilah, by which he became dim, if not totally blind, with respect to spiritual sight and discerning; thus he lost his place in the mystical body, and became a fruitless branch in the Lord's vineyard! May the sight and sense of such objects as this arouse us to vigilance and diligence, that in the end we may be blessed with a mansion in the realms of light and immortality!"

33

There is often much comfort to be derived from the dying testimonies of those who have endeavored to serve the Lord while in health; and who feel on the bed of death that they are not forsaken by their gracious Master. Such faithful servants are often made to feel that their salvation is not from any merit of their own, and are impressed with a sense of their own unworthiness, and that there is no room for flesh to glory in the Divine presence, yet they are enabled to rejoice in the mercy of the Lord extended to them.

John Richardson* testifies of his wife Priscilla, that she "loved retirement much, and waiting upon the Lord, and the enjoyment of his internal and living presence, and especially with the Lord's people, that they might also be made partakers with her of the like special favors. This was as her crown and kingdom in this world, *even from her childhood;* and to see Friends prosper in the truth was matter of great rejoicing to her. When we had been married scarce three years, the Lord raised her up to bear a public testimony amongst Friends in their meetings, which was very comfortable and acceptable to them; and also she had the spirit of grace and supplication measurably poured upon her, so that many with me did believe she had access to the throne of God, and to that river which maketh truly glad the city of God. She always freely gave me up to answer the service I believed the Lord called for of me.

"She was taken from me when we had been married but about five years, in the twenty-eighth year of her age, and died in a sweet frame of mind and was sensible to the last; and her last words were, 'He is come, He is come, whom my soul loves; and my soul rejoices in God my Saviour, and my spirit magnifies Him.'"

Thomas Story† relates that when he was at Philadelphia, in 1699, the city was afflicted with an epidemic of fatal sickness, which carried off much people. He says: "I

*See note, p. 77.
†See note, p. 111.

found my companion well, but many Friends on their sick and dying pillows; and yet never could be more of the settled remaining presence of the Lord with them, or scarce any where, than was with them at that time. Such is the goodness of God to his own people, that in their bodily or any other afflictions, his holy presence greatly abates the exercises of nature by its Divine consolation. O the love that flowed in my soul to several in the times of my visits to them! in which I was lifted over all fear of the contagion, and yet not without an awful regard toward the Lord therein.

"My companion and I remained in town till the twenty-third of the month, visiting the sick Friends from time to time, as we found necessary or expedient. And great was the presence of the love of God with his people, in the midst of this trying visitation; which gave us occasion to say, 'Good is the Lord, and greatly to be feared, loved and obeyed; for though He suffers afflictions to come upon his own chosen people, in common with other men; yet that, which otherwise would be intolerable, is made as nothing, by how much the sense thereof is swallowed up and immerged in his Divine love. Oh, the melting love! Oh, the immortal sweetness I enjoyed with several, as they lay under the exercise of the devouring evil (though unspeakably comforted in the Lord)! let my soul remember it, and wait low before the Lord to the end of my days!'"

Mary Fletcher relates of her estimable husband, John Fletcher,* that when near the end of his life, "he told me he had received such a manifestation of the full meaning of those words, *God is love*, as he could never be able to express. 'It fills my heart,' said he, 'every moment, Oh, Polly, my dear Polly, *God is love!* Shout, shout aloud! I want a gust of praise to go to the ends of the earth!'"

Of Peter Gardiner (an anecdote of whom is narrated on page 327,) it is recorded that he "made a very sweet and heavenly end." To one who came into his sick chamber,

---

* Born in Switzerland in 1729. Became a clergyman in the Church of England. Author of several religious works. Died in 1785, beloved for his piety and amiable qualities.

he said, " I am sick in body, but the Lord reigns gloriously in Zion : His power is over all his enemies." His last message to be sent to Friends of his own neighborhood, is very touching : " I have sweet peace with Him that is the Redeemer of Israel, and am now waiting for my Pilot to conduct me to my long home."

When John Churchman,* of Nottingham, was on his death-bed, although his pain was often great, he would many times in a day, break forth into a kind of melody with his voice, without uttering words, which, as he sometimes intimated was an involuntary aspiration of his soul in praise to the Lord, who had again been pleased to shine forth in brightness after many days of poverty and deep baptism, which though painful, had proved beneficial to him, being a means of further purifying from the dross of nature. A few hours before the close of life he said, " I am much refreshed with my Master's sweet air ; I feel more life, more light, more love and sweetness than ever before," and often mentioned the Divine refreshment and comfort he felt flowing like a pure stream to his inward man, saying to those who were with him, " I may tell you of it, but you cannot feel it as I do."

These and thousands of others have verified in their experience the testimony borne by the late Samuel Cope in one of his public testimonies, that the Christian religion is one " to live by " and " to die by." One of the weakest · points in the system of those who reject it, is the absence of any light or hope as to the future, when this stage of existence ends. There all, to them, is darkness and doubt. A. T. Rankin gives the following narrative of one whose sceptical views on the approach of death could not give him the support which he then felt to be necessary. He says :

In the early part of my life, travelling in Eastern Virginia, at one of the interior towns I was introduced to Colonel W., a gentleman of wealth and eminence in the

* See note, p. 14.

community where he lived. Surrounded with the blandishments of social and domestic life, often called to bear the honors and reap the profits of office, he seemed happily situated. Some years afterward a newspaper, containing an account of his death, was sent me. When death approached and eternity opened, he felt the folly of living without religion. In his last hours a pious slave directed him to the Saviour of sinners. When the minister, for whom he sent, entered his room, he said, "There sir, you see a faithful old servant, who has answered the end of his being better than I have. He is a Christian, and I am a lost sinner. I would rather now be what he is than what I am, though I possessed the wealth of the Indies. I have been a wretched disciple of Paine; and, what is worse, I have endeavored to make others as bad as myself. What have I gained by all the deistical works of which I once was so fond? Nothing but the horror and distress of mind which I now suffer. Now they seem to me as the poison of the serpent."

To his associates in disbelief he said: "I once held the same opinions, I hold them no longer. I cannot die an infidel. God have mercy upon me, a poor, mean, vile sinner!"

What a contrast with such a case is furnished by the following narratives:—

Mary Griffin, a native of Connecticut, was a minister who labored in the Lord's cause in her early life, and continued to be employed in his blessed service to a very advanced age. When eighty-two years old she travelled several hundred miles on horseback on a religious visit; and in her one-hundreth year the energy and clearness of her mind continued so unimpaired, that although so weak in body as to be unable to stand alone she performed a religious visit among the families of Nine Partners' Meeting in New York. In the flowing of gospel love she was often led tenderly to point out to the young the great advantage of choosing the Lord for their portion. As she drew towards the close of her earthly pilgrimage she seemed absorbed in the love of

33*

her Saviour, in whose service she had been so long engaged; and her conversation was much about the things pertaining to an everlasting state.

One day, while sitting retired and meditating alone, as she was accustomed to do, she was overheard saying, "I hope ere long to rest eternally in the arms of thy love." Reviving from a fainting fit, she exclaimed, "I feel love to flow to all mankind, and I believe this love will increase, and Truth prosper and spread through distant lands, even where they sit as it were in darkness; and that the knowledge of the Lord will cover the earth as the waters do the sea. My heart is filled with praises to the Lord, that He not only called me in my youth, but enabled me to follow Him; and is yet with me in old age. Oh! it is well, when we can say with the Apostle, "I have fought a good fight, I have kept the faith, henceforth there is laid up for me a crown of righteousness, which the Lord, the righteous Judge, shall give me at that day; and not to me only, but to all them also that love his appearing."

Her strength gradually wasted away, and she remained in a very sweet frame of mind to the close. Her last words to her children and her grandchildren, who had gathered round her dying bed, were, "Fear the Lord above all things, and keep up your religious meetings."

Comfort Collins was another of the aged servants of Christ, who found by happy experience, that the Lord does not cast them off in the time of old age, when their physical and mental strength fail. One who visited her in 1812, when she was more than one hundred and one years of age, thus describes the interview, "All her faculties have in a manner, fled, save religious sensibility. She has no recollection of ever having had a husband or children, houses or lands; nor any remembrance of her nearest friends, when named; yet her sense of Divine good, and the religious fervor of her mind, appear unabated. We stayed about an hour with her; the whole of which time she was engaged in praising her Maker,—in exhorting us to love the Lord, and to lay up treasure in Heaven;—several times saying, 'one hour in the Lord's presence is better than a thousand elsewhere. I know it, Friends, I know it by experience.' Then her voice would settle away into a kind of melody; and, after being still a minute or two, she would again lift it up with angelic sweetness in praising the Lord, and advising us to love and fear Him."

INDEX.

Acknowledgment of wrong made helpful to a stranger to religion. The, 67.

African woman. Kindness of a poor Christian, 170.

Amusements. Remorse of a dying woman who had wasted her time in worldly, 154.

    The Light of Christ leads those who obey it out of worldly, 156. 158.

Ashton, John. Noble resolution of, and his wife to walk in the way of everlasting happiness, 41.

Atheist. No man can be an, before he acts contrary to knowledge, 98.

Bacon, David. Composure of, in time of danger, 226.

Baily, William. The love and religious concern of, for his persecutors, 270.

Ball. The attendance of a, contrary to convictions of conscience, 95.

Banks, John. Concern of, to be diligent in temporal, as well as spiritual things, 342.

Baptism. True, that of the Holy Spirit, 43, 371.

    Illustration of the nature of true, 54.

Barclay, Robert. Remarks of, on the visitations of the Spirit of Christ which come upon all men, 39.

    Convinced of the Truth by the secret operations of the Divine life, 305.

Bathurst, Elizabeth. Concern of, for her acquaintance, 270.

Beer. The sale and use of given up, 86.

Benton, Thomas H. Tribute of, to his mother, 75.

    led to obtain a reconciliation with those with whom he had been at variance, 174.

Benevolence, 160.

Bettle, Samuel, Sr. Account related by, of the efficacy of prayer, 140.

Brantingham, Mary. Incident in the ministry of, 308.

Bray, William. Benevolent acts of, 166.

    Faith exemplified in the life of, 232, 233, 234.

    Love of and concern for others, 268, 284, 285.

    acknowledges his inability to preach without Divine help, 346.

Camm, Thomas. Ascription of praise and rejoicing of, at the close of life, 384.

Capper, Mary. Experience of the teaching of the Holy Spirit by, when a child, 25.

Card Playing. Effectual reproof given to, 79.

    draws away the mind from heavenly things, 157.

    The practical effects of, injurious in any and every home, 158.

Carlett, S. Providentially relieved from anxiety respecting the payment of a debt, 56.

Chalkley, Thomas. Testimony of, that card playing, music and dancing should be shunned by Christians, 157.

Chaplin, Jeremiah. Kindness of, in his business dealings, 170.

Child. Submission and confidence of a tender hearted and loving, 191.

    The unhesitating trust of a, 240.

Christ by his Spirit visits all men, 9.

    The light of, reveals sin and leads to repentance and amendment of life, 27.

    The light of, guides man's steps in the way of peace, 250.

    Experience of the healing virtue of, 198, 199, 200, 201.

Christmas. Solemn warning against spending the day called, in a riotous and sinful manner, 58.

Churchman, John, instructed when but eight years old to choose the path of obedience and peace, 14.

    restrained from making a voyage in an armed vessel, 78.

    Loss sustained by, through unwatchfulness, 98.

    Concern of, to turn people to the Witness for Truth in their own hearts, 181.

    relieved from apprehensions of danger by the fear of the Lord, 224.

    led to illustrate the work and effects of religion by comparisons drawn from the outward world, 289, 290, 291.

Churchman, John, called to visit England, &c., in the love of the gospel, 300.

> instructed to attended closely to Divine openings in his ministry, 346.

> Illustrations of Divine guidance in the ministry of, 349, 350.

> Divine refreshment and comfort felt by, on his death bed, 388.

College student. Visitation of Divine grace to a, obeyed, 28.

> Visitation of Divine grace to a, disregarded, 118.

Collins, Comfort. Happy experience of, when physical and mental strength failed, 390.

> Elizabeth. Narrative by, of an instance of Divine mercy and justice, 59.

> Instructed to be more faithful in the exercise of her gift as a minister, 119.

Compassion overpowering the love of life. Incident of, 172.

Compliments. The use of, declined by David Ferris from religious conviction, 152.

Confession of wrong doing the way to peace of mind. The, 121, 123, 125, 126.

Conversation on religious subjects not to be lightly entered upon, 375.

Cowper, John. Testimony of, to the need of Divine help to understand the way of salvation, 110.

Dahl, Endre. Remarkable preservation of, and companions at sea, 202.

Danger. The fear of removed, 224, 226, 227, 228.

Deist instructed, A. 334.

Delay in performing religious duties dangerous, 114, 247.

Dewsbury, William. Willingness of, to suffer for his religious testimony, 219.

Divine grace. The visitations of, extended to all, even to barbarous people, the ignorant, the young, &c., 9.

> Illustrations of the operations of, 10–40.

> On the importance of yielding immediately to the visitations of, 117.

> Repentance for past sins one of the early effects of yielding to, 121.

> mercy and forbearance. Instance of, 97.

Divine guidance, 242-262, 318, 323, 344.

    guidance and sanction in regard to marriage. On the importance of seeking, 263.

    revelation not ceased, 323.

Dreams used at times to convey spiritual instruction, 49.

Dress. Plainness and simplicity in, enjoined upon the followers of Christ, 143, 146, 147, 148.

Drinking of healths refused by Thomas Story, 198.

Drunkard. An habitual, solemnly warned by a dream, 57.

Ellwood, Thomas. The spiritual growth of, hindered by religious performances in his own will, 106.

Emlen, James. Remarks of, on Divine favor often enjoyed early in religious experience, 193.

Everard Barbara. The power of Divine grace displayed through, 319.

Example of an upright Christian life. The good effect of the, 64, 65, 66, 67, 68, 69, 70.

    An evil, often very hurtful to others, 66.

Faith. True, 23

    exemplified in the life of William Bray, 232, 233, 234.

    of a slave woman, 235.

Faithfulness to convictions of duty, 88, 94, 214.

    The rewards of, 381.

Ferris, David. Instruction conveyed to, in a dream, 49, 51.

    ascribes all his knowledge in Divine things to the teachings of the Holy Spirit, 110.

    Convinced of the impropriety of the plural language to a single person, and of hat honor, 152.

    Remarks of, on the injurious effects of talking too much on religious subjects, 375.

First day of the week. The conscientious observance of the, 83, 94, 214.

Flavel, John. The ministry of, made effectual to a hearer after many years, 31.

Fletcher, John. Experience of the love of God, near the close of life, 387.

    Mary. Testimony of, respecting plainness of dress, 148.

Foreign travel. The insidious dangers of, 181.

Forgiveness of injuries. Powerful effect produced upon others by the meek, 69.

Fothergill, John. Experience by, when very young of the manifestation of the light of Christ against sin, 26.

Samuel. Instructive dreams related by, 52.

Friends. The example and appearance of, blessed to others, 18, 151.

On the testimony of, to plainness of dress, 149.

Fruits of the Spirit, 121.

Gardiner, Peter. Instances of Divine revelation in the ministry of, 327, 328.

Account of the heavenly end of, 387.

Gibbons, Hannah. Instructive incident in the life of, 114.

Gobat, Bishop, remarkably delivered from death, 216.

Gough, John B. Remarkable instance of the power of Divine Grace related by, 35.

Green, Jacob. Instructive incident recorded of, 148.

Grellet, Stephen, instructed in regard to the washing of regeneration, 54.

Solemn warning by, against spending the day called Christmas in a riotous and sinful manner, 58.

Griffin, Mary. Happy retrospect and experience of, in advanced age, 389.

Griffith, John, delivered from a delusion of Satan, 107.

Grubb, Sarah [Lynes]. Account by, of a tendering religious opportunity, 367.

Halhead, Miles. Illustration of the continuance of Divine revelation in modern times in the case of, 329.

Hat honor. David Ferris required to bear a testimony against, 152.

Healy, Christopher. Incident in the ministry of, 315.

Help providentially extended, 211, 212.

Helping others. On the duty of, 163.

Hill, Rowland. Illustration of one of the devices of Satan by, 293.

Holy Scriptures made instrumental in solacing the heart of an aged widow. The, 62.

Good effect upon others of an example of reading the, 71.

Holy Scriptures. The, are to be rightly understood only by the openings of the Spirit of Christ, 111.

The, instrumental in saving the life of a young woman, 313.

Hoag, Joseph. Experience by, of the temptations to and dangers of infidelity, 100.

Instructive incidents in the experience of, 114, 345, 348, 361.

Testimony of, to the healing virtue of Christ, 200.

Divinely instructed in regard to a change of residence, 259.

answers the objections of a slaveholder, 261.

Encouragement instrumentally conveyed to, 273.

Future events foretold by, 324, 325, 326.

encouraged to trust in the Lord for the support of his family, while absent on religious services, 340.

Holy Spirit. The awful condition of those who reject the visitations of the, 95.

The immediate revelations of the, alone give a right understanding in spiritual concerns, 110.

Hone, William, reclaimed from infidelity, 24.

Honesty of Abraham Lincoln. The, 133.

which flows from the fear of God. Illustrations of, 135, 137.

Hooper, Geraldine. Reproof administered by, 286.

Hornold, William. Faithfulness of and thankfulness of, to the Lord, at the close of life, 383.

Horse racing. Solemn instance of Divine mercy and judgment on a young man addicted to, 59.

Humility one of the fruits of the Spirit, 180.

Indian woman. The prayer of an, 353.

Infidel reclaimed through the instrumentality of his daughter. An, 24.

convinced through the example of an upright Christian. An, 64.

A converted, led to make restitution, 127.

An, answered, 287.

Infidelity. Disobedience and unwatchfulness lead towards, 98, 99, 101, 187.

renounced on the death-bed, 388.

Influence. Observations upon our unconscious, over others, 72.

Influence. On the importance of guarding our, 72.

On the responsibility upon all for the, they exert over others, 73.

Intoxicating liquor. The influence of a child against the use or sale of, blessed, 22, 23.

Remarkable reformation of a woman addicted to the use of, 35.

The power of natural affection used to reclaim a father from the use of, 139.

A prominent professional man induced to abandon the use of, 139.

Prayer for Divine help to resist the temptation to use, answered, 140.

Bravery, unassisted by Divine grace, not sufficient to resist the temptation to use, 141.

Johnson Dr. Samuel. An act of contrition by, for disobedience to his father, 129.

Remark of, on the effect of luxuries, &c., at a dying hour, 159.

Jordan, Richard. Instance of the baptizing power of the ministry of, 318.

Religious concern of, in social intercourse, 379.

Kennedy, James. Consistent, upright course of, 91.

Kindness to a poor widow in her distress. An act of, 160, 162.

Knox, John. The Scottish reformer, saved from death by obeying an internal admonition, 245.

Language. The plain Scripture of thou, &c., enjoined, 145, 149, 152.

Law. The practice of the, declined by Thomas Story as a dangerous obstruction to his religious progress, 262.

Leddra, William. The joy of, on the eve of martyrdom, 220.

Legislature of Virginia. A member of, preserved from death, by attending his week-day meeting, 206.

Lewis, William. Observations of, on the constant need of watchfulness against self love, 376.

Lincoln, Abraham. Illustrations of the honesty of, 133.

The kind feelings of, 164, 165.

The dependence of, upon an overruling Providence, 235.

Lord's care over his people. The, 196.

Love and concern for the welfare of others, one of the fruits of the
      Spirit, 267.

      at times requires the administration of severe reproof, 276.

Lybrand, Joseph. Divine intimation to, obeyed, 249.

Marriage. Sad consequences to a Christian woman from, with an
      irreligious man, 183.

      The importance of seeking Divine guidance in regard to, 263.

      The experience of Frederick Smith of the blessings of religious
      fellowship in, 265.

Marsh, John Finch. Incident in the ministry of, 317.

Martyrs. Adrianus, one of the early, 70.

      Heavenly consolations of the, 220, 221, 222.

Mazarin, Cardinal. Anguish of, near the close of life, 156.

Ministry. Illustrations of the effects of true gospel, 41, 304, 307, 310,
      311, 318.

      The, of the word of life truly baptising, 43, 44.

      Sorrowful result of a refusal to appear in the, 97.

      Warning to those in the, against highmindedness, 184.

      Account by Thomas Story of his call to visit America in the
      work of the, 299.

      The exercise of, not to be undertaken without an evidence of
      the fresh extension of Divine help, 302, 303, 321, 322, 331,
      332, 344, 345, 346, 351.

      The beneficial effects of, largely dependent upon the state of
      mind of the hearer, 305, 317.

      Gifts in the, bestowed on women, 308, 319.

      Illustrations of unity of exercise in the, 315, 316.

      Gifts in the, at times bestowed upon persons of weak mind, 319.

      On the outward maintenance of the, as showed by Christ, 336.

      Diligence in their temporal business advised to those engaged
      in the, 341.

      Outward information at times hurtful to the exercise of the,
      348.

      A, without words, 351.

      The unsatisfying character of that, which does not proceed from
      the Source of all good, 359.

Moffàtt, Robert. Account related by, of the kindness of a poor African woman, 170.

Mother. The influence of a pious, 75.

Mott, Richard. The effect of the example and conversation of, upon a boy, 18.

Music ought to be refrained from, 157.

Naylor, James. Testimony of, against deceitful prayers and worship, 109.

Extract from, on love to the lost, 276.

Divine authority attending the ministry of, 310.

Neale, Samuel. Account by, of his yielding to Divine visitation, and appearance in the ministry, 44.

instructed to give up gunning and such amusements, 83.

experiences conversion to be a gradual work, 105.

respected for using the plain language, 153.

Remarks of, on the preservation of spiritual greenness, amid the decay of the mental powers, 384.

Oaths. A faithful testimony borne against, 89.

Obedience to the Spirit of Christ in the heart necessary for the reception of the Divine blessing, 80.

Prompt, to requisitions of duty necessary, 114, 119.

One step in the right direction opens the way for another, 86.

Operations of Divine grace, 9.

Opportunity for doing good. Watchfulness in improving an, 116.

Parker, Theodore. Instructive incident occurring in his childhood related by, 13.

Peckover, Edmund. Solemn religious opportunity of, with Friends, 367.

Penington, Isaac, convinced of the truth by the power of God, 321.

Remarks of, respecting disputes on religious matters, 373.

Penn, William. The love of, for the Truth, 365, 366.

Pernicious reading. Illustration of the sorrowful effects of, 124.

Pierce, Jane. Instance of Divine forbearance and mercy related by, 97.

Pike, Joseph. Account by, of the baptizing power attending the ministry of William Edmundson, 43.

Plain Scripture language of thou to one, &c. The, 145, 149, 152.

Plainness and simplicity in dress and behavior enjoined upon the followers of Christ, 143, 146, 147, 148, 149, 150.

Poor and afflicted. Instances of holy faith in the, 221, 222.

Prayer. True, the breathing of the soul to God, through the operation of the Holy Spirit, 107, 296, 353, 358.

How, may become abomination, 109.

The efficacy of true, 140, 206, 212, 272, 296, 297.

Prayers and praise of a poor laboring man blessed to a sinful woman, The, 61.

Privateering. A faithful warning against, disregarded, 60.

Profanity reproved, 70, 274, 278, 279.

Prophecy. The spirit of, not withdrawn from the church, 323.

Quietness and composure in times of danger, 219.

Rachel, Joseph. Kind act of, 166.

Railroad. Faithfulness to convictions of duty of a conductor on a, 83.

Providential preservation of a train from wreck on a, 205.

Redman, Elizabeth L. Incidents in the life of, showing Divine guidance, 246.

Religious opportunity of, with a slave-dealer, 314.

Religion. The essence of, consists in being brought under the dominion of the life and power of Christ, 106.

Nothing in, can be accceptable to God but the genuine product of his unerring Spirit, 108.

On the difference between a theoretical assent to the truths of, and a living conviction of their reality, 112.

A travail of spirit to be experienced in the work of, 194.

Honesty one of the effects of, 214.

Illustrations of the work and effects of, by comparisons drawn from the outward world, 289, 290, 291, 292, 294.

not only preserves the mind from undue cares, but leads to industry, 341.

On the care necessary on entering into controversy concerning, 368, 372, 373, 374.

The injurious effects of talking too much on religious subjects, 375.

The Christian, that to live by and to die by, 388.

Removal of residence. The importance of seeking to the Lord for counsel in, 257.

Renwick, James. One of the Scottish martyrs, 221.

Repentance one of the fruits of the Spirit, 121.

Reproof at times a religious duty, 269.

The administration of, 274, 277, 278, 280, 282, 283, 286, 287, 312, 357.

Restitution of property wrongfully taken one of the effects of yielding to Divine Grace, 121, 123, 126, 127, 128.

Retirement of soul before the Lord. Blessings to be derived from frequent, 305, 354, 363, 365, 367, 386.

Rewards of faithfulness, 331.

Richardson, George. Instructive incident in the ministry of, 260.

Richardson, John. Experience of, in the work of regeneration, 104.

convinced about hat honor, bowing the knee, and finery in habit, 144.

Observations of, on the need of constant watchfulness, 183.

Experience by, of the virtue of Christ in healing physical ailments, 198.

preserved from the fear of death, 228.

Divinely instructed in removing his residence, 258.

Remarks of, on seeking Divine counsel in regard to marriage, 264.

Divine opening to, respecting future events, 323.

Remarks of, on the maintenance of ministers, 336.

Observations of, on declining to say " grace," before meals, 359.

Tendering religious opportunity of, with a family in Bermuda, 364.

Testimony of, to the religious character, and happy death of his wife, 386.

Robbers. A religious man preserved among, 224.

Roberts, John. Future events foretold by, 330, 331.

Robson, Michael. Account by, of his convincement of the principles of Friends, 151.

Routh, Martha, when quite young made sensible of Divine displeasure, 11.

Salvation to be known only through the gospel of Christ, 109.

Scott, Job, when very young instructed in Divine knowledge, 14.

Scott, Job, convinced that true baptism is not that of water, **43.**

> Experience by, of the dangers of infidelity, 99.

> Experience of, in the work of regeneration, 104.

> led to adopt the plain Scripture language of thou to one, &c., 145.

> Earnest religious concern and supplication of, for the souls of others, 271.

> Divine openings on the mind of, 301, 372.

> instructed in silent exercise in religious meetings, 302.

> Rejoicings of, in a sense of Divine favor in the retrospect of a religious visit, 381.

Scotton, Robert. Account related by, of the prayer of an Indian woman, 353.

Secret Society. A member of a. Divinely required to withdraw from it, 81.

Self-love. The constant need of watchfulness against, 376.

Self-indulgence. On the danger of yielding to, 185.

Services to be performed by the followers of Christ, 267.

Shackleton, Richard. Remarks of, on the blessings derived from frequent retirement of soul before the Lord, 305, 354.

> Caution by, upon writing or speaking on religious subjects, 377.

Shipton, Anna. Relation by, of the Christian life and services of a girl of seventeen. 15.

> Account by, of the effect of the prayers of a poor laboring man, 61.

> Remarks of, on one who had become entangled in the snares of the world, 181.

Shipwreck. Remarkable deliverance from, 207, 209.

Singing praises to the Almighty in an irreverent manner reproved, 46.

Simpson, James. Incidents in the ministry of, 332, 333, 334.

Simpson, John. Concern of, to be industrious in business as well as fervent in spirit, 343.

Slave-dealer. Religious opportunity of Elizabeth L. Redman with a, 314.

Slave-holder rebuked. A former, 283.

Slavery. Observations of Abraham Lincoln upon the suffering caused by the late civil war in connection with, 239.

Smith, Abigail. Warning by, against a haughty spirit, 184.

Smith, Frederick. Experience by, of the blessings of religious fellowship in marriage, 265.

Stanton, Daniel, immediately instructed by the visitations of Divine Grace, 34.

Remarks of, on the baptizing ministry of John Estaugh, 42.

Illustration by, of the effects of silent exercise of spirit, 42.

Warning given by, against privateering, 60.

Exercise of mind of, respecting horse-races, stage-plays and other evils in Philadelphia, 154.

Providential deliverance of, from shipwreck, 207.

concerned to be diligent in his business, 341.

Story, Thomas. Testimony of, to the Word of God, as that which enables man to understand the Scriptures, 111.

Remarks of, on bearing the cross in using the plain language, &c., 148.

assisted by Divine grace in time of trial, 197.

Composure of, in time of danger, 227, 229.

declines the practice of law from religious conviction, 262.

called to visit America in the work of the ministry, 299.

Remarks of, on the maintenance of ministers, 337, 338.

Remarks of, on the injury done in the church by messengers unsent of God, 344.

Divine refreshment experienced by, in a meeting without words, 351.

Advice of, against dwelling on the failings of others, 355.

Account by, of tendering religious opportunities, 365, 366.

Care of, to wait for the Spirit of Christ before entering into controversy on religious subjects, 368.

Testimony of, to the Divine consolations experienced by Friends in Philadelphia during an epidemic sickness in 1699, 386.

Submission. The want of due, implies a rebellious spirit, 189.

Submissive spirit. On the need of a, 190, 192, 193.

Suffering. Through a dispensation of, man is made willing to submit to the government of Christ, 104.

Taulerus. Experience of, in learning the truths which he preached, 113.

Temptation. Warning given by a criminal against yielding to the
    first, 185.
    A, resisted, 186.
    Those who have experienced, themselves, qualified to advise
        against it, 287.
    to self-destruction overcome, 313.
Thomas, Abel. The gospel ministry of, blessed to Joseph Hoag, 101.
Thompson, Thomas. Dedication of heart of, to the Lord, and tri-
    umphant end, 383.
Thorp, John. Caution extended by, to a person depressed in mind,
    108.
Tobacco. Temptation of a child to use, resisted, 19.
Todd, Dr. John. Repentance of, for an act of disobedience and false-
    hood to his father, 130.
Trust of a poor weaver justified. The, 203.

Unfaithful forfeit the esteem and respect of others. The, 77.
Unfaithfulness to convictions of duty. The sorrowful consequences of,
    114, 115, 118, 119, 183.
Unkindness to a poor woman deeply repented of, 131.

Waln, Nicholas. Composure of, in time of danger, 226.
War an evidence of the spiritual blindness which has overspread Chris-
    tendom, 179.
    Testimony of the Duke of Wellington against, 179.
    Compunction of a soldier who had killed another in, 180.
    Damage providentially prevented during a, 217, 218.
    Trusting in the Lord during an Indian, 229.
Waring, Thomas. Divine intimation to, obeyed, 251.
Warning conveyed by a dream, 52, 53, 55, 57.
Warren, Matthew. Incident in the life of, illustrating Divine guid-
    ance, 245.
Watchfulness. Illustration of the need of, over their conduct, by pro-
    fessors of religion, 78, 184, 187.
Webster, Daniel. Anecdotes of, 174, 175.
Wesley, John. A prayer of, answered, 206.
Wheeler, Daniel, submitting to the visitations of Divine grace, led in
    the path of self denial, 143.

Williams, William. Account related by, concerning a little girl, 20.
    led to reprove a young woman for singing praises to her Maker
      in an irreverent manner, 46.
Wilson, John. Reconciliation of, with Thomas H. Benton, 175.
Wilson, Thomas. Notice of the powerful ministry of, 41, 46, 321.
    Peace of, in his dying hours, 382.
Withy, George. Incidents in the life of, illustrating Divine guidance,
    245, 309.
Wine. The excessive use of, found to be an obstacle to peace of soul,
    81.
    and spirits. The sale of, abandoned under a requisition of duty,
      84.
Worship. The advantage to young children of silent, 15.
    The faithful attendance of meetings for, in the middle of the
      week, 73.
    Experience of a Friend tempted with drowsiness in a meeting
      for, 288.
    Blessings attending a silent exercise of soul in meetings for,
      302, 305, 351, 356.
    Advice against indulging a drowsy or wandering spirit in meet-
      ings for, 355, 357.
Worth, Ebenezer. Instance of the long suffering and goodness of the
    Lord, related by, 33.
Wright, Edward. Remarkable conversion of, 37.
    Remarks on actions of, while in spiritual darkness, 141.

Young. Incidents showing the effects of Divine grace upon the, 11–27.
    The, made instrumental for good in the Divine hand, 22.
Young woman. Account of the religious awakening of a, 30, 31.

Lightning Source UK Ltd.
Milton Keynes UK
UKHW021521050119
334855UK00008B/1279/P